# BLONDIE

By the same author:

Falkland Islands Shores

Reasons in Writing
A Commando's View of the Falklands War

Amphibious Assault Falklands
(The Battle of San Carlos)

# BLONDIE

———————— • ————————

## A BIOGRAPHY
## OF
## LIEUTENANT-COLONEL

## H G HASLER

DSO, OBE, Croix de Guerre,
ROYAL MARINES

by
## EWEN SOUTHBY-TAILYOUR

with a Foreword by
## HRH The Duke of Edinburgh

LEO COOPER

First published in Great Britain in 1998 by Leo Cooper
Reprinted in 2003, in this format, by
LEO COOPER
an imprint of
Pen & Sword Books Ltd
47 Church Street
Barnsley
South Yorkshire
S70 2AS

ISBN 0 85052 950 6

A CIP catalogue record for this book is available
from the British Library

Typeset by Phoenix Typesetting
Burley-in-Wharfedale, West Yorkshire

Printed in England by
CPI UK

FOR
BRIDGET, DINAH AND TOM


not forgetting
*Violet, Mandy, Trivia, Catfish, Tre Sang, Petula,*
*Jester, Sumner* and *Pilmer.*

# Contents

Anyone with more than a passing interest in yachts and yachting will have heard of 'Blondie' Hasler, but, as this biography makes very clear, there was much more to his life than 'Tre Sang', Petula' and 'Jester'; ocean racing, self-steering gear, junk rigs and reefing systems. His life-long passion was small boats, which his commission in the Royal Marines did nothing to abate. What became famous as the 'Cockleshell Heroes' raid on German shipping in Bordeaux could only have been conceived and led by someone with a deep understanding of – and faith in – small boats.

'Blondie' shared the inventor's perception that there must be a better way of doing practical things, but he also seemed to be able to conjure original ideas from his restless and far-seeing mind. Add to that, prolific author, portrait painter, cartoonist, musician, gifted amateur hydrographer and diligent searcher for the Loch Ness Monster. The author has taken all these ingredients, stirred them well and has served-up an exceptionally rich and tasty biography of one of the great characters of this century.

# Acknowledgements

As can be imagined many people have helped me to write Blondie Hasler's biography.

Bridget Hasler was kind enough to ask that I tackle this immense project after I had rather presumptuously (with Mike Richey pushing hard from the side-lines) suggested to her that someone should do so. Once I had agreed, with alacrity it has to be admitted, I sat back to consider the honour of delving into the life of a man who is regarded as the founding father of two spheres of life not totally unconnected as far as human endeavour and fortitude are concerned – maritime special forces and short-handed ocean sailing. Inevitably these two worlds have brought me into contact with a fascinating selection of men and women all anxious to ensure that Blondie's story would be told accurately and fairly. If it has not been, then that is entirely my responsibility and no fault of those who gave their time so generously.

My greatest thanks go to Bridget who has willingly, but not, I think, without some natural hesitation, allowed me access to all Blondie's papers. I made two promises; first, I would discuss with her any "skeletons" that I might find before they reached even the first draft and, second, she would have the final veto on every word written. I am glad to say that I found no skeletons and apart from correcting various 'family' details she has been remarkably abstemious with her criticisms. She did, though, insist on one or two caveats: Blondie would not be referred to as the 'Cockleshell Hero' – an expression he felt was not only inaccurate but also embarrassing – and the Bordeaux raid would not emerge as the prominent feature of his life. For his part, he regarded it as an almost insignificant incident in the overall war effort, although he did accept that the techniques used were to prove invaluable in subsequent operations.

Nor did he like one of the two names given to him and in that respect I bowed to another of Bridget's requests which is why 'Herbert' does not appear in the title. Indeed the following anecdote is typical: shortly after announcing their engagement Blondie wrote to Bridget approving the wording of the wedding invitation but added, "How unfair that I should be the only one who has to display all his names. I wish I was Marmaduke Lancelot de Lacey Hasler. You wait till I start naming my sons (but in the meantime) I think Lieutenant-Colonel Herbert George Hasler will have to do."

The Hasler family have been fully supportive and helpful, particularly John Hasler (who, very sadly, has not lived to see the result) with boyhood tales of cranky craft, mud flats and Southsea Beach, while Bridget's eldest sister Susanna Nockolds, and Geoffrey, filled in many gaps.

At the very beginning Jock McLeod (Chinese rig expert and business partner), Michael Richey (owner of *Jester*) and David Astor (late of the Royal Marines and the *Observer* newspaper) provided vital background help to the great moments in Blondie's life so that, before one word was written, a balanced priority could be taken and the various episodes put into context. Once started, and in no order of preference, Christopher Brasher, late of the *Observer*, Commander Lloyd Foster, author of *OSTAR*, Major Dacre Stroud from SOG and early, post-war sailing days and Brigadier Jack Richards (from the earliest days as Second Lieutenants together) were able to provide details. Superb help came from Lieutenant-Commander Bill Ladbroke, whose encyclopaedic memory of the RMBPD, canoes, Explosive Motor Boats, *Sleeping Beauties* and other, less successful, ideas made research even more of a pleasure. Over pints of beer in his Somerset local I enjoyed lunches with Dick and Joan Raikes while listening to tales of wartime submarine operations that made the back shiver but the heart proud to be British; and again with Hardie Telfer in Argyll, except it was whisky, Popski's Private Army and crofting. General Sir Peter Hellings (who, sadly, did not live to see some of his anecdotes in print) provided a marvellous insight into the life of a pre-war Royal Marines young officer – much of which, regrettably, is unprintable! Oliver Patch, who joined the Royal Marines with Blondie, provided personal reminiscences – but he, too, has not lived to see them in print. Donald Peyton Jones who, with Norman Tailyour, shared many training and sailing experiences with Blondie has taken a lively interest and been able to confirm a number of incidents quoted by Norman Tailyour and Pat Phibbs before they died. Johnnie Coke, who read from Chaucer at Blondie's Thanksgiving Service, has kept in constant touch, for they shared many amusing times together.

Before he died, Nigel Clogstoun-Willmott sent tapes and letters covering his wartime involvement with Blondie for which I am most grateful – but his own story would be worth recording as well: likewise Johnny Bull (*Tuna's* First Lieutenant) with his memories of 'the raid' and submarine operations in the Far East. He, too, has since died.

Major Richard Clifford deserves especial mention for not only has he sailed a number of 'Blondie's races', but he was himself a Royal Marines SBS officer of note, able to develop further some of Blondie's original ideas through modern materials and technology. Concurrent with this biography Richard has been writing the 'classified' history of the SBS and the interchange of information has been helpful to both of us. It was he, too, who presented Blondie with an SBS tie in a pub in Poole – a happy occasion as he often reminds me. Jock Stewart, Jock Swan, James Buxton and Johnny Horner – brave men from the RMBPD and SOG days – were unstinting with their letters and photographs. Pug Davis helped with wartime contacts and present addresses and I must pay tribute to Sir Lyonel Tollemache who arranged the wonderfully lucid meeting with his father, Sir Humphrey, in a nursing home a few weeks before he died. It was Lyonel who wrote later of the only time he sailed with Blondie, in words which seem to me to sum up so much – and not necessarily to do with sailing:

> I instantly felt the difference in the feel of the boat when Blondie took over the helm – she seemed to become part of him as we covered the course with reduced effort: she now seemed to possess more stability requiring less apparent exertion from himself.

Among dozens of other correspondents, Hugh Bruce, John Arnold, the late Gordon Sillars, Sally (Rayne), Peter Hamilton (whose own single-handed trans-Atlantic crossing did much to inspire Blondie), Raymond Andrews, Tom Haydock, Bill King, Ken Wylie, Tony Newing, the late José Ferrer and Bryan Forbes (respectively, actor/director and script writer of the film *Cockleshell Heroes*), Belinda Martin, Rachel Lambert, Gill Heard (Bill Sparks's daughter), Lawrence Hornby and E.C.B. Lee all supplied snippets that add up to more than the whole and I am grateful for all these grace notes to the general theme. Others not mentioned above will find acknowledgement in the text, and to those whose names I have inadvertently omitted, my sincere apologies.

The staff of the Royal Marines Museum, Ed Bartholemew and Matthew Little, led by their Director, Colonel Keith Wilkins, have been especially helpful with archive material – not forgetting Linda Coote who will, I hope, help with the sales! General J.L. Moulton,[1] James Ladd,[2] Charles Messenger,[3] Wellington College, Dr. C.M. Woolgar (Mountbatten archivist at Southampton University), the staff of the Public Record Office and the Imperial War Museum were all equally forthcoming with assistance.

Throughout the text there are numerous quotes from unknown or untraceable sources. These are taken from snatches of conversation at the most unlikely times and in the most unlikely of places (literally, all four hemispheres) over the last eight years and from drafts found among Blondie's papers, drafts which may well have found their way into formal print. Where this is known credit is given but some papers give no clue to their destination (if any) or source. If a particular passage was printed and I give no acknowledgement, again I can only apologize.

Three important people each in many respects, representing main pillars of his life, were, to my immense regret, unable to contribute to Blondie's story: Rosamund Pilcher, (playwriting); Bill Sparks (*Operation Frankton*) and Eric Tabarly (single-handed ocean-racing). The first absence worried me for Blondie fell out with Mrs Pilcher – believed to be the only person with whom this occurred – and yet it would have been interesting to know why or how they parted and would have stopped me making fascinating, private speculations. We only have his notes and they are very vague indeed. The 'other side' would have added a vital ingredient (and balance) to the story.

Bill Sparks was a different matter, for having failed to answer a number of letters I eventually received a verbal message via a third party that, simply, he would not help. Ordinarily I would not mention this for fear of sounding petty but find myself forced to do so to pre-empt enquiries asking why I do not include his name in the acknowledgements. I have relied instead on anecdotal evidence from other sources and Blondie's brief notes.

Eric Tabarly probably did not receive my letters and all other methods to contact him have, similarly, failed.

As always Leo Cooper and Tom Hartman have shown remarkable patience, while the backing of my agent Jüri Gabriel has been crucial.

To everyone my sincere thanks – but above all to Bridget for sharing her memories with me: it cannot always have been easy.

---

[1]  Major-General, (RM) CB, DSO, OBE. See Bibliography.
[2]  See Bibliography.
[3]  See Bibliography.

# Author's Notes

*Hasler – that fascinating combination of man of action who is also a man of ideas, capable of high self-dedication where action and idea meet.*[4]

During the early days of research David Astor told me, "You have many problems. Two of which are that Blondie would have died rather than hear himself praised and unless you can find something nasty to say about him no reader will believe you and the story will lose all credibility."

David was right but I was not prepared to fabricate or embellish slight imperfections with research of doubtful quality in order to gain what would have been a *false* creditability. While I needed to give praise where it is due and criticize where necessary, search as I did, I could find no one prepared to offer the slightest adverse comment or hint of dubious action to form that vital counterweight. Conversely I have tried not to put Blondie on a pedestal and have attempted to offer few comments but rather let his deeds and the words of others portray the man. I may not have succeeded, with the result that Blondie could be regarded as having been 'too good to be true': yet nobody is that, and he certainly had his faults, but they tended to be negative ones. He had, for instance, no business acumen; he was too generous for his own financial good; he was too willing to share his commercial secrets with the unscrupulous; he found the initial stages of any relationship awkward and he was modest and diffident to a remarkable degree – with these last, interactive aspects of his character occasionally forcing others to regard him as difficult to get to know or even aloof. But they were, too, his greatest strengths: friend-

---

[4] *British Ocean Racing.* Douglas Phillips-Birt. Privately published for the RORC by Adlard Coles Ltd.

ships, once made, were made for life, while his reticence kept him humble and approachable.

An example of a genuine attempt to turn the spotlight occurred in November 1972, when Blondie was honoured by the Royal Marines through a letter from the Commandant General[5] announcing that they wished to name one of two new buildings at the Amphibious Training Unit, Royal Marines,[6] at Hamworthy, near Poole, after 'the founder' of the post-war SBS.

> We would very much like to mark the special position that you hold in the eyes of all those who have served in the Royal Marines Special Boat Sections.

Blondie was flattered but his reply was noticeable for the manner in which he quickly changed the subject:

> You have some fine seamen amongst your serving officers these days, and chaps like Mike McMullen[7] and Richard Clifford[8] earn a lot of respect for the Royal Marines amongst sailing people. It was different when I joined in 1932 and found that Patrick Phibbs was the only serious sailing man in the whole Corps! We are hoping to send off some hot Royal Marine entries from Plymouth on the Round Britain race in 1974.[9]

He was not one who, in the cliché, "did not suffer fools gladly" for he would see the good in all, and those who were particularly stupid he would counsel with a non-patronizing humour until they understood perfectly what it was he was trying to demonstrate. I know! It took him

---

[5]  Lieutenant-General B.I.S. Gourlay, OBE, MC. Later General Sir Ian, KCB.
[6]  Previously the Joint Services Amphibious Warfare Centre and now simply, Royal Marines, Poole.
[7]  Captain Mike McMullen RM, who had come 13th in the trans-Atlantic race of that year and who had won first prize on handicap in the 1970 round-Britain race. He came second in the 1974 race to which Blondie refers and was lost at sea in the 1976 trans-Atlantic.
[8]  Captain (later Major, MBE) Richard Clifford RM who came 25th in the smallest boat then to finish in the 1972 trans-Atlantic race and who is a regular competitor in that and the round-Britain races. He was awarded the RCC's Seamanship Medal for his performance in the 1976 trans-Atlantic race. An SBS officer (now retired) he has written the official (but classified) history of the post-war SBS.
[9]  Eight in all, including three NCO's.

considerable time and wonderful patience to explain to me how his steering gear worked as I laboured many days attempting to master its simplicity prior to the 1970 two-handed round Britain race.

I had the privilege to know him throughout my life and sailed, briefly, with him in *Petula* in the Hamble during a weekend out from my local prep school. I also had to remember that it was Blondie's story and not the story of the SBS nor of modern short-handed sailing, but, due to his total involvement in both, that too has been difficult.

Throughout I puzzled over what makes a man famous, what tangible, practical signs are there to indicate that this man or that woman is publicly acknowledged as one who has achieved distinction or position. There are, of course, the usual trappings of fame more often associated with dubious 'celebrities' rather than genuinely famous people – signs of little real consequence such as an appearance on a Desert Island, 'This Is Your Life', a profile in the colour supplements or an entry in *Who's Who* (although he has now been accorded a lengthy piece in the Oxford University Press's *Dictionary of National Biography 1986–1990)*.

Apart from his wartime decorations few accolades came Blondie's way – and if he had been asked to appear on Desert Island Discs (and, more improbably, accepted) his music would have been jazz-orientated, his book probably one of Claud Worth's or Slocum's and his luxury one of his own steering gears; he would have made the boat to go with it from the natural resources available. Yet Blondie was more deserving than most and although there were two attempts by the Cruising Association to have his contribution to the sailing world nationally recognized by the award of the civilian OBE his name never caught the eye of those responsible for such decisions. Worthy of the highest honours given to other members of the sailing fraternity, he was never singled out for such awards which tend, anyway, to be bestowed upon those who break records or win races. Exceptions need to be made occasionally and it is a pity that Blondie was not one of them for his achievements – every bit as much as those who were so honoured – were equally 'to the greater glory of the nation'.

Surprisingly, too, there are few sailing trophies named in his honour. The *Jester Trophy* for the smallest monohull class in the trans-Atlantic race and, comparatively recently, the *Hasler Trophy* for monohull yachts under 46 feet sailed by close members of the same family in the round Britain and Ireland Race are the only two – and even the *Jester Trophy* is now in jeopardy as the lowest size limit is probably being raised.

The British Canoe Union's *Hasler Trophy* was originally presented in

January, 1958, to the Royal Marines Canoe Club by Lloyds subscribers who wanted to maintain their interests in all waterborne activities: later the trophy was presented to the British Canoe Union for long-distance racing. The silver statue is of two cast and carved silver figures, one representing a Royal Marine in the uniform worn during the Bordeaux raid and the other a civilian canoeist.

In December, 1995, the SBS introduced an annual dinner for Officers and SNCOs. Known as the *Frankton Dinner*, towards the end of the evening the RSM reads an account of Blondie's Bordeaux plans and their results, a fitting and lasting tribute from the men he continues to inspire.

He was elected to the Royal Cruising Club in 1948, an organization to which he gave much time and a club that was to honour him with its Medal for Services to Cruising in 1970. He was particularly fond of the RCC and in the 1970s wrote the following in the course of an article (not believed to have been published) he titled *Small Boat Voyaging – Everything Changes*.

> A new breed of amateur sailor could be found . . . who owned small cruising boats and were demonstrating that it was possible not only to sail but also to make coastal passages without any paid hands. . . . The most accomplished of these cruising men tended to belong to the Royal Cruising Club, founded in 1880 with a limited membership, all of whom were required to show nautical as well as social qualifications. The scarcity of such gentlemen at that time is implicit in the first Object in the Club Rules: "To associate owners of yachts, boats, and canoes used for cruising on sea, river or lake and other persons interested in acquatic amusements". I suppose an aquatic amusement could be held to include taking an actress for a picnic up the Thames in an electric canoe, but the Club very firmly developed the other way into a pioneering group of amateur seaman steadily evolving the boats and techniques for sailing themselves around the coast of Europe and, gradually, across the oceans. It seems a modest enough achievement nowadays but in the climate of the times it was a great endeavour.

It springs to mind that he would have been an ideal candidate for the Yachting Journalists' Association's prestigious *Yachtsman of the Year* award – given to Francis Chichester after the first trans-Atlantic race, but never to Blondie: yet it is difficult to recall (I hope the YJA will forgive me trespassing on their territory) a more suitable recipient, even if most are honoured for some form of individual achievement in competition or trial.

In his book *Cockleshell Heroes* Brigadier Lucas Phillips offers a near perfect summing up of what might be called The Hasler Philosophy: it is worth repeating for although written of his wartime exploits it also presages the introduction of his finest inventions: *Jester*, her Chinese-lug rig and self-steering gear, and his most enduring idea, the single-handed trans-Atlantic race.

> The impulse of the moving waters was in his veins. Together with this passion went an ardour for contriving and devising things. He was not content to accept things ready-made but worked them out for himself, and they had to pass every test. He was fascinated by 'all trades, their gear and tackle and trim'. He loved making things with his own hands, from the beginning up, and to whatever problem he turned – whether it was a point of ceremonial drill, the rig of a dinghy, the fastening of a ski, the modification of a car, the diet needed for a long cruise – he devoted to it an intensity and singleness of purpose that was not satisfied with any ready-offered solution but impelled him to probe the smallest details of invention, whether it were a screw, a cord, a strap or a grain of wheat.
>
> All this means that Hasler was, and remained, very much an individualist; in both senses of the term, he liked to paddle his own canoe.

He was, too, at home with Agur's "Confession of Faith" in Proverbs 30:

> There be three things which are too wonderful for me, yea, four which I know not.
> The way of an eagle in the air, the way of a serpent upon a rock; the way of a ship in the midst of the sea; and the way of a man with a maid.

Unlike Agur, he made it his passion to know the ways and means of these four 'wonderful' things – despite some taking a little longer than others!

Finally, his legacy will not be found in such places as honours lists, 'celebrity' celebrations or reference books for 'achievers', his legacy can be seen each time a yacht puts to sea or an SBS-trained Royal Marine slips on a face mask, launches his canoe, or emerges from a submarine.

Above all though, writing this has been fun and that is entirely because Blondie himself was fun.

Ewen Southby-Tailyour
*"Black Velvet of Tamar"*
South Devon. Summer 1997

# Glossary

Those items marked * are more fully explained in the text.

| | |
|---|---|
| ALC | Assault Landing Craft – infantry |
| CCO* | Chief of Combined Operations |
| CODC* | Combined Operations Development Centre |
| COPP* | Combined Operations Pilotage Party |
| COSRO | Combined Operations Small Raiding Organization |
| COXE* | Combined Operations Experimental Establishment |
| DSEA | Davis Submarine Escape Apparatus |
| HCO | Head of Combined Operations (SEAC) |
| MLC | Motor Landing Craft – one tank |
| MNBDO* | Mobile Naval Base Defence Organization |
| MSC* | Motorized Submersible Canoe – the *Sleeping Beauty* |
| NRDC* | National Research and Development Corporation |
| OSTAR | Observer single-handed trans-Atlantic race |
| RA | Royal Artillery |
| RAMC | Royal Army Medical Corps |
| RE | Royal Engineers |
| Rhumb Line | Line on the earth's surface that crosses each meridian at the same angle. A straight line on a Mercator chart |
| RM | Royal Marines |
| RN | Royal Navy |
| RMBPD* | Royal Marines Boom Patrol Detachment |
| RMFU | Royal Marines Fortress Unit |
| SACSEA | Supreme Allied Commander South East Asia |
| SEAC | South East Asia Command |
| SCOBB | School of Combined Operations Beach and Boat Section |
| Sod's Opera | Evening of 'self-help' entertainment in overseas units and ships |
| SOG | Small Operations Group |
| SRU | Sea Reconnaissance Unit |

# CHAPTER ONE

## Canoes, *Violet* and Battleships

On 3 May, 1917, the 14,348 ton Anchor Line troopship SS *Transylvania* sailed from Marseilles carrying 2,860 officers and men in addition to her crew. A submarine threat had delayed her in the French port, but she was bound at last for Alexandria with an escort of two Japanese destroyers, the *Matsu* and the *Sakaki*. At 10 o'clock the next morning, while zig-zagging at fourteen knots, south of Cape Vado in the Gulf of Genoa, this overladen vessel was struck in the port engine room by a torpedo. The Master, Lieutenant S.Brennel, Royal Naval Reserve, immediately turned his ship for the shore two miles away, at the same time ordering the *Matsu* to lie alongside to take off the troops. Meanwhile the *Sakaki* steamed round in an attempt to keep the submarine safely below periscope depth, but she was unsuccessful, for twenty minutes after the first, a second torpedo was seen approaching. To save herself and the embarking survivors the *Matsu* went full astern giving the torpedo an unhindered run into the already stricken liner. The *Transylvania* sank within an hour of the first attack.

Along with her captain, one ship's officer and ten of her crew, twenty-nine military officers and 373 NCOs and men were lost. Among this number was Lieutenant (Quartermaster) Arthur Thomas Hasler, MC, Médaille Militaire, Royal Army Medical Corps, returning from leave in England to rejoin the British and French campaign in Salonika where the Allies were supporting Serbia and where he had been serving since 1915. In addition to his British and French decorations, won during the retreat from Mons when he had commandeered lorries to evacuate the wounded under fire, Hasler was mentioned in despatches in October, 1914; a second "mention", earned in Salonika, was gazetted after his death.

Arthur Hasler was born on 11 March, 1875, joined the Royal Army Medical Corps in 1895, was commissioned on 6 February, 1915, and led a reasonably typical army career for that era, serving in Egypt between 1898–1900 and Ceylon between 1900–1903. On 14 September, 1907, then a Staff Sergeant, he married Annie Georgina Andrews[1] at Charlton Parish Church, near Woolwich, three months before being posted to the Province of South Africa for six years with his school-mistress bride. The three of them – a first child, John, was born in December, 1908 – returned to the United Kingdom a year before the outbreak of the Great War in 1914. On 27 February that year a second boy, Herbert George, was born to Arthur and Annie at Sandford Avenue, Dublin.

Six months later Arthur, now a Warrant Officer, was mobilized for war and stationed under canvas in nearby Phoenix Park, Dublin, before being sent to France in October as a member of the British Expeditionary Force. He returned in April the following year on receiving his commission in the RAMC, upon which he moved his family to his parent's house in St Andrews Road, Southsea, but shortly afterwards moved to his own house at 13 Winter Road, via a brief stay in 77 Devonshire Avenue; all three houses being within an eighteen-month-old's pram-ride of the beach and the sea.

On *Transylvania's* foundering Arthur Hasler was posted as 'missing presumed drowned' and the standard War Office telegram was duly handed to Mrs Hasler starting with the dreaded words, "Deeply regret to inform you that. . ." Annie, now widowed, was offered a six-month teaching post by the army and so moved her family to Empshott Road, Aldershot, and when that ended she moved them back to Southsea.

Arthur Hasler had not been a seaman and had had no deep love for the sea to pass on but he did have courage and determination and by marrying an equally intrepid woman of great fortitude these attributes were distilled with considerable interest in their two children. Fifty-one years on, the younger Hasler would, too, choose a wife of equal tenacity, but although John was destined for a career of some distinction starting with a Bachelor of Arts degree from Cambridge University before reaching the rank of Colonel and subsequently being decorated with the American Legion of Merit in the Degree of 'Officer',[2] he would never marry.

While still in his twenties Arthur and Annie's younger son was to change the style of covert nautical operations in wartime and by his thir-

---

[1] Daughter of Major and Mrs Andrews
[2] Citation by the President of the United States of America: "Colonel JA Hasler, British Army, was senior member of the Executive Staff of the Munitions Assignments Board from May 1944 to October 1945 and British Secretary, Munitions Board, from June to October 1945. He was of the utmost assistance to the Board and materially contributed to the prosecution of the Allied war effort. Signed; Harry Truman".

ties would have begun to influence and guide the rather more peaceful, but no less demanding, ocean racing world into equally radical methods and designs unimagined before his appearance. He linked these two careers through an inventive and fertile mind unchecked by boundaries and convention until his death in 1987.

On the instructions of his mother, who considered the abbreviation "appropriate, wholly suitable and to be taken seriously by the rest of her family",[3] Herbert George was known as Bert until his teens when he asked that he be called George, the name by which all members of his family – except his mother – would know him for the rest of their lives. However, in his early twenties he was nicknamed 'Blondie' by his naval and marine contemporaries due to his thinning fair hair and luxuriant golden moustache, and it is by that name that he will now be referred. As a very small child with a near-cherubic face beneath a mass of blond curls he also looked the part.

Blondie began life as he was to live it, with modesty and equanimity, although this last attribute was not always appreciated by those with a more stressful outlook. On Southsea's shingle beach he and a young friend were playing contentedly until his companion suddenly, and certainly without physical provocation, hit Blondie hard in the face. When asked why, the assailant's reply was simple and truthful, "Because he looks so happy!" Later Blondie boxed for his school but not always with the necessary success: violence, especially personal violence (even if under strict sporting control) was not to be his style.

Blondie's aunt and her three sons lived close by, allowing the five cousins to spend as much time as they could together on the beach, a beach that faces the eastern Solent and the English Channel beyond. It was here that Annie Hasler learned quickly that she should not take her eyes off her 'Bert', for whenever Blondie detected a slackening in vigilance he would head seawards very fast. He did not crawl on hands and knees in the accepted fashion for his age but, already true to his future, 'invented' a better and more effective method of propulsion by skidding across the shingle on his bottom in a form of rolling, rowing motion. He would practice this to perfection by sliding around the house still attached to his pot yet remaining in the upright position. His mother was always horrified, but it amused her visitors.

Another influence on the youngest Hasler, and one as important as the beach and the sea beyond, was Southsea Canoe Lake, also within pram-walking distance; here he would sit fascinated by the men and boys

---

[3]  Author's interview with Colonel John Hasler who died on Boxing Day, 1990.

trundling their magnificent model yachts to the stone edge from where they were launched, to be kept on course by rudimentary wind vanes resembling huge goose feathers.

In due course the question of schooling arose, while Annie struggled on her widow's pension, determined that only the best was suitable for her late husband's sons. With financial assistance offered by the army to the children of those killed in action, she was able to send John to Portsmouth Grammar School for one year before he took up a place at Christ's Hospital, the Bluecoat School. Blondie, aged five, was enrolled in the local school as a day boy for two years, before moving to de Gresly Lodge (where he was to be the head boy of nine), which itself then moved to Soberton Towers in the Meon valley in 1925.

As he grew older and able to make his own way through Southsea's quiet suburban streets much of Blondie's spare time was spent on the edge of Southsea Canoe Lake watching, talking and questioning until the caretaker, realizing that the only way to satisfy a twelve-year-old's quest for knowledge was to start him with some practical gift, presented him with a pair of dinghy paddles. Grateful though Blondie was for this present, he believed oars to be useless without a boat (which is what the caretaker, with some prescience, had foreseen) and so with Colin Ellum, a friend from school, and aided by their Deputy Headmaster, Mr Fiddian, he set about building his first sea-going craft. While he would certainly have built something that floated without the impetus of two free oars it is a convenient moment to establish the first practical beginnings of his love of small ships and the sea.

This canoe, a two-seater and canvas covered, would roam the local waters with Colin and Blondie embarked while, in his diaries, Blondie recorded these first forays across the medium that was to dominate his life:

> Proud owner of a canvas canoe built at school; tried to sail it in Langstone Harbour during the holidays.

'Tried' may have been the correct word for although rowing was the prime method of navigating the local tides and mud flats, this was hard work for two young boys and a waste of good, free winds. Experiments with various rigs, contrived out of any lengths of cloth they could scrounge, produced some very basic forms of propulsion and, as a contemporary note admits, even that was downwind; nevertheless, the die was cast. Just seventeen years later Lieutenant-Colonel H.G.Hasler was designing similar craft and their sails for less peaceful purposes in the Far East.

John Hasler had by now been offered a commission in the Royal Engineers and, while attending courses with the Royal Artillery at Woolwich noted in a letter to his mother that "all the people he admired came from schools such as Wellington College at Crowthorne, Berkshire". He suggested that Bert should apply, but money was short and Wellington one of the leading public schools with fees that matched its status. Nevertheless, with her customary determination, she did apply and Wellington responded, equally positively, by offering Blondie the chance to sit a 'special scholarship' examination. He failed, but so impressed the headmaster that he was offered a bursary instead and in the Lent Term, 1928, joined Wellington's Lyndock Dormitory under the tutorage of G.T.Griffith, the housemaster.

Blondie's years at Wellington were notable for distinguished performances in various activities, but especially swimming, rugby and cross-country running. His first term, though, was an unhappy one for he was teased about his name Bert and his Portsmouth accent to such an extent that the holiday was spent persuading his mother that he should be called George while he learnt to speak more like his public school contemporaries. A victory was recorded on both accounts, allowing him to adopt a happier mien more in keeping with his character.

Once settled, he bought a Boy's Own Paper publication, *How to Make Canoes, Dinghies and Sailing Punts* – the well-thumbed copy still sits on his bookshelves – and set about constructing, in his own words, "a sort of flat-bottomed punt". With an overall length of ten foot, dart-shaped in plan and only one plank in depth she was not likely to be very seaworthy but he knew no better way to discover the whys and hows of this fundamental requirement than to sail her across the shoals of Langstone Harbour. During her building in the back garden of 63 Festing Road (to where Annie had moved the family after Aldershot) the tenant, a handyman of considerable talent, watched carefully. His plan had been to offer practical advice and hints but he realized that he had nothing to offer the young lad and so sat back and watched admiringly.

She (no name was given to her, nor the canvas predecessor, whose fate is unknown) was first launched off Southsea's beach from a borrowed hand-cart at which precise moment it became clear that she was badly in need of ballast and some form of centre-board. John Hasler and, of more importance, his Bull-Nosed Morris motor car, were pressed into service while Blondie scoured Old Portsmouth and the camber area. Eventually after much negotiation, and poorer by five shillings, he appeared with a 'monstrous piece of metal'. This centre-board severely tested the Morris's springs but it was exactly what was needed by the 'punt'.

In thanks for this help, John was offered a clockwise sail around the 'island' of Portsmouth which was planned to end at the Eastney pontoon of the Hayling Island ferry where there would be a rendezvous with mother, young female cousin and the borrowed hand-cart. It was Easter and not warm. The tides were right for his purpose, Blondie having meticulously checked them, and the brothers set off on the nine-mile, clockwise passage. The draft of the vessel was minimal but even so there was not enough water at the north-west corner of Langstone Harbour where Blondie discovered that Portsmouth was not always as much of an island as it believed itself to be. They attempted to remove the centre-board altogether so that it could be carried by hand across the shallowest parts, thus raising the draught of the vessel for this phase of the journey, but something went wrong and the monstrosity dropped into four feet of water. Now drawing only one foot the punt was easily pushed across the shoal while Blondie dived to recover his five shillings worth. With no harm done they continued towards mother and cousin but by then nobody was waiting and they sailed on the two miles to Southsea Beach. Blondie wrote in his notes:

> Learnt to sail from books, trial and error, in Langstone Harbour with school friend.

Empirical observations of the need for freeboard forced the addition of a second plank after the first summer's trials, thus increasing considerably (a comparative term!) the punt's sailing ability, stability and safety.

With the second summer and the increased freeboard he was able to venture further along the south coast, extending the length of his cruises to the point that he would be away for 'days at a time'; on one memorable occasion sheltering up an Isle of Wight creek. Many mothers might have fussed and, although Annie did worry immensely, she was anxious that her active and intelligent sons were not stifled by too much motherly concern. In George's case she would recall, "I knew that he would always turn up." The freedom, and particularly the maternal confidence in his ability, was a vital component of the younger Hasler's formative years that allowed him the freedom to "cruise all over the Solent with a tent to fit over the boat."

If Wellington did not teach Blondie to sail[4] it did give him the opportunity to excel in other sports that were to be useful in later life. Swimming brought him the greatest recognition when he was capped in

---

[4] He designed and built another slab-sided canoe for use on the College lake.

1931, to become Captain of the College team the next year; he was also capped for cross-country running in 1932, his last year. The only ball game at which he showed any real prowess was Rugby football but team games were not to his liking, although he did play well enough to reach the first fifteen in 1931, his report at the end of the season suggesting, enigmatically, that he was, "A sound hardworking forward if somewhat inconspicuous; does not use his hands enough but makes up for this by being able to convert tries with confidence". He boxed at the College but no records exist other than, "In the senior boxing (1931) under 11 stone HGH had a walk-over from Tweedy". Later he boxed in the Royal Marines with, in his own words, "disastrous results". Diving was more successful with, "Hasler as good as usual."[5]

His first dabble into the publishing world occurred while still at school. On 30 May, 1931, the editor of the *Illustrated Sporting and Dramatic News* publically corrected a statement made in a previous issue describing a Mme Heriot's yacht, *L'Aile,* as being the former German schooner *Meteor V* when she was, in fact, the *Ailée,* having been designed and built for Madame in 1929. The editor "was pleased to be able to correct an error", little realizing perhaps, that his correspondent was a seventeen-year old schoolboy. Precocious it might have been but it demonstrated an early concern for correct detail.

The first time his name actually appeared in print as a by-line was beneath a letter published in *Yachting World* of 11 December, 1931, in which Blondie argued that the gaff rig was preferable for cruising when compared to a Bermudian sail plan. Writing in response to an article from Conor O'Brien[6] he sought to offer the Irish nautical sage support. Having done so, he launched into a technical discussion on the heights of Bermudian masts and their 'moments of inertia', finishing with a discourse on the effects of drift on a yacht's rudder.

With his fascination for the sea it might have been natural that Blondie's first choice of career would be the Royal Navy but he "warmed to the idea of becoming a Royal Marine for the simple and practical reason that he could join directly as a Second-Lieutenant and Second-Lieutenants were paid more than Royal Navy cadets".[7] He took the appropriate exams, attended the required interviews, was gazetted as a

[5]  Wellington College records.
[6]  One of the most experienced yachtsmen of his age with an inventive mind which he used to improve the rigging and gear of offshore yachts, often favouring gaff or even square rig.
[7]  Author's interview with General Sir Peter Hellings, KCB, DSC, MC. Commandant General, Royal Marines, 1968–1971.

Probationary Second-Lieutenant on 1 September, 1932, and appointed to Royal Marines' Barracks, Stonehouse, for two months' initial training. On 1 November he and the others of Plymouth Division joined Royal Marines' Barracks, Eastney, where they met those from the Portsmouth and Chatham Divisions for the start of their officers' courses.

Seven officers joined that September for the three-year training period with Blondie "passing in" at the top. By the end he was to slip a place or two, although it was acknowledged that this had nothing to do with a lack of military ability or poor attentiveness but much to do with the time he spent sailing. As was the custom, the September batch of young officers would be joined by the succeeding January entry for most of the courses, and in this case the full list, in order of initial seniority, was: from September, 1932, Hasler, Price, Bowen, Patch, Teek, Pitts and Clifford and from January, 1933, Matters, Courtice, Tyndale-Biscoe, Peyton Jones, Richards and Tailyour.

Young Officers were paid on the assumption that they received paternal help in such matters, so that a private income, while not as in some army regiments vital, was considered so near to being essential as made no odds. In company with his contemporaries, he was required to buy his uniforms out of an initial allowance, although it was not then the practice to part immediately with this sudden wealth in favour of a tailor. As a direct result of this 'fortune' and with no time to build one himself, Blondie searched for his first 'bought' boat. A Second-Lieutenant's pay was 7/6[8] a day but suffered a compulsory deduction of 3/6 for messing and an additional 1/- for breakfast which left just three shillings for mess-bills and life! or £4.50 a month in modern terms. Officers were required to dine in each night unless they had permission to be "ashore", but such dispensation was not given lightly by the President of the Mess Committee. The formal nature of these dinners meant almost compulsory pre-prandial drinks and wine and port with the meal, ensuring that even less ready cash was available to sustain a life-style beyond the boundaries of Eastney Barracks.

Blondie's love for the sea was absolute, so to maintain his hobby while keeping up with the others he had to miss breakfast, thus saving seven shillings a week, or one pound, eight shillings a month.

In May, 1933, he met his first recorded love. Female but inanimate, she came in the form of a small, half-decked, retired, gaff-cutter-rigged fishing smack of about twenty feet (plus a substantial bowsprit) and after

[8]   37½p

agreeing a purchase price he sailed to collect her in the still commissioned, but still nameless, sailing punt. A series of poignant photographs in his album show the punt arriving in Portsmouth Harbour camber, and the newly acquired *Violet* towing her out under sail; all this above the caption, *Last voyage of Violet from Camber to Langstone.*

As the album's caption implies this was her one and only outing with her new owner:

> One magnificent sail around the Solent before bringing her to an anchorage in Langstone Harbour where that night there was a bad storm. By the morning all that could be seen was her mast.

*Violet* had cost £35, or considerably more than two month's pay even before mess-bills and compulsory deductions, but he was not the first officer to spend his uniform allowance on items other than his tailor's bill and certainly not the last.

As *Violet* was uninsured, it was a major blow and, although Blondie had lost a great deal of money, of more significance, he had lost a vessel. He never lost another.

Not even ocean racing, let alone cruising, was considered then to be a sport of great value as far as the instilling of courage, self-confidence, endurance and leadership qualities under arduous conditions were concerned, for all sailing was regarded by senior officers as a pursuit of pleasure to be conducted only in spare time. To make a favourable impression it was necessary to play tennis or one of the accepted games such as Rugby football, cricket, hockey or golf.

But there were attractions other than small boats as Oliver Patch[9] remembered that a particular pride of Blondie's was an old 500cc Norton motor cycle with which he spent hours tinkering. This was an enforced pastime as for some minor infringement of the law he had had his licence removed for six months. Together they bought a 1921 water-cooled, Morgan Grand Prix with a great brass radiator for £1.10.0.[10] which they shared for pub crawling. Unfortunately the brass radiator was better looking than it behaved and leaked so badly that it could only be kept watertight by adding increasingly large quantities of ground ginger to the cooling water:

[9] Later, Major O.Patch DSO, DSC, Royal Marines – a distinguished Fleet Air Arm pilot – in a letter to the author shortly before he died in January, 1991.
[10] One pound and ten shillings or, today, 150 pence.

Blondie drove the open roads and I did the towns as his six months' suspension were not yet up. Going over Telegraph Hill – west of Exeter – Blondie was driving; with the old machine finding it a bit tough I jumped out and walked up. I well remember seeing Blondie's pork-pie hat moving slowly up Telegraph Hill above a cloud of steaming ginger beer.

The Morgan met its end after one guest night when, as six people hung on, it overturned in a race around the Officers' Mess against an elderly Wolsely. High spirits were acceptable as an ingredient of relaxation from intensive training, although many of the pranks would certainly not be tolerated now. "More is the pity," as a number of Blondie's contemporaries have since testified. For instance, late one night an Austin 7 'inadvertently' found its way onto the dodgem-car arena on Southsea Pier after which the owner, the Chief Royal Marines' Gunnery Officer at Whale Island, was taken to hospital. Episodes such as this were considered part of life and not a block to an officer's career in those rather more carefree, but no less professional, days. General Sir Peter Hellings, who was to join a few months after Blondie's joint batch, later remarked that it would

> quite unnecessarily cause a great deal of fuss if one did it now! The balls-aching seriousness of life today comes from America and is terrible. In those days everybody was in plain clothes by lunchtime and then the officers and men would have a splendid time playing games or shooting – and we still won wars.[11]

An enlightened small-arms instructor of the time was Major Patrick William O'Hara Phibbs.[12] Pat Phibbs, who had made his mark as a young officer with a small converted Polperro 'hooker,' *Elizabeth Mary*, encouraged his subalterns to cruise at every opportunity for the sheer fun of it and because, he believed, seamanship helped form a strong character. Brought up with yachts since birth, Pat was also a near-unbeatable racing dinghy and cutter helmsman who encouraged

---

[11] Interview with the General shortly before he died when he was delighted to hear that in the Royal Marines there are still pockets of firm resistance to this attitude.
[12] Later Lieutenant-Colonel, OBE.

Norman Tailyour[13] and Donald Peyton Jones[14] (both of whom had also been brought up with boats from a very early age) to buy for £5 a small wooden sailing yacht called *Witch* that they found lying in the mud of Fareham Creek. They and Blondie would sail together, sometimes reaching as far as the Channel Islands, but Blondie's desire to be master of his own craft bettered him and in 1933 he bought a more affordable, fourteen foot Bermudian-rigged dinghy.

The fitting-out of *Witch* provides a typical insight into the off-duty life of a young officer. By good fortune, and a desire to save money, Tailyour and Peyton Jones shared a captain's double-roomed quarters in Eastney Officers' Mess and by both sleeping in the bedroom they were able to use the day cabin for the construction of a coach-roof for their half-decker. When completed it had to be hoisted out through the first-floor window under Blondie's helpful and supportive guidance.

On 27 May, 1934, Blondie's batch of young officers (without the second half) joined the Royal Marines' Depot at Deal in Kent for the 19th Military Course in which he was to gain first place despite, apparently, not doing a stroke of work moving Divisions and Brigades on paper from one part of Kent to another. Instead he read a copy of *Yachting World* underneath his desk and out of sight of Gerry Ross[15] and the Directing Staff. His colleagues, irritated by his temerity and *sang froid,* looked forward to a personal set back for him, not to say retribution, so there was much chagrin when the course results were announced. In practice they all appreciated his company and were extremely fond of him, if not a little in awe of his natural talents, which did not extend to his ability on the saxophone and the only two tunes he seemed to know, *Sweet Georgia Brown* and *Georgia on my Mind.* He could get away with much because he never made the rest of the batch feel inadequate – "which, of course they were not!"[16]

He was already establishing himself as something of an eccentric in a few of his personal habits by practising, for example, long periods without sleep while living in primitive conditions in his boat or on a handy beach. To suffer, quite willingly, the cold and wet conditions in

[13] Later General Sir Norman, KCB, DSO and Bar. Commandant General, Royal Marines 1964–1968, Honorary Lance Corporal in the Zouaves, Admiral of the Texas Navy and Captain of Deal Castle.
[14] Later Major, DSC. After retirement, the Reverend.
[15] Later Lieutenant-Colonel G.W.Ross, Royal Marines and the father of Lieutenant-General Sir Robert Ross, KCB, OBE, who retired as Commandant General, Royal Marines in 1996.
[16] Author's correspondence and discussions with Oliver Patch.

dinghies or small, leaky, retired fishing craft for days on end was not the norm even in an era without the domestic luxuries now taken for granted, and, although Blondie was not alone he took this way of life to an extreme that the others did not. There was nothing 'macho' about it (to use an expression more understood these days), it was simply his chosen style of practising self-sufficiency.

Royal Marines Young Officer training is varied and, in addition to the normal parade ground work and basic military skills, many of the courses were then designed around service at sea with the large Royal Marines' detachments or ashore with one of the Mobile Naval Base Defence Organizations. The MNBDOs, which traced their antecedents back to the autumn of 1923 at Fort Cumberland, close to Eastney Barracks, were responsible, as their name implied, for the landing of guns and heavy equipment over piers constructed from scaffolding in order to establish and then defend makeshift bases wherever the Royal Navy had need for them in times of international crises.

There was the Seamanship and Chartwork Course to be passed, the wonderfully named Electricity and Searchlight Course, Naval Gunnery courses at Whale Island, Portsmouth and, in Blondie's case a preliminary exam in German. The Young Officers served in HMS *Iron Duke* to give them their first taste of life at sea with the Royal Navy although this was, in practice, a frustrating month as the emasculated ex-battleship of 26,000 tons was employed as a Gunnery Training Ship. Having been 'demilitarized' in 1931 under the London Treaty she was no longer the proud Flagship of Jutland.

This short introduction to life in the world's most powerful navy had more to do with seamanship than gunnery for on the last day, 10 November, 1933, the combined batches sat their exams in seamanship in which Blondie gained 807 out of 1000 available marks, just beating Norman Tailyour but being easily beaten by Donald Peyton Jones.

Blondie was a popular but unconventional officer under training and one acknowledged to possess charm, charisma and leadership qualities beyond the norm. He is remembered from those days as being a modest, intelligent man with impressive physical strength and powers of endurance. In practice, though, he abhorred violence and although more than able to defend himself against most odds in a fight he was careful never to get into a position where he might have to use his fists.

He enjoyed a 'good run ashore' as much as any other, although an endearing diffidence made him better company in small groups he knew well rather than in large parties. He made friends slowly and very surely, not through any stand-offishness on his part but a desire to "get it right first time": true friends, he believed, were for life. Almost pathologically shy in the company of women that he had only just met, he found the initial stages of a friendship an ordeal, but once the ice had been broken, with either sex, he was a loyal ally who would support in the foulest weather as well as the fairest.

He showed no great ambition to reach the top of the Royal Marines; indeed few officers at that stage looked beyond commanding a capital ship's detachment of several hundred, which was a goal that suited Blondie well. Not yet able to describe himself as an "inventor", it must have crossed his mind (for it had certainly already crossed those of his colleagues) that that was where his talents lay. Inventing can take many forms, from the practical solution to a hitherto unsolved mechanical problem to an erudite discussion on paper expounding a revolutionary theory for carrying out some complicated military or nautical evolution; Blondie was to range between all limits of the spectrum.

Although all young officers and recruits are shaped into similar moulds, the Royal Marines expects its young men to be individuals. Blondie's batch of young officers was no different. His main interests were, it is true, regarded as eccentric for their day but not particularly unusual. The primary difference between him and the others was his *avant-garde* views on almost everything, and his inability to accept standards at face value. He wanted to know the reason behind 'things', such as equipment, plans and events, whereas most were able to accept the *status quo*. If there was a way to improve on a design or procedure Blondie needed to analyse and discuss it.

For much of these early days his brother, though five years his senior, was part of Blondie's life and would spend many happy weekends with his Royal Marines colleagues. John Hasler, by now a Captain in the Royal Engineers, remembered, with not a trace of jealousy, being in his brother's shadow, admitting that George would have made a much better engineer than himself. He would say, "It was Blondie's inventive streak and analytical mind that more easily fathomed out the problems that came the way of sappers."

John recalled with great pleasure and undisguised pride being approached at social or military gatherings (some far removed from Royal Marines' circles) with the question, "Are you Hasler's brother?" to which he would reply amicably, as far as any older brother can under such cross-examination, "No, I'm Hasler!"

Throughout his life John remained Blondie's most fervent admirer.

# CHAPTER TWO

## *Trivia* and War

Heedless of official displeasure, sailing predominated, for these were the halcyon days of empty waters, alcohol stoves, mud berths, beer at almost nothing a pint – even by the standards of a young officer's pay – and the continual worry of being late back for courses. Few young officers could afford an engine and it is doubtful whether they would have used one anyway.

History does not relate the fourteen-foot dinghy's fate but she was replaced for £15 in 1934 by a twelve-foot day-boat that Blondie named *Trivia.* This latest love was to be a great favourite for it was she that took him offshore for the first time and, although she landed him in an amount of trouble and took up much of his time and money, not once did he regret either. He was not alone, for Donald Peyton Jones and Norman Tailyour, first in their *Catherine* and later in *Witch* would often act as stores carrier to Blondie, although *Trivia* would usually reach the chosen destination first!

If any vessel taught him seamanship it was this one, particularly during an unusual duo of voyages along the English south coast. *Trivia,* an open, clinker-built dinghy carrying 100 square foot on a tall gunter-rig was not built for speed, but in Blondie's hands was certainly good enough for the occasional handicap race. Designed by George Feltham[1] some years before, Blondie believed her to be the forerunner of the present Seaview One-Designs. She was painted white, "went through the water well", especially in a good breeze and with her home-made drum and line roller-reefing and powerful sections was easy to handle: she had a good carrying capacity and pulled very easily under a pair of seven-foot oars.

Between February and June, 1935, Blondie's batch were stationed in Plymouth but due back in Eastney at the beginning of August for more

---

[1] Whose family were to build another yacht associated with Blondie's international sailing endeavours – *Jester*

courses, including the major one of Land Artillery. Moored alongside *Witch* in the Stonehouse Barracks Camber, there was only one way *Trivia* could return avoiding expensive road transport. *Witch,* with her rudimentary accommodation and two owners, could make the journey with comparative ease but not so the dinghy who would need staging points along the coast.

By Thursday 27 June, 1935, four days were left in which to complete the 145 miles and while Tailyour and Peyton Jones set off eastwards without much ado, Blondie converted a bivouac tent, loaded *Trivia* with food, water and camping gear and prepared to sail single-handed. To reef the mainsail or raise or lower the centre-board from his position at the tiller he led all lines aft to the helmsman's position, an arrangement that was to be particularly useful when running onto an open beach in a rising wind and sea.

Writing in his log he made the journey and its preparations sound easy, almost casual, but taking seamanship casually was not Blondie's way although he never liked to appear to be making much fuss. This was to be a meticulously planned journey that remained a personal (and, in some respects, national) bench-mark for many years. Convinced that a small open boat was far safer for coastwise passage-making than a cranky, larger vessel bought for the same sum of money, it was better, he argued in 1935, that £100 be spent on the best most seaworthy dinghy than on

> a third-rate cabin boat worse suited to coastal passages than a good open boat. Not for us to grow hairs as we feverishly work out depth of water. We see the bottom before we hit it and will always know exactly where we are by day and have a very good working idea at night.

With youthful arrogance unbecoming of his later years he dismissed the idea of sleeping ashore each evening, regarding this as an unsatisfactory compromise that put those who did so in the same bracket as hikers and cyclists. The tent, which folded into a bag the size of a rugger ball, was supported not by a ridge pole but by a single, hooped length of bamboo stuck into the two midships crutch sockets to form a curved dome. The whole structure had, according to Blondie, more headroom than a four-ton cutter and did not leak as much as those that he knew, for he had in mind *Witch's* home-made coach-roof!

His bunk was a seven-foot bottom board lifted up and laid along the thwarts on one side while the other side was kept clear for cooking. When sailing everything was kept out of the ends of the boat and stowed either side of the centre-board casing, giving *Trivia* a comfortable motion. The only item outside the midships section was the bent bamboo pole that lay curved beneath the stern sheets and totally out of the way.

Following *Witch* at 0700 into the tail-end of a south-westerly gale that had left a residue swell off the entrance, Blondie found that it was too much for the twelve-footer, even with six rolls in her mainsail, and he was forced to return north across Plymouth Sound. As many have found, the weather outside Plymouth Breakwater can appear benign when viewed from north of Drake's Island, but by 1000 the wind really had eased and, although a fair sea was still running in the Channel, "the sting was gone from the blow". Blondie kept the original rolls in the mainsail and with her shallow draft *Trivia* sailed round the Shag Stone – "that spouting fang of rock" – to turn to port and the shallow passage between the Mewstone and Wembury Bay to the north:

> Here was grand sailing with the great cliffs away to leeward fringed with white along their base and a good fresh breeze on the quarter to take the boat along at four knots under her short-ened sail.

Three of the rolls were shaken out off Bolt Head before another delay took charge, best told in his own words:

> Alas for human frailty; my subconscious brain began to receive mild complaints from a lower region. In short, I felt ill, and having no wish to allow the process to come to its undignified conclusion I rounded Bolt Head and anchored at 2.30 pm inside the entrance to Salcombe in calm water.

After twenty-four hours at sea and with a promise of fair weather for the morning, *Trivia* made one and a half knots close-hauled on the star-board tack while her skipper lay smoking a pipe "varying his siesta with periods of goofing over the side at shoals of jellyfish of all sizes as the sun got hotter and hotter". At Lyme Regis he secured *Trivia* inside the Cobb and repaired ashore for, "a much needed pint of mild". As dusk fell they were able to make sparkling progress towards Portland Bill but, by dawn a south-easterly breeze freshened until they were beating along the coast with heavy spray and a disturbed sea and (as he noted in his log) without breakfast. With thirteen miles dead to windward and mindful of his new Commanding Officer's views on such adventures, he decided to run back for Bridport in order to continue overland.

Once *Trivia* was secured ashore the wind began to moderate allowing them to set off again but it remained back-breaking work and after fourteen miles and ten hours of pounding to windward they had only reached a little beyond the village of East Fleet by 8.00 pm. *Trivia* was again secured ashore, yet, fickle as ever the wind now backed to the east and moderated. Blondie's determination took charge immediately so that, as he was to remark later, St George could approach the sleeping dragon.

The west-going ebb stream was due shortly after sunset at 2111 which allowed an hour to cover the five miles to the Bill; in the last of the twilight and about three quarters of an hour later than planned, his ambition was achieved and they were out into the true wind; but now the dragon awoke for he had, truly, missed the tide and, despite tacking close inshore between the rocks and the increasing and notorious Portland Race about half a cable offshore, he had a problem:

> It was now almost too dark to see the outlying rocks and as I was making no headway against the tide I was forced to pay off and run back round the Bill. I was dog-tired, having done quite a lot of sailing in the past three days and this must be my only excuse for the grotesquely unseamanlike manoeuvre which I now perpetrated. Instead of running back to the safety of the beach at the northern end of the peninsula, I could wait only until I was about a cable in from the end of the point on the west side before dropping anchor close inshore under the lee of the cliffs and turning in all standing. A change of wind during the night would almost certainly have had me guessing, but the Deity who looks after fools in small boats was in a tolerant mood and I slept soundly for the remaining four hours of darkness. (see p. 22)

The 'Deity responsible for nautical fools' had indeed taught the young Blondie a lesson and then let him sleep soundly, and safely, on it. He was learning fast and, by his mistakes, in the best possible manner. Many years later he was to recall this experience with a little more honesty:

> Anyone who could anchor a dinghy there in the dark and then sleep soundly for four hours must be quite out of his mind. But it certainly wasn't my conscious mind that had put the helm up that night, run back round the Bill close to the rocks in the dark, lowered the jib and anchored. Yet it proved under the circumstances to have been the perfect course of action. The conditions

that may have led to this hallucination and blackout seem to be mental and physical exhaustion stretching back over two and a half days of sustained effort with little sleep; anxiety to make progress and frustration at failing to do so; the alternation of hope and despair, and finally fear, experienced in a sinister location on a dark night.[2]

The remainder of the journey was reasonably straightforward. With a fine east-north-easterly breeze they rounded the Bill for the second time and by mid-afternoon had made a landfall at Lulworth Cove where the clock and thoughts of his future Adjutant forced him, finally, ashore.

> Left *Trivia* on a good mooring inside the Cove and caught my train exactly on time. Since leaving Plymouth I had covered 127 miles in 3½ days and of that time only a total of about four hours was spent out of the boat. Best of all, I found I liked it!

The following Friday he returned to Lulworth and after a boisterous sail arrived at Portsmouth on Sunday evening after meeting up with *Witch* off the Isle of Wight.

This had been the first real adventure and one that had been approached with a little trepidation and much planning, all of which brought him to the absolute conclusion that no matter what military work was to come his way small boats would always take the top priority in his life.

He passed the Land Artillery course with 184 marks out of 200 and on 13 August was re-appointed back to Plymouth, whence he returned in *Trivia* on 19 August.

This was a reverse journey of June's up-Channel expedition, but now he was wiser and more knowledgeable, the significant difference being that he was on summer leave and could afford to stop for sleep. By and large he considered that the efforts to sail at night on the way to Portsmouth had been unprofitable; not only had he made little headway but he had tired himself out for good, daytime passage-making.

"The man-eating race of Portland Bill" produced no more than a series of overfalls on the east side that, "would hardly have worried a duck-punt" before he was on his way into Lyme Bay where the night was spent, courtesy of some fisherman, above the highwater mark, and so leisurely progress was made towards Plymouth.

[2]  Hasler papers.

He slept at anchor inside Teignmouth's 'training wall' and at the village of Beesands where:

> every able-bodied man and boy turned out to help me haul the boat under the shelter of the cliffs. I had foreseen a series of violent thunderstorms during the night and as I lay in my bunk and felt a fine spray falling on my face I sorrowfully disrated my tent, a converted hiker's contraption, from waterproof to showerproof.

His summing up was as cheerful as that for the outward leg:

> Plymouth Sound was a lovely sight in the autumn evening, and I felt completely at peace with the world as *Trivia* drifted on with the dying breeze through the eastern entrance and up past Drake's Island to her old berth.
>
> It had taken me about six days to cover the 180 miles from Portsmouth, just a fraction more than I needed for the passage the other way in June. The passage as a whole thoroughly confirming my enthusiasm for dinghy cruising . . . The smaller the boat the better fun.

"Plymouth for courses" ran his orders, along with promotion to Probationary Lieutenant with a seniority of 1 September, 1935, followed, at long last, by his first 'operational' posting to date from the 28 December, 1935. The battleship HMS *Queen Elizabeth,* Flagship of the Mediterranean Fleet mounting eight 15-inch and twelve 6-inch guns, was Blondie's lot and he was delighted. The appointment was to last for nearly two years[3] during which time he was loth to be parted from his beloved *Trivia*; however, as he had discovered, if you do not ask you certainly will not be granted and so a letter to the Commander followed his "duty" letter to the Captain that had acknowledged his appointment, and all was well. His twelve-foot dinghy was probably less trouble in the battleship than the polo pony (owned by her Commander) aboard the cruiser HMS *London* to which Norman Tailyour was appointed.

On 24 August, 1935, the British Cabinet had re-affirmed its policy of sanctions against Italy if she invaded Abyssinia, as seemed likely by the volume of Italian shipping passing south through the Suez Canal, and began to take practical moves to prepare for this and the likely retaliatory

[3] Until 7 June, 1937

consequences. Late on 5 September, during their summer leave, a number of the officers from the joint 1932/1933 batch received priority telegrams ordering them to report forthwith to Plymouth Division Headquarters. Blondie's official records are vague during this period and he made no reference in his own notes but anecdotal evidence is positive that he took part in the early stages of the move of the MNBDO to Alexandria. Certainly Norman Tailyour, Donald Peyton Jones, Peter Hellings and Jack Richards[4] were among those who recalled his presence. The liners *Neuralia* and *Lancashire* were requisitioned as troopships and stood by; Jack Richards takes up part of the story:

> We were just finishing training and the Royal Marines were mounting the guard at Buckingham Place when the MNBDO was mobilized. They formed up at Fort Cumberland so that an 'auction' for marines could take place as officers picked and chose their teams from a cast of about 2,000 in the manner of a school sports afternoon. In four days the MNBDO was brought up to strength of 1600 under the command of Brigadier W.H.L. Tripp DSO, MC.[5] with Major E.J.B. Noyes[6] as the GSO1.
>
> From Fort Cumberland we marched to Fratton Railway Station to disembark at Southampton from where we marched to the Bibby Liner SS *Lancashire* for the journey to Alexandria.

They marched ashore in Alexandria four abreast on the 28th September dressed in pith helmets (not the Royal Marines ceremonial 'helmet WP') bush jackets, Sam Browne belts, khaki shorts, boots and puttees wound up to the knee and carrying side arms. The MNBDO was equipped, initially, with four 6-inch guns, "many" anti-aircraft guns, thirty-three searchlights, boom nets and mines fired electronically from the shore with the task of controlling the passage of ships in and out of Alexandria: Moustapha was the main base and batteries were sited along the coast line at Raz el Tin.

For the younger officers and men recreation was, as expected, centred around the sailing dinghies that could be hired from the Royal Yacht Club of Egypt at Alexandria, close to Raz el Tin, and the British Boat Club. It was here that Norman Tailyour and Donald Peyton Jones spent their uniform allowance on building a twenty-one foot gaff-cutter, *Sea*

---

[4]  Later, Brigadier, CBE.
[5]  Later Lieutenant-General, CB, DSO, MC.
[6]  Later, Major-General, CBE.

*Vixen,* designed to the same lines as the already famous *Dyarchy.* Unfinished by the time the crisis was over, she would be shipped back to the United Kingdom, along with the guns, in the freighter SS *Lyminge.* Whalers and dinghies were also available for racing, as were punts crewed by Egyptian guides for duck shooting, with the "locals" always adding more to the bag than the officers.

Various windfalls came the way of those interested in boating, one occurring after the liner *Ausonia* caught fire on 18 October, to sink at her moorings on the 20th. It was indeed an ill wind for one of her lifeboats was salvaged and soon re-rigged as a schooner with a "cabin conversion" for cruising. At weekends there was also racing in the Jewel Class day boats in Alexandria Harbour, otherwise the officers and men of the Mobile Naval Base Defence Organization kept fit man-handling their guns and climbing the pyramids.

With the threat over, the MNBDO in Alexandria was wound up in spring, 1936, to travel home on board the British India Steam Navigation Company's SS *Neuralia,* leaving nothing behind except Dog Wuppity, the mascot. The MNBDO's primary tasks had been to thwart any aspirations that Mussolini might have had towards Egypt and the sighting of heavy guns had been part of the counter-move while the positioning of these guns and the building of scaffold-piers instilled in Blondie two life-long fascinations, that of moving very heavy equipment and under-water diving.

Blondie arrived home in time to join, with *Trivia,* HMS *Queen Elizabeth* before she sailed from Plymouth on 19th May for a year's cruise in the Mediterranean. At each anchorage he would race against the service dinghies and cutters also carried on board or take friends for picnics on the more isolated beaches. They also spent a month back in Alexandria. On *Queen Elizabeth's* return for the 1937 Coronation Review (prior to a "truck to keel rebuild") he was asked to draw the illustrations for the ship's programme, a task he was delighted to accept.

Blondie was posted to Plymouth on 8 June, 1937, but by now news of his nautical attributes had reached those responsible for appointing young officers and so he was quickly back in Portsmouth to take up two appointments that were to shape his career and, by keeping him in the "boating and writing world", part of his civilian life as well. The military appointment, on 15 December, 1937, was as Fleet Landing Officer to the nucleus of the Mobile Naval Base Defence Organization, then re-forming, and the second was Assistant Editor of the Royal Naval Sailing Association's journal.

As a preliminary to his military work, and remembering the uses to which the equipment had been put in Alexandria, he attended a Davis Submarine Escape Apparatus course at HMS *Dolphin* with every intention of adapting it further for diving rather than escaping.

On 23 May, 1939, he was promoted Captain and, in those last months before the war, sailed as much as possible and notably in *Wanda*, a forty-foot gaff-cutter built by the Berthon Boat Company in 1930. As a result he was elected to the Royal Ocean Racing Club.

War with Germany was declared in September, 1939. Immediately the Home Fleet was despatched to Scapa Flow in the Orkney Islands to be protected, in part, by the Royal Marines' Special Gun Mounting Party of the MNBDO. This party was quickly enlarged, renamed the Royal Marines Fortress Unit (RMFU) embarked in the requistioned merchant ship the SS *Mashroba* and sailed north with anti-aircraft guns.

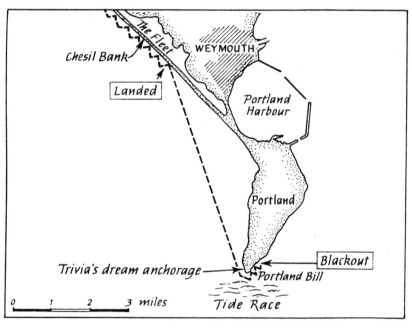

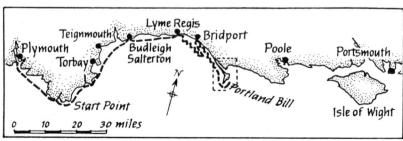

# CHAPTER THREE

## LCUs, Trawlers and *Puffers*

To understand events north of the Arctic Circle in 1940 it is necessary to look briefly at the background. Once war had been declared Mr Winston Churchill, appointed First Lord of the Admiralty for the second time, advised that an economic blockade of Germany would need to be established and that the export of iron ore through Narvik from the Swedish mines at Gallivare was a suitable start.

Two-thirds of the enemy's needs could be satisfied by these northern orefields, with Norway controlling one of only two exporting options: the ore could only travel south through neutral Sweden or west to Narvik's railhead and thence by ship to mainland Germany via the inner leads of the Norwegian coastline.

Unable to deal with Sweden the Home Fleet was ordered to mine the entrance to Vestfiord, leading to Narvik, disregarding the fact that these were Norwegian waters, while a landing force (it could hardly be termed amphibious) was formed in the Scottish naval bases to follow on if the mines failed to prevent an enemy occupation.

Germany began her invasion of Norway on 3 April, 1940. On the 7th German naval forces, including *Scharnhorst* and *Gneisenau,* put to sea to cover the invasion and were sighted at 0848: the British Home Fleet was sailed at 2015 to intercept but the enemy landed at Narvik on 9 April and, although Norwegian resistance was brave and determined, it was quickly overrun.

The first British troops to land in Norway, elements from the Brigade of Guards, did so at Harstad on 14 April from ships under the command of the Admiral of the Fleet Lord Cork and Orrery with a view to investing Narvik and eventually capturing it. By May these men would be augmented by over 25,000 from France, Poland and Norway.

On 28 April, 1940, Churchill sent Personal Minute No 315[1] to the

---

[1] RM Archive: 7/19/19

First Sea Lord and the Vice Chief of the Naval Staff asking about moving anti-aircraft guns up to Narvik, even before the town was taken back, as, he suggested, "the surrounding hills are capable of affording gun-sites". He was also anxious to know whether or not the aerodrome to the north-west was being extended to take Hurricanes . . . Churchill was indeed back again as First Lord of the Admiralty and, with a clear aim, continued, "We must expect early and increasing air attack."

On 26 April Churchill established a Narvik Committee[2] under the chairmanship of the Civil Lord to:

> Prepare in outline a plan for converting Narvik and its surround-ings (if and when captured) into a Naval, Military and Air base of high importance. We may well have 30,000 troops operating from Narvik on or beyond the Swedish border this summer. Strong defences must be mounted on the approaching fiords . . . (These men will be) brought to bear on the Gallivare orefield . . . questions of Swedish neutrality need not be settled yet.[3]

The committee held its first meeting on the same day at 2.30 pm and was able to report that a naval base was "now in the Narvik area with Lord Cork": things were moving as the First Lord wished.

Blondie Hasler, as Landing Officer of the RMFU since 20 October, 1939, had been sent to Scapa Flow to help install the guns and port defences for the Home Fleet, a main *raison d"etre* of the MNBDO in general and of the recently-formed RMFU in particular.

In Scapa, and in common with a number of other young officers, he occasionally came under the influence of the eccentric Commander Newcombe who, among his more formal duties, would take parties of young officers duck and snipe shooting. Newcombe had lost a leg in the First World War but never regarded that as a hindrance to his career or chosen sport. When flighting conditions were suitable and he had coerced the right companions, he would look up from his desk at a Wren secretary (who had yet to be issued with uniform) and say, "Right, we go! Bring me my driving leg," and she would do just that, while never forgetting his shooting leg with holes drilled in it to let the bog water out. The party would then set off led by the Commander with his spare legs tucked under each arm.

[2]  RM Archive: 7/19/19 (7)
[3]  RM Archive: 7/19/19 (8)

On 12 April, 1940, MNBDO, now strengthened to include anti-submarine and medical facilities, was placed on one month's notice for overseas duties and, as expected, the RMFU component, under the command of Lieutenant-Colonel H.R. Lambert, DSC, Royal Marines,[4] joined the Norway campaign on 10 May, basing itself at Harstad on the north-east corner of the island of Hinnoya.

On that day the Landing and Maintenance Group (LMG) moved forward to the near-island of Skänland, south of Harstad, to help establish the airfield from which Hurricanes could, if they arrived in time, operate in support of the imminent attack on Narvik. The LMG had deployed from Scapa Flow in SS *Mashroba* from which they now unloaded material needed for the operation on to Harstad's jetties, fortuitously as it was to turn out, for the ship was about to be bombed. Additionally, *Mashroba* possessed workshops, stores and carried guns, landing craft and the equipment for building a pier. Blondie shipped a considerable amount of this equipment, including that belonging to the RAF, across the Skänland beaches using two slow landing craft placed at his disposal.

Landing from HMS *Effingham*, the attached French Demi Brigade captured the small, but strategically interesting, village of Bjerkvik, at the head of Herjangsfiorden, on 13 May, 1940. Bjerkvik straddles the road between Skänland and Narvik and would provide a useful, and reasonably close, embarkation beach for tanks, while control of the head of the fiord would stop any land-borne, pre-emptive strike against Skänland, should the Germans have been so minded. Allied troops were now able to concentrate ashore around Saegnes and Emmenes from the 22nd onwards.[5]

On 22 May the Commander in Chief ordered the Officer Commanding Royal Marines Fortress Unit to "provide experienced personnel to assist in running landing craft for the assault on Narvik town". After twelve days of logistic work, there were no shortages of volunteers for this operational task allowing the Landing Officer to pick and choose the best that same day:[6] on the next he was ordered to take two Motor Landing Craft, MLC 20 and MLC 18, south through the

[4] Later, Major-General, CBE, DSC.
[5] *The Royal Marines – Admiralty Account of their Achievements 1939–1943.* (*HMSO 1944*).
[6] He chose: Temp 2nd Lt G.W.H. Andrews RM, Sub-Lieut R.G. Sturdy RNVR, Mne A. Caiels, Mne J. Maclaren, Mne J.R. Garthwaite, Mne H. Johnson and a few naval ratings for the 2 MLCs – regrettably their names are not recorded.

narrow, twisting and strong-streamed Ramsundet[7] channel that separates the mainland (of which Skänland is the westernmost peninsula) from the island of Hinnoya. (see map p. 41)

Having embarked two crews, enough food, water and ammunition for at least a week and one anti-aircraft Lewis gun for each landing-craft, Blondie's tiny force sailed on 23 May through this difficult passage under tow of two *Skoyter;* meanwhile, back at Harstad, *Mashroba* was bombed and then beached. The ubiquitous *Skoyter* are best described as the Norwegian equivalent of the Scottish *Puffer* and, with one single-cylinder oil engine, were about as manoeuvrable, but they were to play an invaluable part in the whole campaign as Blondie, and others[8], would testify.

The Naval Orders[9] for the forthcoming attack were written on 22 May and were contained in just four pages of large type; having established the ground rules for the attack on Narvik they allowed for much individual interpretation and initiative as, without likelihood of air parity, let alone air superiority, any firmer plan was bound to be distrupted. The airfield at Skänland was still being constructed to take the long-awaited Hurricanes that should have offered the air-support so essential to amphibious operations, so while this airfield was under construction a small strip further north, capable of operating Gladiators, was brought to readiness despite the Commander-in-Chief, Home Fleet's, continued scepticism over this aircraft's usefulness:

> The Gladiators sent to Andalsnes area have all been destroyed having only accounted for one enemy machine as far as I know, this being due, apparently, to difficulties starting their engines.

There were other problems, particularly with the planning. Without any doctrine for joint or combined operations and with sparse amphibious and air assets the day would only be saved by the weakness of the enemy on the ground, the well-trained (but erratic) French Foreign Legion and the determination and bravery of the Royal Navy. Meanwhile, the naval orders had a three-fold 'Intention'.[10]

---

[7] To this day still "restricted", as much for the difficulty of navigation as for military reasons.

[8] *The "Puffers" at Narvik.* Peter Dalzel: *Army Quarterly Review.* 1965.

[9] Hasler papers. *Flag Officer Harstad's Naval Operation Order for the Attack on Narvik.*

[10] The forerunner of, first, the "Aim" and later the "Mission" in operational orders.

First:, It is the intention to capture Narvik by means of a landing by infantry at Orneset and by tanks between Ormesvik and Taraldsvik. This force will then advance into the town of Narvik.

Second: A simultaneous advance will be carried out on the Ankenes peninsula by infantry and tanks.

Third: Both operations will be supported by naval and land artillery.

The landings, due to begin at Orneset at 0001 on 25 May, were delayed until the 28th to await the arrival of the Hurricane Squadron. There were also continuing differences of military and naval opinion over the manner in which the landings should be conducted; differences not helped by Major-General Mackesy, the military commander, and Admiral of the Fleet Lord Cork, being at odds from the very beginning and, then, compounding this unfortunate state by refusing to meet. The naval commander, understandably wanting to capitalize on the navy's success of 13 April,[11] had originally planned to attack on the 15th, the day after Mackesy's arrival, but the General did not consider a military attack necessary at all.

Nor did General Mackesy's decision find favour in London, for, while he had been ordered not to land "in the face of opposition", the CIGS agreed with Lord Cork that advantage should be taken of any naval action and that, ultimately, "boldness is required". In his book *The Second World War* Winston Churchill's view was blunt:

> The sea-borne attack, brilliantly opened by the Navy, was paralysed by the refusal of the military commander to run what was admittedly a desperate risk.

In the event Mackesy was replaced by General Auchinleck on 13 May and planning could continue with more agreement and equanimity. The main point at issue was the Royal Navy's desire to reinforce success against the army's view that a blockade to starve the Germans out would be the most likely way to succeed. Yet the opposition was small when compared to the Allied ground and naval forces while, in the air, the Germans continued to dominate.

---

[11] The second battle of Narvik and the landing of the French Foreign Legion at Bjerkvik.

By the time the attack was ready to be launched British and French troops held all the land surrounding the Narvik Peninsula and, thanks to the Royal Navy fighting, and winning, the two battles of Narvik (10 and 13 April) both coasts of Ofotfiord also lay in Allied hands.

The British Army had trained and equipped Independent Companies for guerrilla operations in the region yet had overlooked the probability that at that time of year thick snow was still liable to cover the ground; hence the troops had not been issued with suitable camouflage material for the conditions. To exacerbate matters, the snow that year lay later than usual, although by May it had begun to recede to about 1000 feet above sea level. The Royal Navy had made great sacrifices to set the scene for a military assault and viewed with concern the lack of determination by the military to follow suit. In the end no British infantry took part.

Allied naval forces for the amphibious attack on Narvik were tabulated as: three cruisers, five destroyers, 2 MLC and one Assault Landing Craft while the ground forces were made up from a French force of two battalions of Foreign Legion and one of Chasseurs, a battalion of Norwegian infantry on the north side of Ofotfiord and a Polish force on the south. All British troops had by now been withdrawn from the zone (the South Wales Borderers in the ill-fated HMS *Effingham* who hit an uncharted rock on her way to Bodo) except for one or two light AA sections, Field Artillery Sections, a small RAMC detachment and detachments of signallers. Allied re-supply forwards from the Harstad and Skänland bases was either by the indifferent roads skirting the fiords with their innumerable weak bridges or by painfully slow *Skoyter,* a large fleet of which provided most of the intercommunication in the area.[12]

The occupying German forces consisted of miscellaneous infantry units landed from ships at the time of the original invasion which, by the end of May, had been pushed back on both sides of Ofotfiord so that only Narvik was entirely in their hands. They possessed no armoured vehicles, only one field gun and had three possible supply routes, one by rail via neutral Sweden (the border is about twenty miles to the east of Narvik), by parachutes or by seaplane, and it was this last that they used most.

The only armoured fighting vehicles in the Allied force were about a dozen French tanks which had to be transported by landing craft as their thirteen-ton weight was beyond the capacity of the local bridges and car ferries, both of which were vulnerable throughout the campaign to an almost uninterrupted air superiority enjoyed by the enemy. Daylight

---

[12] Lt (later Lt Commander) Patrick Dalzel-Job RNVR in command.

bombing was a daily occurrence, mostly directed at ships and carried out from a high altitude. From 20 May onwards the Allied forces gradually concentrated in the areas east of Saegnes and Emmenes which, being thickly wooded, was well adapted for concealment although under twenty-four hour enemy observation from points sited at about 1400 feet on the heights to the east of Narvik. Troop movement by anything other than very small parties was impossible, enforcing high standards of concealment and camouflage.

Once south of the Ramsundet Channel and with the attack on Narvik delayed until the 28th, Blondie was ordered to pre-position two French tanks and two field guns at Emmenes on 23 and 24 May and with the naval forces due to move into position off Tjelsundet, at the western end of Ofotfiorden, by 2100 on 27 May all would be ready.

The two Motor Landing Craft under Blondie's command were of very different design. MLC 18 was an obsolete vessel powered by a rudimentary form of water-jet propulsion that gave it a maximum speed of about four knots laden, providing that the jets were clear of weed (a rare condition) and whose heavy bow ramp could only be raised slowly by three men. With a draught of four feet and a wading depth for the tanks of three feet, the choice of beaches was restricted to those with steep gradients – of which there are very few in that area. Blondie's other craft was slightly more suitable for the task with a shallower draught, twin-screw propulsion and a higher speed.

As he had had experience with water-jet propelled landing-craft and as he rightly believed that it was the one most likely to cause trouble Blondie elected to command from MLC 18, with 2nd Lieutenant Andrews as a back-up, and gave MLC 20 to Sub-Lieutenant Sturdy. Two marines were attached to each MLC as beach party. Their first task was to transfer two French tanks and two field guns and tractors to Emmenes from Sandtorg and Bjerkvik respectively. The military staff had selected Emmenes Bay as the landing beach because it was conveniently situated and had a road running along the shore, but on arrival it proved to be impossibly shallow and studded with large rocks for several hundred yards out to sea and, while this was evident from the map, the point had been missed owing to ignorance of landing operations on the part of the staff. This simple operation took over five hours and included one drowned tank that had become bogged down on a rising tide. Blondie was to comment later, as have so many in his position before and since, that throughout these operations it was evident that no army officers and only a very few naval officers had any appreciation of the practicalities of amphibious work.

For a subsequent load the landing craft managed to marry-up with a car ferry landing place at the entrance to Skjomen Fiord which, as they still do, consisted of a sort of drawbridge that they lowered into a MLC, causing the bows to submerge, an operation that had earlier led to the loss of a landing-craft but which, this time, was conducted without damage.

With these preliminary pre-positionings completed on the 24th the small force was ordered to lie low in Herjangsfiord where three Assault Landing Craft (ALC) of the Landing and Maintenance Group were also waiting for the assault. Ashore Blondie was appalled to find the crews bivouacking "in a state of some savagery, having no officer to look after them", although great ingenuity had been exercised in camouflage by lying bows-on to the shore with a kedge astern and covering the whole arrangement with foliage.

Four days of "enforced idleness" followed, while everyone awaited the arrival of the promised Hurricanes. This time was not wasted by the MLC crews who equipped their craft with light, wooden brows about fourteen feet by three to assist with the dry passage of troops across shallow beaches, the French infantry officers considering, quite rightly, that it was undesirable to begin an operation in mountainous, snow-clad country with boots full of water. Blondie commented:

> Nothing much of interest occurred. We drew rations and rum indiscriminately from the navy and the French army and our interests were well looked after by Lieutenant D.Duff, Royal Navy, the liaison officer at French HQ who indeed appeared to be controlling the whole operation (including the French military staff) in a most masterly manner.
>
> 2nd Lieutenant Andrews took an armed party ashore one day with the intention of shooting a sheep to supplement our rather monotonous rations but returned empty-handed. The scheme had already been worked to death by the Foreign Legion and all he found was one sheep (evidently the last in the area) closely guarded by its owner who also had a gun.
>
> The French troops remained completely concealed. Walking along the roads there was no sign of occupation at all but on proceeding into the woods one came across vehicles, ammunition dumps and troops all completely covered in brushwood. The Foreign Legion were in splendid form eating tinned horse, drinking apparently unlimited quantities of rum (which they carried in their water-bottles) and discharging their rifles at all

hours of day and night apparently for the dual purpose of cleaning the barrel and keeping their eye in. We were not keen on the latter practice since they usually chose to do a sort of "throw-off" shoot at our boats in the fiord.

Then, at last, on 27 May two Operation Orders were received, one covering the naval bombardment and one the French attack on Narvik peninsula, and indicating that these would take place on the following day. After agreeing with Blondie the most convenient embarkation points for his men and vehicles and the best beaches for disembarking them in the assault, Lieutenant-Colonel Magrin Vernerey, Commandant la 13ème Demi-Brigade de Marche de Légion Étrangére, issued his orders[13] on 27 May, accompanying these with written schedules for the landings.

Colonel Vernerey's plan was to load the French and Norwegian troops at Saegnes and Oifiord and, supported by two tanks, land them immediately east of Orneset, to the east of Narvik, under cover of the naval bombardment. A portion of the force would then push the enemy west along the south side of Rombaksfiord while Polish troops in the Emmenes area, supported by another two tanks, were to attack eastwards through Ankenes along the southern side of Beisford.

The naval bombardment opened at 2200 on 27 May with the arrival of three 6" cruisers and five destroyers taking up their positions to the north and east of Narvik and immediately engaging their pre-arranged targets at close range. "Adding to the fun," as Blondie put it, was a battery of French 75mm guns sited on a reverse slope immediately south of Saegnes. A major target for all weapons was the entrance to the railway tunnel immediately east of Orneset known to shelter the only field gun that the enemy possessed.

Blondie's landing-craft had to complete eleven waves between 2300 on the 27th and 0700 on the 28th, and, as tactical surprise for the first wave was vital, this one was planned from Saegnes in order to give a little initial cover from enemy observation while most later waves would depart from Oifiord to give a shorter turn-round time.

The assembly point for the first landing craft wave was half a mile due east of Langstrand and north of the line of destroyers stretching along the fiord while the three cruisers formed an arc from west to north-north-west of Narvik. The signal for the attack to start was given promptly by

---

[13] Copy in Hasler papers.

the Flagship at 2350 and with three-quarters of a mile to run there was not much time for things to go wrong to make an H-hour of midnight.

The landing at midnight was easier than anyone had hoped for, especially as the bombardment had achieved part of its object by drawing attention away from the area. A few scattered rifle shots greeted the first ALCs, but by the time the MLCs arrived with 100 men in each there was no opposition. Blondie could see nothing of the progress of the troops once ashore, for they disappeared up the thickly wooded slope of the mountain, but "from the lively rattle of musketry it appeared that things were not quite as quiet as had at first appeared.".

Having landed the first waves without loss the landing-craft returned to Oijfiord where they loaded men across the open beach in full view of the enemy. They might have got away without interference but for the solitary German field gun (a captured French 75mm gun mounted on a railway carriage) which, once the naval bombardment had lifted, emerged from its tunnel. As MLC 20 was backing off six high-explosive shells fell in rapid succession around her. The landing-craft escaped unscathed but 2nd Lieutenant Andrews, now of the shore party, was wounded and several Frenchmen killed.

Blondie dashed ashore from MLC 18 to find out what was happening and although the German fire had ceased (thanks to a prompt response by HMS *Coventry*),[14] the beach was already deserted. Finding a field telephone, he managed to speak to Lieutenant Duff at French HQ who brought him up to date and promptly told him to embark a company of Norwegians, if he, Duff, could find them – which he did, in the woods and after a long quarter of an hour. It took a great deal of persuasion in bad French to motivate them as they were by now very frightened not having, in Blondie's words, "foreseen the possibility of any danger being attached to the operation".

As MLC 20 made her second trip to the east of Narvik the Germans counter-attacked and, gaining the high ground to the east of the landing beach, opened fire with machine guns. One legionnaire was killed in the landing craft forcing the embarked French officer to insist that Sub-Lieutenant Sturdy land them on a beach 300 yards further west; this they did without further casualties.

Both MLCs now returned to Saegnes to embark a tank each, an evolution that was only possible on such a shallow beach as the flood tide had begun to make. Having loaded the armour successfully the two boats

---

[14] Donald Peyton Jones, in charge of one of her guns, was responsible for this target.

steamed direct to Taraldsvik at the dignified pace of four knots. But the gradients at Taraldsvik beach were an unsurveyed quantity, so, with the tank commanders' ready concurrence, it was agreed that no attempt would be made until they heard a blast from Blondie's whistle. The approach was unmolested and the two MLCs ran gently on to what, as feared, was a shallow, weed-encumbered coastline. Blondie, in the water-jet-propelled craft, tried to go astern but the inlets became clogged, instantly preventing any further movement until they could be cleared.Deciding that a delay in getting the armour ashore was inadvisable he, rather doubtfully, blew his whistle. Both tanks immediately charged over the ramps into four feet of water "discharging their cannon and machine guns all over the landscape", an action that could have ended in disaster as the area was already occupied by Allied forces. Nevertheless, and much to his surprise, the tanks did negotiate the water-gap successfully, only to become irretrievably bogged at the top of the beach – and thus, in Blondie's words, "the tank offensive was terminated" leaving him little choice but to leave them to it.

MLC 20 returned at once to Saegnes to lift ammunition, stores and reserve troops in company with the Assault Landing Craft while MLC 18 succeeded in leaving the beach to 'amble' at about a knot as the engine room staff made a determined effort to clear the jets. The Luftwaffe now made a belated and vigorous arrival to bomb the warships and the French artillery, forcing the cruisers and destroyers to take violent avoiding action. One 6" cruiser received a hit amidships, but, apart from setting fire to some ready-use cordite, she was little damaged.

MLC 18 experienced several more near misses, this time from enemy mortar fire, but managed to reach the other side of the fiord unscathed where she was beached for four hours at the bottom of the tide so that her jets could be cleared. While she was 'out of battle' Blondie took the opportunity to embark in one of his *Skoyter* carrying petrol and ammunition from Bjerkvik to Orneset, a fateful decision, for, although all went well across the fiord, when they arrived and had secured alongside MLC 20 enemy aircraft began bombing runs along the beach.

Still fully laden with ammunition the *Skoyter* slipped from alongside a beached landing-craft and steamed as fast as she could towards the middle of the fiord in order to achieve 'a little dispersal'. Although this was the correct action she was now prey to a formation of three, previously unnoticed, ME 110s flying in close formation at about 100 feet who promptly machine-gunned her before wheeling and repeating the process from the opposite direction. Fires broke out immediately as the incendiaries punctured the full petrol cans still loose on the upper deck which, in turn, set fire to the wooden ammunition boxes. Bullets had also hit the reserve MLC coxswain in the leg and his seaman in the base of the spine.

The vessel and her crew were now in grave danger. With the Norwegian crew sheltering in the forepeak and the wounded men being attended to, the blazing *Skoyter* was steered for Langstrand by a Royal Marine, while others feverishly attempted to prevent the fire igniting the ammunition or reaching the engine room. With buckets of water against blazing petrol it even began as a losing battle. By good fortune rather than remarkable seamanship she was run on to the beach allowing the crew to scramble quickly over the bow. At the after end, and as they approached the shore, Blondie mustered his uninjured men to haul in the skiff they were towing, and with that safely secured, they manhandled the wounded over the side but just as they cut themselves free the fire reached its goal and the ammunition exploded, disintegrating both wooden vessels. Apart from the discomforts of a short, cold swim towards the beach, nobody was further hurt.

By this time the main attack had developed well, with the whole of Narvik in Allied hands and the Germans retreating into the mountains to the east. The MLCs continued to work intermittently, ferrying supplies and second-line troops, finally re-embarking the two tanks (which had been de-bogged) from Orneset and returning them to Bjerkvik.

Blondie's part in the assault on Narvik was now over and, once the tanks had been delivered from whence they had come prior to the assault, his small force sailed for Harstad, satisfied that they had achieved all that was asked of them. So it was an unpleasant surprise to find that, instead of a warm welcome, not only had their 'home' been sunk in their absence but everyone else in the Royal Marines Fortress Unit had already left for England!

Blondie's Norwegian adventures were not yet over, for on 26 May the evacuation of the British Expeditionary Force across the beaches of Dunkirk marked a new start for Britain's war effort. 'Side-shows' such as Narvik would now take second place while the country licked its wounds and its leaders planned the next moves from a 're-grouped' position. Consequently those left behind in Harstad were ordered to prepare to evacuate the men and equipment they had spent so much care in landing.

The landing craft detailed for this next operation were now MLCs 14 and 20, plus two ALCs, but this time with only one crew each. A welcome improvement on the *Skoyters* as depot and support vessels was a trawler they were able to requisition and re-name His Majesty's Trawler *Man o' War*.

The German forces had been pushed back almost to the Swedish border and were no longer capable of mounting a serious counter-attack, but, to compensate for their defeat on the ground, bombing sorties increased steadily with their main objectives, as they had been throughout, the allied shipping.

The plan for the withdrawal of troops in the Narvik area was based on a series of orders which Blondie tabulated as follows:

a. The withdrawal to be carried out in five days.
b. Each night a proportion of the force to be embarked in a fleet of *Skoyter* at various local jetties and taken out to destroyers lying as close inshore as possible, each destroyer taking up to 500 men.
c. The destroyers then to steam down Ofotfiord to rendezvous with troopships lying well out.

Inevitably this simplicity had been subject to a number of restrictions, the troopships keeping well away from Narvik in order to maintain a semblance of secrecy and to avoid a greater risk of heavy bombing. Under these circumstances, and much against the Principles infused into Royal Marines, it was considered by the commanders that all equipment should be destroyed rather than evacuated.

The *Skoyters* were now organized into five groups of eight, with each group in the charge of a naval officer with military guards on each vessel "in case coercion of the Norwegian crews should prove necessary". The landing craft under Blondie's specific command were required to prevent destruction of any jetties by Norwegians and then to embark the final rearguards from the chosen evacuation beaches. His small flotilla arrived at Skjomenfiord, about two miles south of Emmenes, the day before the withdrawal was due to start.

The weather, which up to then had been in the bomber's favour, now degenerated into low cloud, preventing further action. It is reported[15] that during the first four days of this phase the organization "worked like clockwork" and that, consequently, Blondie's landing-craft crews had nothing to do except help throw guns, equipment, vehicles and ammunition into the sea, not all of which was given the 'float test' for HMT *Man o' War* acquired a fair cross-section of useful *matériel* including two

[15] Blondie's post-operation report – Hasler papers.

Bofors guns which were quickly mounted on her forward well deck to add to her 4" gun, while light machine guns were fastened "in great profusion" all round the superstructure. They regarded themselves as the most formidable trawler afloat.

The routine was occasionally broken by the arrival of aircraft to bomb Narvik through gaps in the cloud, but this was largely a waste of ordinance as most troops had been evacuated; only the civilian population suffered. During one such attack *Man o' War's* newly acquired Bofors "claimed a large share in a Heinkel which was seen to come down about two miles to the westward".

Towards the operation's end MLC 14 and one ALC, both under command of Sub-Lieutenant Sturdy, were detailed to embark the rearguards from Straumsnes, in Rombaksfiord, and transfer them to HMS *Veteran*. HMT *Man o' War* was to accompany her using her 4" gun to give covering fire if necessary and to sink the landing craft on completion. Meanwhile MLC 20 and one ALC under Blondie's command were to embark rearguards from the east end of Beissfiord and transfer them to HMS *Firedrake*, lying west of Narvik town, after which they were to rejoin their depot ships and sink the two landing craft in the same way.

This operation went without disruption and once all troops were embarked in the waiting destroyers Blondie's party "spent an amusing ten minutes sinking the landing craft by gunfire, with the exception of one ALC which we decided to tow all the way home". This lucky vessel was secured with new hemp hawsers before they set off north through the Tjelsundet in company with two other trawlers.

They were the last men to leave and, like most rearguards, felt a strong impulse to lose no time in the process, but as *Man o' War's* speed was hampered by the landing craft it was obvious that she would have to drop her tow. With the 4" gun unable to be trained on to the ALC unless the trawler stopped and turned "an interesting half hour was spent doing the job with a couple of rifles firing tracer into her petrol tanks." When finely ablaze, she was cut adrift by concentrating the rifle fire on the knots at the outward end for the trawler skipper was keen to lose as little of his new ropes as possible.

With no further opportunity to put their AA armament into action, the journey home was uneventful and the three trawlers arrived safely at Scapa Flow from where Blondie returned overland to rejoin the RMFU at Eastney.

On his arrival he still sported a ginger-red beard which would have been removed during the passage from Harstad had he been with the

RMFU's main party and read the standing orders for the unit's return. But he was proud of the growth, especially the colour, and risked his luck by appearing in service dress at Eastney where he was promptly ordered to shave. He did, but not before posing for a photographer!

So Blondie came home from the war for the first time, not that he would be telling anybody about his experiences, for he knew that many of the older officers had seen much worse in the First World War and that many of his own contemporaries were at sea facing more difficult odds. But one person to whom he did confide his feelings, but not the details, was David Astor,[16] a Royal Marines Hostilities Only officer serving at Eastney. David was surprised by the lack of confidence in his friend after such an experience, and equally surprised for the reason behind it when Blondie confessed that, now he had been 'tried by fire', he was doubting his ability as an officer.

This lack of faith in himself stemmed from a belief that he had let his men down. They had, on occasion, not been up to scratch (when he had found them "living in some savagery" was an example) and for that he would only blame himself.

"Was it," he asked David often over a drink in the MNBDO Officers' Mess, "a fault to punish myself for the failure of the men under my command when, in practice, it was my lack of leadership?"

Realizing that example, not threat, is the greater stimulation and, guided by his friend, from now on, if his men let him down, Blondie would push himself to even greater limits of endurance or levels of skill to show what was possible and what the standards were that he sought.

Blondie knew, too, that training men, only to dismiss them after some otherwise hidden flaw had risen to the surface, was expensive in money, but in war especially expensive in time. When the time came to choose his own teams for specific tasks he would devise methods of selection which were to rely heavily on an ability to see through pretence, baloney and even shyness. His capacity[17] to see the hidden depths – or lack of them – in a volunteer would astound his contemporaries, thus sending a man back, once accepted, would be a rare event, and when he did have to take that action he would chastise himself for making a poor choice in the first place.

Another aspect that worried Blondie after his first operation was the lack of any blood-lust he had felt, and that this non-aggressive attitude (as far as personal violence was concerned) was not a good

---

[16] To be awarded the Croix de Guerre in 1944 and of whom much more later.
[17] Contemporary reports and personal reminiscences.

attribute to possess in war,[18] when, as Admiral of the Fleet Lord Fisher had once said, "The essence of war is violence. Moderation in war is imbecility." Those few weeks north of the Arctic Circle proved to him that this maxim was not to his style and, while certainly wishing to "engage the enemy more closely", the Narvik campaign had set him thinking of ways to do so in such a manner that the minimum number of lives would be lost for the maximum amount of material damage inflicted.

While few were aware of what had happened in the fiords around Narvik the news crept out through the *London Gazette* of 11 July, 1940, when the award of an OBE was made public. This was followed by the French Croix de Guerre from General Belthouart, lately commanding the French forces in Norway, and again his name appeared in the *London Gazette*, on 26 September, when he was Mentioned in Despatches. The British had recognized his flair for organizing a minor amphibious operation and the French acknowledged his bravery and tenacity while under fire. The 'mention' was for saving his crewman's life after the ME 110 machine-gun attacks.

Despite these signs of public recognition (the citations were sparse) his part, he thought, was so insignificant to the overall campaign that it was not worth reporting, beyond the few lessons learned, and that he did largely through verbal de-briefings and two very short papers[19]. Tabulating lessons for the future was one thing to Blondie, but the telling of his own story (even officially, let alone in the Officers' Mess) did not come so easily.

The Royal Marines Office knew, of course, of the landings and would have read Colonel Lambert's reports in which Captain Hasler's name fleetingly appeared but it was still well over a year after his return from Narvik before a letter from the office of the Adjutant General Royal Marines was despatched:

> To the Commander 2 RM Gp MNBDO dated 29th October 41:[20]
>
> It is understood that Maj[21] H.G. Hasler OBE was in charge of an operation in the Norwegian Campaign of which a full account is not held in this office. It is therefore requested that

---

[18] Conversation with David Astor.
[19] Hasler papers.
[20] RM Archive: 7/19/19 (30)
[21] He had been promoted to Acting Major on 18 March, 1941.

Maj Hasler may be instructed to prepare and forward an account
of this Operation to AGRM.

Blondie's report was despatched to the AGRM's office on 8
December, 1941 and his Commanding Officer received an acknowledgement dated 19th December, 1941, signed by the AGRM himself.[22]

Military lessons would continue to be drawn from this campaign, but
two of Blondie's personal comments highlight the need for a certain *sang
froid* in difficult times. The only times he came under fire, and was frightened by the experiences, he explained, were when the French Foreign
Legion "while bored and having had too much of the rum they carried
in their water-bottles, a seemingly endless supply!" would use his landing
craft for target practice. The second was that the German bombs
produced more fish for his men than he ever could with rod and line and
in that respect were occasionally welcome!

As a finale to the amphibious aspects of Narvik in 1940 it is interesting
to read a paper written in 1939 that highlighted the inability of Britain at
that time to conduct swift amphibious operations:[23]

> With the material at present available it is impossible to stage any
> landing operation on a hostile shore, with a force of a brigade or
> more sooner than six months from the time that the order is
> given.

When the editors of the *History of the Combined Operations*[24] presented
this quote in 1956 they added their own summary:

> By 1939 therefore . . . we had no means of putting an army
> ashore in face of opposition and the technical problems of
> achieving a greater rate of build-up than the enemy had scarcely
> received any attention at all. Any question of tactical or strategic
> surprise appeared hardly worthy of consideration as any likeli-
> hood of it being achieved was remote. The events of 1940 were
> to compel rapid and unconventional solutions to all these
> problems.

[22] Hasler papers.
[23] Deputy Chiefs of Staff (Inter Service Training) paper 35 dated 30 June,
1939.
[24] One of whom was Norman Tailyour.

The business of taking the war to the enemy had yet to be properly addressed, but through his actions in Norway Blondie had played a significant part in highlighting the amphibious deficiencies that then existed and, through his thoughts and ideas, soon to be given substance, he was to become a driving force in the "unconventional solutions" so obviously needed.

Two short pages of observations from the Norway landings had been written by Blondie on his return and were eventually incorporated into his comprehensive report for the Adjutant General:

Some General Observations on the Operation
1. The landing operation was made comparatively easy by no appreciable enemy fire directed on to the beaches . . . Had it been otherwise, there would have been heavy casualties in the MLCs before they ever reached the beach. Thus:
2. If the opposition had been heavy it might have been impossible to use the MLCs at all in the early stages . . .
3. The French 13-ton tank proved to be difficult to load and unload because:
   a. The beaches were in most cases insufficiently steep-to . . .
   b. Except when actually going into action, the tank commanders were extremely cautious . . . It is important that the military staff realize that it needs

---

[25] Later Rear-Admiral Ralph Lindsay Fisher CB, DSO, OBE, DSC. A member of the Royal Cruising Club with extensive experience of square-rigged sailing. He had also canoed 900 nautical miles down the Danube with his wife in 1936. His remarkable naval career included the command of HMS *Wakeful* at Dunkirk. Shortly after picking up her second load of soldiers all 650 were killed when she was sunk by torpedo from "E" boat S.24 (Oberleutnant Zur See Hans Detlessen – later wounded and captured while commanding S.38). Fisher, one of the few naval survivors, was rescued by a Scottish drifter but the destroyer she had moored alongside to transfer survivors was torpedoed. Fisher held on to the drifter but, with no one on deck and now steaming in a circle at seven knots, he was obliged to let go. Mistaken for an enemy vessel the drifter was then shelled by a destroyer and brought to a stop. Once again Fisher tried to board but the destroyer now decided to ram, and as she did so he dived to come up astern, having avoided the propellors. He floated till dawn before being rescued by a Norwegian steamer that transferred him to another drifter bound for Dover. Later he conducted some remarkable cruises and in 1978, at the age of seventy-six, won the RCC's prestigious Romola Cup (for the second time) for a two-handed round Ireland cruise with his wife. He died in 1988.

more than a road running near a beach to make a
site for loading or unloading tanks.

Meanwhile, and unknown to Blondie, on 20 April, 1940, a girl was
born to Ralph and Ursula Fisher at Salterns Quay, Mengham Rythe,
Hayling Island; at the time Bridget Mary Lindsay Fisher's father[25] was
commanding HMS *Wakeful* and about to win a DSO at Dunkirk.

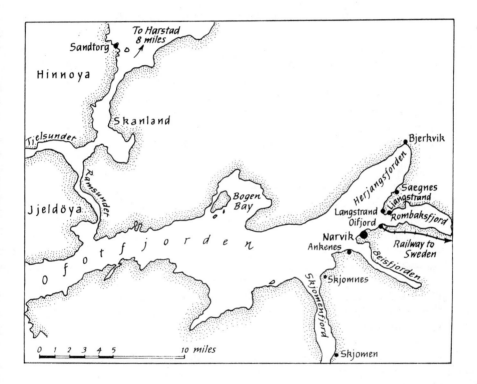

# CHAPTER FOUR

## Explosive Motor Boats and Cockles

While Blondie remained with the MNBDO for the rest of 1941 combined operations were very much on the move. In order to put the next two phases of Blondie's war into context the genealogy of the Combined Operations Headquarters needs to be examined.

After the First World War combined operations (particularly due to the Gallipoli campaign) had suffered from a bad press:

> It was regarded as suicidal to approach a defended beach in small ships' boats, the only craft available. Further, the awful prospect of having to get out of these open boats to land on an enfiladed beach was not considered, quite rightly, to be 'an operation of war'.

Since 1921 combined operations had been studied at the three services staff colleges where, if not in practice then at least in educated theory, some of the principles were kept alive. In 1936 the Director of the Royal Navy's Staff College at Greenwich wrote to the Admiral President of the War College:[1]

> The Staff College fully realizes the importance of the part the navy will play in any amphibious expedition and . . . as a sea power the predominant partner in any operation will be the navy. As such the navy should take the initiative for the design and provision of craft in the organization required for mounting an overseas expedition and in the supply of any special equipment required.

The Admiral forwarded the letter with a further recommendation that "a permanent committee be established to consider the subject and that

---

[1]  Captain B.C. Watson RN to Rear Admiral R.M. Colvin, 22 February, 1936.

a small training and development establishment of the three services should lead to real and rapid progress".[2]

Consequently a Combined Operations Sub-Committee was established and agreement reached for an Inter-Services Training and Development Centre (ISTDC) to be formed on 2 May, 1938, at Fort Cumberland, Eastney, under the command of a naval captain with, among others, a staff-trained, Royal Marines Adjutant. Work began in June with the first exercise held later that summer by a cruiser squadron landing soldiers from open boats propelled by muffled oars onto Slapton Sands in South Devon. So:

No progress in technique had taken place since the Crimea.[3]

Eventually combined operations were to receive the necessary momentum under the leadership first of General Bourne,[4] secondly, Admiral of the Fleet Lord Keyes and then most significantly, under Commodore (to begin with) Lord Louis Mountbatten:

After the defeat of the Allied armies in France and the Low Countries in May, 1940, it was apparent that the only way of returning to the offensive other than by bombing was by means of amphibious operations. In Europe, at this juncture, the policy could only be one of raiding the occupied coasts with the aim of causing the enemy to disperse his forces and equipment uneconomically. Further, the successful execution of a raid is excellent for morale at a time when a country must be strategically on the defensive.[5]

On 14 June, 1940, the Adjutant General of the Royal Marines, Lieutenant-General A.G.B.Bourne, CB, DSO, MVO, was appointed by the three Chiefs of Staff to be Commander of Raiding Operations (originally Offensive Operations). Additionally he was to act as Adviser to the Chiefs of Staff on Combined Operations and remain Adjutant General of the Royal Marines. General Bourne's remit from the Chiefs of Staff Committee was:[6]

[2] *History of Combined Operations Organisation 1940–1945.*
[3] Ibid..
[4] Later, General Sir Alan, KCB.
[5] Ibid..
[6] RM Archive: 2/14/1.

to harass the enemy (by raiding operations) and cause him to disperse his forces and to create material damage particularly on the coastline from Northern Norway to the western limit of German-occupied France . . . You are to keep the Chiefs of Staff informed of the operations you propose to carry out.

The Inter-Services Training and Development Centre was brought under General Bourne's command and with it the following instruction:

In addition we wish you to press on with the development and production of special landing craft and equipment and to advise us when the occasion arises, as to its allotment.

By mid-1940 General Bourne, now Director of Combined Operations, was not considered to be senior enough for the task, so it is interesting, in the light of the rank of the third head of Combined Operations, that the following letter was sent by Mr Churchill on 17 July, 1940:

Prime Minister to General Ismay and Sir Edward Bridges.
I have appointed Admiral of the Fleet Sir Roger Keyes as Director of Combined Operations . . . General Bourne should be informed that . . . it is essential to have an officer of higher rank in charge . . . and in any case the Royal Marines must play a leading part in this organization . . .

No new directive was issued to Admiral Keyes who, recognizing the need to move away, physically, from the Admiralty, placed his Headquarters in the War Cabinet Annex at 1a, Richmond Terrace. By the end of July 1940 he had under command about 500 men in commandos, 740 men in the Independent Companies,[7] 15 Assault Landing Craft and 4 MLCs. Northney Camp on Hayling Island had been requisitioned by the ISTDC on 15 June, 1940, to be re-named HMS *Northney* on 26 January, 1941. Then, on 14 March, 1941, the DCO was made responsible, under the direction of the Prime Minister, as Minister of Defence, for, *inter alia:*

The command and training in irregular warfare generally, and in landing operations in particular of the troops specially organized for this purpose, ie the Special Service Troops.

[7] See Charles Messenger's *The Commandos.*

But Admiral Keyes did not last long as DCO for he disagreed with the Chiefs of Staff over the conduct of *Exercise Leapfrog* in Scapa Flow and, among other factors, with a recommendation of his that a properly equipped headquarters ship was vital to success. Churchill replaced Keyes with Captain Lord Louis Mountbatten, who would be promoted to Commodore 1st Class and appointed Adviser on Combined Operations. There was yet to be a fourth title.

On 16 October, 1941, Mountbatten's directive ordered him to:

> Note that it is incumbent on you to give technical advice upon all plans for combined operations at all stages from their inception to the point when they are finally approved. It is equally incumbent upon the Commanders and Staff to seek your technical advice at all stages of planning.

Churchill required Mountbatten to "mount a programme of raids of ever-increasing intensity with the invasion of France the main object" and for this over-riding priority he was to "create the machine, devise the appliances, find the bases, create the training areas and select the site for the assault." In Mountbatten's own words he was to "think defensively but at all times to concentrate on the offensive".[8]

Back to Blondie: during his absence with the Royal Marines Fortress Unit and on the day before he landed the first troops of the Foreign Legion into Narvik he had been re-appointed, *in absentia,* to the Base Depot of the MNBDO and so it was to this unit that he had reported shortly after his return. By 8 January, 1941, MNBDO 2 had formed on Hayling Island under the command of the now Brigadier Lambert. Impressed by the young landing craft captain's performance, Lambert had him transferred from the Headquarters on 9 January to command the Landing Company with the rank of Acting Major, to date from 18 March.

Blondie's mind had been working fast, and in detail, on how he could improve current amphibious techniques and equipment. He was aware of the army's Special Boat Sections (attached to Lieutenant-Colonel Bob Laycock's[9] army commandos) and their use of Folbots[10] to gather intelligence and conduct sabotage attacks in the Mediterranean. By

[8] *Mountbatten.* Philip Ziegler.
[9] Among other appointments to become Chief of Combined Operations in Dec. 1943.
[10] Civilian-style canoes, discussed in detail later.

coincidence, Lieutenant-Commander Nigel Clogstoun-Willmott, Royal Navy[11], had also been in Norway during that spring of 1940 and had become equally as concerned as had Blondie (although they had not met in the fiords) over the lack of sensible beach intelligence and the absence of any plan, or method, to gain it.[12] In March 1941, Clogstoun-Willmott and Major Roger Courtney,[13] of the King's Royal Rifle Corps, carried out a comprehensive beach reconnaissance by canoe launched from the submarine HMS *Triumph* off Rhodes prior to the Allied landings of *Operation Cordite,* landings that were cancelled after Germany occupied Greece.

Although canoes were used by the army SBS in the Mediterranean on fifteen submarine-launched operations throughout 1941 the first using limpet mines against an enemy ship was from HMS *Taku* during the night 21/22 July in Bengazi harbour. Then, two Royal Marines, Sergeant Allan and Marine Miles, who, although captured after their canoe was holed on a rock, paved the way. It was four months before limpets were to be used again in such a manner by Tug Wilson[14] and Marine Hughes at Navarino. Sadly this mission had to be aborted and another four months were to pass before the third such attack was made, this time in Boulogne and, for the first time, by an all-army team.

In the spring of 1941 Blondie's ideas firmed-up into a simple combination of canoes and, the main difference between his ideas and those of the SBS, underwater swimmers who could attack enemy shipping in their harbours. These divers would be launched offshore from surface craft or submarine that could wait to pick them up on completion.

The paper[15] was forwarded via a non-receptive Admiralty to Combined Operations Headquarters and rejected on the simple, but erroneous, grounds that the equipment for such attacks did not exist. As Blondie knew personally, the canoes did exist, in modified civilian form with the army, and the ability to breathe under water was certainly extant. His compatriots in Alexandria in 1935 had used the Davis Submarine Escape Apparatus not only to inspect underwater obstructions but for sport.

[11] Later Captain RN, DSO, DSC and Bar.
[12] Taped interviews with, and letters to, the author.
[13] Later to win the MBE and MC with the SBS. Both these officers appear later.
[14] Then a Captain, later Lieutenant-Colonel Robert Wilson, DSO, Royal Artillery.
[15] This paper no longer exists although official references to it are made. There is no indication of the exact date (probably May) that Blondie wrote it. In his own diaries it is simply: *Early 1941 submit paper on underwater, canoe attack.*

The Italians were known to possess motorized 'human chariots' and although Blondie was suggesting an even more covert form of approach, he retained a high regard for the Italians and their inventive means of prosecuting attacks against large ships in secure bases. Their determination and ingenuity, and especially that of Commander Belloni, knew few bounds; in the end, though, it was faulty intelligence that led to failure after spectacular, early successes. Between the frogmen astride their chariots and the almost suicidal performance of the Explosive Motor Boat coxswains, these men inflicted grievous harm to British and allied ships.

The Explosive Motor Boat used by the Italians at Crete, and later against Grand Harbour, Malta, offered a one-way journey. d'Annunzio's original First World War concept had been developed into a high-speed craft capable of planing while carrying a 500-pound warhead in the bows. The coxswain aimed his craft at the target and, when satisfied that he was on course, pulled a lever and jettisoned himself and a small balsa-wood raft into the wake. This raft was not designed to effect any form of escape but merely to keep the man out of the water as his motor boat exploded against a ship's side. Conducting a raid which automatically implied surrender and imprisonment did not meet with the British concept of operations, and certainly not with those of Blondie Hasler.

The final catalyst to Blondie's ideas occurred on 26 March, 1941, when six Italian Explosive Motor Boats attacked and sank the cruiser HMS *York*[16] and damaged the Norwegian tanker *Pericles,* but not her cargo, in Suda Bay, Crete.

Later in the year, long after Blondie's paper had been despatched to the Admiralty, the Italians sank two ships in Gibraltar and on 19 December, 1941, the crews from three 'two-man human torpedoes' succeeded in placing delayed action charges on the hulls of the battleships HMS *Queen Elizabeth,*[17] and HMS *Valiant,* the destroyer HMS *Jervis* and the tanker *Sagona,* in Alexandria Harbour. The *QE's* log for 19 December, 1941, records the event with a remarkable lack of drama:

> 0550. Explosion in the stern of oiler *Sagona* on starboard beam.
> 0610. Explosion amidships. Ship listing to starboard and settling in the bows. Lighting failed.

[16] The only 8" cruiser in the Mediterranean Fleet. She was beached but then bombed again.
[17] The C-in-C (Admiral Cunningham) was on board at the time and, determined to prove to any "spies" that the damage was less than it was, ordered morning colours and daily routines to be seen to continue as normal.

0750. HM Subs *Trusty* and *Triumph* secured port and starboard quarter[18]. 1 chief stoker PO and 3 stoker POs and 4 stokers died as result of explosions.
Leave . . . continues.

This audacious attack by three 'slow-running torpedoes' or *maiali* (the Italian for pig) was led by twenty-four year old Lieutenant-Captain Luigi de la Penne and was launched from the submarine *Scire:* not unnaturally, the actions of de la Penne (now a prisoner of war in Palestine) caused Churchill to agitate for similar action:[19]

18 January, 1942. To General Ismay for the Chiefs of Staff Committee. Please report what is being done to emulate the exploits of the Italians in Alexandria Harbour and similar methods of this kind.

At the beginning of the war Colonel Jefferies[20] had a number of bright ideas . . . which received very little encouragement. Is there some reason why we should be incapable of the same kind of scientific aggressive action that the Italians have shown? One would have thought we should have been in the lead. Please state the exact position.[21]

Blondie's views were well-known in COHQ, if previously considered a little far-fetched, but now his name was once more brought to the attention of the Adjutant-General of the Royal Marines and, through him, to that of Lord Mountbatten as he began his trawl for suitable officers and men to help him meet his remit: his "outlandish" ideas fell exactly into the scheme.

From my point of view it was a sheer stroke of luck that (a) the Italians demonstrated that ship attacks by clandestine small craft

---

[18] To supply emergency power.
[19] Oliver Patch had won his DSO on 22 August 1940 – a year and a half before this attack – when he sank the Italian submarine *Iride* which, unknown at the time, was ferrying frogmen to attack the British fleet in Alexandria with limpets. Paradoxically, if they had succeeded, it has to be presumed that Blondie's original paper would not have been ignored and he would have started his work that much earlier!
[20] For further information see *Above Us The Waves.* C.E.T. Warren and James Benson.
[21] *The Second World War. Volume IV.* Winston Churchill.

could be successful and (b) that somebody at COHQ remembered having turned down similar proposals made by an unknown Captain, RM, serving in a non-combatant unit.[22]

It was, therefore, no coincidence that at the age of 28 Acting Major HG Hasler, OBE, reported to the Combined Operations Development Centre (CODC), Southsea, at 1030 on Monday 26 January, 1942, for duties on the staff of the Commodore, Combined Operations. Captain TA Hussey, Royal Navy, was the CODC's Commandant and, as Blondie's immediate superior, they were to work closely over the next months.

Before lunch that first morning Hussey, Hasler and Peter du Cane[23] of Vosper Shipbuilders, visited Gosport to inspect an Italian EMB captured after the abortive attack on Grand Harbour, Malta.

Now with some practical understanding of the Italians' methods of attacking shipping, Blondie could begin his most important work so far and that evening wrote a proposed Terms of Reference, an outline plan to meet those terms and what he described as Questionnaire Number 1. Blondie would ask Mountbatten to approve the three papers the next day when he and Tom Hussey took the 0830 train from Havant to Waterloo on 27 January, 1942, in time for a meeting with the Commodore at 1045, a journey he was to repeat dozens of times over the next year and a half.

Lord Mountbatten's verbal briefing required Blondie to concentrate on "the development of a British version of the explosive motor-boat paying particular attention to methods of attacking ships in harbour." This was, to the letter, what Blondie wanted to do and what he had been thinking about for so long; it also tied in neatly with the "Terms" he had just presented (approved without question by the Commodore) including the study of more covert methods of inserting small raiding parties into enemy territory other than fast boats. This meeting marked the beginning of a relationship that lasted each his lifetime and which was founded, instantly, on mutual respect.

The next day was spent with Naval Intelligence and the evening in discussing suitable counter-measures should the Italians try again. That

---

[22] Letter to Tim Wiltshire Lt RM, 1985.
[23] Commander Peter Du Cane, OBE. Later CBE. Managing Director of Vosper and designer of Motor Torpedo Boats and high-speed racing boats, including *Bluebird II,* world speed record holder, 1939. Began the war as a Fleet Air Arm Pilot.

night he was home in his mother's house, now at Catherington ten miles north of Eastney, in time to spend one and a half hours on his initial report and first impressions of the way ahead.

The report was ready on 30 January but after a meeting that morning with Tom Hussey it was clear "further action was necessary" so the next day he called on Rear-Admiral Horan[24] and Special Operations Executive (SOE)[25] officers to discuss details of mutual interest. First thoughts concentrated on the captured Italian EMB with a view to improving it, developing methods of delivering it to the operational area, getting it past booms and harbour defences and, finally, rescuing the coxswain. Although still fascinated by the combination of canoes, limpets and underwater swimming, the Boom Patrol Boat (BPB) – to give it its British, and purposively deceptive, code-name – had to be Blondie's first priority, but he could not suppress thoughts of his own preferred method of attack.

He saw small parties of men using guile and stealth, rather than brute force, to destroy economic targets, a *modus operandi* more in line with his self-confessed lack of blood lust. He believed that silent, surprise attacks were sapping to an enemy's morale and, while he knew that such operations would not bring about Germany's defeat, to come silently out of the night and to disappear without trace would have damaging consequences out of proportion to the effort expended.

His report caused concern and although he worked on a new version throughout Sunday 1 February, on the Monday he had to agree with Hussey that further modifications were still necessary. There was time, though, that afternoon to meet and help one of the few men with experience of submarine-launched canoe operations:

> Visited HMS *Vernon* to discuss the accommodation of Gerald Montanaro's boys. (Lately of 101 Troop and now of 2 SBS.)[26]

This is their first recorded meeting and while Blondie admired, and may even have been secretly jealous of the experience that he, himself, still lacked, he felt that the methods the army's SBS were using were crude. For their part Gerald Montanaro and Roger Courtney had equal respect for Blondie, although they both believed him to be too gadget-

[24] Rear Admiral, Landing Craft and Bases.
[25] Whose remit was to "set Europe ablaze" by inserting and recovering agents as well as destroying economic and stratregic targets by sabotage.
[26] See, *inter alia,* Courtney's *SBS in World War II.*

minded and on these aspects they agreed to differ. They were, though, together on much more.

On 6 February, and during the course of his searches, he met a man who had been playing a vital role in the development of underwater weapons systems for many years. Commander Cromwell Varley DSO, RN (retired) had, among other things, designed a diving suit. Blondie, though, had more than suits to discuss for the Commander was largely instrumental, during the 1930s and 1940s, for the design and development of the two-man, then three-man, midget submarine with the two-man chariot being one offshoot of his original ideas. His sponsor in the Admiralty was Admiral Sir Max Horton and his earlier collaborator in these matters had been the Colonel Jefferies mentioned in Churchill's letter to the Chiefs of Staff on 18 January, 1942. Varley, Horton and Hasler were to meet often.

On 10 February he had his second meeting with SOE officers for, by now, they were clear that the Royal Marines Major could help them meet their own remit of "setting Europe ablaze". Although many months away, it is probable that the seed of an idea for the future Motorised Submersible Canoe (to be known as the *Sleeping Beauty*) was sown about now and by these men. What is certain is that while the re-designing of the Italian Explosive Motor Boat into a British Boom Patrol Boat (BPB) was proceeding, the use of canoes was also being studied, in tandem, as a method for guiding the BPB over booms and for recovering the pilot once he had jettisoned himself and climbed aboard his tiny balsa raft.

With the staff requirement for the BPB ready on 16 February a long relationship with Vosper Shipbuilders, then based in Portsmouth, began. An early design priority was the delivery of this craft for there was little point in continuing if no method of transporting it existed; thus the BPB's drawings would need to reflect the options for transport, one of which was the bomb-bay of the Lancaster bomber from where it could be parachuted.

All the while, though, Blondie's mind kept returning to the use of canoes which, in the form of the Cockle Mark 1, a barely modified civilian Folbot, was in use, slightly confusingly, with the army's Folboat Troop. The open-cockpit Folbot was constructed of rubberized canvas stretched across a plywood frame; sixteen feet long, and weighing just fifty pounds it could not pass, fully-rigged, through the torpedo loading hatch of a submarine due to its beam of thirty inches. The most successful military version then in service, named the Cockle Mark 1**, could be semi-collapsed to fit but once erected on the casing prior to launching would need buoyancy bags fitted at its waterline level. All this erecting and inflating with the submarine on the surface took time: time that a submarine Commanding Officer had to keep to the absolute minimum.

While it was desirable that all canoes (especially those that needed to operate from submarines) should have the same overall dimensions, requirements differed. The army's SBS operated in coastal sabotage; the SOE landed and recovered agents; the embryo Combined Operations Pilotage Parties[27] would work in surf off open beaches and Blondie's ideas for transporting underwater swimmers would differ again in small but significant aspects that mostly involved long distances and increased payloads. Thus, 9 March was to be a useful day in the life of wartime canoe development:

> To London . . . 1415 – meeting with Courtney and Montanaro
> to discuss Mk II Tadpole[28] staff requirements.

The design of all future military canoes stems from this meeting held at Combined Operations HQ and attended by just Blondie Hasler, Roger Courtney and Gerald Montanaro, Tug Wilson and Clogstoun-Willmott being the only significant absentees. Since having his paper rejected in 1941 Blondie may not have gained the experience of the others but he had pushed himself up a very steep learning curve through the study of every type of canoe then available from the Eskimo Kayak to the German civilian Folbot and including the army's Cockle Mk1, Mk 1* and Mk1**: none had the characteristics that he sought. The army members acknowledged that, despite his lack of operational canoeing experience, the Royal Marine member of the committee was in the ideal appointment to push through ideas for a definitive canoe and even the plans for its operational use, thus the minutes of the meeting reflect the views of three different characters with three different purposes but with a common aim.

It was agreed that there was no reason why a single type of boat should not be able to fulfil all existing requirements for canoe operations. The following were considered to be the Staff Requirements for such a boat.

a.  To be of decked canoe type propelled by two men using double paddles.

---

[27] Formed and led by Clogstoun-Willmott.
[28] Blondie's original codename for canoes.

b.  Maximum load to be two 13 stone men plus 1 cwt of cargo
    – total 480 lbs.
c.  Weight of boat to be, ideally, less than 70 lbs . . . but in any
    case less than 100 lbs.
d.  To be easily driven for long periods at 3 knots fully loaded
    with a maximum speed of 5 knots in a light condition.
e.  To be able to stand up to a wind of force 4 blowing in the
    open sea and to be able to be beached through surf.
f.  Strength of skin to be such as to withstand indefinitely
    grounding on shingle and working alongside other vessels.
g.  Length to be in the neighbourhood of 16 feet.
h.  Beam. Sufficient stability to satisfy a. above must be
    achieved without prejudice to the ability to get out of the
    forward torpedo hatch of a small submarine.

Note. The boat can be partially collapsible if necessary to
achieve this but there must be no loose parts and it must be
capable of complete assembly in 30 seconds in the dark. The
boat is not required to be collapsible for any other purpose . . .
Provision to be made for slinging the boat with 1 cwt load
distributed about the midship section . . . Draft to be not less
than 4" or more than 6" when loaded.

After consultation later, Blondie added a rider that the maximum
overall length could not exceed 17 feet and that the canoe had to pass
through a circular hatch of 28½" diameter with clearance of at least ½"
all round.

Ideas and trials came in profusion. Experiments with captured Italian
face masks and underwater breathing sets (based on the British Davis
Escape Apparatus) were tested in the submarine escape chamber at
HMS *Vernon* and the hatches of the H class submarine, surfacing procedures, diving times, trimming, stowage of canoes, men and gear, were all
studied and puzzled over. The subjects were wide-ranging: the camouflaging of canoes, including the ability to change the colour scheme
depending on changing light and angles of observation; navigating in the
dark without charts; the length of limpet fuses; carriage of canoes to the
operating area; effects of exhaustion and how to combat them; underwater telescopes; audible underwater defences using waterproof
microphones along the boom nets to listen for enemy submarines; the
wading depths of tanks (now at five feet) . . .

Even the amalgamation of the BPB and the canoe were given

substance on his drawing board in the form of an "explosive Tadpole"! Although laughed at as being beyond even Hasler's dreams this single-seater, submersible canoe with a detachable explosive warhead was the forerunner, in principle, of the *Sleeping Beauty*.[29] Tom Hussey was a patient man and while allowing his assistant full rein, clearly had to view things from a wider perspective and just occasionally it was necessary to apply the lightest of brakes:

> Tried idea of explosive Tadpole on Hussey – *not* well received.

On 18 March, 1942, Commodore Mountbatten was appointed Chief of Combined Operations in the rank of Vice-Admiral, Lieutenant-General and Air Marshal with a seat on the committee as the fourth Chief of Staff: thus he now had the rank and the prestige to develop, at the highest level, a long-neglected and often-maligned martial art.

In April Hussey's title also changed to that of Co-ordinator of Experiments and Developments (CXD) and in August, 1942, it was to change, finally, to Director of Experiments and Staff Requirements, or DXSR. To help and advise in these tasks DXSR was given three scientists, Professor Bernal, Professor Zuckerman and Mr Pyke: additions to the team that Blondie was to find immensely stimulating, a view that was reciprocated – although, initially, he was a little "disenchanted" with their "old-fashioned" views.

To assist his trials Blondie obtained two canoes of unspecified but different types to which he gave the names *Cranthorpe* and *Blondin:* he was also given a small Experimental Party of two commando-trained marines on 21 March, but as neither had any background in nautical work they had to be taught the very basics of seamanship and were immediately introduced to canoeing. *Cranthorpe* ended the day with severe damage and *Blondin* "not such a good idea for training either"; nor, apparently, for anything else:

> *Blondin* tried for the first (and almost the last) time. This boat is only to be used as a joke. 1300 sent *Cranthorpe* to Fort for repairs.

With the arrival on 24 March of two Folbots CODC could now "take their lines off" prior to re-designing in accordance with the agreed Staff Requirement, but designing was one thing, building in numbers was

---

[29] Of which more later.

quite another. To their aide came a gentleman to whom much praise would become due. Mr Fred Goatley was, by trade, a boat designer and builder, living and working on the Isle of Wight were he was employed, in 1942, as the manager of Saro Laminated Wood Products Limited.[30] Among other craft, Goatley had designed in 1937 a 12-foot 4-inch assault boat, one thousand of which were already in service and, since July 1941, had been in correspondence with Tom Hussey over the improvement to an earlier 'Goatley Boat'. Hussey ended one letter with the words:

I think I shall be asking you to design a folding canoe to carry two persons . . . but I have not yet received the specifications[31].

Without further prompting, Goatley designed a fifteen foot canoe and sent Hussey the drawings. The main dimension of interest was the 28-inch width making it possible to pass through a submarine's hatch. However, Hussey was not optimistic and ended his letter of acknowledgement on 17 September, 1941, with the comments:

Many thanks for your enterprise in anticipating the 2 man folding canoe. For the time being the demand does not exist but if it does I will communicate with you at once.

For someone of Goatley's experience this was as good as an order and on 10 March, 1942, he wrote back:

We now have much pleasure in submitting drawings of a canoe to carry 2 persons, this canoe when folded is designed to pass through a 24" circular hatch.

Clearly Blondie had to meet this perceptive man and did so for the first time at Cowes on 27 March when it became obvious they held different views on life, for while Fred projected a serious outlook seldom leavened by humour, Blondie, equally serious and determined, was able to laugh at himself. But they did share one invaluable attribute, neither felt the need to overburden themselves (nor, particularly, the various Ministries) with unnecessary paperwork that might delay the swift introduction of a suitable canoe.[32]

[30] Saunders Roe.
[31] Hasler papers.
[32] An unsucessfull attempt was later made to have Fred Goatley appointed MBE.

This meeting brought Fred Goatley, partially, into the whys and wherefores, but not the exact uses to which a new-look, two-man canoe might be put – factors that continued to be withheld on 30 March when he was sent a copy of the Staff Requirements for 'An Improved Design of the 2-Man Canoe' already confirmed by Goatley as being feasible. Blondie included a second sheet to his letter:

> Miscellaneous Comments on Proposed Goatley Design . . .
> Gunwale to fold clear outside of chine. It appears as if this will enable a boat of 27½" beam at the deck to pass through the hatch in the extended position. This would be a great advantage.

Thus was the Cockle Mk II conceived out of the Mk 1**, and with the concept now firmly in SARO's hands Blondie rushed that day to CCO's London offices *en route* for a meeting with Gerald Montanaro at Dover and participation in a night exercise.

After an hour of talks before lunch with 101 Troop (now part of the newly formed 2 SBS) Blondie watched an attack in the harbour by both the Mk1 and Mk1* canoes, which included placing limpets with a 'placing rod', before being invited to test his own skill at the art in the fresh south-westerly wind.

Although he knew that the canoes used by the SBS were not, *pro tem,* what he was looking for, he was interested in their methods of attack and especially procedures for fixing a limpet six feet below the waterline of an enemy ship. Satisfied with what he had seen and tried he returned home the next day full of even newer thoughts.

Luckily the peripatetic nature of his job was recognized by the allocation of his personal service motor-cycle which he was able to use for excursions to Hayling Island, usually on Saturdays. It was on that day that he would choose to make his weekly visit to the landing craft base at HMS *Northney* (and the dances with the Wrens and ATS girls stationed there) while he continued his search for the ideal canoe, if it existed. As a result many Sunday mornings were marked by an invigorating eight-mile walk, usually via a pub, and would precede an almost daily ritual of tending his mother's garden at Catherington. Few Sunday evenings did not end without a dip, on oxygen, in the *Vernon* submarine tank.

But experiments continued unceasingly: stability trials on Assault Landing Craft; slings for the BPB; could the proposed BPB fit inside the *Hamilcar, Hotspur, Hengist* or *Horsa* gliders; could it be made to jump over booms; would it remain aerodynamically stable beneath a parachute; could Raymond Quilter[33] of GQ Parachutes make one large enough; more diving in the tank at *Vernon*; discussions on revolutionary techniques with Roger Courtney of 2 SBS; what about submersible main battle tanks for the army . . . ?

To Blondie two things were certain: the BPB was not going to rely on stealth for success and it would never fit inside a submarine, both of which were factors that he believed to be of paramount importance in taking the war to the enemy. The canoe, he was convinced, had to be the answer.

Then, on the night of 11/12 April, 1942, Gerald Montanaro and Trooper Preece of the Royal Tank Regiment,[34] proved the point with limpets against a damaged 5500-ton bulk ore carrier in Boulogne Harbour during *Operation JV*. Their canoe had been carried to one mile north of the harbour entrance by *ML 102*, which waited to deliver them safely back to Dover in time for breakfast. As with the two previous anti-shipping canoe attacks, it was a daring and brilliantly executed operation. No wonder Blondie was in a hurry.

[33] Later Sir Raymond Quilter Bt.
[34] Awarded, respectively, the DSO and DCM. See *SBS in World War Two*.

# CHAPTER FIVE

## *Mandy* and the Boom Patrol Detachment

Blondie was indeed in a hurry, for the army canoeists were achieving success through an idea he had suggested to the Admiralty nearly a year before. He would, though, always give credit for the establishment of the canoe as a British war machine to Montanaro, Clogstoun-Willmott, Courtney and Wilson (with his near-permanent crew, Marine W.G. Hughes) who had developed their ideas in isolation of his. Courtney and Wilson had, too, developed the limpet mine and Montanaro the placing rod.

If he felt any frustration it was towards the Admiralty for dismissing a mode of attack that the army had been using successfully while he persevered with the Explosive Motor Boat, yet it was these craft that would eventually hold the key to his finest wartime "invention".

Some diary entries for these middle days of April, 1942, reveal the inevitability of the decision to branch out:

> 15 April. Started paper on BPBs . . . 16th: Took draft of paper to Du Cane . . . 19th, Took paper to Hussey . . . got it torn up. pm editing with a pair of scissors and preparing speech for the morrow. 20th . . . to London bearing revised script and completed memo on BPBs.

By the next morning he had sorted things out and, through frustration, had also clarified ideas for his own future.

> 21st April 1942 . . . Birth of embryo idea (in the bath) for more active service role for yours truly.

If the boom Patrol Boats were to be a success then, clearly, an organization would be needed to man them. Additionally, as it had been accepted that they would need canoes to help them negotiate booms and assist in the pilot's escape, they would need underwater swimmers. Work with the CODC would continue but there would have to be a formation to undertake operational trials and, of more importance, operations themselves as soon as targets became available: in other words the operational wing of the CODC.

> 23 April. Discuss new boat party with Hussey (who) originated the idea of an all-Royal Marines unit.

Armed with this support Blondie called on Colonel G.E. Wildman-Lushington,[1] Mountbatten's Royal Marines' Chief of Staff (and former Fleet Air Arm Pilot) to:

> Put across the idea of the Royal Marines Harbour Patrol party.

In fact Blondie intended to concentrate mostly on attack by canoe and divers. Trials using canoes to assist the BPB cross the boom showed him, convincingly, that if the canoe can get through, why waste time with all the paraphernalia inherent in a BPB operation? They would have their uses but not in the form of attack that Blondie had in mind. Additionally, delivering the BPB was throwing up many questions that were not easy to answer and while the delivery of canoes was no less fraught, they posed challenges more suitable to Blondie's thinking.

His enthusiasm for the motorboat, although less than that for the canoe, remained, but if he was to be the guiding light behind the operational use of such craft, it was necessary to gain experience, so on 22 April he planned the requisition of suitable fast motor boats for trials, adaptation and training.

In this respect an officer with whom Blondie was to work closely was entering the arena. One of the Italian EMBs that had beached itself outside Malta's Grand Harbour had been inspected by R.W.Ladbroke and it was this craft that Hussey now had at HMS *Vernon*. Although trained as a Lysander pilot with the RAF, Bill Ladbroke's wartime significance was to be more nautical than aeronautical, for he had raced power boats in the 1930s against many of the famous names of that exciting era; thus he had the experience for which Blondie was looking, knew the exponents of handling craft at speed and where such vessels could be found. Discharged from the RAF for "being blind", Bill was employed by the 23rd Technical Training Group (Civilians) and it had

---

[1] Later Major-General CB, OBE.

been that organization which had sent him to inspect, select and recover the Italian EMB from the Maltese beach. On 24 June he would don the uniform of a Sub-Lieutenant (E) RNVR and join the CODC.

Meanwhile, the more Blondie dived the more he became fascinated by the possibility of using the Davis Submarine Escape Apparatus for long-distance swimming. Sir Robert Davis was interested in the work of the CODC during these early days and, while encouraging their inventiveness, he expressed concern over the horizontal, underwater distances that Blondie was proposing. Rising to the surface from a stricken submarine or sitting astride a 'chariot' were two methods of 'propulsion' but free-swimming over long distances using his gear was a different and worrying matter, and one that was to be brought up again in 1945.[2]

By 25 April Blondie, through the Admiralty, had ordered six of the new-design (but interim) Goatley canoes from Saro and that day allocated two to CODC, one to 101 Troop at Dover (Montanaro's SBS team) two to Greenock for the submariners and one to Major Gus March Phillips of the Royal Artillery for the Small Scale Raiding Force – alias 62 Commando (a cover name) which had originally formed as part of the SOE's sabotage unit. At the last minute there was still confusion over their name for Folbot had changed to Cockle but the Admiralty's letter allocating these first six referred to them as 'punts', yet ended with the statement:

> Would you please note that the official term for your two-man punts is Cockle Mk 1[3] . . . will you please use this term in future correspondence.

Blondie continued to prefer 'tadpole' sufficiently strongly to draft a letter to CCO indicating that he was 'indignant' at such a term as 'cockle'. This prompted a half-hearted attempt to change the name back to canoe, but cockles they remained.

Whether by BPB or by canoe a boom would always need to be crossed and so, determined to lead in this matter, Blondie began practising on the eastern Solent boom that stretched, in solid form, from Lumps Fort above Southsea beach to Horse Sand Fort, then, as a conventional boom across the fairway to No Man's Land Fort from where it was again a solid obstruction to the Isle of Wight west of Nettleston point. To add realism

---

[2]  Chapter Ten.
[3]  Still designated a Mk 1 but, in effect, the prototype for the final version, the Mk II.

to his patrols Blondie did not, to begin with, obtain permission. These exercises were threefold: the study of booms under all weather and tidal conditions, canoe handling under realistic, operational circumstances and the avoidance of patrols. Naturally this was a risky business not always regarded with equanimity by the authorities: Sunday 25 April being a fairly typical day:

> Out in *Cranthorpe* – boom dodging, warping off in smart SE wind. Glorious day. Got arrested on arrival back. Home by staff car.

There was a deadly seriousness to his 'boom dodging' as he perfected his methods, ideas, fitness and endurance for these were all aspects that needed sound study before he could allow his Experimental Party a free rein at evading the armed naval patrols.

On 13 April the patient and supportive Tom Hussey had been appointed to the newly formed post of Co-ordinator of Experiments and Developments at Headquarters Combined Operations while CODC acquired a new Commandant with Lieutenant-Colonel (Royal Artillery) HFG Langley's arrival a fortnight later. Blondie called immediately to impress the importance of the parent unit he was proposing as part of the BPB and canoe package. Of course, having been briefed by the outgoing Hussey, Langley, unsurprisingly, was convinced and promised to forward his own endorsement.

Meanwhile, Fred Goatley and his team were working at full stretch on the first pilot model of the Cockle Mk II ready for Blondie's inspection on 30 April. Little escaped Blondie's eye during his visits and telephone calls: the painter, for instance, was detailed down to the last inch in length; a breakwater was needed to face the stern for beach landings and the cockpit coaming was to be flared all round. The reason for this last modification was that he was perfecting a waterproof jacket that would double as a seal around each individual cockpit with the skirt of the coat slipped round the cockpit coaming to be drawn tight in what today is known as a 'spray deck'. The paint scheme received his close attention with the first boat required in light and dark grey for which he would supply two tins of flexible paint.

On 8 May Blondie was granted 48 hours leave and the ideal opportunity to head for London and the Arts Theatre Club – believed to have centred around nothing more salacious than Jazz – which he promptly joined and where he was to spend many hours entertaining friends to lunch or a dinner-time drink. But not even leave came before future plans and the next day between 1430 and 1700 he was at COHQ "to put across the idea of the Royal Marine Harbour Patrol Detachment".

Encouraging him to develop his plans, Lord Mountbatten, with one minor alteration, approved the proposal and forwarded it to the Admiralty's Director of Training and Staff on 26 May, having altered the name to Royal Marines Boom Patrol Detachment which, he felt, better reflected the cover-plan. Despite a growing resistance to the proliferation of 'private armies', progress was swift and Blondie was granted authority to commission the RMBPD on 6 July, by which time volunteers would need to have been sought, chosen and appointed.

Patrolling the booms covertly in canoes to test techniques of stealth was a vital part of Blondie's work but he also needed to study the booms overtly at all times of day, states of the tide and weather conditions. The ideal vessel was *Mandy*, *Trivia*'s replacement, and, although laid up, it was time she joined the war effort while at the same time giving him some well-needed sailing under cover of this military work. On 10 May he inveigled Johnnie Coke[4] to help him:

> 1215 . . . Left in *Mandy* . . . for maiden voyage. Leaking very considerably . . . wind fresh NE . . . 1420 – start back . . . raining hard.

Johnnie remembers it as a miserable afternoon, but at least he was spared the Wren's cap which, in the future, would be clamped firmly on the head of the current girl friend every time the naval patrol vessel approached. With Blondie in uniform he felt that this gave him the necessary military cover for the work he was undertaking, although the boom crews were hardly fooled and would simply comment, "Oh, it's the Major out with a floozy again" – which was, precisely, the second aim of the exercise and an activity for which he was becoming well-known![5]

The first Cockle Mark II was launched into the Marina River from Saro's yard on 13 May, and although there were many additions yet to come, the basic dimensions of sixteen feet in length and twenty-eight and a half inches in width had been adhered to. Goatley had worked his skill to perfection with a rigid canoe capable of being 'flat-packed' for ease of stowage with the sides constructed of three-ply, rubber-proofed canvas

---

[4] Later Colonel J.C.d'E. Coke, CBE, DSC, Royal Marines. A life-long *bon vivant* who, interestingly, was not to marry until he was 54 – a point he often makes in Blondie's favour.

[5] Various reminiscences forwarded to the author.

and the bottom and deck of 1/8th marine plywood to give strength when being lifted fully laden. A vertical, collapsing, internal strut reduced the canoe's height from eleven and a quarter inches to just six.

This newest cockle was tested, briefly, on the river before being brought back to Eastney and the CODC's own cordoned-off section of the shingle beach from where Blondie had, a mere twenty-five years earlier, experimented with launching himself into the sea on his bottom.

Trials could begin with an enhanced purpose, for Blondie now had his weapon and approval to form the organization that would take it to war.

> 14 May . . . took the Mk II boat out, single-seater, 150 lbs ballast. pm races versus Mk I boat. Maximum loading tests . . . 1800 . . . took Mk II out with 500 lbs ballast . . . 15 May . . . Experimental Party testing Mk II – flooding and rough treatment. Broke forward deck beam.

In order to give credence to his boom patrol training Blondie devised a series of exercises he called, variously, *Patrol* or *Exercise Margate* and, with a view to killing two or three birds with the one stone, he sought and was granted permission to establish a genuine harbour defence rôle. By this work he could test his team in patrolling friendly booms, thus matching their cover, while providing ideal training under quasi-operational conditions. Prior to the arrival of the RMBPD's men the Experimental Party, who would form the nucleus of the training teams, would conduct these patrols within the parameters laid down in the training memorandum he issued[6] in which was also contained genuine instructions for dealing with intruders:

> Human torpedoes. SMG attack until it submerges, then depth charge . . . Capture crew alive if possible. Mark position . . . but keep clear.
> EMB. SMG attack on stern end . . . capture crew alive if possible. Mark position but keep clear for at least 1 hour . . . Then anchor boat by stern avoiding bumper bar.
> Other small craft. SMG attack until boat stops and no resistance is visible. Board with grenades and SMG.

Trial followed trial and all the time they canoed to improve upper arm strength, techniques for embarking and disembarking while at sea, paddling with double paddles for speed and with one, thus lowering the

---

[6] Hasler papers.

silhouette, for stealth. For hours on end he would make his crews sit, crouched and motionless while the canoe drifted as a log. Apart from 'camouflage', the secondary purpose to this last exercise was to practise control of cramp and alertness and if he was hard on his embryo training team in all this he was certainly harder on himself.

Trials with HM Submarine *Unbeaten's* torpedo-loading hatch showed that the Cockle Mark II could be widened by 1½ inches at the gunwale and the lower chine and still fit through in the collapsed condition with this extra width improving payload and stability. More instructions followed for Ted Goatley:

> Stern to be made identical with the bow . . . small (bilge) pump on the bellows principle to be operated by the knee of the man aft.

And, with guile and stealth being Blondie's overriding prerequisite for covert operations, it is not surprising that sailing equipment (mast and standing-lug sail) were specified but:

> this will be supplied only if demanded for a specific purpose.

In fact Blondie had already designed the sailing rig which, if successful, he would ask Saro to manufacture in bulk. The canoe's disadvantages (light, slow, small payload, vulnerable) were, to Blondie, its greatest assets, especially when compared to the alternative that would need an aircraft to convey it, huge parachutes to deliver it, a large, noisy Lagonda engine to propel it and, the biggest drawback, the certainty of capture unless rescued by a canoe.

Then, on 19 June, Blondie dined with an officer on whom he had had his eye for some time and with whom he had served in the RMFU: Lieutenant J.S . (Jock) Stewart, a 'Hostilities Only' Scot from London, was a quick learner, physically strong and an excellent choice to take much of the administrative and trials burdens from Blondie. He agreed, readily, to the proposal put to him over a glass of port and the next day Colonel Lambert of the Royal Marines' Headquarters concurred with the idea.

With the formation of the Royal Marines Boom Patrol Detachment only weeks away the trawl for volunteers 'for hazardous service' was well in hand. Blondie did not seek, necessarily, those already skilled in small boat work – indeed he knew that there were probably none left un-committed to the RNVR, army SBS, the Commandos and the like – but he did seek "men eager to engage the enemy who were indifferent to personal safety and free of strong family ties". Later he was to write[7] that he was lucky to be sent enough men of the right calibre despite coming from units where "the COs were reluctant to let them go unless they didn't like them".

In particular he did not want what would nowadays be called the 'macho type' nor those men for whom the opportunity to serve in 'special forces' would be an excuse for slack discipline or outrageous behaviour. High spirits were one thing to be encouraged among his men but poor discipline was quite another matter. He wanted men with genuine character culled from an adventurous spirit not from 'bottle-bravado'. He sought potential, not experience, from officers and men alike, which is why, late on the afternoon of 25 June, he put this principle into practice by interviewing ten volunteer 2nd Lieutenants at Browndown[8] "and selected Mackinnon and Pritchard-Gordon": there was certainly no experience here.

In addition to the continuing trials of such diverse equipment as diving suits, rota-chutes, swim fins, explosive charges and firing distress signals from the water, baling out the cockles with high pressure $CO_2$ bottles and firing the Lewis gun from the forward cockpit, he found time to sew the eyelets for the sails and, when ready, attempting the first sail, which was only a partial success for she (not a girlfriend, Val, whose name, ambiguously, appeared in the same diary entry) was "slow and made too much leeway".

The next week was much as the previous one (including a "marvellous solo dive from a canoe in the Solent to test the procedure") but with the added excitement of travelling to Plymouth to interview the NCO and marine volunteers from among whom he chose, in this first trawl, one sergeant, one corporal and four marines as suitable for training to be instructors.

Things were now speeding up: his Training Manual, a small, buff notebook[9] from which he would instruct his training team and eventually his men, now tabulated, in progressive lesson form, the basic training of what was eventually to become the Royal Marines Special Boat Service. Not surprisingly, and still relevant today with only marginal differences, he started at the deep end with:

[7]  Letter to Tim Wiltshire, 1985.
[8]  The Royal Marines Small Arms School on the north Solent coast west of Gosport.
[9]  Hasler papers.

> Cockle Mark I Lesson. 1 hour. Stores required: Cockles Mk I.
> Double paddles . . . Forbid racing or full speed practice. Crews
> proceed independently for 20 minutes.

Blondie was to insist, often, on his 'no racing' policy for he was
conscious of the damage that can be done to young men, untrained in the
art, from muscle sprain and torn ligaments and, anyway, stealth and long-
term endurance was what the RMBPD was to be about, not racing. From
the moment of their arrival, the newcomers' first lesson was a practical
one aimed to bring the more cocky down to earth and get them all starting
from a common, and publicly demonstrated, level of inexperience.

Basic swimming lessons, basic seamanship lessons, familiarization
with the local seas, tommy-gun practice, pistol shooting, unarmed
combat, navigation, the layout of naval dockyards and how ships are
moored were all included. Nothing was left out: speed boat training; field
sketching and note taking; limpet mine operations and the five pound
depth charge; coding and decoding, until slowly, painfully slowly, the
lessons would begin to include camouflage and operational approaches
to an objective when training in the different methods of attack and
attention to every detail would be meticulously taught, rehearsed
and practised.

Speed boats were not Blondie's first love, but he did love nautical
challenges, which is why his first solo experience in the Italian EMB,
under Bill's instruction, nearly brought the whole business to an end.
Deciding that the British would operate differently, Blondie removed the
balsa-wood raft at the stern (it hinged horizontally to port to let
the coxswain board) and left it lying on HMS *Northney's* jetty. Now, and
with his engineer's full blessing, Blondie disappeared seaward down
Hayling Island's Mengham Rythe[10] at full speed, but not to reappear as
planned. After half an hour a concerned Bill Ladbroke set off in a rowing
dinghy to see if he could find his CO, which he did sunk on a shallow
mud bank. At twenty-five knots Blondie had shut the throttle to measure
the craft's stopping distance, which turned out to be very short; indeed
so quickly did the EMB come to a standstill that the wake swept across
the open stern that should have been protected by the raft. It was
immediately decided to refit the raft if only to stop future sinkings.

Then, with the arrival of the officers at Eastney on Saturday 4 July,
came tangible proof that the "embryo idea for more active service for

---

[10] And, unknown to him, in front of the house where Bridget Fisher had been
born.

yours truly" had finally reached fruition, and now that a beginning had been made not a moment should be lost for, in many ways, eighteen months had already been wasted. Although Val (the current *amour*) had, too, arrived that day to stay with Blondie at his mother's house, he left her so that he could:

> Demonstrate drawing stores from the dockyard. pm. Laid *Mandy* at top of beach and filled her with water.

The treatment meted out to *Mandy* was in preparation for a sailing trip with the frustrated Val which was re-planned for Sunday. As with all wooden boats that have been left ashore this evolution was to prevent leaking and to ensure that Val (whose love of sailing was still an unknown quantity) was as comfortable as possible: in the end, though, it was another phenomenon that spoilt her day:

> 1420. Left beach in *Mandy* with Val . . . Beat across to Ryde Sand via Normansland Fort. Anchored and sunbathed. Crew feeling *ick*. Ran back same way. 1930 Back on beach. Took Val around town.

The advance party of the RMBPD's non-commissioned officers and marines arrived on 6 July to receive a medical inspection at 2100 before an introductory talk on the football pitch and the next day they were straight into training as laid down in the buff-coloured book. These, then, were the first men to answer the call for hazardous service, men without family ties and keen, as Nelson put it, "to engage the enemy more closely". Blondie was happy:

> 10th July . . . am . . . instructing up till 1150. pm. Instructing swimming. Feeling grand. 1800-0100 – Val to ballet and dinner.

The rigid 'fold-flat' canoe had been devised by Blondie so that it could be handled fully laden, dragged across beaches, fit through the hatch of a submarine and yet be 'constructed' in quick time. To demonstrate the value of the design he had a five-foot working model built which he took to HMS *Forth*, the submarine depot ship on the Clyde, via COHQ, on 20 July. It was vital to persuade the submariners that the Mark II was an improvement and, having done so, to suggest a safe and efficient method of launching it.

One method that had been tried with the soft-skinned canoes in the 'calmish' Mediterranean was the 'float-off' technique[11] where the canoes, manned and ready, would rest on the casing while the submarine dived, leaving the canoes to, literally, float off. The more usual method was for the laden but unmanned canoe to be lowered by bow and stern ropes across the ballast tanks into the water. The crew would then slide down and man their craft, which was not always practicable, especially if the submarine was wallowing in a swell. Blondie's canoes, though, were designed to be craned, fully laden and manned, but submarines do not have cranes: they were, though, fitted with 4" guns that could be trained and elevated and, with this concept accepted, trials would be attempted.

Returning from this successful public relations exercise Blondie held an evening conference at Portsmouth on the reception of the main body of RMBPD's marines due to arrive on the morrow. They would be billeted around Eastney and Southsea as was the custom with 'commando troops' – which they were not, although given similar status. The two chosen establishments that would be home to the first two sections were Mrs Leonora Powell's guest house, The White Heather at 27 Worthing Road and Mrs Montague's at 35 St Rownan's Road, while the officers would live at 9 Spencer Road.

Blondie addressed the new arrivals for an hour at 0815 on 24 July and then, in accordance with his Training Manual, sent them to sea in the various canoes and assault boats the RMBPD's Experimental Team and Training Team had now collected; it was nearly a disaster:

> New troops almost drowned themselves. pm . . . Salvaging boats . . .

And two days later the same happened again:

> Troops doing Mark I, lesson 4. Finishing by sinking one Mark I and one 12 man assault boat, held against boom by a spring, ebb tide. pm . . . Salvaged boats with duty section . . .

The Royal Marines Boom Patrol Detachment was now in being and, initially, consisted of thirty-five men divided into a Headquarters Section, a Maintenance Section and two Boat Sections, each of six, two-

---

[11] This is the method used with today's rubber assault craft which are not so prone to capsize, especially if the submarine has to have forward speed for better control.

man canoe teams. In establishing the formation, Blondie decided to maintain standards based on the parade ground on the understanding that instincts initiated there would be equally vital in battle. From the beginning the RMBPD was a firmly disciplined force, much in contrast to other "special forces" who adopted a more *laissez faire* attitude to such things as the use of Christian names, smartness of dress and saluting which they considered secondary to military prowess: Blondie believed they were inseparable.

Normal service civilities were the order of the day with, consequently, no lack of mutual respect. The younger officers would occasionally meet the men in a pub after a particularly arduous training period, but Blondie, although not disapproving, would only join by invitation. That is not to imply that he did not like a drink (his diaries often mention "trips around town with so and so") but he preferred the company of those he knew well and then in small groups; drinking with his marines was kept for special occasions.

The aims of the RMBPD are best told in Blondie's official report at the time:[12]

> RMBPD – 16th August 1942. Most Secret.
> 1. Functions.
> a.   To operate Boom Patrol Boats with or without attendant canoes.
> b.   To be capable of undertaking at short notice any other form of specialized small boat operation.
> c.   To provide expert personnel for carrying out small boat trials, experiments and development.

To which he added the following notes:

> 1.   It is intended that this Detachment should concentrate chiefly upon small boat seamanship, navigation, underwater work and transport by air with the object of evolving new methods of attacking ships in harbour.
> 2.   It is not intended to specialize in small scale raids on coastal positions, demolitions ashore, reconnaissance of beaches, routine patrols in submarines or the landing and re-embarkation of agents since these functions appear to be adequately covered by others.

[12] Hasler papers.

3. It will be seen from the above that the role of the RMBPD is more of a naval one and less of a military one than that of (others) . . .

The two officers Blondie had chosen to command the sections were J.W.(Jack) Mackinnon, whom he also called Jock, and W.H.A. Pritchard-Gordon with Colour-Sergeant W.J. (Bungy) Edwards as the Detachment Sergeant Major (DSM). All were to be much respected for their different talents: the public-school educated Pritchard-Gordon, for his athletic prowess which few could match and Mackinnon for his almost exceptional swimming ability, although his performance on the jazz drums met with Blondie's approval: he had been commissioned from the ranks and had passed out towards the top of the young officer batch. In his inimitable way Blondie had chosen well and wisely with a fine mix of talent.

Blondie was also pleased with the men who had volunteered, although sad that the total lack of 'boating experience' would mean longer in training: "they are just a good cross section of average young fellows". Some of them were to be very good indeed.[13]

Unknown to the RMBPD, and, anyway a few days before its formal existence, Lord Selbourne, the Minister for Economic Warfare had written to Mr Attlee, the Deputy Prime Minister, on 22 June, exercising his concern over the fast Axis merchant ships that were then operating out of Bordeaux some miles inland from the French coast. These ships were carrying to Japan the latest fuses, wireless and radar parts, machinery, ball bearings, prototypes of naval and military materials, special chemicals and expert instruction. They were known to return with rubber, wolfram, tin, hides and vegetable oils unavailable to the Germans. In the summer of 1941, after the closing of the Trans-Siberian rail route, this two-way traffic had become entirely dependent on the sea[14] to the extent, Lord Selbourne pointed out, that there could be up to ten ships alongside the Bordeaux wharves at any one moment.

COHQ's Examination Committee studied the problem but had not felt that it was a viable task for them, so it was passed on to the Search Committee who, too, were lukewarm about a combined operation against such a target; however, on 27 July, this committee again

---

[13] For instance, Sergeant King of Number One section and Marine Ruff were to form a formidable canoe team, especially at Leros later in the war.
[14] War Cabinet Chiefs of Staff Committee, dated 7 August, 1942.

discussed Bordeaux, only to confirm that a combination of measures would be needed to immobilize the blockade runners:

1. Bombing – but it was a large target and therefore a large number of bombs would be needed and dropped in close proximity to the civilian population.
2. Mining the mouth of the Gironde: the RAF did this not only inaccurately but without any noticeable decrease in any ships, military or civilian, using the river.
3. A submarine patrol off the mouth of the Gironde; which would be fine if the intelligence was accurate, which it was not, otherwise a large number of submarines would be needed and they were not available in such numbers for such an indefinite target.
4. An SOE or commando raid landed on the coast by submarine and Folbot – which would be the easier if combined with an air raid and that was not contemplated for the reasons above.[15]

The Search Committee was charged with, among other things, the execution of a "small raid" every two weeks but the Bordeaux problem seemed to suggest a little more than that. A third letter from Lord Selbourne on 5 August met nearly the same lack of enthusiasm but, as will be seen, it was saved from extinction by a chance meeting in September. On 7 August, 1942, the War Cabinet Chiefs of Staff Committee also discussed Bordeaux but came to no firm conclusions other than to endorse those mentioned above.

Meanwhile, back on the Solent on 25 July, *Patrol Margate* was "cancelled for the n'th time" and if that was professionally frustrating then Blondie was unexpectedly free to:

Go over to Hayling Island – attended dance – slept at office.

On the 27th *Patrol Margate* was conducted for the first time by the officers and SNCOs much to their Commanding Officer's relief. A full moon and calm weather made this introduction to their work a useful and instructive one with the only problem encountered, and noted by Blondie, being 'wetness' in the Mark I canoes. 'Wetness' in canoes in calm weather is usually a function of inexperience, so if that was their

[15] Hasler papers.

only real problem that first night then Blondie had reason to be satisfied that the training was getting off to a good start. Certainly he was becoming happier with the Mark II to the point that he would soon be able to introduce it to his men:

> 28 July. 0500 came ashore. 0545-0645 sleep. 1000-1230 Cowes with Goatley testing new seat backrest and cockpit covers for Mk II. The end is almost in sight, I think . . .

A cockle was not just a canoe; it was the home, transport and logistic base for its occupants as well as being their main armament. Every ounce of ammunition, explosive, food, spare clothing and safety equipment to be carried was tested, weighed, re-designed if necessary and re-trialled before Blondie would agree to its inclusion in the 'order of battle' and only then, when he was satisfied, would he allow his officers and SNCOs and eventually his men to practise. Among all his idiosyncrasies and demands, petty and great, it was his thoroughness based on personal experience that remains the longest lasting memory of those who served in the Royal Marines Boom Patrol Detachment. He knew, as did none other, that if just one man was to be lost or injured, or an operation was to fail, through a lack of diligence on his part, it would be regarded as an indictment of his leadership and attention to detail.

While it might be easy to argue that his almost pernickety concerns were, in the modern vernacular, 'over the top', nothing was too insignificant to demand his total scrutiny. If the men for whom he was responsible were to risk their lives using the equipment he had designed or the ideas that he had dreamed up and to which he had given substance, then they would have the best.

No German ship sunk was worth a man killed needlessly through faulty leadership, unreliable canoes, imprecise training or ill-thought-through procedures – and all of this was his responsibility alone.

# CHAPTER SIX

## *Frankton* and *Tuna*

Each day brought new ideas and the testing of new or re-designed equipment with 30 July representing a 'normal routine' when he spent the morning in London discussing dummy boats and decoys with Douglas Fairbanks[1] before more talks on the Mark II cockles and the choice of parent craft for inserting them. Over tea he called on Professor Newitt to air his ideas for an 'underwater glider'[2] and that evening he was back on the water practising wire climbing and sinking mooring buoys. Many nights were spent paddling the Mk II Cockle single-handed, sometimes fully laden, sometimes fully flooded apart from a buoyancy bag at bow and stern and sometimes with the help of sails; occasionally he would drift for hours as motionless as the semi-submerged logs he hoped to emulate.

The correct compass for the task concerned him and, after much searching, the RAF's P8 was chosen, largely for its grid and luminous markings that made it near perfect for the dark and difficult circumstance he expected. The problem with all compasses was a common one and not of their making, for each canoe would carry eight mines and one magnetic holdfast with each of these nine 'limpets' containing six large magnets. While the limpets would be carried as far aft and as far forward as possible during the approach to a target the distance from the compass would never be sufficient to negate their influence.

Camouflaging techniques were practised with the marines often watching their colleagues from the deck of a ship where they learned that at a distance and with a shallow angle to the horizon, the canoe could be hidden by the use of darker colours but close-in the canoe had to blend into lighter colours. To match these changes Blondie experimented with

---

[1]  COHQ staff officer as an adviser on landing craft and, later, on deception plans and camouflage.
[2]  The *Sleeping Beauty*.

hinged flaps, dark on one side and light on the other, attached to the canoes' upper hull.

He taught the men the best direction for a low-visibility attack depending on the phase and height of the moon, whether the wind was with or against the tide and how to deal with the problems of phosphorescence. Burial ashore and temporary scuttling offshore were well-rehearsed options for concealment, and all this, and more, was driven home through night exercises and the *Margate* patrols.

> Lesson 1. Double paddles fastest and least tiring for our types of craft. Always used when noise and visibility can be accepted. Paddles always feathered. To reduce silhouette change to single paddles. Always feathered with paddle horizontal. If challenged by sentry or searchlight "freeze up" and turn directly towards or away, preferably the former. If possible allow wind and tide to carry you clear, otherwise allow pause for observer to lose interest, then paddle gently away, keeping end-on. If fired at from a stationary position, paddle away diagonally at full speed, formation scattering. If approached by patrol boat, "freeze up" with faces turned away, prepare grenades and pistols below cockpit cover. Board on No 1's order. Keep lookout astern at all times . . .
>
> Lesson 2. Lying Up. Aim at arriving at beach one hour before morning nautical twilight. Thorough recce up to 100 yards radius. Beware coastal footpaths. Lie up several hundred yards inland if necessary. Carry up equipment first, boats last. Sleep in canoe for extra warmth and shelter or when in mud. Always recce again at first light . . . leave no trace on departure . . .

As with so many "special forces" raised during the Second World War the individual unit resembled the character of its founder and the RMBPD was certainly no exception. The men admired Blondie for his human qualities as much for his professional attributes and, particularly, for his ability to mix the two when necessary. He knew that it has to be a fine balance especially with men chosen for "hazardous duty" who believe themselves to be set apart from others by that simple expression. Contrary to other "special" units, the overriding impression gained by

---

[3] Various letters to the author.

visitors, expecting the contrary, was of an organization that was at once relaxed, professional and very highly disciplined.[3]

But to Blondie this was all meaningless without a target and he fretted over whether or not, and when, his Detachment would be ready. His men were being taught to work in an unfamiliar medium, from first principles and while they never let him down with their enthusiasm and spirit they were not seamen nor navigators, and in some respects never would be:

> 10th August 1942 . . . am. Rescuing 6 of No 1 section from watery deaths.

which accounted for the next entry:

> pm. Lecturing on tides.

His belief that the basics of seamanship and navigation could be instilled into his men in two weeks was optimistic and not shared by Bill Ladbroke who found his leader remarkably intransigent, to the point of stubbornness, on this matter. With progress frustratingly slow, even Blondie had to admit that his faith in his own ability to impart nautical knowledge was misplaced and so reluctantly agreed that a civilian, the pre-war Olympic yachtsman[4] Charles Leaf, be employed solely for this task.

*Patrol Margate*'s simple format was now replaced by a more advanced night exercise, *Grundy*, which included endurance tests and the trial of drugs to keep the men awake: Blondie and Corporal Bick being Professor Solly Zuckerman's[5] initial guinea pigs on the first night vision and endurance tests with Paradrene and Dipthal.

> 16th August. 2030. Dope inserted in eyes. 2130–2230. Paradrene tests – not very convincing. 2325 – onwards, exhaustion test. Marching all night. 17th Sep 42. 0645 finish marching. 0745. Swimming. 0920–1315. In Cockle Mk II to Isle of Wight and back. 1400–1600. Being tested before and after Dipthal. Fairly convincing. Office work till 1830. Turned in early.

---

[4] Six metre yachts. Appointed Lt RM.
[5] Later Lord Zuckerman. Among other tasks, then, he was Lecturer in Human Anatomy at Oxford.

The RMBPD's HQ remained with the CODC in Dolphin Court. Conveniently, Blondie's own office was suitably large to double as a bedroom on the rare nights that he was not in London or a canoe. Snippets from his diaries give a flavour of these hectic days during which he occasionally had to look over his shoulder, as well as ahead to yet unknown tasks. Visits to London to see the latest West End plays with Val (*The Springtime of Others* was playing in August) were interspersed with trials on limpets, high speed navigation and boat handling in the requisitioned *Spider Boy*,[6] discussions on underwater propulsion for the "glider" and, not for the last time:

> 17th Aug: Conference with Laycock, Hussey, March Phillips and Courtney re amalgamating the three units. Managed to stave it off for the present but I fear CCO will overrule it.

Lord Mountbatten did not overrule the decision but there remained a continual worry that his RMBPD would become just one part of a larger organization with the amalgamation of all SSRF,[7] COPP, SOE, SBS, RN/RM canoe-borne operations. Blondie had known that the proliferation of seemingly similar organizations was not viewed with enthusiasm by COHQ, and for some good reasons, one of which was the conflict over submarines. However Clogstoun-Willmott, Courtney and Hasler believed that there was room for their own separate organizations as their aims were, after all, different. Nor did it escape the COHQ's notice that the units were all commanded by highly individual men who would not easily be subordinated to another like-minded character. Each unit, too, relied heavily for its individual success on its individual leader. Towards the war's end some form of amalgamation did take place in the Far East, and then largely, for administration purposes only.[8] Some duty days were more of an oasis of relaxation than others:

> 24th August . . . embarked in HMS *Camperdown* at Bursledon for first full-scale drop of Uffa Fox rescue dinghy off Cowes. Pleasant day consisting of big eats and free beer.

This was the forerunner of the airborne lifeboat developed by the yacht and dinghy designer Uffa Fox for use by the Royal Air Force,

---

[6] Seventeen foot Chris Craft.
[7] March-Philips' Small Scale Raiding Force.
[8] See Chapter Ten.

the drawings of which had been offered to Blondie for comment. He was immediately interested, for if such craft were parachuted safely from the adapted bomb-bay of a Lancaster bomber then the BPB could be made to do so and, of greater appeal, so could Fox's vessel containing canoes.

On 7 September the production Mark II was at last "showing better results than the pilot model" and with that the long search for perfection neared the end. The results of the latest tank tests were conclusive and encouraging: the hours of detailed, painstaking observations, evaluations and re-designing were paying off. With 480 pounds of load, including two crew, the original 'pilot model' had been lower in the water by 1¾ inches forward and by 1¼ inches aft. The improvements now resulted in an extra ¾ of a knot at sprint speed with double paddles and a reduction in towing effort from five pounds seven ounces to four pounds ten ounces.[9] The whole exercise being one of balancing speed and carrying capacity against stability and strength.

By now the crane arrangement discussed during his recent visit to the Clyde had been devised and trialled by HMS *Forth* using a "T" class submarine whose engineers had bolted a girder extension to the submarine's 4" gun barrel. Now it was Blondie's task to produce the sling and for this he constructed strips of webbing between longitudinal wooden struts across which the canoes would be slid while on the submarine's casing. Wire strops at the ends were then brought together to a single lifting point above the middle of the canoe, and once in the water it would simply float out forwards allowing the sling to be hoisted inboard for the next one.

Then, quite suddenly, the future "took charge" during the evening of Friday 18 September as Blondie was "discussing prospective schemes" with Colonel Robert Neville in Richmond Terrace. Anxious for the RMBPD not to be placed to one side, he asked to study a list of possible options as, he suggested with optimism rather than conviction, his men were now ready, "providing it's not a job needing very good navigation or seamanship": but there was nothing suitable and he returned, empty-handed, to Southsea.

However, on Monday he was summoned back by Lieutenant-Colonel Cyril Horton,[10] Royal Marines, for, unknown to Blondie, the previous Friday's visit had not been as wasted as he thought. Over the weekend Horton, who was about to write off the Bordeaux problem as being

[9]  Although no account was taken for operating in a high percentage of fresh-water – as they would.
[10]  Later, Major-General F.C. Horton, CB, OBE.

unacceptable, had heard of Blondie's visit and decided to take a second look.

Bordeaux is a substantial port sixty miles inland on the west bank of the Garonne River. Twelve miles downstream the Garonne joins the Dordogne, together forming the Gironde River that flows north-west into the Bay of Biscay. The Gironde, fed from the rains of central France and the melt waters of the Pyrenees, is fast flowing, muddy, encumbered with logs and edged with low-lying reed banks beneath gently-sloping, undulating ground which, for the most part, is planted with vineyards producing the world's highest quality claret.

In COHQ Blondie was shown a document headed "*Frankton*" and became interested immediately. During the afternoon he studied other proposed operations but by the evening remained convinced that *Frankton* was precisely the type of problem which he had formed the RMBPD to solve. He sought out Neville to air a few initial thoughts before retiring to the Royal Ocean Racing Club in St James's Place where he sifted idea after idea until the dawn by when he was certain he had the outline of a solution. He returned to Richmond Terrace, eight minutes walk away, to present his roughed-out plan to a receptive Colonel:[11]

> Most Secret. From: OC RMBPD. To: COHQ
> Date: 22nd September 1942
> Operation "FRANKTON".
> Outline Plan by RMBPD.
>
> 1.  The attached outline plan has been produced without close study of the natural features of the locality or of the defence measures which might be encountered.
> 2.  Before proceeding with detailed planning it is requested that I may be informed whether the proposal, made in the outline plan, that a carrying ship should drop 3 cockles Mk II not more than five miles from the mouth of the river, in the dark, is practicable.
> 3.  At first examination the Cockle side of the operation appears to have a good chance of success, and it is hoped that RMBPD may be allowed to carry it out.
> H.G. Hasler, Major RM

---

[11] Hasler papers.

It is interesting to study the simple outline plan exactly as Blondie wrote it, with the covering letter above, for from such simple concepts often grow the greater successes:

Nature of Operation
1.   Limpet attack on cargo vessels lying at Bordeaux, using Cockles Mk II.
Forces Engaged. (Own troops)
2.   Submarine or Surface Vessel (carrying ships)
3.   Cockles Mk II.
Attacking force. 6 Ranks RMBPD.
Intention
3.   To sink between 10 and 20 of the cargo vessels lying alongside in the Bordeaux area.
Method
4.   Timetable.
    D.1. Not later than 2300. Carrying ship drops Attacking Force not more than 5 miles from the mouth of the Estuary.
    D.2. Approx. 0600. Attacking Force lands and goes into concealment.
    Approx. 2000. Attacking Force resumes passage.
    D.3. Approx. 0600. Attacking Force lies up.
    Approx. 2000. Attacking Force resumes passage.
    D.4. Approx. 0600. Force lies up at advanced base (within 10 miles of targets).
    Approx. 2000. Final approach commences.
    D.5. Not later than 0230. Commence withdrawal to advanced base.
    0600. Limpets explode.
5.   Escape.
Either (a). Sink or destroy all remaining equipment, escape overland.
    or (b). Return down the Estuary on successive nights to rendezvous with carrying ship not earlier than 0300 on D.8. at position not more than 8 miles from mouth of Estuary. (This alternative may be impracticable in view of the probability of the programme being delayed by bad weather).
6.   Dates . . .

Blondie wanted to approach using a full spring flood tide in the dark, ideally about the time of a new moon and if he could find a week with the right combination it would, he assessed, be a four-night journey using the strong favourable tides. Although suggesting the use of a submarine he knew that Flag Officer Submarines[12] was never attracted to ideas that involved his boats in anything other than sinking ships – which was precisely what Blondie was also about to attempt!

Interestingly, he was proposing to use only half a section – 6 men in all – and yet his aim was to destroy in excess of ten ships. Estimates of how many ships there were at any one time varied but, for instance, in October of that year, and well before the earliest time that Blondie could launch his attack, it was reported that 102,800 tons of shipping lay alongside the inland port.

A factor that had to be considered at an early stage was mines, both German and British. While they were not considered a threat to the canoes they would certainly be a major planning consideration to a surface ship and even more so to a submarine. The RAF had laid various minefields off the entrance to the Gironde but the position of these had not been plotted accurately.

On the assumption that all canoes would make the objective and with eight limpets per craft, a total of twenty-four limpets were available. Blondie's permutations were based on a minimum of three limpets per ship to ensure success, thus a more realistic aim might have been eight ships, but he was not advocating caution in his initial planning for fear that too few ships attacked would, once more, push *Frankton* back into the 'not on' category.

His work on *Frankton* that second day did not end when he left Neville's office for although the rest of the day was spent at a COHQ conference on 'small boat development' he was dragged off the 1745 train, just before it left Waterloo, to discuss the parent craft for his proposal: obviously his outline plan had already hit the mark. He caught a train an hour later and was back at work in his own office by 2145. Colonel Neville later remarked that Blondie's response had been noted as the quickest operational plan then on record.

On Thursday he was granted seven days' leave but this did not last beyond the following day which was spent "digging holes in his mother's garden and answering the telephone" because on Saturday he drove to Fordingbridge to witness the first full dropping trial of a 4,000 pound load by parachute in advance of trials with the BPB. This experiment was not a success as, according to Bill Ladbroke, separation occurred almost

[12] Admiral Sir Max Horton.

immediately and the weight buried itself in the Hampshire countryside and is still there to this day.

Blondie did then allow himself some rest:

> 27th. September. (Sunday). Digging more holes. Sleeping in the sun . . . 28th pm. Cutting sails for Mk II. 29th. am. Playing saxophone, sewing sails. 30th am. Still playing saxophone.

All the while *Frankton* dominated. One factor that remained paramount to any success of this nature was the accurate prediction of tides and inshore currents and for help in this and other associated factors Lieutenant-Commander D.P. L'Estrange RNVR[13] had long since been co-opted to the staff of CCO. On 12 October Blondie met this man who was to be the vital planning cog for the forthcoming operation: they were to meet many times over the next weeks and formed an excellent relationship which was, in large measure, responsible for so much that was to go right. Officially, L'Estrange was the COHQ Staff Officer responsible for co-ordinating raids but his responsibilities went beyond supplying the ephemeral data needed; he was also responsible for briefing on enemy positions, equipment and strengths as well as local topography. Having discussed the area under scrutiny, they called on Flag Officer Submarines himself and in particular Captain Raw. Raw had much experience in the use of submarines for 'special operations' having been Captain (S) in the Mediterranean with responsibility (in addition to starving the German Afrika Korps) of landing army SBS canoes for sabotage duties. Following this initial meeting with the submariners on 18 October, Blondie and L'Estrange re-wrote the outline plan that afternoon, still working on the deployment of three canoes deployed from a submarine of the 3rd Submarine Squadron.

Despite giving his full support to the outline plans, Admiral Mountbatten believed the risks to be so great that he did not expect any of the *Frankton* team to return; he did not doubt that some would reach their targets but he was certainly not sanguine about their ability to get back safely to the United Kingdom, especially as, from the outset, no vessel was earmarked for the return journey. A great distance lay between Bordeaux and Spain, the nearest neutral country, and with the French Gendarmerie under orders from their Vichy Government to give the Germans all assistance, conditions were not conducive to easy escaping.

---

[13] In happier days, a Malay rubber planter.

Nevertheless, planning was to continue, but on 21 October (Trafalgar Day) Blondie was told that CCO had, himself, decided that the Commanding Officer could not be put at such risk. Blondie chose to ignore the possibility of this decision being made final although, as a pre-emptive strike, he did approach Colonel Neville with a strong plea that he should lead this first operation.

> If they go without me, sir, and don't return, I shall never be able to face the others again.[14]

Neville agreed to speak to Mountbatten but Blondie was determined to put his case in person and so approached, formally, the Royal Marines' Adjutant-General whose staff copied his memo direct to COHQ.[15]

1.  Operation is an important one, and appears to have good chance of success. Main difficulty is a question of small-boat seamanship and navigation on the part of the force commander. My second-in-command has only been using small boats for about 4 months and chances of success would be materially reduced if the most experienced officer available were not sent.
2.  A failure would prejudice all future operations of this type.
3.  In a new unit the OC can hardly gain respect if he avoids going on the first operation.
5.  If I am not allowed to go on this operation what type of operation will be permissible for me? The case of Major Stirling[16] in Egypt is thought to be similar.

    H.G. Hasler.

Blondie buried himself in training on the assumption that he would be leading *Frankton*. Without explaining why to any of his men, this training was subtly changed to reflect a long approach through enemy-held territory; consequently the marines of RMBPD now began a series of exercises across and through the mud flats of Hayling Island's many creeks in preparation for the lying-up that would be necessary along the Gironde River.

---

[14] Lucas Phillips's *Cockleshell Heroes*.
[15] Hasler papers.
[16] Founder of the SAS. Later Colonel Sir David, DSO, OBE.

Then the single most important 'conference' of his career to date.

> 29 Oct . . . 1700 – conference with CCO, Haydon, Selly, Neville[17] to decide if I should be allowed to go. Won after a ding-dong battle. Quick supper at the RORC. 2115. Train to Glasgow.

He travelled north with, no doubt, a great sense of relief that this final – and unexpected – hurdle had been cleared, but only just. The meeting had been convened to discuss the plans for *Operation Frankton* which had not altered in major detail since the first draft mulled over during the evening of 21 September and written on the morning of the 22nd at the Royal Ocean Racing Club. CCO and his team had found little with which to disagree until they reached the 'Command' paragraph of the Operation Order which stated, without ambiguity, that Major H.G. Hasler, OBE, Royal Marines, would be leading the operation.

"But should he," Mountbatten had queried, "when there is little and, most probably, no chance of returning?"

Blondie argued that it was his command; it was his idea; they were his specially selected and trained men; the canoes were, largely, of his design; the techniques were his brainchild and if the Detachment's first attack was to fail because he was not leading it he would not be able to face his marines nor continue as their Commanding Officer. It was not Blondie's style to ask any man to do anything he had not himself first tried and trialled to absolute perfection and that, he contested, included the raid itself. He finished by declaring that future operations could only benefit from his first-hand experience.

Blondie had just one ally around the conference table at 1A Richmond Terrace that day, his fellow Royal Marine Robert Neville – and when all present were asked to give their judgement and all but Neville sided with Lord Mountbatten Blondie feared the worst. Having listened to the arguments 'against' (there were none 'for') the Chief of Combined Operations then looked straight at Blondie and said, "Much against my better judgement I am going to let you go."

The next day Blondie's outline plan was forwarded to the Chiefs of Staff Committee to be approved six days later on 3 November . . .

---

[17] CCO – Admiral Mountbatten; Major-General FC Haydon – Vice Chief of Combined Operations and Lt Col R.A.R. Neville RM – responsible for the co-ordination of planning and Blondie's main ally on these occasions.

NATURE OF OPERATION:

2. A small party, six strong, will be disembarked from a submarine approximately 9 miles from Cordouan Light. The party will paddle up the Gironde Estuary in Cockles Mk II, lying up by day and paddling by night to the Bassens–Bordeaux area, where they will carry out a limpet attack on blockade runners in the Port. The party will escape overland to Spain . . .

INTENTION:

5. To sink between 6 and 12 of the cargo vessels in the Bassens–Bordeaux area . . .

FORCES REQUIRED:

6. a. One submarine carrying three Cockle Mk II
   b. Six all ranks, Royal Marines Boom Patrol Detachment.

METEOROLOGICAL CONDITIONS:

7. a. No moon is essential.
   It will only be possible for the Cockles to proceed on the flood tide or during slack water.
   c. Wind maximum force 3 . . .

COMMAND:

10. a. Operation will be under command of Flag Officer Submarines.
    b. Naval Force Commander, Officer Commanding HM Submarine.
    c. Military Force Commander – Major H.G. Hasler, OBE, RM . . .

EVACUATION:

12. The Party will escape overland through occupied France to Spain as per special instructions . . .

TRAINING:

17. Special training began on 20th October and will include . . .
4. Full-scale rehearsal on British estuary (if possible) . . .[18]
5. Training for escape.

A few days later Mountbatten decided to increase the force to a full section of six canoes, but in the meantime and late in the morning of

---

[18] *Exercise Blanket* – of which more later.

30 October a much happier Blondie arrived at HMS *Forth* on the Clyde. On board the submarine depot ship he was ushered immediately into the office of Captain H.M.C. Ionides (Captain S3) to discuss the previous day's decisions. With the certainty that the Chiefs of Staff would approve the operation, they began at once to work on the details.

So happy was he with the excellent arrangements that Captain S3 and his team had been preparing since his last visit that Blondie telephoned Robert Neville that evening to thank him for his support and then rounded off a thoroughly satisfactory day drinking with Tommy Lambert,[19] the submariner son of a Royal Marines General. For RMBPD's first operation Blondie chose Number 1 Section under the command of Lieutenant Jack Mackinnon. The other ten members were: Sergeant Samuel Wallace, Corporals A.F. Laver and G.J. Sheard and Marines James Conway, Bill Ellery, Rob Ewart, Eric Fisher, Bill Mills, David Moffat and Bill Sparks. Blondie made up the twelfth man: six canoes, two men in each.

The men arrived shortly after noon the next day to begin a period of training more intense and comprehensive than any they had so far undergone. Even if they did not know what their task was to be, it was clear that this had to be a prelude to the real thing for Blondie gave them no time to sit and romance about the scenery of a Scottish loch nor the local lasses, despite being Friday night and Glasgow a short bus-ride away.

The stores arrived during the afternoon of the 31st and at 1500 the marines had their first glimpse of the latest Cockle Mark II with Blondie's numerous refinements and attachments. By 1830 all was set for training the next day and while they relaxed on board HMS *Forth* Blondie prepared his lectures until nearly midnight.

On Sunday the Section was introduced more formally to their steeds for the raid that they guessed had to be imminent and by the end of the afternoon they had conducted the first limpet attacks and were pleased with the result. All agreed that the Mark II was a distinct improvement.

The vessel that was used for much of their work and for the initial practices of hoisting and lowering into the sea was the Dutch ship *Jan van Gelder*. While No 1 Section overcame inevitable teething troubles, and a certain nervousness at sitting in their canoes while swinging beneath a crane, two submarines, *P 339* and *P 223*, were being prepared for more realistic trials with their four-inch guns.

Blondie was anxious that training conditions were close to those that

---

[19] Later lost at sea.

they would find in the Garonne river and so *Jan van Gelder* would steam slowly ahead at between one and two knots to represent the likely tidal streams while they placed limpets six feet below her waterline with the placing rods. That night, Monday, the men were given a much-welcome all-night leave pass, but the next morning, 3 November, it was back to reality.

> Am, hoist out. 1000 all boats leave ship in formation for long day trip up Loch Long. 2 boats fully ballasted . . . 1630 returned to ship. Very exhausted. Total distance approx. 13 miles. 4th November. am, 1100. Hoist out. 1330 over to *Jan van Gelder*. Hoist in on quarter davit. 1430–1700 Practise daylight hoisting out fully loaded. Limpet attacks against *Jan van Gelder*. 1900–2100 repeating (in the dark) with southerly breeze and lop. Good value. 2330 return to *Forth*.

When, on 5 November, Mackinnon's men were instructed to paint their canoes in a disruptive camouflage scheme to Blondie's specification their suspicion that something 'real' was afoot intensified and once that artistic task was complete their belief was absolute as they embarked for their first trials in a sea-going submarine. *P 339*, under the command of Lieutenant-Commander Wingfield, was loaded with canoes and stores during the dog watches, while that evening, on board HMS *Forth*, Blondie and Jack cut up maps and charts and drafted the orders for *Exercise Blanket*. Unknown to Number One Section Commander and, of course, to his men, this was to be the major testing ground for the real thing, for by taking place up the river Thames from Margate *Exercise Blanket* was designed to mirror the distances and, in places, the topography that would be found along the Gironde.

At 0740 the following morning all ranks embarked in *P.339* which then sailed into a fresh south-easterly wind to seek a lee off the western coast of Arran where they practised, for the first time at sea, hoisting out the canoes on the gun-barrel extension.

The next evening the Detachment returned south for *Exercise Blanket*, happy with their progress, but for Blondie, in London, it was business as usual with the continuing fight to keep the RMBPD as a naval formation:

> Put in mild protest at proposal to put unit under army command.

However strongly he might have felt about amalgamating with the SBS or coming under army command Blondie had more important things on his mind. While he was confident that his men were ready, and he certainly was not going to send untrained men to war, he knew that the success of *Blanket* was vital and that the performance of himself and his team would be critically studied and closely analysed in Richmond Terrace.

The exercise lasted from 2055 on the night of 10 November to 0600 on the morning of the 14th and has been described, even by Blondie, as a complete failure – but it was not.

Blondie was determined that the exercise would be conducted under operational conditions and that meant carrying the correct gear over similar distances to those they would travel in France and although some of the navigation (especially that of Mackinnon) could be described, politely, as 'creative' some did reach (but not as a team) as far as Blackwall Point, just a few miles short of their destination, Deptford. The initial weather was mist over a flat calm sea which, no doubt, contributed to the Lieutenant's late arrival at the first staging point up the Swale, although initially steering on a reciprocal bearing had much to do with this as well!

> 0600 reached highest point, Blackwall Point. Picked up Mackinnon and three boats at Greenhithe and returned to Chatham. pm. Cleared up exercise at C-in-C's. Evening to Wrens' party with Mackinnon – very weary.

At that time Blondie did not refer to the exercise as a failure; at least he never used that word on paper until long after the war when, in a private résumé of the events that led up to *Operation Frankton*, he wrote:

> No 1 section start exercise in Thames Estuary from Margate to Deptford. Complete failure.

What is certain is that vital lessons were learned – as is the object of such endeavours – with plenty of time to put these right before the real thing. Blondie had also been able to exercise his well-known reaction to what others might see as disasters: "Ah, good! Now we know that that is not the way to do such and such!" Clearly, though, it was not the success for which he had hoped, but some, if not all, canoes had reached close to their destination, unchallenged, and they had covered a much longer distance than ever before.

However weary from the Wren's dance and the canoeing, Blondie was not too tired the next morning to report to COHQ for his debriefing where, according to Lord Mountbatten's biographer,[20] he met the Chief of Combined Operations in the canteen. When hearing that the exercise had only been a success because it highlighted the shortcomings, Mountbatten professed delight that these same mistakes would not now be made up the Gironde: as a result *Frankton* was not to be cancelled or even postponed.

Mackinnon still knew nothing other than that there was to be an operation and he certainly did not believe that they were training for anything in France while rumours among the men suggested a raid against German warships holed up in the Norwegian fiords – a view that Blondie did nothing to dispel. With rising excitement, and not a little apprehension, Number One Section returned to HMS *Forth*, but with the submarine depot ship now full of submarine crews accommodation was found in the nearby Indian merchant ship, the *Al Rawdah*, where a final round of packing and stowing gear was begun.

The canoe cargo bags were packed, emptied, re-packed, stowed and re-stowed with the cycle being repeated in the dark until every weapon, item of clothing or piece of equipment could be reached and instantly identified by touch. Fusing and setting of limpets continued unabated until this, too, could be done safely and accurately in the dark. More attacks against the *Jan van Gelder* were conducted, as was shooting with the service issue .45 Colt and the silent Sten gun. Fighting with the seven-inch, double-edged Fairbairn-Sykes fighting-knife[21] was perfected and there were interminable, long, cross-country, forced marches.

Considerable thought had been given to the uniforms they would wear and which had now been manufactured to Blondie's design after months of wet, cold, hot and sweaty experiments with cloth, shape and practicability. The suit had to be all things for all conditions but mostly at night and, naturally, always in the wet. They were, though, particularly designed for use with the Mark II cockpit and were practical, hard-wearing, waterproof, camouflaged and, inevitably, called the 'Cockle Suit'.

The question of badges of ranks and formation symbols for raids of this nature was the subject of much discussion within COHQ since 18 October, 1942, and Hitler's "infamous order" dictating that all "commando saboteurs" whether in uniform or not were to be shot: while

---

[20] Philip Ziegler, *Mountbatten.*
[21] Known, colloquially, as the commando dagger.

not, strictly speaking, commandos, it was felt that the members of such raids would probably be treated in the same illegal manner. In the light of such a probability some at COHQ suggested that raids should be conducted in civilian clothes as the treatment meted out to members, if caught, would be the same; to start, ran the argument, wearing appropriate escape clothing would save time and provide less risk of compromise. But that was not Blondie's view and he regarded it with contempt – his men would fight as Royal Marines and, if that was to be their fate, they would die in the uniform of a Royal Marine. To go dressed in clothes that would automatically ensure they would be shot as spies if caught was a defeatist attitude with which he had no sympathy, so badges of rank were carefully sewn onto the Cockle suits as were 'Royal Marines' flashes on each shoulder above the Combined Operations badge of a superimposed anchor, rifle and wings. There would be no mistaking that they were members of a conventional military unit.

Commander L'Estrange arrived from London with air photographs of the Gironde estuary from which Blondie was now able to select his daytime hides in advance. He also brought with him the latest geographical, topographical and meteorological data needed for the final stages of planning and the latest information on the enemy's defences and ship dispositions. For the sake of security Blondie did not, at this stage, write any orders but he did keep copious notes on the tides and the terrain through which they would pass.

The name of the submarine earmarked for the operation had been given to Blondie but no others for officially, there was no raid in the offing. The chosen boat, HMS *Tuna*, commanded by Lieutenant Dick Raikes, was on patrol and would remain so until a few days before sailing for the Bay of Biscay.

In fact *Tuna* was completing the last of a series of "abortive patrols mostly in appalling weather in Northern Waters" following a summer refit with Swan Hunter Shipbuilders on the Tyne.[22] Now, with little notice she was ordered to prepare for a 'Special Operation', yet her crew did wonder what could be more special than the work in which they were ordinarily engaged. For the time being, though, they and the First Lieutenant were told no more but guessed that it had to be something particularly unusual as the submarine was degaussed[23] three times in the intervening days – a fact that did not go un-remarked by the sailors, who

---

[22] Letter to the author from her First Lieutenant.
[23] A process whereby the magnetic field of a steel ship is altered to allow "safe" passage through a minefield of magnetic mines.

believed her to be the most heavily degaussed boat ever to serve in the Royal Navy![24]

In the early evening of 25 November, after a long day practising his men in fusing limpet mines, Blondie boarded *Tuna*, now alongside the depot ship HMS *Forth* to meet her First Lieutenant, Johnny Bull[25] who knew only that he was to prepare for a party of thirteen marines. After this meeting he knew little more except that he also had to find space for six canoes and a mass of stores. The only detail to be discussed that evening was the method by which the canoes would be launched.

Initially unaware of the earlier trials, Johnny suggested the "floating off" technique, but Blondie explained his tested method and handed over the slings. *Tuna's* First Lieutenant was convinced and later wrote:

> We went ahead and bolted a piece of rolled steel girder on to the barrel of the gun having first welded an eye to the end of the girder to which we bolted a two-part purchase that could be used to hoist the canoes out from the casing into the water. When doing so we used the gun's normal training mechanism to swing the canoes out before lowering them into the water.[26]

Much of the 26th was spent packing and re-packing the stowage bags until the evening when all compasses were swung with the canoes fully laden for war. The order of loading the canoes had to be strictly adhered to, not only for speed and ease in the dark, but also to ensure that, once afloat for the final journey, there would be no differences in compass deviation from when they were swung.

The 27th was yet another day of packing, unpacking, compass checking and, finally, a walk ashore, but it did not end quite as planned for, in a rare admission that a party might have got out of hand Blondie ended his diary entry with the words:

Evening – drinking in *Al Rawdah* with Poles. Disastrous results.

At the end of supper, and just about to turn-in, Blondie and the RMBPD's second in Command, Jock Stewart, had been joined by a collection of Polish submarine officers. At first the two Englishmen refused the offer of a nightcap, but, after being pressed, agreed to "just

---

[24] Interview with her Commanding Officer.
[25] Later Commander J.R.H. Bull, MBE, DSC and Bar, American Bronze Star.
[26] Letter to the author.

one glass of port". However, the Poles believed they could do better than port and produced their own national version. Eventually Blondie and Jock retired to their bunks helped by Blondie's MOA,[27] Marine Todd: both awoke in the morning unaware of what could possibly have produced such a kick – they never did discover.

With a hangover just when he needed one least, Blondie left his team touching up the camouflaging of their boats and reported on board *Tuna* to meet, for the first time, the man on whom the delicate and dangerous task of getting the raid off to a good start would depend. Dick Raikes had had an eventful war so far, winning a DSO while with HM Submarine *Sea Wolf*. He also knew the coast for which they were heading and, even if Blondie had wanted to use the 'floating off technique', would have vetoed the idea:

> Neither of us was going to try the floating off technique but we did discuss it. I had landed a couple of spies on the coast in 1940 when we ran aground – we weren't very good at it in those days – and launched a Folbot, probably one of the first to ever be used on operations. The team were an Englishman who had lived in France all his life and who spoke English like a Frenchman, the Frenchman was of Gallic temperament who, when we got close inshore and had just touched the bottom (we were trimmed right down so perfectly safe) insisted on going around the whole crew shaking hands saying *"Vive La France"* and that sort of thing. Finally we got these two chaps onto the casing with their wireless set and told them which way to head. The idea was for them to paddle the canoe ashore and then light a blue lamp in our direction when we would pull the canoe back in so we would leave no trace. To our horror when we got the last *"Vive La France"* out of them they started paddling in the wrong direction straight out into the Atlantic. Do we shout to them to get back or do we wait until they get to the end of the 500 yard rope and ignominiously pull them back in?
>
> We were very close to the shore so we pulled them back in again in silence, directed them in the right direction and set them off again. Eventually we recovered the canoe safely.

Dick Raikes knew his submarine's destination of course, so much of his discussion with Blondie ranged around the 'how and precise where'

---

[27] Marine Officer's Attendant or, in army parlance, batman.

of the launch. The 'how' had been decided more or less and just needed practice but the 'where' was less certain due to the mines and the ability of the submariner to navigate through enemy-controlled waters with accuracy. Blondie knew, geographically, where he preferred to be launched and that was in the middle of the RAF's inaccurately plotted mine field. There were, too, the enemy mines to consider, but with his heavily degaussed boat and the belief that the Germans had only used magnetic mines, and old ones at that, Dick was less concerned about 'theirs' than 'ours'.

From that first meeting Dick Raikes's positive and determined attitude impressed Blondie Hasler immensely and every bit as much as Dick was impressed by similar traits in Blondie. These were two men of very different build but united by many other characteristics. Their overriding similarity was perfection and both achieved this in their men by calm, cool example, each officer's personality being felt at the lowest level of his command: Blondie very fit and tall and Dick Raikes fit and short, but with an equally commanding presence and penchant for going without sleep for long periods. Both possessed that indefinable ability to command without issuing orders and if things went wrong both were able to put them right by quiet deliberation and discussion. As with the best submariners and their boats so it was with Blondie and his RMBPD: control was exercised directly at all levels, a far cry from normal 'military' discipline where responsibility is, quite rightly, delegated downwards through junior commanders. With the RMBPD, as with *Tuna*, safety and success for the whole was invested directly in the commanding officer. A life-long friendship began that day.

By now the canoes had been given names and the crews paired off after swapping and changing over the months as everyone learned each other's strengths and weaknesses. Finding matching 'couples' had not been easy, for although the men were friends and colleagues, some, when on long patrols and tired, hungry and exhausted, would get on better with others.

One such was Marine Bill Sparks, a lively cockney but not always the most companionable of men for he had already fallen out with one or two others in Number One Section. Nevertheless Blondie considered him to be worthy of the task, but for the sake of overall harmony decided to take him as his own number two in the lead canoe. As for Blondie, he needed a strong canoeist willing to engage the enemy and who would do as he was told without comment or query; this relationship was to be well-tried before they returned to England.

The final day was spent packing the operational clothes which they would don before launching, checking the compass deviation for the Gironde area, sewing on the last of the badges and a final touch-up of the camouflage. Blondie and Sparks took all the bags now containing everything the six canoes would carry on the operation across to HMS *Forth* ready for loading in the fore-ends of the submarine that afternoon and at 1100 a final meeting was held between Blondie, Captain Ionides, Lieutenant Raikes, the ever-vital Commander L'Estrange and *Tuna's* navigator.

Blondie's last duty that night was to pack his personal papers and effects and leave them with Jock Stewart to await his return. He also left a list of various jobs that he wanted finished or progressed in his absence: work was to proceed on underwater ship attacks for he was sure that once *Frankton* had been successfully completed the Germans would be prepared for the next one and that would need to be conducted by "frogmen" covering the last few hundred yards to place limpets; thought was to be given to the submersible, one-man canoe that Blondie had been considering with his counterparts in COHQ, SOE and HMS *Dolphin*; a suitable underwater suit needed to be developed; further targets for the RMBPD needed to be sought; the delivery of BPBs and canoes needed to be progressed – as did the construction of the delayed BPB itself. Jock Stewart would not be idle during Blondie's absence.

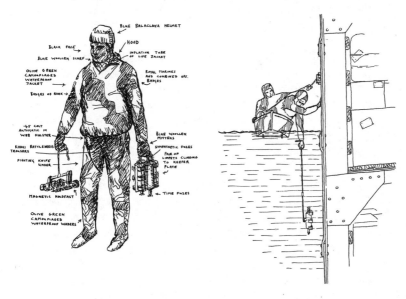

Blondie's sketch of a 'limpeteer'.      Placing the Limpet.

# CHAPTER SEVEN

## *Catfish, Crayfish, Conger, Cuttlefish, Coalfish* and *Cachalot*

At 1030 on 30 November, 1942, HM submarine *Tuna* slipped from alongside HMS *Forth* as Captain Ionides, Lieutenant-Commander L'Estrange, and Captain Stewart waved goodbye from the depot ship's deck.

Below, the collapsed canoes had been carefully secured, on their sides, in place of the re-load torpedoes while the sealed cargo bags and pre-packed personal bags were stuffed into every other conceivable space. The sailors had given the marines their cramped bunks, Blondie was offered the Captain's cabin and Mackinnon was allocated one of the officer's bunks in the wardroom, a curtained recess off the port side of the main passageway.

Once the formalities of leaving had died away and with the submarine an hour down the Clyde and still on the surface, Blondie called his men together in the fore-ends to face them with the truth.

He had the latest intelligence on enemy positions, he had the up-to-date escape route details arranged with the French Resistance, together with French money, and, of most importance, he had information on the targets available at the Bordeaux docks and the secondary docks a mile or so downstream at Bassens North and South. He did not reveal all at that first talk but just enough for his men to take in the emotional import of what they were being asked to achieve; there was plenty of time for the fine detail later. The target, even the country, was a surprise, as was, in particular, the method of recovery – an overland escape: this was some-thing for which the men had not been prepared, although they quickly accepted that the submarine would be unable to wait the eight or so days off an enemy-held coast.

Up to that moment there had been no clue that this was not another training exercise, for Blondie had allowed no opportunity for goodbyes, farewell letters, nor last minute telephone calls; nothing had indicated that this was for real.

The six canoes had been christened with names beginning with "C" to reflect their status as Cockles and divided into two Divisions each with a specific target. "A" Division would be *Catfish* with Major Hasler and Marine Sparks; *Crayfish*, Corporal Laver and Marine Mills and *Conger* with Corporal Sheard and Marine Moffat. "B" Division, led by Lieutenant Mackinnon and Marine Conway in *Cuttlefish*, had Sergeant Wallace and Marine Ewart in *Coalfish* and Marine Ellery and Marine Fisher in *Cachalot*. Marine Norman Colley was embarked in the submarine as "spare man".

At 1519[1] that Monday afternoon *Tuna* stopped in the Inchmarnoch South exercise area to conduct two hoists of the canoes and, as this was the marines' last practice and the first and only one for *Tuna's* crew, the trials did not end until well into dark at 2000.

The best time for five of the six boats to reach the water from first being brought on to the casing was thirty-one minutes. *Coalfish* was not launched as she was torn coming out through the torpedo loading hatch and *Cuttlefish's* compass was damaged as she was brought in manually over the sides of the ballast tanks, an evolution which all hoped would not need to be conducted during the operation.

Immediately after these trials Blondie and Dick Raikes sat and considered the effect the timings would have on the outline plan and concluded that they should aim to surface in a position eighteen miles west of Pointe de la Negade, come to full buoyancy, assemble the canoes on the fore-casing, trim down and steam eight miles due east along the southern edge of where Dick believed the RAF had laid their mines. Using this approach *Tuna* would be on the surface, inshore, for half an hour and about as close as Dick felt he could go towards the river's entrance; it was also as far away as Blondie felt he could start the paddle. As with so many "combined operations" this was to be a compromise and, as with compromises, it suited neither party particularly.

With the final rehearsals over, *Tuna* headed south and the next day was rolling heavily down the Irish Sea with all her passengers, except the officers and NCO's, "pretty useless"[2] and fast asleep between meals and visits to the heads, but at 2115 that night all were forced to their feet to re-stow and check their craft.

By 2 December the men had recovered sufficiently for them to attend

---

[1]  PRO. ADM 173. Log of HM Submarine *Tuna*.
[2]  Hasler diaries.

lectures on the escape procedures and the first rudimentary attempts at the French language. While this may have been useful for breaking the ice when in contact with a genuine French resistance worker the amount learned would not convince the Gestapo or Gendarmerie of their innocence as Breton peasants. For his part Blondie would be at a rare disadvantage, although speaking French passably well it was with a distinct German accent!

Two days later Blondie was ready to give full orders for the attack from notes which he then transcribed into a written "Summary of Verbal Orders Issued by Military Force Commander"[3] and, having done his sums, then asked Dick if he could aim for a first attempt during the night of 6/7 December.

> Submarine will arrive off the entrance to the Gironde approximately 5th December, and will hoist out entire force on first suitable night after 5/6th December, starting point being approximately 9½ miles 259° from Pointe de la Negade . . . Force will enter the estuary and proceed towards Bordeaux by stages lying up by day and travelling by night on the flood tide. On the first convenient night the attack will be delivered with limpets at HW slack, after which force will withdraw down the estuary on the ebb as far as possible. At LW slack crews will land on the east bank, scuttle boats and equipment and escape overland via Spain to the UK . . .
>
> . . . Disembarkation Drill . . . Before giving the order to commence hoisting out the captain will give a last-minute estimate of the magnetic bearing and distance of the headland 2½ miles NNE of Pte de La Negade. This will be set on compass grids.
>
> Approach Course. Will be as stated (above) until 1 mile offshore after which boats will follow the coast to point X which is a point one mile due north (magnetic) of Pte de Grave. At this point the CO will decide which side of the estuary is to be taken for the first lying up place by each division . . . At some stage during the first night's passage the Force Commander will give the final instructions to B Division (3 boats) which will then

---

[3]  It is generally assumed that there were no written orders but these are among his papers. In his diary for 5 December he states: "Then spending evening writing fair copy of orders and studying advanced bases."

proceed independently under its own CO for the remainder of the operation.

The orders continued with a miscellany of facts and instructions:

Whilst both Divisions are together, formation within A Division is arrrowhead followed by B Division in arrowhead. When the leading boat stops, B Division will close and each boat will come alongside the boat ahead . . . Passage making will only take place in darkness. No attempt will be made to move in daylight or in foggy weather . . . boats should keep out of the buoyed channel but must not move close to the coast.

Search areas for targets were allocated as follows:

Bordeaux west bank: *Catfish* and *Cuttlefish*. Bordeaux east bank: *Crayfish* and *Coalfish*. Bassens north and south: *Conger* and *Cachalot*.
   The Objectives of each boat are as follows:
a.   Primary. Two limpets on each of the four largest merchant ships (excluding tankers) in their target areas. The two limpets are to be placed 5 foot below the waterline in the following positions:
   A Division Boats. On the up-stream end of each ship, one limpet just short of amidships and the other between there and the up-stream end of the ship.
   B Division Boats. On the down-stream end of each ship, one just short of amidships and the other between there and the down-stream end.
   In addition *Catfish* and *Cuttlefish* carry one cable cutter and one wire cutter[4] each to be placed during the withdrawal on any vessel lying in the stream and if of sufficient size these two boats will reserve a pair of limpets each for her.
b.   Secondary Objectives. (Only to be attacked if it is impossible to get at the full quota of primary objectives.) In order of choice:
   i.   Large tanker in the target area (two limpets from each boat all between midships and the stern).

---

[4]   Another of Blondie's devices that he had developed with CODC. These were small explosive charges for fixing to cables and mooring wires in order to add confusion to the chaos by making sure the target was drifting in mid-stream when the limpets went off.

ii.  Any smaller vessel (except submarines) in the target area (one limpet from each boat. A Boats on upstream end and B boats on downstream end).

iii. Any vessel not in the target area which may be encountered during the withdrawal down to and including dumb lighters.

The Withdrawal.

Boats will proceed downstream on the ebb with caution . . . At LW slack they will select a suitable landing place, land their two bags of escape equipment then destroy reserve buoyancy in the boat and scuttle it with all remaining equipment. Then proceed independently in pairs in accordance with the escape instructions.

On reaching a British Consul in Spain he is to be informed that the party consists of Combined Operations personnel escaped from a raid, but no further details.

Action to be Taken in Various Emergencies:

If the submarine should be surprised on the surface with any boats out on the casing the fore-hatch will immediately be closed. Crews on deck will inflate life jackets, load their boats, get in and fasten the cover. If the submarine should dive they will endeavour to float clear and proceed independently with the operation. Or, if ordered by the captain from the bridge, crews will withdraw via the conning tower hatch having first destroyed the reserve buoyancy of the boat.

Once clear of the submarine any boat losing the remainder of its formation will take the prescribed action to rejoin. If this fails it will continue the operation independently.

If approached by any vessel evasive action may be taken until the vessel gets nearly close enough to see the canoes. At this stage boats will stop and remain stationary in the lowest position.

If the patrol boat appears to be coming alongside both members of the crew will prepare hand grenades and will endeavour to capture the patrol boat by boarding. All other boats will take evasive action and proceed independently.

If hailed or fired at from the shore, boats will stop in the lowest position and allow the tide to carry them clear. They will never attempt to paddle away or shoot back.

If approached by a person of apparent French nationality

whilst lying up, crews will remain concealed until sighted then get hold of him (or her) explain they are British and instruct them not to tell anybody that they have seen you. Children should be told to tell the above to their parents and nobody else. Do not detain such people long or harm them unless they are behaving suspiciously.

If approached by one or more soldiers of apparent German nationality remain concealed until sighted. Then kill them as silently as possible and conceal their bodies preferably below the HW mark. Get away as soon as it is dark, regardless of the state of the tide . . .

If the alarm is raised during the attack boats will not withdraw but will use their own initiative to press home the attack at the earliest opportunity.

Everything, apart from the unmarked sections of charts that Blondie and Jack Mackinnon had been preparing, was committed to memory, nothing incriminatory or compromising would be carried in the canoes. Throughout 5 December *Tuna* remained dived with the NCOs and marines given a stand-off from lectures and briefings during the morning while the two officers continued work on the timetables for the attack and studied air photographs for lying-up positions. That evening each Division was briefed on its second night's lying up area and given practice in the Number 3 code – an ingenious method of sending signals back via the resistance movement or, as a last resort, from a prisoner of war camp.

6 December was a Sunday. During the morning Dick Raikes brought *Tuna* in towards the coast for a visual fix to ascertain his position since rounding, unseen, the island of Ushant. Above, the sea was flat calm with a slight swell making periscope work hazardous, while below the tension began to rise as the time for action approached.

Dick's plan was to close the coast twenty or so miles south of the Gironde's entrance to make certain of his position before approaching the southern edge of the minefield. Land was sighted at 1340 through the search periscope but it is low and featureless along much of that seaboard and difficult to identify for a positive navigational fix. As it was vital that he establish his position without doubt, Dick began creeping his submarine northwards looking for some identifiable feature, but the sky was too overcast for a sun-sight and the coast just a long line of houses and churches impossible to connect with objects on the chart.

Unable to fix his position accurately, Dick called Blondie to the

Control Room: a delay of twenty-four hours was advised and readily agreed, although in his personal diary Blondie records that there was "slight reaction on all sides."
The First Lieutenant wrote later:

> The captain was forced to postpone till the next day . . . we would retire from the coast during the night and try and get a star fix in the morning. The Captain and Hasler were obviously most concerned about this but took great pains to conceal their misgivings.

Blondie was anxious not to delay one moment more than was necessary and Dick Raikes was anxious not to risk his submarine. Both understood each other's position perfectly, their reactions being those of professional frustration rather than of exasperation each with the other, and, as Dick reported:[5]

> The night of the 6th/7th proved impossible as I was completely unable to establish my position with sufficient certainty and it was imperative to be dead accurate. This was unfortunate as conditions were quite perfect, a nice mist coming down after dark.

Thankfully the weather cleared during the night allowing a good star fix at dawn on the 7th and, according to Johnny Bull:[6]

> We renewed our reconnaissance of the coast, finally getting a sight of the lighthouse at the mouth of the River Gironde (the Pointe de Grave). We then started to move towards the agreed point of disembarkation some four or five miles offshore. . . . There were a large number of fishing boats and we had to use the periscope with tremendous care to avoid being reported to the Germans.

Dick spent the whole of 7 December tip-toeing *Tuna* along the coast until finally obtaining another accurate fix at 1345. Air patrols by Me 110s, Me 109s, Ju 88s and Dornier 18s throughout the day were intense and with the surface an oily calm on top of a long swell the

[5] Operational Report of HM Sumbarine *Tuna*. Hasler papers.
[6] Letter to the author.

chances of being spotted were high. At 1800 a patrol trawler was heard, and then seen patrolling along a line south-east to north-west and running almost through the intended disembarking position.

> It was decided, to the evident delight of the OC Military Force, to try and disembark close to the coast and near the RAF's badly laid mines. . . . I don't think those mines could have been laid in a more embarrassing position as they seemed to interfere with every plan of action from the start. This plan quite evidently required extreme accuracy in navigation even allowing for the rather touching faith of the authorities in the accuracy of the positions given by the RAF – a faith which I did not share. Further, this plan entailed coming to full buoyancy four miles off the coast and ten miles from the RD/F station and doing the whole operation in one, cutting out the approach at low buoyancy. But the most important considerations were that in that position the boats had a fair tide for an extra hour and that our position would be dead accurate.[7]

Blondie records simply:

> *Tuna* right inshore trying to obtain a fix. Succeeded about lunchtime. Self slept most of morning and afternoon. 1700, final talk to troops. 1745, supper. All set for disembarking.

This was the final, pencilled entry in the diary that Blondie now left in the safe keeping of Dick Raikes.

At 1515 on 7 December, four hours before the time for surfacing, the canoes had been turned from their sideways 'flat' stowage and made ready for disembarkation. The first four canoes to be lifted out would be those of the NCOs and marines; once on the casing they would be moved forwards of the hatch, making room for the two officers' canoes to be lifted straight aft. Blondie's would be the penultimate canoe on deck to be placed immediately beneath the gun and thus first into the water followed by Mackinnon's. The two Division leaders would then be afloat ready to take charge of the others as they were swung outboard. There was, too, another reason why the officers needed to be the first; if the launch had to be aborted while only half completed they would continue with the operation.

---

[7] Taken from *Tuna's* Operational Report. Hasler papers and PRO ADM 173.

Once on the casing those bags that could not be stowed into the canoes in the 'flat' condition would be stowed in the strict order required for the river passage. This juxtaposition would be altered for the attack itself when, for instance, the limpets and escape bags would be brought closer to the cockpits – and the compasses. Two limpets would then be loose between the legs of 'number one' plus a placing rod and grenade and the six remaining limpets, magnetic hold-fast and second grenade between the legs of the 'number two' in the stern.

Buoyancy bags would be inflated at bow and stern, the paddles fixed in their clips down the side decks and the remaining bags pushed into place. In the meantime faces were blackened, weapons loaded and, unknown to Blondie, a few small flasks of rum smuggled into the canoes as presents from the sailors. At 1917 Dick Raikes ordered the First Lieutenant to 'surface'.

Dick was first on the bridge before the hull of the submarine disturbed the calm, anxiously scanning the two or so miles to seaward for the patrol vessel that he had been watching all day through his periscope. With his boat trimmed down and probably invisible against the shore lights Dick felt that it was as good a set of circumstances as any and so called Blondie up.

"Are you happy to go?"

A slight pause.

"Yes."

They wished each other luck and shook hands but Blondie had one last request: "I'll be back in March. Will you fix a table at the Savoy for lunch on the 1st April?"

Holding the view that All Fool's Day might not be appropriate, Dick replied, "Not bloody likely but I'll book one for the 2nd."

They laughed and parted. The order was passed and the canoes were immediately lifted through the torpedo loading hatch where Blondie's, fully-manned and weighing, as they all did, 480 pounds, was fitted into the sling beneath the four-foot gun barrel extension and carefully hoisted over the side onto the low swell. Four others followed. A mixture of Dick Raikes's Operation Report and *Tuna's* log[8] take up the story where Blondie's diary left off:

> 7 Dec. 1345. Psn 45° 22'.5 N; 1° 14'.1 W. Further fixes approx every half hour till 1735 . . .
> 1917. Surfaced DR 45° 21'.8 N; 1° 14'.1 W.

[8]  PRO. ADM 173. 17677 and 17678.

1919. Stopped both.

1930. Commenced operations. Sea flat calm. Patrol boat in sight about four miles away . . . a beastly clear night. All boats were in the upper hatch by 1945, only one being damaged while coming out of the hatch. Trimmed down and disembarked the remaining five. As the first canoe was placed in the slings searchlights began sweeping the sea from the Pointe de la Negade and down the coast, but there was no light opposite us. There was an uncomfortable feeling that this reception may have been due to the RD/F station plotting us and this feeling was strengthened by the fact that the trawler was evidently closing. The last boat was waterborne in position 45° 23' N; 1° 14' W just after eight that evening.

2003 Operation completed . . . a time that reflects great credit on Lieutenant Bull and his upper-deck hands. Waved "au revoir" to a magnificent bunch of black-faced villains with whom it has been a real pleasure to work. Proceed on main motors course 200°. . . . Course and speeds to avoid fishing vessels . . .

13 Dec. Secured to D Buoy. Plymouth Sound.[9]

The boat damaged in the hatch was *Cachalot* whose crew, Marines Ellery and Fisher, were forced to return and, in effect, live to fight another day, which Eric Fisher was to do with spectacular success at Leros in June, 1944.[10]

From here the narrative is based on an amalgamation of Blondie's private synopsis of events and two official reports written on his return to the United Kingdom.[11]

The five cockles moved off in two arrowhead formations with A Division, led by *Catfish*, steering 035° Magnetic to pass two miles to the west of Pointe de la Negade. The sea remained calm beneath a clear, moonless sky; the land was covered by a slight haze.

At about 2350 the canoes passed over the Banc des Olives whose presence was evident from soundings and the sea building into steep rollers. As the force of the flood tide could now be felt Blondie altered

---

[9] *Tuna* had been ordered to Plymouth where she would become the first submarine to be fitted with a radar.

[10] See Ladd's *SBS – The Invisible Raiders*.

[11] *Operation Frankton* Intelligence Report, dated 12 April, 1943; *Operation Frankton* Detailed Report by Military Force Commander, dated 8 April, 1943. Hasler papers. Neither of these reports was available when the book *Cockleshell Heroes* was published in 1956.

course a little towards the east in order to follow, more directly, the line of the coast about one and a half miles away. Shortly afterwards the sound of broken water ahead indicated a tidal race which, never having been apparent from the charts or the Admiralty Sailing Directions, was an unwelcome surprise so soon into the operation.[12] Unable to escape because of the strong tidal stream, they would just have to do their best, but the breaking seas were unlike anything for which they had been trained. Blondie was sure that the Cockle Mk II could weather this obstacle provided it was kept head into the waves with the cockpit cover fastened. He and Sparks went first to wait the other side and check the remainder through, but Sergeant Wallace and Marine Ewart did not appear and a brief, futile search in the race was made. Since both men and the boat had buoyancy equipment Blondie believed that they may not have capsized but had turned further inshore on finding themselves separated from the remainder. Nothing further was heard of *Coalfish*.[13]

A short time later a second tide race was heard ahead. This one was rather heavier than the first and on emerging to the north it was now *Conger*, with Corporal Sheard and Marine Moffat, which had not made it in one piece with her crew in the water holding on to their capsized canoe. As it was impossible to bale out the flooded boat she was scuttled and an attempt began to tow the two swimmers further inshore while the tide carried the depleted convoy around Pointe de Graves through a third but less violent tide race about a quarter of a mile from the beach. To add to their troubles, the lighthouse on the point was now switched on at full strength, lightening up the scene brilliantly.

Unable to haul Sheard and Moffat any further for fear of jeopardizing the whole enterprise, Blondie halted the remaining three canoes about one and a half miles south-east of the point they had just rounded, where after sad handshakes, the two exhausted men were left with a flask of rum. From this position the tide should have carried them very close to

---

[12] Although delighted with the intelligence support he had received throughout the planning he would, in future years, express concern verging on anger, that this fundamental obstacle had been unknown by the hydrographers. Another concern would be the considerable fresh water content of the river closer to Bordeaux that gave his canoes less freeboard and more wetted surface area, thus affecting his precise calculation of the effort required to paddle over long distance.

[13] Wallace and Ewart were captured on the beach at Point de Grave and after failing to give any information were later shot in accordance with Hitler's orders.

the mole at Le Verdon but they were already very cold and unable to swim effectively despite wearing fully inflated life jackets.[14]

This incident wasted so much time that it was now impossible to attempt the east bank of the Gironde especially as the canoes were by then closer inshore than had been intended. The tide compelled them to pass between the Mole at Le Verdon and a line of three or four anchored vessels lying about three-quarters of a mile north-east of it. In order to get through this defile unobserved it was necessary to change to single paddles and separate to several hundred yards.

Clearing this latest danger, *Cuttlefish* lost the formation and while Blondie had no audible or visible clues to suggest that she had come to grief it was another blow, for his original force of six canoes was cut to two before the first night was out.

But *Cuttlefish* was indeed still in good shape and, unknown to Blondie, continued the approach independently – the reason for the delay has never been known. Blondie's orders had been for B Division to paddle independently "at some stage during the first night" and as Mackinnon had studied suitable hides from the air photographs and charts he would have chosen his own first night's stop. Blondie was not entirely unhappy, but with so few boats left he would now have preferred to have continued all together.

After waiting for as long as they dared, the remaining two canoes continued on a course of 196° magnetic to pick up the west bank of the estuary near Chenal de Talais where they turned south-eastwards. At about 0630 the first attempt was made to land but a slight swell breaking over a line of half submerged stakes on a shingle bank about one cable from the shore made it impossible to reach dry land safely. In desperation they continued along the coast until, as day was breaking, they were able to beach on a small sandy promontory near the Pointe aux Oiseaux. A reconniassance showed that there was good low scrub above the high water mark into which the boats were quickly carried and concealed with camouflage nets.

As dawn took charge a number of small fishing craft[15] emerged from the Chenal de St Vivien and, as ten of the smaller ones turned inshore, six people walked along the river's edge to meet them. The marines took

[14] Moffat's drowned body came ashore on the beach at les Sables d'Olonne seventy miles to the north: Sheard's was never found. *Conger* was found fifty miles to the north close to La Pallice.
[15] About 30 craft ranging from 16 foot pulling and sailing vessels to 30 foot motorboats.

cover as well as they could but it became hopeless as preparations for breakfast were made within a few yards.

Certain that they would be discovered, Blondie decided that the lesser risk was to declare their presence rather than try to hide, be observed and consequently reported to the French police as a suspicious group of unknown nationality. Not helped by his German accent, he eventually managed to convince the French that they were British and so, making no promises, the fishing party and their womenfolk left the canoeists alone but only after an elderly man brought them bread, for which they were thankful, not so much for the sustenance but for the implied friendship.

It was not possible to resume the passage up river until well after dark that second night when the flood stream began to run at 2330. As it was low water springs the canoes had to be dragged over three-quarters of a mile of sandy mud before they could be launched, leaving distinctive tracks that would not be covered until after daybreak, but these were not spotted.[16]

Eventually, and extremely muddy, they floated clear and out into the shipping channel where navigation was now easy as the port hand buoys were showing a dim flashing blue light allowing the canoes to keep one cable to the north-east of them: the weather remained calm with no cloud and good visibility but with a haze over both shores – it was intensely cold with the salt water freezing on the cockpit covers and their 'cockle suits'.

Picking up the east bank just north of Porte de Calonge they followed one mile off until the approach of daylight made it necessary to seek the second hide; this time they were fortunate to find a suitable landing at their first attempt with the canoes hidden quickly into a ditch between two hedges. A farm about 300 yards away gave Blondie a little concern, as did a low-flying aircraft, but they were left undisturbed in spite of a herd of cows in the adjacent field. Well-earned rest filled their day in this most perfect of hides, along with hot food and the discarding of certain stores they no longer needed, including Blondie's Tommy gun which he considered an unnecessary weight.[17]

The plan for that night was complicated. After sunset they would have three hours of flood tide to help them, but they would then need to lie up for six hours of foul tide before catching the first of the next flood

---

[16] Pointe aux Oiseaux was not known as such then (according to Blondie's intelligence reports) but is now recognized by that name on the charts and maps. It has eroded since 1942 and no trace of the hiding place now exists.
[17] This double hedge remains as it was then.

three hours before dawn. From the map Blondie chose 'Desert Island' as their intermediate night-time hide and, in order to catch as much of the tide as possible, ordered the start "somewhat earlier than was prudent". He was right. The local farmer watched them, silhouetted against the western sky, as they prepared to launch the canoes; jovial but inquisitive, he walked towards them across the field from the track that runs parallel to the river bank. However, so convinced was he by Blondie's story that he invited the four Royal Marines to the farmhouse for a drink and was rather upset when this was politely refused.

Desert Island[18] was covered in thick reeds six or seven feet high with occasional trees but the landing was difficult due to vertical mud banks on which the reeds for the most part were almost impenetrable. At 2045, and after many attempts, they found a landing place where the canoes could safely be left to dry out as the tide fell. The reeds through which they had to force their way were dry and made loud cracks as they were trodden down but as a fresh saw cut indicated that woodmen worked there Blondie was not too concerned about leaving such tell-tale tracks.

Under way again at 0200 on 10 December they aimed to catch the first of the flood but were forty-five minutes too early and had to wait for the ebb to stop. On their way at last they crossed the ship channel to enter the shallow passage that runs to the west of Ile Verte. This channel was narrow forcing them, despite no sign of life, to use single paddles until 0630 and the approach to the southernmost end of the Ile de Cazeau where they began to look for a lying-up place.[19] With banks similar to those of Desert Island it was only after considerable difficulty that they scrambled ashore near a small pier about a quarter of a mile from the southern tip of the island to come almost nearly face-to-face with a light anti-aircraft position about 40 yards away.[20] They made a dignified retreat but not until Blondie had inspected it from a distance of ten yards for future intelligence purposes.

With daybreak imminent the situation was now urgent and so again, close to desperation, they put ashore at 0730 in a far from ideal position on the extreme southern tip of the island where, without cover, they placed the two boats in the middle of a marshy field and hastily dragged the nets across. Although unobserved, a man and a dog came within a

[18] Properly known as Ile de Patiras, it, too, is largely unchanged.
[19] This long island has four names depending which part is being described – Ile Verte to the north, Ile du Nord in the middle, Ile de Macau on the middle west bank and Ile Cazeau to the south.
[20] Many of these emplacements still exist, much dilapidated.

hundred yards and at one time a herd of cattle stood in a circle looking down at them.

In this precarious position the four of them had to sleep, eat cold food, drink cold water, urinate and defecate from the comparative sanctuary of the canoe cockpits, protected only by the camouflage nets. Throughout that long uncomfortable day light aircraft flew overhead, forcing them to keep very still and preventing any real rest.[21]

It had been intended to carry out the attack on the night of the 10/11 December, but, as they had not yet reached high enough up the river to allow time for withdrawal in darkness afterwards, Blondie decided to move closer to the target area on the night 10/11 and carry out the attack early on the night 11/12.[22] The boats were launched at 1845 on 10 December with considerable difficulty owing to the vertical and slippery banks, but the weather was now good for their purpose with low cloud, the occasional shower and a moderate, southerly breeze.

For the first two miles they kept to the centre of the channel, then changed to single paddles and followed close along the western bank until, after an uneventful passage, they passed beneath the pontoon pier opposite Bassens South and found a small gap in the reeds into which they forced the canoes at about 2300. As soon as the tide began to ebb the boats dried out and they made themselves comfortable for the night.

Daylight proved that they had indeed been fortunate for they were quite inaccessible and well concealed, yet, by standing up, they were able to observe the traffic on the river and, at last, two good-sized ships lying alongside and four cables away immediately opposite them. During

---

[21] This tip of Ile Cazeau and the marshy field with long grass is today very much as it was in 1942.

[22] No account was taken, presumably, of the fact that it was still possible – indeed he was under orders to try and make it so – that Mackinnon would carry out his attack on the original night. This would have made Blondie's attack extremely hazardous. Mackinnon and Conway actually spent that same night on the same island but about three miles or so north up the east bank. It has to be assumed that they too decided to delay their attack until the same night as Blondie. However, while launching from their hide at 2100 *Cuttlefish* was holed on submerged stakes opposite Bec d'Ambes, and sank, with Conway nearly going down with his craft. After somehow making it to the mainland and to the village of Cessac twenty miles east-south-east of Bordeaux they were befriended and helped, only later to be betrayed to the French police while in the hospital at La Reole. A German party was sent to capture them: they were eventually shot.

the day they could rearrange the stowage of the boats for the attack, finishing with the fusing of the limpets which they set for a nine hour delay.

Unfortunately the weather now cleared and by twilight was once again flat calm under a clear sky with good visibility. With moonset at 2132 Blondie considered it essential to delay leaving this ideal hide until 2110 and thus about thirty minutes later than desirable from the tide point of view. Having made up his mind, the fuses were started.

My plan of attack was as follows:

*Catfish*: To proceed along the western bank to the docks on the west side of the river at Bordeaux. *Crayfish*: To proceed along the east bank of the river to the docks on the east side at Bordeaux but if no suitable targets could be found to return and attack the two ships at Bassens South which we had been studying during the day.

2115 Launch. *Crayfish* separates to attack east bank.

2245 *Catfish* along west bank approaching Bordeaux Docks impeded by deck lights and flood lights on ships. Past the entrance to the basins without difficulty except that it was necessary to keep about a cable offshore owing to a good many lights on the shore particularly around the lock gates. Pass 4 ships then put 3 limpet on cargo ship *Tannenfels* and 2 on a Sperrbrecher (German naval patrol vessel). Canoe nearly squashed between bows of tanker and cargo ship *Dresden* but got out and round to put 2 limpets on her stern and last one on tanker's.

Whilst *Catfish* was a little distance from the side of the Sperrbrecher in the act of turning to go down stream we were seen by a sentry on deck who shone a torch on us. Fortunately we were able to get back close to the ship's side and drift along with the tide without making any movement. The sentry followed us along the deck shining his torch down on us at intervals but was evidently unable to make up his mind as to what we actually were owing to the efficiency of the camouflage scheme. We were able to get under the bow of the ship where he could no longer see us and after waiting there for about five minutes everything seemed quiet so we resumed our course downstream. The attack on the second large merchant ship was rather spoilt by the presence of the tanker alongside and the fact that the tide was now running so strongly that I considered it unsafe to get in between the bows of the two ships. This forced us to attack the stern only.[23]

After all limpets had been placed, *Catfish* withdrew down the river without any further incident. Whilst having a short rest in midstream near the south end of Ile de Cazeau we were rejoined by *Crayfish* who was also on her way back, having completed her attack. *Crayfish* sounded like a Mississippi stern-wheeler at full speed but we knew what it was and we laughed aloud. This meeting was purely by chance but it was decided to continue in company until the end of the withdrawal. They had put 8 limpets on the two cargo ships at Bassens South: 5 on the *Alabama* and 3 on the *Portland*. Withdrew together until LW then separated according to orders and landed before dawn near St Genes de Blaye . . . Nothing further is known of *Crayfish* or her crew.[24]

With one and a half hours of darkness left on 12 December, 1942, and a mile or so north of Blaye, the two crews parted company with a final handshake and congratulations as Bill Sparks and Bill Mills, the two 'number twos', each offered to have the first pint ready on their return to 'Pompey'. Blondie ordered *Crayfish* inshore while he took *Catfish* swiftly away to find a separate landing place a quarter of a mile to the north: as they parted, he allowed himself a moment of concern – as he had when saying goodbye to Sheard and Moffat – for on their own in a foreign, occupied country they would have none of the guidance he had so far provided.

A few minutes later Blondie and Sparks landed, without difficulty, across the mud banks into a "fairly deserted area", then, having removed the escape equipment attempted to scuttle the faithful cockle in which they had paddled more than ninety nautical miles over five successive nights. *Catfish's* buoyancy bags were slashed and she was pushed out into the river but neither she nor *Crayfish* (who was then being dealt similar treatment) sank and both were found by the Germans later that day.

---

[23] The two ships did come together briefly with Blondie Hasler "feeling like Atlas" as he pushed the canoe back in the direction of the first of the ebb.
[24] After two days, they reached La Garde, about 20 miles from Blaye, where, still in uniform they were captured by the French police, handed to the German Security police and eventually shot.

The worst of their journey now lay ahead, for it was the phase of the operation for which not even Blondie had been able to plan, and while he knew that he, himself, would find the next weeks difficult he feared more for the others about to make the same arduous journey through occupied France. His thoughts were, too, with the others who had not made it thus far.

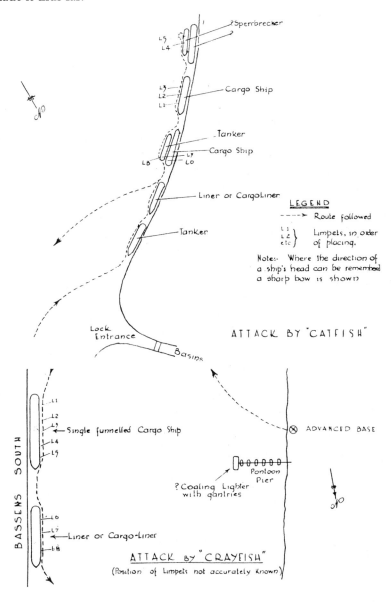

From *Report on Operation Frankton*, 9 April, 1943.

# CHAPTER EIGHT

## *Marie-Claire*

Right now the important thing was for Blondie and Sparks to get as far away from the Gironde as possible and into the escape pipeline, but the start to this momentous journey was not auspicious: the canoe would not sink, they were hungry, tired, filthy and cold and when they did reach their first rendezvous the Resistance knew nothing of them. Blondie kept no record of this phase of the operation and while he would now sit for hours on end going through every detail of the approach and attack for future reports he never committed anything substantial to paper.[1]

> 18 Dec. Arrived Ruffec. Nobody to meet us because signal had not got through. Asked for help at Hotel de la Toque Blanche. Lucky choice. [M. René Flaud collected them at 12.30 on the 19th]

While Blondie and Sparks were making their way towards Ruffec, seventy-five crow-miles to the north east of Blaye, the results of the raid were being speculated in Combined Operations Headquarters.

Initially there was considerable gloom in 1A Richmond Terrace for although Dick Raikes had sent a brief signal (*Operation Frankton completed 2100/7*) there was no more news. For *Tuna's* part she arrived in Plymouth, via some filthy weather that again prevented fixes and almost had her ashore on the Lizard Peninsula. On debriefing, her Commanding Officer could say no more than that five canoes had been launched successfully in good weather and from that moment on there had been silence from the marines. Combined Operations Headquarters were not, of course, expecting news quite yet, nor were they necessarily expecting good news, although Lord Mountbatten did believe that the raid would at least achieve its military object.

---

[1] For a fuller reconstruction see Lucas Phillips' *The Cockleshell Heroes*. Neither the MI9 nor SOE files contain details of this escape.

The first inclination anyone heard came by courtesy of a German High Command Wireless statement which was quoted under the Stop Press column in a London evening paper on 9 December:

> On 8 December a small British sabotage squad was engaged at the mouth of the Gironde River and finished off in combat.

In sending an immediate memo to the Prime Minister, Lord Mountbatten made assumptions that could have been considered premature; nevertheless, they were well meant and aimed at pre-empting an incisive Churchillian query about the wisdom of letting Blondie lead the raid:

> It seems possible that the Germans may have only intercepted one section of the raiding party. The Commander of the party . . . would probably have been with the leading section. The capture by the Germans of one section would not necessarily have compromised the other section since no papers were carried other than charts.

That the raid was a success became clear in February, 1943, from air photographs which, when added to French reports, indicated that six ships had been sunk or severely damaged. Of individuals there was no news and all were reported Missing in Action on 25 January, 1943, with the familiar, dreaded telegram duly arriving at Catherington. Two days later Mrs Annie Hasler received the confirmatory letter:

> Madam, In confirmation of the Admiralty's telegram despatched on 30th January 1943 I am commanded by My Lords Commissioners of the Admiralty to state that they have been informed that your son . . . has been reported missing on active service while engaged in a raid against the enemy coast . . .

It was not to be until 23 February that first-hand information was received in a near-indecipherable signal from Switzerland indicating that at least Blondie and Sparks had survived. The message was sent, ostensibly, in the standard format, but unfortunately Blondie had forgotten how to set up a specific part of the encoding process. Initially the jumbled collection of letters made no sense to the staff, until an off-duty 2nd Officer, Wrens, Marie Hamilton, set to work: many cigarettes later and with a cry to a surprised staff of "It's coming out – it's coming out!" she decoded the following:[2]

> COHQ. *Tuna* launched five cockles seven Dec. *Cachalot* torn in hatch. Pad hatches. In bad tide-race SW Pte de Grave *Coalfish* lost formation fate unknown. *Conger* capsized crew may have swum ashore. *Cuttlefish* lost formation nr Le Verdon fate unknown. *Catfish, Crayfish* lay up in bushes Pte aux Oiseaux. Found by French but not betrayed. Ninth in hedges five miles north of Blaye. Tenth in field south end Cazeau. Eleventh in reeds thirty yards south of pontoons opp Bassens South. Attack eleventh. *Catfish* Bordeaux West three on cargo ship two on engines of Sperrbrecher two on stern of cargo ship one on stern of small tanker. *Crayfish* Bassens South five on large cargo ship three on smaller liner. Back together[3] same night. Separate and scuttle cockles one mile north of Blaye. Sparks with me. Fate of *Crayfish* crew unknown. Hasler.

He put in as much information as possible for he could not know that the submarine had made it home and anyway Dick Raikes would only have reported that they had been launched successfully. Neither was Blondie sure that he would make it home himself, so the main lesson, that raiding of this nature was feasible, had to be passed to COHQ.

While the purpose of the raid was unknown by the enemy until the first limpet exploded at 0700 considerable confusion and extra damage was caused by the French *pompiers* who arrived to help douse the flames but who were then less than cautious with the amount of water they poured into the damaged hulls, adding to their instability. Initially the Italians, whose expertise in underwater sabotage had not gone unnoticed by the Germans, were accused by the Nazis of carrying out "these acts of treachery" in retaliation for not being allowed to use the submarine pens and at least one Italian submarine captain allowed himself to be well-fêted in the local cafés. Postwar there was even talk that the French Resistance were about to blow up the ships themselves and were "a little hurt" that they were beaten to it![4]

The discovery of the two canoes off Blaye and one unexploded limpet offered the Germans the only tangible clues to the nature of the

[2] Hasler papers and letter from Ronnie Sillars of COHQ.
[3] Originally decoded as "back to get her", causing some initial puzzlement.
[4] Various conversations with the author in Bordeaux 1971–1985.

operation. Initially, and due to the intermittent spacing of the explosions, the Germans thought that floating mines had been laid in the river and, contrary to some reports, they were not expecting an attack. Blondie had been worried that, with six men missing and having been seen on at least two occasions by French people, the Germans must have been alerted, which is why, he thought, the targets and docks were floodlit. But, so far from the sea, the enemy were not expecting an attack and felt safe to continue 'working cargo' at all hours.

Blondie never told of the tribulations of his escape through occupied France and Spain other than to suggest that having a man with you in battle for which you have both been trained is one thing but having a man escaping with you while you endeavour to live off your own wits is quite another.[5] So it was clearly an irritating time for someone who preferred his own company and whose skills at survival and subterfuge were far more sophisticated than those of his fellow escapee. He was also desperate to get back, not for the freedom that that entailed, but to put into practice the lessons he had learned.

In the early stages, while the excitement of escape was strong, and before the tedium set in, Sparks's cockney sense of humour and adventure was much appreciated. The approach to Ruffec, without rest since leaving *Tuna*, was arduous and, with one notable exception, unfriendly or down-right hostile. The exception was a communist woodcutter and his family deep in the woods near St Preuil, to whom they made the promise of sending a BBC wireless message "The chicken is good" on their safe return to England.

Arriving in Ruffec to find no trace of a contact and uncertain what their next move should be, hunger drove Blondie to peer into selected windows trying to choose a café where the state of their filthy "borrowed" clothes would be the least conspicuous. He found a near-empty one and ordered soup and wine. Delaying until the other patrons had left and with some trepidation he handed the waitress a pencilled note with his payment which read "We are escaping English soldiers. Do you know anyone who can help?" It was a huge risk but, thankfully, his request was answered in a note folded into his change. "Stay at your table until I have closed the restaurant." Unwittingly, and by sheer good luck, they were about to enter the 'escape pipeline'. However, a good deal of cross-examination lay ahead before they were accepted as genuine escapees.

Before establishing why the Resistance were not at the rendezvous it is necessary to take a brief look at the woman who would, in the end, see

---

[5] See also Chapter Ten.

Blondie and Sparks to safety. Mary Lindell, an Englishwoman of great bravery, but little tact as far as her own safety was concerned, served in the First World War during which she was decorated for bravery under fire by the French and Russians. Subsequently she married the Comte de Millville and, after joining the Red Cross in the Second World War (when she was awarded a second Croix de Guerre), she continued to wear her British medals superior to those from France and Russia, thus indicating, as publicly as possible, where her allegiance still lay:

> We were sick to death of the French and knew that someone would have to stay behind and stand up to the Jerries and see things through . . .

With the unwitting help of the German C-in-C in Paris, who introduced her to the great grandson of Count Von Bismarck responsible for such matters, she obtained passes and a large stock of petrol coupons ostensibly to re-unite babies from the north with their parents on the Riviera. But her real business was as the agent 'Marie-Claire', under which *nom de guerre* she repatriated a number of men before being captured and tortured by the Gestapo in Paris. She managed to escape from Fresnes Prison, via Spain, to England where, on her arrival in July, 1942, she was debriefed in a flat above Overton's in St James's Street by Captain Airey Neave who, himself, had just escaped from Colditz. Determined to return, and against the wishes of some in MI9, (Whitehall's escape department) because she was known to the Gestapo, she was flown by Lysander to a field near Limoges on 21 October, 1942 – Trafalgar Day. She did not have a wireless operator with her as the one suggested did not meet with her approval. Without formal communications, therefore, she did not receive news of the *Frankton* raid until after it had taken place – nor did MI9 know that, anyway, she was lying in hospital with five broken ribs after a car crash. Once she knew of Blondie's predicament she despatched her nineteen-year old son, Maurice, to see him and Sparks safely through the system. Maurice was later captured but released on payment, in two halves, of torn bank notes and she, too, was captured again by the Gestapo, shot in the head and breaking her neck while escaping from a moving train, before being incarcerated in Ravensbrück. Her youngest son, Octavius is believed to have died in Mauthausen concentration camp, while her only daughter also worked for the Resistance. After the war Blondie was to help her obtain recognition from the British Government for compensation for those British-born women who were similarly treated for helping their countrymen. Mary Lindell received the OBE, but not until 1969 by when it was certainly considered far too little and certainly too late.[6]

Meanwhile, on 19 December, Blondie and Sparks were taken to Armand Dubreuille's farm nearby, to spend six weeks in hiding. In doing so the Frenchman ran considerable risks, due, especially, to the proximity of the line of demarcation which was at that time well patrolled but, never daunted, he and his family extended the warmest possible hospitality. He also made contact with 'Marie-Claire' who, while lying in hospital, arranged for Maurice to take on the task of getting them to Spain.

Maurice arrived at the Dubreuille's house on 6 January and, after promising to send a second message which this time was to declare, "The two chickens have arrived"[7] Blondie and Sparks were spirited away by bicycle and train towards Lyons where the three arrived the next day. As the Resistance had had no warning of their impending arrival there was no time to issue identity cards before this journey which, therefore, had been an anxious one. Lyons was two hundred or so miles east of their starting point and even further from the Spanish border for which they hoped to head, but the reason for this out-of-the-way staging post was explained as soon as they were taken straight to 'Marie-Claire's' flat.

This was a meeting that Blondie never forgot, for not only did the legendary Resistance worker remind him of a terrifying fox-hunting, female English aristocratic, but she was openly contemptuous of the Nazis and the French who collaborated with them. Her 'normal' route across the Pyrenees, she explained, had been compromised, forcing her to set up a new one – and that would take time.

Meanwhile they would be accommodated in a northern suburb house where, she stated, there was only one strictly-enforced rule and that was, No girls. With their involvement, "everything goes to hell!" and nobody, not even Bill Sparks, argued against Marie-Claire on that issue.

With Marie-Claire unable to open her new route as soon as she had planned, this was now the start of a long and deeply frustrating time of mixed circumstances including a major move to Marseilles in early February where yet more idling awaited them. Naturally Blondie accepted the reason for the delays and knew well that brave men and

---

[6] Obituaries: *The Times*, 17 January, 1987 and *The Daily Telegraph*, 10 January. She died on 8 January aged 91. See also Foot and Langley's *MI9 Escape and Invasion 1939–1945*.
[7] Both messages were duly sent and received.

women were doing their best to ensure his safe return, but his main worry was now their fitness for a forced crossing of the snow-covered mountain frontier. Then, without warning on 1 March, and escorted by a young Frenchman, they were put on the coastal train for Perpignan where they transferred to the back of a van full of empty wooden crates, among which they were able to hide. Beyond Ceret, in the foothills, the van stopped, the marines crawling stiffly out to be met by two Basque men who immediately took charge.

It was the beginning of a hideous, physical ordeal that on many occasions Blondie was not sure they would, or could, weather. But come through they did, although there were many moments when it was only the thought of what lay ahead, and what lay behind if caught, that kept them going, for there was precious little practical sustenance to supplement their reserves of energy, which were low even before the start. However, once over the border they were in Catalan country whose inhabitants were violently anti-Franco and not likely to co-operate for one moment with the Spanish police; which was fortunate, for the carabinieri would have had no hesitation in locking them up and, most likely, returning them across the border and into the hands of the Gestapo-sympathizing gendarmerie.

The small town of Banolas, a punishing twenty miles down from the border, was the first objective where, much to Blondie's delight, they were expected and welcomed at a small inn. Barcelona, which he now knew to be his destination, lay another fifty-five or so miles to the south-south-west and so, with mounting relief (but after another five days) it was towards that town that they drove in the back of another van, this one laden with china lavatories on a copious bed of straw, which was not only a perfect hiding place but deliciously warm.

Although his arrival in Spain was a cause for gratitude to the French Resistance there was not yet any guarantee of security, despite being under the protection of the British Consul. All Spanish men of military age were required for service and it was possible that Blondie would be rounded up and his real identity discovered, but he looked old for his age and with a nearly bald head (and what was left turned grey) he was able to wander more freely than other escapees.

From Barcelona, and about six weeks after Annie Hasler had been told that her youngest son was missing in action and about two and a half weeks since being told that a message had been received confirming that he was, in fact very much alive, Blondie wrote to his mother. It had been an anxious wait, but for the others of Blondie's team (apart from Sparks) there was to be no such happy, second message.

Hotel Victoria, Barcelona, Plaza de Cataluña,

12th March

Dear Mother,

I am taking this first opportunity of writing to let you know that I am still flourishing and happy. I am sorry not to have been able to let you know before but you know how things are these days! I hope you haven't been too worried about me – I'm afraid it isn't by any means the first time that you have spent waiting for news from me! I am very fit and happy as usual, and enjoying it all very much.

I am supposed to be on my way home, but anything may happen, and I expect this letter will get home before I do. Don't worry about me in any case.

I have had a most interesting time since I last saw you. I have only just arrived here, so the novelty has not yet worn off. I was here for a day in 1936, during the Civil War,[8] but things are naturally much better nowadays.

There is quite a lot of food and drink to be had, but most of the things one can buy are rather expensive and appallingly bad quality. However, there are compensations not to be found in England – no blackout, lots of bananas and oranges, and even quite a few eggs.

There is so little I can write about that I have now exhausted it. Hoping to be with you again soon.

Love George.

At last, and with his identification confirmed to the Consul-General in Barcelona by COHQ, the urgency to get Blondie home was intensified. He was moved to the British Naval Attaché's house in Madrid where he waited a few more days, including an evening watching flamenco dancing in Seville with a number of Germans at the next table, before the final car journey to Gibraltar. Blondie arrived in the United Kingdom by air on 2 April, only one day after he had asked Dick Raikes to book the luncheon table at the Savoy!

As he had warned his mother, he did not return home straightaway,

---

[8]  No details of this visit exist. This is the only reference to it that he made.

for the next day he was in Combined Operations Headquarters to start a lengthy verbal and written debrief. As a finalé to his reports, Blondie tabulated, in very simple terms, the miles covered:

| Night | Nautical Miles |
|-------|----------------|
| 7/8 December | 23 |
| 8/9 | 22 |
| 9/10 | 15 |
| 10/11 | 9 |
| 11/12 | 22 |
| Total: | 91 |

The report was a detailed but dispassionate résumé that ended with the following praise:[9]

> It is desired to draw attention to the part played by the following NCO and men in this operation:
> a. Ply X3091. Cpl A.E. Laver RM who handled his boat skilfully and displayed initiative and coolness in making his independent attack.
> b. Ply X3664. Mne W.E. Sparks (No 2 of *Catfish*) and Ply X 108159 Mne W.H. Mills (No 2 of *Crayfish*) who both did their work in a cool and efficient manner and showed considerable eagerness to engage the enemy.
> No report of this operation would be complete without further mention of the work of the following officers in the initial stages:
> a. Lieut R.P. Raikes DSO, RN, commanding HM Submarine *Tuna* who cheerfully accepted serious risks in order to fix his position accurately and subsequently to launch the attacking force in a favourable position.
> b. Lieut-Cdr G.P. L'Estrange, RNVR, Combined Operations Headquarters, who did the bulk of the detailed planning and personally prepared, with great thorough-

---

[9]  Major-General Tony Simpson of COHQ said of Blondie's *Frankton Report* that it "read like a match report of a golf tournament" – which is probably what Blondie wanted.

ness and accuracy, the actual charts, tide tables etc used by the attacking force.

By the 9th he was back on the south coast picking up, with very little pause for breath, where he had left off. The escape through France and Spain had been an experience but it had wasted valuable time.

At breakfast in Eastney Officers' Mess that morning he ordered a pint of beer, poured much of it over his cornflakes as though it were the most natural of habits (after all, there was strict milk-rationing in force) coerced a number of 'volunteers' into a morning's sail in the Lymington Scows that had been commandeered for training, and, once that was out of his system, was in his office at 1030.[10] By 1700, and after visiting Bill Ladbroke's workshops, now moved to HMS *Northney*, Hayling Island, and spending time with Clogstoun-Willmott of the COPP and Courtney of the army SBS, he was on the water again trying out an improved version of the cockle that had served him so well: at 2015 it was time to change for the Sergeants' Mess dance. Life was back to normal!

The Chief of Combined Operations was personally thrilled to have his doubts about Blondie's survival dashed and, in expressing his admiration in a more official manner, wrote the following citation on 13 May, 1943:

> Major Hasler's cool, determined and fearless leadership was in accordance with the highest traditions of the Royal Marines corps – and he is strongly recommended for the highest recommendation possible for a feat of this nature. Louis Mountbatten. CCO.

There was no doubt that Lord Mountbatten had the Victoria Cross in mind; also on that day he wrote a recommendation for Dick Raikes, copying, exactly, the words Blondie had used. Just over a month later the *London Gazette* of 29 June, 1943, carried the following announcement:

> For courage and enterprise. To be a Companion of the Distinguished Service Order, Captain (Act Major) H.G. Hasler, OBE, RM.

Blondie was disappointed that Dick Raikes's name did not appear in the honours list but, to his pleasure Bill Sparks received the DSM and

---

[10] Letter to author from John Arnold dated 3 May, 1989.

Corporal Laver and Marine Mills were both mentioned in despatches – neither being eligible for the recommended DSMs which could not, then, be awarded posthumously.

Two days later he received a letter from Lord Mountbatten:

> I was delighted to see that you had been awarded the DSO and am writing to offer you my most sincere congratulations. This is a fitting tribute to the conspicuous courage and qualities of leadership you displayed in your recent hazardous operation and I feel sure that there have been few decorations that were more deserved. Yours sincerely, Louis Mountbatten.

What was unexpected was the promotion to Brevet Major. For an operation that even the Germans were to describe as "the outstanding commando raid of the war" a Victoria Cross would have been in order – and appropriate.

The first memorial to be dedicated to the dead of *Operation Frankton* was unveiled twenty-three years later on 3 April, 1966, in the English Church of St Nicholas at Bordeaux.[11] Nobody who was there has yet forgotten the simplicity, beauty and emotion of the service, best summed up at the time by the *Daily Express*:

> Courage is not the prerogative of man alone. In the congregation sat Mary Lindell, no longer young but still aristocratically beautiful, Mme. Pasquarand, her face apple-red, weathered by the sun and Atlantic winds – workers in the French Resistance who defied the Gestapo and faced torture and death . . .
>
> The plaque was unveiled by Lieutenant-Colonel H.G. (Blondie) Hasler . . . No one could invade the privacy of the thoughts of this quiet-spoken, modest man as he tugged at the White Ensign this morning, revealing on the oak plaque eight names. For a few seconds he looked at it intently. Then his head bowed, and the congregation stood in a brief and overpowering silence. . . . These were the names of the young men he had trained for a daring mission involving almost certain death. This was his particular responsibility.

[11] In 1990 the church was sold and, although destined for the Musée de l'Estuaire at Blaye, the plaque is currently lodged with the British Consulate in Bordeaux.

It was not until 11 January, 1984, forty-two years after the raid, that recognition of their deeds was marked in the United Kingdom. That memorial now stands close to the present Headquarters of the Special Boat Service at the Royal Marines base at Hamworthy, Poole, and was erected from public subscriptions largely through the efforts of the MP for South East Essex, Sir Bernard Braine, DL, MP. The Commandant General, Lieutenant-General Sir Steuart Pringle Bt, KCB, led the service with a message from His Royal Highness Prince Philip, Captain General of the Royal Marines, who wrote of the operation:

> The sheer size of an operation has never been a criterion of its importance or a measure of the popular response to its outcome. The ten men who took part in *Operation Frankton* have written one of the most glorious pages in the long history of the Royal Marines. The memorial to those who died is as much a tribute to their personal courage as it is a record for posterity of what can be achieved by human will and determination in the face of adversity.

Lord Mountbatten's words are carved into one of the Purbeck stone blocks:

> Of the many brave and dashing raids carried out by the men of Combined Operations Command none was more courageous or imaginative than *Operation Frankton.*

Fittingly, among the guests, many of whom were relatives of the men whose names were upon the memorial, was Commander R.P. Raikes, DSO, Royal Navy. Later Blondie was to write:[12]

> I would have wished that the memorial could have included some mention of the Captain and crew of HM S/M *Tuna* who took such severe risks to launch us as near to the Gironde as possible. Dick Raikes, her captain, was a marvellous CO . . .

[12] Letter to Tim Wiltshire, 18 October, 1984.

# CHAPTER NINE

## *Sleeping Beauties*

On Sunday 10 April, 1943, Bruce Wright's name first appears in Blondie's diary. He knew of Wright's existence but on that day he first saw one of the 'new' ideas that he had brought with him across the Atlantic.

Sub-Lieutenant Bruce Wright, RCNVR, commanded[1] a launch patrolling the anti-submarine booms guarding St John's harbour, Newfoundland. Among his attributes he was a near-Olympic standard swimmer and while pondering his patrol duties it occurred to him that it would be easier to breach the boom by swimming under it rather than by forcing a way through in a submarine.

Remembering the abalone divers of California who used 'single-window' face masks, fins on their feet, spring-loaded guns that fired 'arrows' and rudimentary surf boards which they would paddle with their arms to preserve energy over long distances, Wright wrote a paper, *The Use of Natatorial Assault and Reconnaissance Units in Combined Operations*. This he dispatched to the Director of Naval Intelligence in London from where it reached the desk of Lord Mountbatten who immediately summoned the Canadian, ordering him to bring samples of the equipment he proposed to use.

Blondie watched Wright demonstrate his paddle board at their first meeting and was sufficiently impressed to take him to London the next morning to develop further a few of the ideas and ask Dunlops to produce special suits and fins to aid underwater approaches and attacks. This was also the day that Blondie was able to renew his friendship with Dick during a debriefing on *Frankton* to the Plans Committee, after which they met Joan Raikes at the promised lunch. It wasn't 2 April nor

---

[1] While his CO had been ill.

was it the Savoy but it was a celebration nonetheless. Dick Raikes later commented:[2]

> As soon as I knew he was back I booked a table at Kettner's in Soho. I felt absolutely at home with Blondie for he was immensely modest, looked you straight in the eye, and said what he thought. Here was a man you could go to with any manner of problem. Despite being very quiet he was also a most dynamic person, which is perhaps very unusual, and shared with me a great sense of the ridiculous which we believed to be more important than a sense of humour – which he possessed in large measure as well.

The lunch was a happy occasion that ended at 1430 for Blondie to attend a meeting on the BPB after which he was "called in as consulting physician on two projected operations" followed by yet more talks on the possibility of "amalgamating all the small boat units", but much to his relief there was "still no result". Other threads closer to his heart and higher on his priority list had to be taken up again and, in particular, improvements to the underwater breathing apparatus, the Mk II* Cockle, the *Sleeping Beauty*, and the two 'civilian' loves of his life – Val and *Mandy*.

Val arrived in Portsmouth during the evening of Friday 16 April, at the start of four days' leave and, in preparation for her visit, *Mandy* was put on her buoy earlier in the day to allow her wooden planking to "take up". That afternoon she was brought ashore and re-rigged but actual sailing took second place to 'country pursuits' until Tuesday when they enjoyed a wonderful day alone, disturbed only by the patrol boat arresting them because Blondie's permit had expired. He was back on familiar ground in more ways than one! – and to honour their renewed relationship Val wasn't 'ick'!

Believing that the canoe remained the ideal method of approach before an underwater swimmer placed limpets, thoughts now turned to delivery from a base area. Tests proved that the standard Admiralty cutter, fitted with an Austin 8 horsepower engine and given a small forepeak, could be adapted to carry two cockles plus their four crew and diving gear at a speed of six knots over a two hundred mile range. Of particular interest to the men of the RMBPD it had a 'minimum silhouette', was silent

---

[2]  In conversation with the author.

under power at four knots, able to set an auxiliary mast and sails, withstand heavy weather and could take the ground with impunity. The stern was cut-away and replaced by a hinged transom with rollers across which the canoes were man-handled, and so impressive was all this that an order for eight was placed with the dockyard and more sailing added to the training programme.

The Motorised Submersible Canoe (MSC), or *Sleeping Beauty*, had featured among Blondie's ideas for development and was one "mechanical but stealthy" craft in which he took a great personal interest: the other was the human torpedo or two-man chariot, but this was not his idea and had, anyway, been in development and use for some years. In early summer, 1943, the first *Sleeping Beauty*, which Blondie had originally named the *Underwater Glider* (itself a more acceptable offshoot of the *Explosive Tadpole*) was produced for the Special Operations Executive to specifications laid down by him.

Much of the initial experimental work was conducted in HMS *Dolphin's* tank before the first were built by Camper and Nicholsons of Gosport. The MSC was, in effect, a one man, open submarine with the crew sitting in the cockpit breathing oxygen when submerged: unlike the BPB, though, it was not an expendable weapon system and unlike the 'chariot' there was no detachable, explosive warhead. Driven by an electric motor it could also be sailed by a simple lugsail.

With a length of 12 feet and a beam of 27 inches it was constructed of "best quality mild steel with a semi-silver finish plate" which was then painted in a disruptive pattern camouflage scheme. Without pilot, limpets and the oxygen breathing apparatus it weighed, on the surface, 625 pounds, but, submerged this weight would treble to 1800 pounds. Able to dive to a maximum depth of 50 feet it had a remarkable range as the handbook describes:

> 12 miles at full speed or 40 miles at cruising speed in still water. Full speed: 4.4 knots. Cruising speed: 3.1 knots. Operational planning range: 30 miles at 3 knots.

For 'general' ship attack the pilot's notes are clear, even if they did suggest, rather optimistically, how easy it was:

> It may be necessary for the pilot to approach his target from a considerable distance, porpoising occasionally to check his direction. Within 150 yards in the 'trimmed down' position the

pilot should conduct a static dive, erect the head-guard under-water, and approach at the maximum depth at which he can be certain of not passing under the ship.

On bumping the target, he will apply full helm to bring the craft alongside, then stop motor and allow the craft to sink stati-cally. . . . When he feels the boat sinking past the turn of the bilge he drives in diagonally to touch the bilge keel with his arm verti-cally upwards as he passes under it. He then immediately stops motor, blows to slight positive buoyancy, coming to rest against the ship's bottom a few feet inside the bilge keel, gets out and secures the craft to the bilge keel by means of the clamp and line.

When charges have been placed he vents to negative buoyancy inside the bilge keels where the bubbles will be trapped and not rise to the surface – and drives off on a compass course. When well clear, and outside the patrolled area, he lays a course for his rendezvous. If he misses the rendezvous altogether he can set sail to assist a long passage.

It is easy to understand why Blondie was taken by this method of oper-ating against enemy ships for it represented a one-man operation that did not rely on others for success or failure; it combined the all-important business of stealth with an acceptable range; it employed underwater swimming – a skill that Blondie was convinced held the key to so much they were considering: it allowed escape hidden from enemy view and, in extremis, a return under sail. Despite all that, Blondie spoke of the *Sleeping Beauty* as being "without doubt, the most dangerous vessel in which I ever ventured to sea".

All this time Bruce Wright was working on an idea that Blondie regarded as a minor incursion into his own field but he saw the value and gave it a free rein during a weekend of contrasts:

> Sunday 25 April. am. Carting manure and making extension box for wheelbarrow. 1430–1545 cycling back to Portsmouth against strong SW wind. 1615 by car to Romsey with Wright. Tea with Mountbatten and family. Discussed Wright's project. Home by 2230 having stopped for supper at the Swan, Bursledon.

Wright's proposal was to use only underwater swimmers for reconnaissance and sabotage duties in those places that canoes, and certainly the heavier craft, could not operate. Mountbatten, taken by the logical progression, insisted that this method he brought under

RMBPD's wing and be known as the Amphibious Reconnaissance Party, although this was later changed to Sea Reconnaissance Unit despite occasional references to the Sea Reconnaissance Section. CCO's office approved the SRU's training syllabus for approaches by divers and paddle boards provided it was conducted under Blondie's guidance and direction at HMS *Northney*. He would also be responsible for the selection of volunteers, with the first candidates due to arrive at Hayling Island on 30 July.

Endurance was going to be the primary key to successful underwater attacks and so the first of many lengthy swims was begun on 23 June when Blondie covered 443 yards on just one oxygen bottle.

While successful in so many areas of 'work', a subject with which Blondie had yet to come to terms was marriage. A number of girlfriends flit through his wartime diaries via weekends, sailing trips in *Mandy*, London theatres, jazz clubs and local dances, usually on Hayling Island. Now with so many colleagues taking their wartime affairs as far as the altar, and though in no apparent hurry to take the same step himself, he did ponder "how to do it".[3] Having lost his father at a young age and then attending a series of traditional boys-only boarding schools, he was naturally shy with women and, consequently, unaware (through lack of opportunity) how to progress an initial, physical attraction to the deeper, emotional aspects of such relationships.

He was admired by, and fascinated with, women and believed strongly that they should always be treated with the utmost courtesy and consideration, but he could achieve neither of these gentlemanly acts during a war that took the greater part of his attention and without the income with which he could lavish the care and devotion he believed they all, and particularly one he might wish to marry, merited. He could, and did, let himself go in mixed company and was well-known for his beer drinking and saxophone playing at small parties but would keep closer ties at an arms length.

> Tuesday 22nd June. . . . Wren drivers dance. Debauching in mess afterwards,

and a medley of similar entries for June, July and August, 1943, continues the testimony to an enjoyment of life, both social and military. But it would be many years before he met a woman with whom he was "on the same wave-length" and who, in return, would appreciate him

---

[3] David Astor.

and not be horrified by the apparent disregard with which he viewed luxuries and danger. Many girls were definitely put off a closer friendship because of this, thus denying him the chance to understand "how to do it".[4] It took him many years to discover for himself.

> . . . Round town [Portsmouth] with Ian Major and Gordon Sillars and back to Mess with large crowd of parasites and Rita . . . Evening out with Jean Blundell, Ian Major and partner . . . Drinking around town [London] . . . Evening, dine at Mirabelle with Bruce, Pat Elliot[5] . . . to Starboard Club. Swimming and drinking. Slept the night there . . . Around the town [Portsmouth] with Graham, Gordon and Cox. Spear fishing with DSEA . . . fin swimming under ship – great fun.

As with his seemingly innocent sailing along the booms, when he could mix business with pleasure without raising eyebrows, military diving too gave him access to a new sport he found fascinating:

> Monday 7th June am. Office work till 1830 1st spear fishing attempt – DSEA, goggles. Cold and good visibility. Saw Bass.

But he did not, that evening, catch his supper for a later entry reads:

> Saw 'Bertram the Bass' yet again.

While this was all 'good stuff', life in a unit responsible for the establishment of equipment and techniques was bound to be onerous without the spur of regular operations, yet, unknown at the time, change was in the air with the imminent appointment of his mentor, Lord Mountbatten, as Supreme Allied Commander South East Asia.[6]

In the meantime, for the Commanding Officer of the Royal Marines Boom Patrol Detachment there were still developments to be processed: there were diving problems with the *Sleeping Beauty* to be addressed: there were longer and longer underwater endurance swims to be

---

[4] Letter from Sally (Rayne) dated 15 January, 1997 – to whom Norman Tailyour proposed at about this time when she was 17: and again in the mid 1970s!

[5] A Wren officer friend of Blondie's in COHQ who had played her part in decoding the *Frankton* signal.

[6] He was offered the post by Churchill on 15 August, 1943, and left England on 2 October.

conducted and the BPB had yet to endure its first parachute drop and always nothing was so trivial that it did not receive the full Blondie attention:

> 16th August . . . Flight Lieut Nicholls arrives re pigeon signals. Stays to lunch.

and hardly a week passed without at least two trips to London for discussions on either the future of the RMBPD, the formation of Bruce Wright's Sea Reconnaissance Unit and, often, the integration of all such formations, Navy and Army, under army control. Even a re-run of *Operation Frankton* was considered, on 19 August, by the COHQ Plans Committee but it was discarded on Blondie's advice until underwater swimming had reached a higher level of evolution.

Now, towards the end of 1943, Blondie became aware that the COPP parties (except those earmarked for the invasion of Europe) and the SRU were being filtered to India, and while the CODC continued to be the focus for innovative thinking in small boat operations, the European theatre itself was becoming less 'receptive' to such work. It did not come as a surprise, therefore, when Lord Mountbatten called for him from Delhi to co-ordinate small boat operations in the South East Asia Command (SEAC) under the catch-all title of the Small Operations Group.

Despite being posted to Bombay over Christmas, Blondie's connection with the war in Europe was not over. The Italians had surrendered to the Allies on 9 September, 1943, and with their equipment now available for study, not least of all, that of their Assault Units that had, in many courageous ways shown what could be done in small boat/ underwater operations, Blondie was despatched to establish if there was anything of value to be learned at first hand. At the beginning of February, 1944, he was able to report to CCO in London, now Major-General R.E. Laycock:[7]

> I visited Taranto on 27th January, 1944, to examine the equipment and technique of the Italian Assault Unit. All members of it appear to be eager to operate against Germany and it is understood the policy is to give them facilities for doing so. I took care not to divulge information of our own organizations and

[7] Hasler papers.

research in this field and was able to gather much interesting information of their equipment and technique. H.G. Hasler. 18.2.44.

The visit had been a fascinating insight, not only into the late "enemy's way of thinking, but for the lack of progress they seemed to have made since their early successes", particularly in the area where they were believed to have had rather more advanced thoughts – breathing apparatus. Consequently, Blondie felt, we did not have much to learn from them and, despite now being "on our side", advised that caution should be exercised in exchanging information while the balance was still in our favour.

# CHAPTER TEN

## Catalinas and *Physalia*

Shortly after his arrival in Delhi Lord Mountbatten,[1] appointed a Head of Combined Operations, HCO, to his staff and issued a number of directives bringing together many of the 'special forces'[2] under one roof.

His aim was for a Small Operations Group to pave the way for the liberation of Burma, Siam, Malaya and Singapore through beach and airstrip reconnaissance and the gathering of intelligence. To achieve this, and even before he had left England, he asked for Combined Operations Pilotage Parties and Groups of the Special Boat Section to be placed under his command. Consequently, COPP 7 arrived in India in August, 1943, to be joined at Cocanada by COPP 8 in the middle of November with A and B Groups of the SBS arriving in February, 1944. To provide the Headquarters and Base Staff and to reinforce the Group, Royal Marines Detachment 385 was commissioned and sent direct to Ceylon.

To gather this diverse collection together for administrative purposes, to ensure that training was not unnecessarily duplicated and that operational tasks were correctly apportioned, Brevet Major H.G. Hasler, aged 29, was promoted Acting Lieutenant-Colonel on 13 December, 1943, and five days later appointed to the Combined Operations naval base of HMS *Braganza* in Bombay as Officer Commanding Special Boats Units, South East Asia Command. This title only lasted a few days for on 25 January, 1944, he was re-appointed Officer Commanding Small Operations Group which, in practice, had not yet formed; for internal Royal Marines administrative reasons he was to be re-appointed on 24 April to RM Detachment 385 but remained, *de facto*, OC SOG until

---

[1] Known to the men of the Far East 'special forces' as Batty Lord Mount.
[2] Known, then, as Irregular Forces. 'Special Forces' is used except when quoting directly.

its official formation under a Royal Marines Commandant on 12 June, 1944.

What now occurs marks the beginnings of the Royal Marines Special Boat Service (as it is known today), for much modern equipment and many techniques are direct descendants of those used in South East Asia Command's Royal Navy COPPs, Sea Reconnaissance Unit, army Special Boat Sections, Royal Air Force Catalina squadron and Royal Marines' Detachment 385. Blondie's earlier worries that his RMBPD would form part of an army command were now dismissed as most like-minded 'private armies' in the South-East Asia Command were about to come under Royal Marines operational control!

The base chosen by Blondie for the SOG in the very early weeks of 1944 was Hammenhiel Camp on Karaitavu Island close to Jaffna in the north of Ceylon[3] and named after the fort two hundred yards offshore that had been built by the Dutch in the sixteenth and seventeenth centuries. To establish this camp Blondie was posted to HMS *Hathi* in Kandy, Ceylon, from where he was able to begin his work in time for the arrival of the COPPs and SBS parties from India in April, 1944. So that no time would be wasted after their arrival he prepared training programmes and pamphlets to meet the 'Function' contained in the Annex to Supreme Allied Commander's Operational Directive Number 14[4] to C-in-C Eastern Fleet, (a document he had helped to draft) which was to:

> Provide parties trained and equipped to operate against enemy coastal river or lake areas, using as their final means of approach various types of small craft . . . inflatable boats, paddleboards or swimmers. The personnel of SOG will *not* be qualified to act as agents nor, of their own, to make contact with local supporters in enemy areas.

The operations would be split into two types: those mounted on behalf of a superior Headquarters would be known as Independent Operations and those for which teams would be detached under command of SEAC Commanders to spearhead or support major operations were to be known as Force Commanders' Operations. There were to be many of each.

---

[3] Now, Sri Lanka. The author was prevented from visiting Hammenhiel in 1996 due to Tamil Tiger activity.

[4] Hasler papers.

In April seven Royal Marines officers flew to Hammenhiel for a five-week course in SOG subjects in order that they might act as instructors and these men, and the two COPPs and two SBS teams, were now joined by COPP 4, but it would not be until July that COPP 3, C Group SBS and the operational members of 385 Detachment would join and, later still in November, when the SRU arrived.

Blondie was aiming for an organization which would look like this:

*Headquarters*

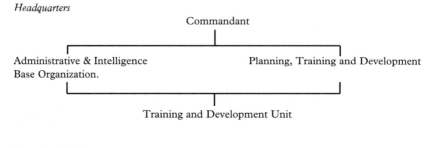

Commandant

Administrative & Intelligence Base Organization.

Planning, Training and Development

Training and Development Unit

*Operational Units*

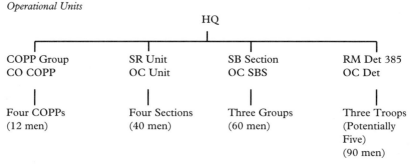

HQ

| COPP Group | SR Unit | SB Section | RM Det 385 |
|---|---|---|---|
| CO COPP | OC Unit | OC SBS | OC Det |
| Four COPPs (12 men) | Four Sections (40 men) | Three Groups (60 men) | Three Troops (Potentially Five) (90 men) |

An early paper titled *Characteristics and Employment of SOG Units* highlighted the skills, particularly of delivery, that Blondie felt needed developing to suit this new environment:

> The common feature of all parties is that some stage of the final approach is by swimming or in very small boats in which arts they are specially trained. Approaches by routes impassable to ordinary troops such as swamps and bogs is also being studied. . . . Usually approach is stealthy and relies on surprise.
>
> The following are types of operations for which parties would require only a short working-up period.
>
>   a.   Reconnaissance either before a landing or to facilitate planning including water approaches, obstacles

      under water and above water bearing surface of land
      and exists from the shore area. Also reconnaissance
      of special areas to locate defences, dumps and
      supply routes.

b. Capture of individuals for identification and
    interrogation or of material for intelligence.

c. Ferrying of agents and their stores . . .

d. Markers and Guides . . . for airborne or assault
    landings . . . placing of time delay markings to indi-
    cate targets for air attack.

e. Diversions. . . . Destruction by explosives or incen-
    diaries of bridges, railways, dumps, aircraft, boats
    and ships. . . . In the latter two cases the actual oper-
    ations might be carried out underwater . . .

f. Aid to 'Isolated Forces' by running communica-
    tions and by carrying or ferrying limited equipment
    or supplies.

g. Long Range Penetration for fulfilment of any of the
    above roles which are relevant . . .

Training of all units was to include jungle and anti-malarial training; additionally, the four 'arms' of the SOG would study skills that might otherwise not be considered "their part of ship": the SBS were to parachute; the SRU would learn canoe handling and navigation; the COPPs were to make a special study of surf problems and Detachment 385 would act as "larger teams with varying proportions trained in difficult special subjects", this last, slightly ambiguous expression, giving them the freedom of manoeuvre between the various operating disciplines that the Royal Marines enjoy!

Despite having had a Commanding Officer appointed on 25 January, 1944, and the arrival of various COPP and SBS parties early in the year, the SOG was not formed, officially, until the day before the arrival of the Commandant at Hammenhiel on 13 June, 1944. Colonel H.T. Tollemache, Royal Marines,[5] had experience of the Far East as a young officer, but, of more importance, he was a patient and tolerant man with a fine sense of humour able to guide and support the diverse talents – and characters[6] – under his command. He was always to insist that he had been chosen to command solely on Blondie Hasler's

---

[5] Later, Major-General Sir Humphrey Tollemache Bt, CB., CBE., DL.

[6] Not least of all the four Commanding Officers.

recommendation to the Royal Marines Office that he, Tollemache, was the man most able to accept Blondie's views on special forces' training and operations. In his own words: "I was happy to be chosen by Blondie to be his Commandant. I knew him well, knew his reputation and admired him greatly."[7]

On the Commandant's arrival Blondie was able to begin the meat of his work unencumbered by command, for he was now the Senior 'G' Staff Officer with additional responsibilities for Training, Planning and Development. Training pamphlets aimed at keeping abreast of new equipment and the enemy's tactics proliferated, starting with *Planning a Small Scale Operation – Common Causes of Failure*, and, although *Frankton* had not failed, there were numerous lessons to be learnt from that operation, as there were from others. He believed that a few prime factors caused failure and, having tabulated them, expanded on each in turn:

> Unsound planning. . . . The leader must ensure that the plan has a reasonable chance of success. . . . Relevant parts of the plan must be discussed . . . with the Royal Navy, RAF, escape organisations . . . The plan must be flexible and not rely on a timed programme. Allow several days for briefings, preferably not at sea where sea-sickness may interfere.[8]
>
> Unpredictable difficulties in execution. . . . Late start . . . rough weather from any direction making a lee shore unsafe for boats . . . barking dogs, cows . . . boats reaching targets at different times, targets vanishing or increasing in number or shifting position . . . capture.

After this item Blondie added:

> It must be made clear . . . which of two things is the more important: attaining the objective or the safe return of some or all of the force.

Loss of secrecy concerned Blondie with the practical aspects of this subject being driven home immediately each man joined the SOG:

---

[7] Conversation with the author, September, 1989, shortly before the General died. Blondie and he had first met on board HMS *Queen Elizabeth*.
[8] Lessons here from HMS *Tuna*!

Only the Force Commander and his deputy should ever know the objective of the operation until the last minute and then only divulge it after it is impossible for any news to leak out.

But his most illuminating comments were reserved for the heading, *Human Weakness of Personnel* with its sub-headings, *Lack of Skill, Lack of Courage, Lack of Intelligence, Mental and Physical Exhaustion*, and in all of these he believed there was no room for compromise. 'Lack of Courage' was the heading that preceded his most strongly felt views, and the views that reveal most about himself and the conduct of an operation:

> Make men visualize for themselves all mishaps that can happen. This will frighten them at the time but will make the actual operation seem like a picnic. Do not mistake lack of imagination for courage – men without imagination nearly always lose their heads when exposed to unexpected danger or difficulty.

Morale was similarly treated:

> The morale of a force depends largely on the degree of confidence and ability shown by the officers. Never show fear, doubt or indecision. . . . You will feel all these things but must conceal them. . . . Make it clear that any man who fails through lack of courage or determination will not be welcome on his return.
>
> Mental exhaustion . . . A man's brain tends to become tired and his powers of reasoning may decline to vanishing point. . . . Keep his instructions down to a few essential points, eg. if you rub it into him that he should pass a buoy on a certain course he may lose his head if he fails to sight it, although he may, in fact, be very close to his correct course . . .

Blondie believed that physical exhaustion was the most vital problem a leader had to overcome:

> A man who is physically exhausted gets sleepy, careless and short-tempered and is liable to take absurd risks simply because he has ceased to care whether he succeeds or fails . . .

His views on escape would be discussed at a private meeting with each key member of a team before he left for an operation, when Blondie would advocate two, personal, views. The first, and most extreme, was that if in a position of responsibility while escaping with someone likely to compromise the endeavour that man might have to be 'ditched'. The second, made not entirely with tongue in cheek was: "The only time I thought of giving myself up while escaping through France was when I realized that I had to shack up with Sparks."

Transport from the SOG base across the one thousand or so miles of the Bay of Bengal was to be a constant worry and one he had identified within three days of his arrival in Ceylon. As most Special Force operations involved transporting a few men and a small quantity of stores significant distances inside an enemy-controlled area, a number of methods would need to be adopted, each compatible with the other down the line for ease of passing the teams onwards.

Firstly the force would have to be taken by ship, submarine, flying boat, parachute or land to within striking distance of the objective from which position they might have to change to canoe, small craft, underwater swimming gear or simply, feet. Having reached their objective there was then the withdrawal to consider, possibly under fire or observation, to pre-arranged pick-up points with alternatives depending on enemy activity and the degree of compromise that had occurred. Finally there was the transport back to base.

No possible method of 'terminal' approach was dismissed: wading with a range of one to two miles; surface swimming for two to four miles at night, with aids; swimming underwater with oxygen up to a maximum of five hundred yards; canoes with a range of ten to twenty miles a night; inflatable boats carrying two to ten men for five to ten miles per night; rigid and folding assault boats for ten to fifteen miles a night; rigid and inflatable paddle boards or rafts with ranges of between three and ten miles a night;[9] mud flats and swamps across which the enemy would least expect an approach – "special equipment for crossing soft mud is being developed"; the *Sleeping Beauty* "available at 3 months notice"[10] and even X craft – the midget submarines. To this list Blondie added what he called 'country craft' among which he included dugout canoes.

As a training ground Hammenhiel camp

[9] The range of these could be greatly increased by the use of the strap-on, Wellborne electric motor and small propellor.
[10] Although the first of twenty-one had been delivered to the RMBPD before he handed over command and others were sent to the Far East for Australian forces, none were ever received by the SOG.

was quite good with sheltered waters and no distractions. The climate is hot but dry with exercises being postponed only rarely through bad weather. A dry jungle fifty miles away was useful, with its only pest the tick which caused great irritation.[11]

But the area did have its drawbacks for there was a lack of variety in the coastline with a notable absence of surf, nor were there rivers in which to practise and, with a negligible rise and fall of tide, conditions did not mirror those under which the teams would be operating. As there were no cliffs or hills within 150 miles, nor 'wet' jungle, such 'operational' training had to be conducted around Adam's Peak and the coarse forests of the hill country.

Two places were identified for surf training, one on the southern shore of Pamban Island which lies between Mandapan and Mamnar at the India end of Adam's Bridge and the other at Bentota a town about forty miles south of Colombo with both these beaches only suitable during the south-west monsoon.

During the First World War Uffa Fox had worked on flying boats when with the Royal Naval Air Service and had now designed a self-bailing, self-righting craft for dropping to pilots in order that they might deliver themselves to safety, or, at the least, survive. This airborne lifeboat was not Blondie's idea but he certainly believed that it would make an ideal 'intermediate carrier' to replace the Admiralty cutter so, before leaving England, he and Uffa Fox had batted ideas back and forth to produce four designs including a 30 foot vessel that could carry 20 men. Fox called this 'Blondie's Version', and for which, in September, 1943, he had drawn the arrangements for carriage beneath a USAF Flying Fortress.

The Research and Development Department had confirmed, on 10 December, 1943, to Squadron Leader Peter Levy, RAF, of COHQ, with a copy to Blondie, that

> The Mk II boat may be regarded as substantially finalized. The overall length is 30 ft with a maximum beam of 6' 6". The weight of the boat complete with all marine and signalling equipment is about 3,000 lbs. . . . Some thought has been given to dropping a man with a boat and I have little doubt that this can be brought to an operationally satisfactory conclusion . . .

[11] Hasler papers.

With this acceptance in principle Blondie and Uffa Fox had then drawn up a 'staff requirement'[12] (published by COHQ's Head of Operational Research on 31 December, 1943, under the code-name *Suitcase*) announcing that the craft (with the men following independently) should be designed "to be parachuted from the heavy bomber which will be in general use throughout the Pacific area from Summer 1944 onwards". It was to have a range of at least three hundred miles under power at a cruising speed of five knots with a maximum speed not exceeding seven. It had to be self-draining and unsinkable, and was to be fitted with oars and sails. Precise almost to the point of pedantry, Blondie and Uffa insisted that it should sail efficiently up to five points off the wind with a load of four men and eight hundred pounds of stores – which would probably include canoes – all of which would be strapped in during the parachute descent. A final requirement was that the craft, when empty, should be capable of being scuttled in thirty foot of water without damage and lifted again when required.

Once trained for land jumps, parachuting into the water, in company or not with an airborne 'intermediate carrier', was the next logical step for the men of the SOG. Wishing to develop this technique further, Blondie raised various ideas in a letter for Mountbatten's staff:

> Dropping a 'stick' of men in company with a standard airborne lifeboat as a means of long-distance approach and withdrawal. . . . Dropping men with inflatable boats for shorter approaches. . . . Dropping men with . . . containers to carry out an approach by swimming. . . . Dropping men into water close inshore in order to avoid difficult country for parachute landing. . . . In each case withdrawal would, of course, form a separate problem.

There was interest in SEAC for the use of such a delivery method and so *Suitcase* continued to be developed with an added option of being dropped close to a submarine if it could come within the ten fathom line – then considered to be the shallowest, safe, operating depth. However, as late as July, 1945, Colonel Tollemache was still pushing for two airborne lifeboats without success: they were never received. Two other methods, mentioned briefly above, are worthy of a little closer study: midget submarines and flying boats. In a letter dated 16 October, 1944, Colonel Tollemache raised the possibility of their use, although already appreciating the limitations of the XE craft.

[12] Hasler papers.

1. Blondie's father, Lt (QM) A. T. Hasler, MC, RAMC.

2. Blondie *(left)* with his mother, Annie, and brother John, c. 1916.

3. "A sort of flat-bottomed punt" (p.5).

4. Blondie with his friend Colin Ellum on Eastney beach: "proud owner of a canvas canoe" (p.4).

5. 2/Lt Hasler competing in the Arbuthnot Trophy, Bagshot Heath, on his 500cc Norton, August, 1933 (see p.9).

6. Modelling Field Service Dress for th Royal Marines, 193

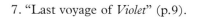

7. "Last voyage of *Violet*" (p.9).

8. "Plymouth Sound was a lovely sight in the autumn evening" (p.19). *Trivia* returning after her epic voyage from Portsmouth.

9. Norman Tailyour *(right)* the author's father, wearing the DSEA before inspecting an underwater obstruction in Alexandria (see p.46).

10. HMS *Queen Elizabeth*, flagship of the Mediterranean Fleet, in Grand Harbour, Malta, 1936.

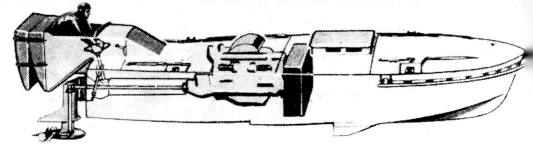

11. British Boom Patrol Boat powered by Lagonda V12 engine (see p.47).

12. The *Sleeping Beauty* with Blondie at the controls: "without doubt the most dangerous vessel in which I ever ventured to sea" (p.127).

13. Placing the limpets (see p. 127).

14. The prototype Cockle Mark II being constructed in Fred Goatley's Workshop, April, 1942 (see p.61).

15. Blondie *(right)* and Jock Stewart in the prototype Mark II.

16. " . . . the canoes quickly hidden in a ditch between two hedges" (p.106).

17. "An Englishwoman of great bravery" (p.116). Mary Lindell (Marie Claire) with Blondie *(left)* and Bill Sparks *(right)*.

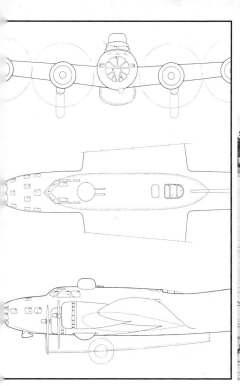

18. "Fox called this Blondie's version" (p.139). Uffa Fox's 30ft airborne lifeboat carried by a Flying Fortress.

19. Training at Hammenniel Camp, Jaffna Peninsula, Ceylon, early 1944.

20. " . . . a small platform bolted beneath the port, after cupola" (p.143). Catalina flying-boat and Mark III canoe; note swim-fin on wing.

21. "Sailing was taught as a military skill vital for stealth and speed" (p.154). The Mark III canoe in Ceylon.

22. Blondie's successor, Donald Peyton Jones (left) (see p.165).

23. " . . . sailed by men of iron" (p.170). *Tre Sang*, 1947.

24. *Petula* under the RCC burgee, "the beautiful, well-mannered Scottish lass" (p.181).

25. Playbill for *The Tulip Major* which "brings lots of laughs" (p.200).

26. Rockall from the west-south-west: "the rock suddenly appeared dead ahead at 1400" (p.183).

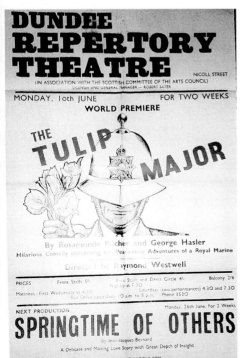

27/28. During the filming of *Cockleshell Heroes*: *(above)* Blondie *(at rear)* with *(from left)* Bill Sparks, Trevor Howard and José Ferrer; *(below)* Joan Raikes, Dick Raikes and Blondie (see p.191).

. Prototype Lapwing rig fitted to a Firefly dinghy: reaching *(left)* (p.211).

30. The Lapwing rig fitted to *Jester.*

31. *Jester* with a Chinese lug rig.

32. Prior to the first single-handed trans-Atlantic race, May, 1960. Blondie in *Jester (left)* meets David Lewis in *Cardinal Vertue* (see p.235).

33. Loch Ness Patrol Recce Group, 1961: Jock McLeod, Bridget Fisher and Blondie (see p.255).

34. "Tacking across Urquhart Bay", 1962 (p.263). *Jester* passes Urquhart Castle.

35. *Tum Tum*, the model that grew into *Sumner* (p.293).

36. The Wedding, 30 October, 1965. *Left to right:* Ursula Fisher, Meg Fisher, Jane Heaton Armstrong, Blondie, Bridget, Jock McLeod, Annie Hasler, Ralph Fisher.

37. A sticky moment as *Sumner* inches her way across a muddy field at Bosham (see p.296).

38. *Pilmer*, "a fibreglass potty only 22 foot long" (p.315).

39. *Galway Blazer II* in which Bill King attempted the first single-handed, non-stop circumnavigation of the world (p.355).

40. Blondie with Dinah and Tom on board *Pilmer*, 1981.

41. A model of the Hasler Floating Breakwater (see p.382).

42. Hardie Telfer "had at some time been seconded to Popski's Private Army as the Colonel's bodyguard" (p.313).

43. "Preparation of the fields continued into late spring" (p.317). Blondie on his Fergusc tractor.

The team must also be trained and act as part of the crew, thus the numbers who can leave the craft to operate ashore are limited. The craft is suitable for close periscope reconnaissance and for offshore soundings and similar operations.

But it was the thought that Sunderland and Catalina aircraft could deliver canoes and inflatable dinghies that was to find great favour among the men of the SOG, although, when available, conventional submarines and some of the other craft mentioned earlier would be used.

The Sunderland had the greater carrying capacity, higher landing and taking off limits in surf and swell and a far greater range which would, assuming that navigational and detection difficulties could be overcome, give the maximum time of darkness on shore in a single night and a quicker return to base for the SOG teams.

In practice, though, the Catalina was to become the well-used method of approach to an enemy shore, with Tollemache's paper already paving the way.

> Discussion and limited trials have been held locally with Catalina aircraft. A report of these trials was forwarded under HC 431/1 dated 5th October 1944. The conclusions may be summarised as follows:
>
> Carriage of requisite men, canoes and equipment is possible by making minor modification which would take about a week to accomplish. Reconnaissance would be necessary in any particular area to determine: Surf and swell conditions which might make landing and take off impossible . . .

Meanwhile Blondie continued to give their employment considerable thought, for although they had been used for various 'special forces' work elsewhere nothing quite on the scale and regularity envisaged by the SOG had been conducted. At that stage of the war the primary role of the Catalina was with Coastal Command's anti-U boat patrols, being described in the COHQ Bulletin X/54, *Carriage of Canoes in Flying Boats*, as:

> twin-engined, high wing flying boats capable of carrying 4,000 pounds of bombs or depth charges. At 122 mph in still air at a cruising height of 5,000 feet their maximum range is 3400 miles without payload. They carry a crew of nine when operational on their primary task. Normal means of entry and exit are through

the port gun cupola situated between the trailing edge of the main plane and the leading edge of the tail plane.

Trials of the Catalina in SOG-style operations were conducted at Kankesanturai and China Bay in September, 1944, under Group Captain King, the Commanding Officer RAF Station, China Bay, aided by 324 Squadron, Royal Netherlands Navy Air Service, and members of Hammenhiel Camp's Training and Development Staff led by Blondie with, among others, Major John Maxwell, Royal Marines, the Commanding Officer of Detachment 385 and Captain Dacre Stroud, Royal Marines.[13]

Prior to these trials Blondie had prepared a series of loose minutes, two of which are headed, *Flying Boats – Things we want to Know* and *Imaginary Problems – Use of Flying Boat (Catalina)*. This last outlined a fictitious operation by Catalina and compared this solution with that using a submarine. There were no conclusive results to suggest that one was operationally more efficient than the other. However, the Catalina option was put forwards as the marker by which the experiments should be run, for Blondie was "pretty certain" that the flying boat would be the answer to many of his problems; problems which, for the most part, centred around the lack of suitable submarines, the long passage times to and fro and, leading from that, the loss of physical fitness among his men.

But there were also problems with flying boats; for instance, being noisy it was necessary to know how far away and under what wind conditions and at what heights they could be heard from the shore. What degree of accuracy could be guaranteed in selecting landing sites? How would the north-east and south-west monsoons affect landing and taking off? Did the pilots need moonlight? Could they home onto tiny, screened lights shining from canoes. Could the Catalinas launch and pick up swimmers? What means of escape would be available if an aircraft failed to RV? The list was long and detailed.

The RAF's support was absolute, entering into the experiments, adaptations and alterations of their aircraft with total conviction.

Trials showed that a load of four men, two canoes and equipment added up to 1,500 pounds – a 'light load' – allowed the *Catalina's* range to be extended to about 2,000 nautical miles or even to 2,500 with extra tanks, although it was normal for a 15% safety margin to be deducted. The aircraft could land at first or last light or by moonlight during the

[13] Later Major, DSC.

second or third quarter providing the moon was well above the horizon. Short seas would not prevent landing or take off but swell would, landings and take-offs being possible across or down wind up to Force 2. The Royal Netherlands Navy Air Service's experience showed that much of the west coast of Malaya was without swell during the north-east monsoon and that landings in such offshore-wind conditions could take place two or three miles to seaward without being compromised by sight or sound: prior reconnaissance of the sea conditions would be prudent. Detection ranges were not trialled fully at this stage but were estimated for various wind strengths; different cover and deception tactics were discussed with the aim of hiding the intention of a single aircraft that might be deploying SOG parties.

There were no problems with the inflatable boats tested, and it was estimated that even eight to twelve surface swimmers with six paddle boards could be launched in quick succession through the perspex, blister door pods on either side of the hull, with, if operationally necessary, the aircraft taxiing up to fifteen knots. Recovery using portable ladders or a net was possible at five knots.

Methods of carriage included stowing the canoes on top of the aircraft's hull and abaft the main wings. Practice launches from this position were interesting, but eventually dismissed due to the likelihood of damage, for the canoes would be assembled on top of the main plane and by retracting one of the wing floats the *Catalina* would tip to one side allowing the fully-manned canoes to slide down the 'ramp', over the wing tip (now at water level) and into the sea.

After a number of experiments (including Dacre Stroud puncturing the perspex pod with a canoe's bow section "much to the annoyance of the RAF") a small platform bolted beneath the port, after cupola was found to be the best method for manhandling canoes in and out.

Built in three sections, the Cockle Mk III's hull could be dismantled on this tubular platform outside the Catalina before being brought inboard where three (one built and two un-built) could be carried provided a few small pieces of the Catalina's hull were cut away: an operation that most certainly would not have been sanctioned by the RAF in peacetime, and, perhaps not even in wartime – had the Air Marshals known.[14] By various modifications, therefore, all manner of combinations for every mark of canoe were eventually possible. Dacre Stroud, the 'Chief Trials Officer', and the RAF aircrew earned much praise for the inventive manner in which progress was made.

[14] Author's conversation and correspondence with Dacre Stroud.

The possibility of radar detection by the Japanese was not considered great as COHQ's Bulletin X/54 pointed out:

> Japanese radar is inferior to Allied and German equipment . . .
> The best tactics for avoiding detection against any type of radar
> is for aircraft to fly in at as low a height as possible.

An aircraft flying at 300 feet was only radar-visible at 26 miles to the very best Japanese radar – an acceptable range to the British – with the problem of flying low over the sea at night merely another difficulty to be overcome.

As far as other methods of transport to the operational area were concerned the Commander in Chief Eastern Fleet did not approve of the use of submarines for 'irregular forces' work but welcomed ideas that would enable SOG units to operate from surface ships as, he believed, this would increase the scope of operations and relieve his submarines for their normal duties. Due to the considerable superiority of naval aircraft in the theatre the C-in-C foresaw no difficulty in sending a surface vessel to one hundred miles of the enemy coast, but no closer unless conditions and necessity required. Approval for the use of X-craft was not forthcoming for the rather more understandable reason that they had to be towed close to the operational area by a conventional submarine. In practice British submarines were released for a number of SOG's sorties but there were numerous other calls on their time.

So far only the training, trials and methods used have been discussed for they were the meat of Blondie's work but also because he never, much to his embarrassment, left Ceylon. However, as no operation by the SOG took place without him assessing its chances of success, and without him then approving and often conducting the necessary training before giving the final authorization, it is helpful to view a tiny sample to offer a flavour of what was being achieved – not least of all because, through these operations, based on his ideas and principles, we see the practical beginnings of the modern SBS.

For instance one independent operation – *Confidence* – carried out by COPP 3 from the submarine *Seadog* was part of a trio of beach reconnaissances made in North Sumatra, Phuket and Malaya[15] in advance of 34 Corps' landing over the Morib beaches. Four of COPP 3's canoes carried out this recce during the night of 9/10 June, 1945, but only two made the return rendezvous. In common with so many other similar

---

[15] *History of The Combined Operations Organisation*

actions, the missing men were able to meet up with local guerillas to return safely later.

A Detachment 385 operation, *Ngayokkaung,* was conducted during the night of 23/24 February, 1945, when 2 Troop, led by Major D. Johnson, landed in a twenty foot surf boat and "intruder" rubber dinghy from Fairmile ML 315, commanded by Lieutenant-Commander Cole. Their aim was to "snatch one or two locals, preferably the village headman, together with a sample of the enemy force present, from the village of Ngayokkaung". This operation was not a full success as the "party was rumbled ashore and ordered to retire before the village could be reached". Valuable intelligence was gained, although for the loss of the patrol commander, shot while approaching the surf boat on the beach and Corporal Smith who was posted as 'missing presumed drowned'.

Captain J.F.M. Steele's Number One Troop's *Operation Bruteforce One* provides an example of a Detachment 385 patrol that did not succeed. The task set by SACSEA was to land by Catalina aircraft of 240 (SD) Squadron RAF off the coast of Bilguyn Island, north of the mouth of the Salween River as a deception raid to "give the impression that a larger force had surveyed it for airfields, landing beaches etc". What happened after the landing has never been ascertained but 385's war diary comments: "It is probable that all the tell-tale signs were planted. The party, however, did not return and were lost. This is thought to have been due to natural hazards rather than to enemy action". As they were still 'missing' in 1956 this assumption seems the most likely.

Between 1 and 4 April a rescue operation, *Bruteforce II* was mounted under the command of Lieutenant R.T. Onslow using two Mark IIIs and two two-man rubber dinghies from a Catalina to "attempt to rescue Captain Steele and his men". A number of similar 'rescue' operations were conducted throughout the existence of the SOG but more usually in support of other, larger operations.

A cross-section of objectives for other patrols emphasizes this theme: "In pursuance of an overall Deception Plan by 15 Corps, a canoe containing marked maps and air photographs to be anchored . . .; to pick up four Chinese; by simulating a genuine SOG beach recce to lead the enemy to believe that a landing in force was imminent and to plant ashore delayed action Very lights and drop offshore a signalling device to lead the enemy to believe that a part of the force was in difficulties."

Deception landings were also made on the Andaman Islands and along much of the mainland coastline.

In November, 1944, and not put off by the apparent lack of

submarines, Blondie drafted a letter for his Commandant to send to the Commander-in-Chief Eastern Fleet with a copy to Lord Mountbatten's Head of Combined Operations.

> It is submitted that the ability to launch underwater swimmers direct from a submerged submarine might be of value on occasions. This evolution has been used operationally by Italian and by Russian swimmers in the present war. A preliminary survey of this project suggested that torpedo tubes could be used for both launching and recovery of swimmers. It is requested that approval may be given for trials to be conducted.

But the staff were unimpressed by this suggestion and demanded to know what the object of the proposed trials was, and while Blondie thought that this was obvious it was also clear that those responsible for sanctioning such experiments needed time to find some way of saying no. The Commandant replied, expressing "anxiety that without submarines the SRU's primary purpose was being stunted". This letter, drafted by Blondie, and the paper that follows on attacking shipping, are repeated at length for here lie two of the foundation stones of the modern SBS:

> The object of the proposed trials is to develop a technique which could be applied to the following operations:
>
> a. Launching and recovering swimmers from a submarine close inshore in daylight or moonlight the submarine remaining submerged (presumably on the bottom). On suitable deep-water coasts this would appear to make it possible for the submarine to launch a party very close to the shore without risk of detection and for underwater swimmers to carry out a daylight recce of underwater obstructions, including coral reefs with a minimum of risk.
>
> b. When recovering swimmers or any other small party at night the submarine to "bottom" and use a floating lookout connected by telephone to the Control Room. This would enable the lookout to make homing signals, identify and muster the party before calling the submarine to the surface. A lookout of this type was used in the Italian attack on Algiers . . .

This request for trials of an operation that had been used successfully by the Italians arrived on the desk of the Senior Officer Fourth

Submarine Flotilla, now Captain Ionides, who remained unimpressed and, perhaps, there the matter might have lain, but, in response to a separate, but related paper, Blondie commented:

> This problem of rate of change of pressure is of direct interest in our proposed trials of exit and entry via a torpedo tube. I was told in the UK that all tubes had a large air-lock built-on which would assist in slowing down the rate of pressure change.

But Ionides was firm and dismissed the request on 12 January, 1945:

> All previous operations with swimmers have, so far as is known, been conducted through an escape chamber. This can be flooded under control and is specially designed for getting out of a submarine alive. . . . Whilst it is not denied that it may be possible for a swimmer to get out of a submarine through a torpedo tube it is my considered opinion that such a proceeding would be attended with the gravest risks and that only a percentage would emerge alive.

Colonel Tollemache had no option but to simply 'note' the outcome of the correspondence although it was held among the SOG officers that the refusal had more to do with the reluctance to use submarines with 'irregular forces' than with the dangers inherent in such a delivery method.

Attacking coastal shipping supplying the Japanese front line in Burma featured on Blondie's priority list with the task of studying the problem given to a junior officer who returned a comprehensive paper titled *Suggested Additional Role for SOG.*

In his original remit Blondie laid down the ground rules:

> . . . to sink ships outright, capture ships followed by selection of prisoners, removal of papers, charts etc, inspection of cargo and removal of samples then scuttling in deep water or across a fairway and . . . by cutting out. The bulk of the coastal traffic is carried in vessels of between 50 and 500 tons, many of them wooden ships and a high proportion of these are junks or other country craft manned by Malays, Siamese or Burmese but always with Japanese supervisors on board. Some of these will be armed. . . . Anywhere within 300 miles of Allied Airfields such craft will normally move only by night lying up in chaungs

under camouflage by day. Beyond 300 miles aircraft radius they will tend to be concerned more with avoiding allied submarines than aircraft. This will also tend to make them travel by night only except in localities where the water is too shallow for submarines or where covered by coastal batteries. . . . Ships should be attacked either in harbour by day or at sea by night. . . . In either case attackers must lie in wait for periods up to ten days.

Methods. . . . Attacking in harbour by day . . . boarding with smoke and/or covering fire . . . Shoot-up from the shore with Piats, Bazookas, 2" mortars, LMG, flame throwers etc . . . swimmers (preferably underwater) placing charges by stealth . . .

Attacking by night . . . using standard 25 ft fast motor boat, shoot up and boarding, shoot-up alone (same weapons as above – possibly heavier).

In both cases the essential feature is that the SOG party is put into an advanced base concealing its boats during the day and operating against targets as they appear. Such an operation could be easily mounted under favourable conditions.

In various amplifying notes attached to the original paper Blondie added further snippets:

We should first discuss how the shipping can best be attacked ie by day – night. Underway – anchored. Small floating mines – limpets – bottom charges . . . boarding by stealth – boarding by assault. Internal sabotage and scuttling – cutting out. Swimmers – canoes – *Sleeping Beauties* – BPBs.[16]

I would . . . favour capture intact if possible so as to get ship's papers etc and select prisoners and then to take ship to suitable deep water for scuttling. You will also want to rifle certain food and equipment from it. . . . The object being to neutralize the bridge and upper deck without doing unnecessary damage. Smoke is obviously a great asset – suggest mortar firing smoke and floats ahead of the target ship – or is there any chance of getting generators lodged on deck. I doubt it. Special light scaling ladders required for boarding. . . . Add to list of subjects

---

[16] Neither of which they would possess in the SOG.

(for training of party): boarding, ferreting out crew, internal sabotage and scuttling, ship handling . . .[17]

. . . If on the other hand quick sinking is the object suggest dropping a string of mines across the path of the enemy ship – or a 10 lb charge towed 30 yards astern of you as you cut across her bows.

Blondie's self-confessed lack of blood-lust was not in such evidence against the Japanese as it had been against the Nazis. In Bordeaux he had purposefully chosen a method of attack that caused the minimum of human casualties – if any at all – but in the Far East fewer holds were barred.

Diving with self-contained, underwater breathing sets formed a significant part of SOG, and particularly the SRU's, work and was still based on the British DSEA. Initially, at least with the SOG, all trials and their subsequent developments progressed smoothly until September, 1944, when a report was received from the Captain (S) Fifth Submarine Flotilla, who was also Chairman of the Admiralty Diving Committee at HMS *Dolphin*. The news seemed bad and emphasizes how rudimentary some ideas and perceptions were in those days of underwater work:

A considerable number of mishaps have occurred to divers swimming under water with rubber fins whilst breathing from self-contained oxygen apparatus. It is considered that this method of swimming introduces a number of problems, particularly with regard to consumption of oxygen and production of carbon dioxide which are not altogether explained by present knowledge and it is therefore considered that until further research work has been done this method of diving is dangerous and training in it should be discontinued.

The use of fins on the feet does not in itself introduce any danger to divers while swimming on the surface breathing air, swimming underwater whilst holding the breath or when used to obtain better control under water, such as diving down to the bottom of ships or coming up from the bottom to the surface. The danger appears to lie in attempting to swim considerable distances under water in a horizontal direction whilst breathing oxygen from self-contained apparatus.

---

[17] All now practiced by the SBS.

Due to the amount of work – and long distances – that the SOG was putting in to this method of attack the report was met with some incredulity in Hammenhiel Camp. Major John Maxwell wrote in the minute sheet alongside this letter, simply: "What does the Wop use?" a reference, once again, to the advances, and successes, enjoyed by the Italian frogmen. A Nelsonian eye was turned on this directive allowing the SOG's divers to continue pushing their horizontal, underwater distances further and further.

Having reached the shore, by whatever method, the business of moving through the swell and across the coral or mud exercised the minds, yet was a factor often ignored by Force Commander's planning teams. Suggestions for traversing mud were contained in a report, dated April, 1944, by Captain R.H. Harrison where he described an unlikely mode of transport thus:

> The Chinese mud skitter is a shallow flat-bottomed box about 6'foot symbol × 2' long, 2" wide and 6" deep. The front is slightly flared and pointed and the back left open. Propulsion is by small paddles (like ping-pong bats) strapped to his hands. The occupant lies face down . . . and shoots . . . along the mud surface in excess of walking pace . . . becoming indescribably filthy in a short space of time . . . 6 miles during the heat of the day is not too heavy going.

The stealthy crossing of mud was so vital to the success of many operations that special "Mud Courses" were arranged where skis and mud shoes were tried, but found not to be worth the effort, while skids and mud mats for hauling heavy equipment ashore met with some success. Similar studies were conducted for crossing coral and surf. Of equal practical concern were the dangers of shark, crocodiles and jellyfish. Drills for dealing with them, or preferably avoiding them altogether, were evolved by empirical, and sometimes painful, experiments as extracts from a SOG paper reveal.

The Sea Reconnaissance Unit's Medical Officer, Surgeon-Lieutenant D.E. Robertson, RNVR, detailed a comprehensive report on sting cases concluding that as these were so severe and so frequent a study had to be undertaken and protection arranged. On one operation, for instance, out of the eight participants, seven were so severely stung that they were of no operational use for some hours due to

> Redness and swelling over the abdomen 6 inches broad above the umbilicus and over the right and left arms consisting of white

raised patches of local oedema and surrounding erythema . . .
bitter pain in muscles of his back and buttocks . . . vomiting after
45 minutes . . . difficulty in breathing . . . the face . . . swollen
and bloated . . . profuse sweating. . . . Two hours after the sting
. . . settled mentally and generally quite fit again.

It was to these symptoms that Blondie and others subjected themselves. Three volunteers, of which the supervising doctor was one, had
jellyfish wrapped around various unprotected parts of the body while the
results were clinically observed and tabulated. Likewise, a further three,
including Blondie, wore a protective suit while a fourth was smeared with
a protective grease of thick tallow. The chosen jellyfish, preserved by
members of the Ceylon Fisheries Department in a tin bath, were "of the
order *Siphonophora*, *Genus Physalia*, species unknown" (but known to the
SOG, as the *Portuguese Man o' War*). Those volunteers with tentacles
wrapped around their wrists, forearms and ankles presented the
predicted symptoms outlined above but what was not known in advance
was whether the suit would form a barrier or, conversely, trap the poison
against the skin making the effects longer lasting and worse. Blondie's
suit was immersed in sea-water immediately before the tentacles were
rubbed on to the right forearm for about five minutes. Slow to react, the
animal was encouraged to discharge its batteries of nematocysts by being
spat upon, yet it still took about four minutes before Blondie could feel
a faint, almost unnoticeable, irritation which then lasted for about one
and a half hours.

While much the same was felt by another suited volunteer – Able
Seaman Robson – poor Able Seaman McKeller, with the tentacles
rubbed against his protected left side just above the rib margin, suffered
as badly as those who had the tentacles rubbed against bare flesh. The
greased volunteer suffered marginally less than those with no protection.

McKeller had been rubbed in an area made from elastic material
which, clearly, gave no protection: a recommendation was made that the
suits be adopted in two sizes and that the elastic areas be replaced by the
thicker fabric as in the remainder of the suit.

A second series of trials was recommended but the war came to a close
before they could take place. However, these first and only experiments
had been successful, if painful, and led to this comment in the final Staff
Minute Sheet by 'HGH':

I have been unable to resist writing some short verses on this
subject:

To Physalia – in her bath

O Languid Temptress, form divine,
Reluctant in thy Bath of Brine
Those yielding curves and rainbow hues
Do more than Capers me bemuse.*
Let Nematocysts all discharge**
And P. Utriculus roam at large
Grease me or paint me, rain or shine,
My Heart's Allegiance shall be Thine.

As Parkin's henchman, clad I am
In 2 mill, thick Madapolam;
A web, sneers Totton, to protect thee
Strangely though her charms affect thee.

Yet let my heart control my hand
When singly by thy Bath I stand;
Tear off the suit! And raving mad
Embrace thy favours all unclad.

*Capers. A non-alcoholic form of Brandy
**Nematocysts. The stinging cells.

Anon 1945

And now to crocodiles, but without the practical experiments! On SOG's request the Marine Biological Section of the Department of Admiralty Research and Development (India) based in Trincomalee corresponded with the Zoological Survey of India to obtain information on the dangers, or otherwise, of the Estuarine Crocodiles.

An extract of the report is reproduced for the value of such knowledge and for the final sentence, alongside which Blondie wrote in pencil: 'Brilliant'

Two species of crocodiles are generally met with in the East Indies: *Crocodilus porosus* and *Crocodilus siamensis*. The Estuarine Crocodile (*C. porosus*) inhabits the east coast of India . . . Ceylon . . . the Malay Peninsula and lives in the mouths of muddy rivers and canals near the sea. It is the largest of the living reptiles and specimens up to 33 feet in length have been recorded. The huge size to which it grows enables it to over-come large and powerful animals. When once these crocodiles have acquired man-eating habits they appear, like man-eating tigers to have a preference for human beings. Considering their aggressive nature these reptiles are positively dangerous to swimmers. The Burmans and the Karens of the Irrawaddy delta are said to be fond of the flesh of this crocodile. The most usual method of catching it is to bait a small raft with a duck or a puppy and hang large hooks on either side. The hooks are attached to a rope and to prevent the crocodile from biting through it, the end of the rope is frayed into numerous threads to each of which a small hook is tied. The threads get between the teeth of the crocodile and cannot then be bitten through. B.N. Chobra.

So life continued in Hammenhiel Camp with the tolerant and placid Colonel Tollemache orchestrating the activities of the COPP, SBS, SRU and Detachment 385 and supporting his Training and Development Officer. Much to his chagrin, though, Blondie was never able to gauge for himself, under live conditions, the efficiency of the equipment whose designs he had guided nor the techniques he had so assiduously taught his teams to use. The loss of friends and colleagues was, therefore, all the harder to bear on the, thankfully infrequent, occasions that they occurred.

In his letters home he admitted to hard work and long hours alleviated by Sunday sailing races. At the end of his first year he wrote to Gordon Sillars, then serving in HMS *Jamaica*:

By the time you get this you may have seen that John Maxwell is missing. My best friend, curse it. And me sitting back in the office chair waving goodbye to the brave boys as they go. However, we have by no means lost hope of seeing John again – he is one of the trickiest things ever sent out of Ireland and will make it if anybody could . . .[18]

This outfit is doing quite well on the whole but ye gods it has been hard work for Tolley and me. Fortunately it is interesting and when I am in camp I get a swim every morning before break-fast and boating during the lunch interval every day and best of all a weekly sailing race of sorts on Sunday afternoon. The black women here are comely, but somewhat reserved since the

Portuguese left in 1654.[19] There are innumerable horrid Wrens all over the place but not, thank God, within 100 miles of this camp. Every now and then we receive extremely mirth-provoking general orders explaining how the pale-face squaw has always been celebrated in the Orient for dignified, not to say, queenly behaviour, and how rotten it is of the chaps to whistle at these very unqueenly Wrens in the street. For myself, I have not even made a hand signal to one of them since I came.

To David Astor he wrote at the same time, April, 1945:

Nobody has ever even fired a gun at me, except for the Foreign Legion who used to use my LC(M) for rifle practice in the Narvik area when they got tired of drinking rum in the woods.

There was little social life in Hammenhiel Camp. SOD's opera's were popular, especially when enlivened by the presence of the occasional token female performer, as was beetle racing, but for bright lights it was necessary to take the train to Colombo or Trincomalee, yet they were too full of 'people', and the Wrens he so feared, that Blondie would only visit briefly and on duty.

James Buxton, then a Royal Marines Corporal with 385's 3 Troop, remembers Blondie well and especially the lengths to which he would go to reach perfection: an example was his habit of taking more and more salt with his meals in an attempt to train his body to accept sea water in an emergency. Sailing was taught as a military skill vital for stealth and, where necessary, speed. To achieve these twin ideals canoes would be lashed together to form catamarans fitted with 27 foot whaler masts and sails and given twin names such as Swan and Edgar, Dickens and Jones and, inevitably, Fortnum and Mason – an exhilarating form of progress to those used only to twin paddles. James, as does everybody, remembers the Sunday afternoon sailing races with the Mk III canoes when Blondie would work out the handicapping based on previous results, start the race, jump into his own canoe and then come in first – in order

---

[18] He did not see John Maxwell again for he was captured and beheaded by the Japanese. For details see The Royal Marines Historical Society's *Behind Japanese Lines*. It was he that introduced Blondie to the piano and traditional Irish folk songs.

[19] A hint of his whereabouts that got past the censor.

to check the times of everybody else. "It was great fun and we all bene-
fited in experience by his example and knowledge."[20]

A young naval officer, whose later single-handed crossing of the
Atlantic under sail was to have the most profound influence on Blondie,
joined SOG with his COPP 5 party early in 1945. On his arrival
Lieutenant Hamilton[21] recalls being sent to find Colonel Hasler and
being mildly surprised to be directed to the swimming bath which he
found empty except for a "wildly wobbling, upside-down kayak which,
after a worryingly long time stopped the wobbling and a brilliantly red
and explosively spluttering face appeared:

'Dammit. I CAN'T get that Eskimo trick of righting the brute again.
Oh hullo. You're Hamilton with the new COPP party, aren't you? Sorry
to keep you hanging about.'"

Blondie eventually discovered the secret of the 'Eskimo rightway-
upping trick' two days later, though no one else in the camp, as far as
Hamilton recalls, ever managed it.

There was also the 'Five-Inch Class racing' where tiny models were
constructed and campaigned with nearly as much enthusiasm and
Raymond Andrews[22] (then an Hostilities Only Royal Marines Officer)
remembers Blondie's attempts to invent the modern surf-board when,
after VJ Day, he was sent to Trincomalee to collect lengths of teak,
marine plywood and balsa wood with which to make a surfboard
powered by a sail. The result was similar to the present boards: about
18 feet long, through which was passed a long metal tube as an unstayed
mast with dhow-type sail above and, with a large weight attached, a keel
below. The trick was to sit or lie on the board while operating a small
rudder with yoke lines. As Hamilton concludes: "He was trying to invent
the modern sailboard only he did not think of the collapsible mast with
a universal joint with a wishbone sail counter-balanced by the sailor, for
the technology was not available."

About half way through his time in Ceylon Blondie was relieved of his
staff duties as GSO1 by Lieutenant-Colonel G.W. Ross, Royal Marines,

[20] James Buxton was to sail with Blondie after the war in *Tre Sang*.
[21] Letter to the author, September, 1996. Later Lieutenant-Commander A.G.
Hamilton, DSC, Royal Navy and only the second man to sail the Atlantic
single-handed from east to west: author of *The Restless Wind*. He continued
around the world and eventually formed a partnership with Hugh Bruce. See
Chapter Thirteen.
[22] Later MBE, M Arch, DipTP, RIBA of Andrews Downie and Partners,
London.

his former instructor from Deal, who, although "greatly admiring, did find him somewhat unpredictable!" Other vignettes survive from those days: D.B. (Jock) Swan, then a Sergeant in 2 Troop and later a CSM with more regular units of the Royal Marines recalls that "he had a way of commanding respect from all who knew him for his bearing and ready smile, quiet humour and the practical way he approached any task they gave him, leadership qualities so rarely found in others. I've seen officers and senior NCOs stop what they were doing just to watch him walk from A to B then get on with their job with renewed vigour; it was as if they had received a tonic."

Extraordinarily, due to the 'correct' but mindless application of 'the rules', only one Confidential Report – and of that, only the first page – has survived in Royal Marines records which, considering his career and the certainty that his life would be of interest, is unforgivable. This lone, remaining testament to Blondie Hasler's sixteen years with the Royal Marines is from the report written on 26 January, 1945, at Hammenhiel Camp by Colonel Tollemache and covers the period from 13 June to 31 December 1944. Unsurprisingly it tells us nothing new of Blondie, although it does add an interesting slant to his character as perceived by a senior officer. Under the heading, "General Opinion of Officer" Colonel Tollemache wrote the following on Captain, Acting Lieutenant-Colonel H.G. Hasler, DSO, OBE:

> Thinks clearly and expresses himself well, particularly on technical subjects,and has a lively imagination with a leaning towards development or invention. Despises cant, but is apt to classify in this category too readily. He is intolerant of opinion which he does not share, often despite lack of knowledge or experience to back his own opinion. He has not yet fully realized the need for the petty day to day methods of maintaining good discipline and for this reason appears to lack firmness in dealing with his subordinates. He often fails to hold a balanced point of view on general subjects. He is in the centre of work which borders on a hobby for him and works exceptionally hard and long, and . . .

and at this point the only formal critique of Blondie Hasler's ability as a Royal Marines officer comes to an abrupt end.

He was recommended for 'accelerated promotion' to major which might have been considered a formality as he was already acting two ranks senior to his substantive rank at the time but, in reality, he was not to receive his 'full' majority for another three years, exactly to the day.

Colonel Tollemache felt that Blondie was almost "too good to be true, for the job in which he was employed," but knew, also, that if he had been employed in a more mundane occupation in the wartime Royal Marines the various imperfections he raised in the report might have been of more significance. He felt, therefore, that in his first appraisal of his Training and Development Officer he should "leave room for the obvious improvement as time went by" and what he did write, he believed, "was about as far as he could go in either direction at that moment".[23]

With the war in the Far East brought to an abrupt end by the events at Hiroshima and Nagasaki in September, the SOGs final work was curtailed before spearheading, as had been planned, the amphibious invasions of the mainland areas of the South East Asia Command.

Between its formation as a formal unit in June, 1944, and its disbandment in October, 1945, the SOG conducted nineteen 'Independently Mounted Operations'[24] against the Arakan and Burma coasts, operating frequently with the Fourteenth Army on the Chindwin and Irrawaddy Rivers and with 15 Corps in the Arakan. These could be sub-divided into ten operations involving deception raids and the reconnaissance of beaches and airstrips, two direct action attacks against enemy coastal objectives and seven clandestine landings to collect or deliver agents and stores.

The SOG had also carried out 154 small-scale raids on the Arakan coast in support of 'Force Commanders', including reconnaissance of defences, pre-assault surveys of beaches, bringing back natives for interrogation at base and acting as advance parties. Lieutenant-Commander Hornby, SOG's one-time supply officer, was later to suggest that "Blondie's contribution to allied victory in the Far East has never been adequately recognized" and these stark figures tend to suggest that he is right.[25]

The casualties, although too many, were, considering everything, remarkably light:

Killed: Three officers, three other ranks.
POWs in Japanese hands: three officers and one other rank.
(One officer subsequently liberated. Remainder executed at

---

[23] Conversation with the author, 26 September, 1989.
[24] Three by COPPs, two by the SBS and fourteen by Detachment 385.
[25] Letter to the author dated 6 March, 1989.

Singapore in July, 1945.)

Interned in Thailand: Three officers and one other rank. (All liberated.)

Missing: Three officers and six other ranks (two officers and two other ranks joined up with guerrilla forces and later liberated. One officer and four other ranks still not accounted for).

Wounded: One officer and one other rank (both returned to SBS).[26]

For Detachment 385's individual part their War Diary concludes:

Stage IV Post-Hostility Period – 14 August, 1945, onwards.

With the exception of one occupational operation no further calls were made on the Detachment. Out of RM Detachment 385 and the Naval Parties at Hammenhiel Camp a Small Operations Group nucleus was formed and designed to continue the doctrine during peacetime. This party, in the main an RM Unit and later to be called Combined Operations Small Raiding Organization, left Ceylon in the MV *Athlone Castle* on the 25th October.[27] This day virtually marked the final extinction of the original RM Detachment 385.

But it also marked the birth of what was to become the Royal Marines Special Boat Service, combining, as it was to do, all the skills of the major components of the SOG.

Back in the United Kingdom, Blondie, as did many, whether regular serviceman or Hostilities Only, now questioned his role in a post-war Royal Marines where, in his case, inventiveness (if not drive and enthusiasm) would be less needed while the world adjusted to peace. Officers and men of great worth would be required to cope with the disruption and turmoil that six years of global war had inflicted and Blondie would play his part, but it was to become clear to him that there was much more he could offer a different milieu.

Blondie may not have possessed a lust for blood but he would be a restless peacetime marine, and Colonel Tollemache had known that.

---

[26] *History of Combined Operations Organisation.*

[27] Blondie was appointed to HMS *Appledore* the day after and it is assumed that he embarked in this ship for the passage home.

# CHAPTER ELEVEN

## *Tre Sang* and *The Myth*

With the Royal Marines accepting the post-war 'commando' mantle and anxious to continue the nautical aspects of raiding and reconnoitring in small parties, a skeletal SOG continued into the peace; constant vigilance would be needed as victors and vanquished jostled for a post-war upper hand.

Blondie remained involved and on 24 October, 1945, it was to Westward Ho! in North Devon that he reported for "Duties with the SOG Cadre at Combined Operations Experimental Establishment". COXE had formed on 2 August, 1942, close to Westward Ho!, Instow and Bideford for it was along this stretch of North Devon coastline, and at the conflux of the rivers Taw and Torridge, that tidal and beach conditions most nearly matched those "expected in the forthcoming assault on North West Europe".[1]

As CCO, Lord Mountbatten's first directive to the Commandant COXE on 6 August, 1942, had ordained the study of the practical aspects of amphibious and combined operations and the

> investigation of all problems of assault landings including those arising from flat beaches with a large rise and fall of tide. . . . The handling of stores and conveying these stores across the beaches, the wading of tanks, tracked vehicles. . . . Your investigations should lead not only to the development of special equipment but also to the development in the technique for its use.[2]

Instead of being axed at the war's end COXE's work was now expanded to include the study of the tactical and technical problems

---

[1] *History of Combined Operations Organisation.*
[2] The establishment at Instow is now named the Amphibious Trials and Training Unit Royal Marines – with very much the same remit today as in the 1940s.

of small scale raids and the writing of doctrines and staff requirements for

> experience has shown that the organizing and execution of trials demanded highly specialized and skilled work requiring considerable appreciation of what to look for and how to look for it and, unless personnel employed in this work were continually fulfilling their function, valuable data could be lost through inexperience.

In 1946 Blondie was able to "fill that function" as adviser to the School of Combined Operations Beach and Boat Section (SCOBBS) then forming at HMS *Appledore*[3] out of the nucleus of SEAC's Small Operations Group, now under the command of Major Anthony Rainey. While some argued that, with the war over, there was no need for 'irregular forces', there were still officers, and Blondie was one, who believed such skills should not be allowed to die purely for the lack of an immediate requirement. A cadre of experience and ideas upon which a more formal force could be built if necessary was all that was wanted. SCOBBS original aims were to:

a.  Train ranks of all services in operational small boat work and swimming as applied to raiding operations.
b.  To carry out trials of new equipment for such raids and to develop techniques for using it.

The North Devon coasts and rivers had certainly been useful for trialling the techniques and equipment to land the Allied forces across the Normandy beaches but Blondie did not consider it the best place for the school which he hoped would transfer to HMS *Hornet* in Gosport with Fort Monckton for training and stores accommodation. In the meantime he produced his own thoughts for the future of 'special forces' in a post-war amphibious/combined operations environment under the title *General Notes on the Use of Special Parties*. The opening two paragraphs set the scene for, in effect, the next fifty years, and probably longer:

---

[3]  COXE's main base at Fremington on the southern side of the River Taw estuary four miles or so west of Barnstaple.

1. In future warfare, as in the past, there will be a requirement for infiltration operations by small parties of uniformed troops for the purpose of:
   a. Reconnaissance of enemy held areas, including beach survey, river crossing etc.
   b. Placing markers and guides for assault landings.
   c. Small scale raids, either with independent objectives or in support of larger operations.
   d. Deception.
   e. Transporting of experts or agents and of supplies for them.
2. Such operations will fall into two general categories.
   a. Strategic. Long range operations required by higher planning staff.
   b. Tactical. Short range operations required by Force or Unit Commanders.

   An increasing number of such operations will be entirely airborne, but where stealth and surprise are important the approach by water will still be the only practical method.

He was now in a position to develop the thinking that was to lie behind most 'special forces' operations that would be practised by the Royal Marines and Royal Navy. His idea was that SCOBBS should train self-contained units of not more than twelve men each to form what he called the Combined Operations Small Raiding Organization (COSRO) with a proportion of these ranks serving in regular infantry formations where their experience would be useful in military evolutions such as assault river crossings.

The COSRO parties would operate, in uniform, inside an enemy area or with civilian agents, whereas the Commandos were primarily intended for coastal raiding or beachhead operations in formations of not less than one troop.[4]

He considered the problems of transport and was able to draw on his experiences in three dissimilar theatres – the Arctic, Europe and the Far East – believing that:

A valuable characteristic of well-trained infiltration parties is that they can land through surf, or over cliffs, rocks, or soft mud.

---

[4] Before the early sixties Royal Marines Commandos were divided into five troops each of sixty or so men.

Even on an undefended coast most of the 'easy' landings are
usually in use by natives and are better avoided.

The various climates in which his proposed parties might operate were
dissected, especially those areas which would otherwise be regarded as
the worst for military operations. Although not dismissing the difficulties,
he saw the advantages of rain and fog for canoe operations and preferred
the Arctic snow for clandestine operations rather than the jungle where
such pests as sharks, stingfish, coral, malaria, ticks and jungle sores took
their toll regardless of how well trained or determined the man.

By 25 November, 1946, Blondie's ideas for COSRO had developed
into a policy paper, he headed, simply, *School of Combined Operations
Beach and Boat Section*, that started by quoting the first two full paragraphs of his earlier paper *General Notes on the Use of Special Parties*, and
continued with:[5]

The intention of SCOBBS is to train a pool of men who will be
available in time of war to carry out such waterborne operations.

Method. These operations call for men trained and equipped
to operate in very small boats (such as dories, canoes, inflatable
boats etc) and by swimming and wading. They must be familiar
with all types of coast and be able to negotiate all forms of
natural or artificial coastal obstacle. (Coast is here taken to
include the banks of rivers and lakes.)

Such men must, from the nature of their work, be not only
courageous, but also intelligent and resourceful. Normally the
required standard can only be reached by training specially
selected volunteers with a high proportion of officers and NCOs.

In the past men have been formed into a number of special
units, from which detachments were sent out as necessary to
carry out both tactical and strategic operations. In future,
however, it is hoped to be able to carry out operations more
effectively and economically as follows:

Strategic Operations, by a single small COSRO Unit working
directly under the staff of the Supreme Commander in each
theatre of war. This unit would contain a number of specially
trained RN Officers with navigating or hydrographic qualifi-
cations to lead teams on beach survey operations (former COPP
role).

[5] Both survive among the Hasler papers.

Tactical Operations by specially trained ranks of the Force or Unit concerned. The numbers of such ranks required would not normally exceed 5% of a forward unit, or 1% of a large force. They would carry out normal unit duties when not required for any infiltration work, and their clandestine work would normally be in support of, and under command of, their own unit.

Later in the paper he expanded these points further:

When the balance of power in a particular theatre of war is in favour of the enemy, so preventing large-scale operations by allied forces, small scale offensive raiding becomes of the highest importance, both in keeping up the morale, and in forcing the enemy to deploy large forces in static defence tasks. This means that planners are prepared to risk valuable sea and/or air forces in order to launch such raids, while the fact that the enemy is deployed in strength ensures that there are plenty of good targets. A most effective means of 'launching' parties during this phase is by leaving them behind during a general withdrawal. On the other hand, reconnaissance and deception raids are generally at a discount. Nearly all small-scale operations at this stage are strategic rather than tactical.

On the other hand:

When the balance of power lies with the allies, large-scale offensive will either be in progress or in preparation. Strategic reconnaissance and deception and the transportation of experts and agents gain high priority, but the strategic raiding has little value and in fact if the enemy area is thinly held it may be difficult to find any good target. As soon as a military, offensive is in progress, continual opportunities will arise for tactical operations under command of leading formations.

The ideas first mooted for COSRO, now enshrined in SCOBBS training, contained a statement headed 'Suicide Jobs and Capture':

It has not been British policy to send a member of the armed forces to do work which is certain to end in death or even capture. In 1943–1945 both the Germans and Japanese executed many British ranks who had been captured in uniform on infiltration operations but these men were captured through failure of the plan and not as part of it. Some enemies have an evil reputation for trying to extract information from prisoners by torture and men captured on infiltration work are particularly liable to suffer in this way. These facts cannot be allowed to interfere with the intention to press forward with such operations but the following precautions should be taken.

ending with the chilling observation:

If a man who is otherwise sound has a dread of capture and its consequences he should be allowed to take 'sudden death pills' with him if he wants to do so.

The approved scale of instructional staff for SCOBBS was five Royal Marines Officers, two Royal Navy Officers, ten Royal Marines Sergeants and one Royal Navy Petty Officer. Basic instruction covered, in fourteen weeks, the range of skills exercised by the COPPS, SRU, SBS and '385' although beach surveying now was 'an extra'. Once it moved to a more "suitable training base and the instructors brought up to strength (including the addition of army personnel) SCOBBS would be capable of handling thirty students at any one time with, it is hoped, at least six places being offered to the army".[6]

Small boat navigation remained at the heart of it all with considerable emphasis being placed on 'dead reckoning' in the belief that, in the end, this had to be the last and most readily available 'aid'. Men were taught, incessantly, to read the signs of tides and winds, to calculate, almost subconsciously, the movement of their craft and to gauge the effects upon it of nature's forces and their own muscle power. Propulsion, too, came under much post-war scrutiny from new styles of sails and oars to trials of all possible forms of propeller, sea and air, to paddle wheels, fins and water-jets.

Training was realistic: for instance Devonport Naval Base in Devon was warned in advance for a night raid by 'special forces'. Security was tightened with sentries and ships' defence platoons of seamen and marines on full alert looking seaward, from whence the attackers were expected to come, but the embryo SBS ranks actually came ashore at Whitsand Bay, beneath Tregantle Fort on the English Channel coast, moved across the Edgcumbe Peninsula to Millbrook Creek, com-

---

[6] Brief for CCO Staff dated 1 July, 1947.

mandeered some local boats (a favourite Hasler ploy) and set off for the dockyard. The swimmers then climbed on board their chosen targets and allowed themselves to be captured while the defenders congratulated each other on a successful defence against these specialists: it was not until the interrogation that the captives suggested the cables and mooring warps were checked for cutting charges and only then did the prospect of three cruisers drifting down the Hamoaze on an ebbing, spring tide before steam could be raised take the smile off complacent faces. If it was good training for the marines it was equally instructive for the "old guard" now on the receiving end of a mode of warfare many had once dismissed as being too far fetched and too far removed from normal operations to be given credence. Attitudes changed.

A naval airfield was equally as successfully attacked, from within; this time the men had themselves delivered by post in cardboard boxes!

Donald Peyton Jones, who took over responsibility for COSRO from Blondie, found that he had collected the most unusual and interesting men "he had ever seen from all walks of life and offering every possible specialist skill. You only had to telephone and say, 'I want to break into the Bank of England' and we had just the chap. If we were asked to exterminate 'so and so' we would be able to say, 'OK, what is his name? Ah, yes. We've got just the man for you'. All were individuals that Blondie had welded into a wonderful team without breaking their characters."

There were many private threads to be picked up after the war, with sailing and friends at the top of the list, and while it might be easy to assume that the previous six years had changed him this was not considered to have been so, although some, perhaps out of jealousy, might have made that charge. A letter written to David Astor:

> Thank you for your note, I am keen to come up and spend an evening with you. I must warn you that London has the worst effect on me. I suffer from a severe inferiority complex and spend most of the time on one leg with my mouth open.

London may indeed have had that effect on him and maybe he did suffer from such a complex; either way, it was easier to avoid being embarrassed by keeping to the familiar surroundings of an officers' mess or among his men, where little daunted him. Ironically, though, during late 1946 he moved to Combined Operations Headquarters in Albany Chambers, London, to further the policies of what later was to be known as Amphibious Operations – policies that, naturally, included his views on the training and deployment of 'special forces'. He was also forced to exist in a society with which he found it difficult to cope.

Although few admit to seeing Blondie, immediately post-war, with a permanent girl friend,[7] such companions did exist but, as has been seen pre-war, the physical side of a relationship was easier for him to handle than the emotional, a state of affairs that was reciprocated by his women companions, but, in their case, more in fear of any long-term involvement with small boats and, to quote one, danger. He was not a misogynist, as the ready desire to attend the Hayling Island dances showed, and was good company in small, private parties when he would usually sing sea shanties, accompanying himself on a guitar. The saxophone might still be brought out, although, it is claimed by friends, his repertoire had not improved from *Georgia on my Mind* and *Sweet Georgia Brown* – so no progress on that score since pre-war! Nor is there any record of a girl from this era called Georgia, so it has to be assumed that the songs were played as songs and not as laments for a lost love.

Meanwhile there was a milieu to which he could return with ease. Living and operating conditions of the wartime "small boats" were comparable to those in the offshore racing yachts of the late thirties, now being brought out of enforced retirement; nor did they improve much with the first of the post-war designs, but Blondie was happy with such privations and so it was into this life that he willingly buried himself, but here too he was not to remain in the background for long. In neither his military nor sailing careers did he set out to achieve success for its own sake and when, inevitably, it found him he would run for cover.

Within a week of returning from the Far East Blondie had viewed a yacht that was to bring him almost instant recognition in the rough and tumble of one of the world's hardest sports. The purchase of *Tre Sang* on 28 November, 1945, from Cecil Frank Baker of Eastbourne for £1,000 marked the first and most significant step in Blondie's post war life. Although he was to build and own a more internationally famous yacht, it was *Tre Sang* and her achievements during the 1946 season that launched him into a world from which he was never able to escape (even if he had been minded to do so). It was to be a world in which his inventiveness and wisdom were to have as much impact as had these same attributes in the earliest development of maritime 'irregular and special forces'.

He took delivery of *Tre Sang* in Gosport and sailed her, with two

---

[7] His occasional wartime diaries dried up and his own comments on this subject do not survive.

others, to Harris's boatyard at Appledore, a journey that even Blondie described as "uncomfortable", for she was not, then, fitted for living on board, but it was a useful voyage that set his mind thinking.

There was nothing new about yachts of *Tre Sang*'s design and construction being prepared for ocean racing in British waters. Of the 30 Square Metre class, first developed in Sweden in 1908, she had been built in 1934, shipped to England in 1937 and successfully raced, but only in the Solent. On the outbreak of war she was laid up ashore 'for the duration' and, thanks to her close-seamed, mahogany construction that required no caulking, she was still 'tight' in 1946. Her steamed, rock-elm frames were spaced 9½ inches apart giving her a hull as solid as was necessary for the short seas of the Baltic but not considered man enough by some for work in more exposed waters. At 43 foot with a waterline length of 27 foot 2 inches and a beam of 7 foot 2 inches she was typical of the genre. Long and thin, with a deep keel, she was able to plane on the turn of her bilges when running down wind.

Blondie's aim was to enter her for the Royal Ocean Racing Club's 1946 season of races but first she needed refining for this task and, no doubt, some minor remedial work after five idle years. Harris's yard lived up to its reputation by meeting Blondie's specifications, one of which was to replace the original mast with a lightweight hollow, wooden structure that curved aft towards the truck in order to increase sail area as high as possible: it only weighed 200 pounds. This curve aft, now seen on many of today's lightweight racers, also reduced the twist of the sail for increased efficiency, especially when going to windward.

It was Uffa Fox's influence that had persuaded Blondie to buy a seemingly unsuitable yacht for the British ocean racing calendar and a yacht that would set the pundits scratching their heads – as they were to do. Fox's views were blunt, controversial and often ahead of their time, but the RORC's wise men regarded the 30 Square Metres with scepticism, describing them as "toothpick boats with their long low hulls and tiny rags of sails only suited for the Solent" and, perhaps, the annual round the Isle of Wight races. Fox, though, believed differently and had written in 1935 that the 30 Square Metres are:[8]

> exactly what is wanted for the rough waters generally found around the British coast. With their light displacement

[8]  Hasler papers and *British Ocean Racing*, Douglas Phillips-Birt, Adlard Coles Ltd, 1960.

they climb almost every sea instead of smashing their way
through them.

For some this was too lyrical, but it had made people think. Later, in
the year before the war, Fox made another challenging pronouncement
when he said that he regarded them as

brave little sea-boats . . . for they beat the ocean racers in their
own weather, boat after boat.

With these comments in mind, Blondie set out to prove Fox's views
on the 30 Square Metre correct and *Tre Sang* was chosen to carry that
torch. Blondie's faith in Fox's opinions, plus his own ability and the
plucky little yacht from Sweden, was to be well-founded, but it is
doubtful, in retrospect, if anyone else would have been able to prove the
point so convincingly, a fact that would be acknowledged in the contemporary yachting press.

Between November, 1945, and August, 1946, *Tre Sang* sailed over
2,600 miles of open ocean with no appreciable trouble during which she
entered for six of the seven races in the RORC's Small Class section,
winning three of them. In doing so she also won the Class III
Championships and the *Ortac Cup*, but there was, of course, more to her
performance than these sparse statistics, including his joining instructions which give an insight into his views on how such races, and perhaps
even life, should be approached:

Bring either a ration card or your own supply of butter, cooking
fat, bacon, sugar, tea, jam plus . . . spirits or wines for drinking
purposes . . . Do NOT bring . . . felt hats, or yachting caps,
pyjamas or uniform . . . and note in particular that you can not
carry a spare set of sailing clothes.

You sailed wearing the clothes in which you arrived and, considering
the problems of water below, let along on deck, this was unusual:

One set shore-going clothes suitable for calling on yacht clubs, I
suggest an old suit or blue coat and grey bags. . . . Do NOT bring
suitcase or trunks.

Blondie had read of the arrival of Carruthers on board Davis's
*Dulcibella* in Erskine Childers' *Riddle of the Sands*! On the instructions for
the Plymouth to Kingston race he added to the bottom:

If you have to drop out arrange a relief – a Royal Marines Officer!

He knew where he would automatically find men who could take the pace and the primitive conditions.

At the season's beginning *Tre Sang* was measured by the RORC and handicapped at 30.41 having been penalized for the low freeboard, the length of her fore-triangle and her scantlings.[9] Initially Blondie thought his handicap was crippling but, in the end, was to consider it fair.

A brief résumé is all that is needed to emphasize the nature in which *Tre Sang* was campaigned: the North Sea race on 7 June with just Ian Major as crew; the Southsea to Brixham race of 5 July with Dacre Stroud and Martin Fleay and the Channel race of 2 August with David Tweed[10] and Hugh Bruce.[11] From then onwards *Tre Sang* did not enter a race in which she did not win her class: the Southsea to Plymouth race on 9 August with Ian Major and Major Laxton:[12] the Plymouth to Kingston race with Anthony Rainey and Tom Haydock on 12 August and the Kingston to Cork Race with the same crew.

Faithful to his yacht and his crews, Blondie was fond of demolishing the common beliefs that *Tre Sang's* success was not due to her but to her skipper who, it was written and repeated often, was a man of iron supported by equally strong men. He argued his case in the November, 1946, issue of *Yachting Monthly*:

> These horrid types insist that a 30 Square Metre can not be made into a good sea-going proposition and that *Tre Sang* has only been successful through the superhuman skills and endurance of her crew. I have never had the same crew twice except in the two Irish races; they were young Royal Marines officers with little or no experience of ocean racing.

In the time-honoured fashion of good sea-going captains he gave the credit first to his ship and then to his crew before he would take any share of it:

---

[9]  The dimensions and formulae by which a vessel is constructed.
[10]  Later Lieutenant-Colonel D.G. Tweed, DSO, MBE, RM.
[11]  Later Major H.G. Bruce, Royal Marines (SBS) and lately of Colditz.
Eventually, with Peter Hamilton (see Chapters Ten and Thirteen), a Director of Sea Services Agency – among others, sole UK agents for the Hasler Seabreaker (see Chapter Twenty and Appendix one).
[12]  Major A.L. Laxton, MC, RM.

True, each member of my crew had three priceless assets which are not, I think, universal in ocean racing crews, namely, youth, an un-quarrelsome nature and considerable experience in dinghies and small racing classes . . . I am not suggesting that a 30-Sq. Metre is the ideal light-displacement ocean racer but only that it is the best one so far produced. Let us regard it as a good starting point from which to proceed with the exciting work of developing the sailing boats of the future.

It was to be another year or two before Adlard Coles, Angus Primrose and John Illingworth took up the challenge to design and campaign light displacement craft and while these remain names synonymous with ocean racing in the forties and fifties it was Blondie who led the way through practical example.

One of his great joys in handling *Tre Sang* was with "the wind dead aft and working jib and genoa pulling like horses" she would get up on the plane as though she was a racing dinghy, a performance that encouraged him to see her as a forerunner for future light displacement, ocean-crossing yachts. Blondie saw the future clearly, encapsulating his views in *Yachting Monthly*:

I also believe that in less than 20 years time planing down wind will be a commonplace feature of open-water sailing and that light displacement cruising boats will be designed to steer themselves, able to stay on the face of a wave for hours or even days at a time. I can only say that every helmsman who has had the luck to get *Tre Sang* 'on the step' has been entranced with the experience and is eager to do more of this kind of sailing . . . the tiller goes 'hard', the boat stops yawing and rolling and goes skating forward in a dead straight line with a huge bow wave springing from a point abreast the mast . . . and with the lower parts of the mainsail and spinnaker blowing aft from the force of the apparent wind.

When writing his *British Ocean Racing* in 1960 Douglas Phillips-Birt stated:

Of course it was commonly said that *Tre Sang* achieved what she did because she was sailed by men of iron. To this Hasler would retort that racing *Tre Sang* in Force 8 was a rest cure. From his description you were led to imagine that his crew of three suffered a kind of guilt complex over the sybaritic days they passed afloat wave-riding on the crests of following seas with the tiller gone solid and the hull juddering with the excitement of it, or taking it easy in the luxury of the cabin's lying-only headroom. The truth lay somewhere between the two views.

All that having been said, it could never be argued, even by Blondie himself, that *Tre Sang* was ideal as an offshore racer – she won races but she was not ideal: her ends were long (nearly sixteen feet of overhangs) she was very wet from spray, but seldom 'green seas', and her accommodation was basic. The sleeping arrangements, to be polite about them even now, were eccentric with a 'tent' arrangement over the two saloon bunks, spoken of with some awe by her crews, to keep out the water that came through the fore-hatch and skylight rather than to act as a lee-cloth to keep the off-duty occupant in.

> In those days if there was a gale people would shorten sail and eventually heave-to but Blondie took great pride in never getting that far. He would drive to windward passing considerably larger vessels hove-to and riding out the seas as best they could. She was so wet it wasn't true! Rather like driving a log along. In the cabin we had a kind of tent over the bunks to stop the water actually getting the bunks wet and he would drive to windward through the breaking tops of the waves which meant getting very wet, rather than pushing them aside and stopping as one did in the larger yachts. I'm not quite sure why we had a cabin as it was just as wet below as an open boat would have been.[13] He would certainly have sailed single-handed if the rules had allowed – and his crews would have been happier![14]

There is no evidence that his crews were ever unhappy no matter how rough and uncomfortable the conditions, with David Astor admitting to making the above points for effect. Another, Hugh Bruce (who would become as tough an ocean racing skipper as any),[15] made the same point after the Channel Race:

> Most of the time we seemed to be at periscope depth and I implored him to put in a reef. He immediately came up from

[13] Which is why Blondie called her a 'Squirty Thirty'.
[14] Letter from David Astor to the author.
[15] A lifelong admirer ever since Captain Hasler had stood up for Second Lieutenant Bruce in an argument over dinner with a senior major who regarded Bruce's home-made, aluminium yacht as a waste of time.

below, "I say. She's doing really awfully well, isn't she. No, no. I think we can carry on for a bit, don't you?" I didn't, but by that time he had gone below again. Of course he was right and we neither lost a mast nor broke in half.

Captain Tom Haydock, another of the young Royal Marines officers Blondie described in an article for *Yachting Monthly*, took some convincing that it was supposed to be fun:

> The first impression did not inspire me with confidence . . . Down below in the cabin, food storage jars were lashed to the starboard shelf. There were two berths over which canvas bunk tents were fitted. . . . Forward were sails and a wooden seat with a hole in it rather like a 'desert rose' at the bottom of the garden. It was quite impossible to sleep in the bunks and Anthony Rainey and I worked watch and watch about with a short break by Blondie. We piled sails and life jackets on the cabin sole and slept athwartships when off watch. Blondie didn't appear to sleep and cooked mostly curry, which he continually replenished with anything edible, on a terrifying petrol cooker. *Tre Sang* had no guard rails or pulpits, however the sails were hoisted in Plymouth and were not changed or taken down until we arrived in Dun Laoghaire where we were awarded a first in our class. She was ahead of her time and many a head shook when they saw her. Blondie was reserved and quiet, yet able, by this trait, to instil confidence, for he never raised his voice.

The most successful of all ocean racing skippers, Captain John Illingworth, remarked in his 'bible' of ocean racing, *Offshore*[16] that

> such a small crew would only be efficient when working with a very small and easily handled sail plan and . . . *Tre Sang's* mainsail . . . has very efficient roller reefing. Moreover Hasler did not use a spinnaker but just boomed out his genoa jib, a simplification in handling but a considerable sacrifice in performance under light breeze, downwind conditions.

Illingworth omitted to emphasize that, sacrifice though it might have been, she still won! A summary of *Tre Sang's* performance that season

[16] First published by Adlard Coles in 1949.

comes from the editor of *Yachting Monthly* in his November, 1946, issue:

> In the early days of the Royal Ocean Racing Club, the very
> suggestion that a craft of the form of the 30 Sq. Metre should be
> permitted to compete in such races would have been received
> with horror. . . . Colonel Hasler does not in any way uphold his
> slim Scandinavian as an 'ideal' type for ocean races. In the hands
> of a less experienced and determined skipper such craft might
> well achieve more trouble than fame.

Blondie's own view was that the 'Thirty' was merely a starting point
from which to proceed with the exciting work of developing the sailing
boats of the future, a theme he developed during a talk to the Little Ship
Club on Wednesday 19 March, 1947. Here he announced that, among
other ideas slowly forming in his mind, he was to use his *Tre Sang* experience to study new rigs "with an automatic means of reducing sail area
so that an absurd amount of mast and rigging is not left standing to
support a very small area of canvas, perhaps a revolving mast". He also
intended to consider self-steering gears "so that a better look out can be
maintained by a small crew" and he was considering perspex-covered
cockpits for comfort:

> One does not sit on a roof. Why sit out in the wind, rain and
> spray in discomfort?

Racing yachts, he forecast, would become smaller regardless of the
distances required of them and all lines would lead aft, making it unnecessary for the crew to have to "climb about the deck". All this, he
argued, would make for safer and less effort-consuming ship-handling.

Factors other than the actual business of going to sea in small boats
also caught his interest. The Royal Naval Sailing Association was not then
the governing body for sailing within the Royal Navy, nor was it open to
'other ranks', an outdated anomaly that Blondie believed was destructive
to the burgeoning pool of talent. In a short article published in the
November, 1946, issue of the *Globe and Laurel*[17] under the heading *The
Value of Sailing and Small Boat Work in the Royal Marines* he wrote:

> While it is true that there is little demand for faint-hearts, I
> would prefer to put caution as the chief trait of a good seaman

[17] The journal of The Royal Marines.

– a caution based on respect of the sea and the elements and . . . of his boat and himself. To take command of any sort of boat a man must muster more self-reliance and a greater sense of responsibility than he would need in most other occupations.

If officers who sailed were thought to be seekers after nothing more than pleasure, the service did not then consider it right that the men should be encouraged to do likewise. He ended his résumé of service sailing with the plea

that any encouragement given to sailing in the Royal Marines should specifically include the lower deck.

The next year the 'lower deck' were encouraged to join the RNSA and in 1949 the Association became responsible for sailing throughout the naval service; many of those who had shone in 'duty sailing races' between the cutters and gigs of the fleet were now able to advance their considerable prowess in the wider aspects of the sport.

At the end of 1946 Blondie decided to sell *Tre Sang* amid rumours that he was doing so due to unhappiness with a handicapping system that was targeted against innovation and radical thought, and while there was certainly a truth in this then, the primary reason was John Illingworth's invitation to help campaign his new and experimental ship *Myth of Malham* in preparation for the Bermuda race in 1948. This was an honour Blondie could not refuse and so by selling *Tre Sang* he was merely clearing the decks to make it easier to accept. He quickly found a buyer and on 19 April, 1947, the submariner Bill King[18] acquired *Tre Sang* for £1,350. Blondie sailed her from Cowes to Appledore from where Bill and Anthony Rainey joined for a fast passage on to the Clyde.

This was Blondie's final journey in the boat that, in one season, had helped shape the future of a significant section of British ocean racing. Others may have talked about it but Blondie had "done it" and others, better known than him, would now take up his challenge.[19] He could not say goodbye to the vessel that he admired so much ("loved" might not have been the appropriate word) without a farewell comment or two.

---

[18] Commander W.D.A. King, DSO and Bar, DSC, Royal Navy.
[19] Including Adlard Coles, an internationally admired ocean racing skipper and a "man of iron" in the Hasler mould. His yacht *Cohoe*, also long and slim, won the *Ortac Cup* in 1947, and with that the die was cast.

Some of my more repulsive friends did not hesitate to call attention to what they imagined would be a close similarity between
(Bill's) past and future experiences.[20]

Able to laugh at himself, he acknowledged that *Tre Sang* had indeed
been a wet boat, but she had won races and that had been one of two
reasons for her existence, the other was as a trials horse. She had been a
double success.

If 1946 was the year of *Tre Sang* in ocean racing circles, then 1947 and
1948 were to be the years of *Myth of Malham*, John Illingworth's light
displacement answer to Hasler and Coles. Designed by Laurent Giles
she had no bulwarks, no doghouse, no sheer and, in complete contrast
to *Tre Sang*, no overhangs – or at least the very minimum.

Before setting off for *Myth of Malham*'s Bermuda race Blondie had a
final hurdle to clear, permission from the Royal Marines. His back had
first given trouble during a cross-country race in Malta when he was
twenty-one and serving in HMS *Queen Elizabeth*. Now, after years of
sitting in canoes in European winters and tropical monsoons (not to
mention *Tre Sang's* less than ideal cabin-tent arrangements and lack of
standing room below) the advance of ankylosing spondylitis[21] was
hastening.

Although he was now in a position to expound his 'special forces'
views from a desk without, necessarily, having to do so from a canoe he
was painfully aware, literally, as were the naval doctors, that his condition
would not improve and, as a thirty-three year old officer unable to "go
into the field" his physical value to the Royal Marines would be limited.
So bad was the condition that he spent a fortnight in the Royal Naval
Hospital at Stonehouse being treated, and, although helpful, long-term
complications were predicted, as his medical report of the time makes
clear:

The condition is now arrested but it was found necessary to
manipulate his lumbar spine. For future reference it is empha-
sized that on no account should the rest of the spine be

---

[20] Hasler papers.
[21] Spondylitis is inflammation of the spine. As the inflammation subsides
healing takes place during which the bone grows out of the side of the joints
eventually surrounding them completely. The joint is then unable to move and
this stiffening is called ankylosis. Taken from a booklet published by the
National Ankylosing Spondylitis Society.

manipulated under general anaesthesia. It is possible that there might be a slight return of stiffness and possibly the return of chronic pain in the lumbar region.

He was offered a medical discharge and with no alternative but to accept, would be placed on the retired list on 16 June, 1948, with the "war substantive rank" of Lieutenant-Colonel but the retired pay of a Major with only four months' seniority.

His last "operational" work had been two months over the new year 1947–1948 at HMS *Rosneath*, Dunbartonshire, a Combined Operations Base where John Illingworth had recently been serving, but for much of the intervening months he had been on the Staff of HQ Combined Operations and in November, 1947, had attended the fifth School of Combined Operations Staff Course.

In October, 1947, SCOBBS had dropped the word 'School' from its title, combined with the RMBPD and moved to Eastney to become, the next year, the Small Raids Wing (SRW) of the newly formed Amphibious School, Royal Marines. Here Blondie was able to see the foundations of his work take shape as his friend and fellow pre-war yacht owner, Norman Tailyour, the School's Chief Instructor, established the Royal Marines Special Boat Sections (then largely the demonstration element of the SRW) in the precise rôles that Blondie had proposed for his Combined Operations Small Raiding Organization in his two 1947 policy papers. With the SBS now taking on the operational rôles of, effectively, the RMBPD, COPP, army SBS, SRU, COSRO and SRW[22] he could leave with the future, as he planned it, secure in the hands of Donald Peyton Jones and, later, Lieutenant 'Pug' Davis,[23] a dynamic officer who was to work closely with Tailyour and the Royal Naval Rhine Flotilla in developing the SBS for the future.

Sad at having to leave a service in which he still had so much to offer,

[22] The *Catalinas* of 240 Squadron would, in due course be replaced by the Chinook helicopters of 7 Squadron RAF and the C-130 *Hercules* of 47 Squadron for Special Forces work. Some of the Royal Navy's *Sea King* and *Lynx* from the Fleet Air Arm squadrons would also be trained for SBS work and although there has never been a descendant of the explosive Boom Patrol Boat, fast, long-range insertion craft would be designed and procured to replace Blondie's 'intermediate carriers'. A variety of submersible 'swimmer delivery vessels' would also enter service. Canoes and underwater diving remain at the core of such work.

[23] Later Lieutenant-Colonel who had won a DSC as a landing craft officer on the Dalmatian island of Brac in 1944.

Blondie did not look back, other than with the greatest affection and loyalty. But he also knew that peacetime service, no matter how much he hated war, would not produce the environment in which his talents could expand. On the other hand yachting in general was ripe with post-war optimism and renewed vigour, for here was a 'young world' waiting for innovation, creation and experiment. The war, if it had produced anything positive apart from the destruction of evil intent, had thrown up, in short time, ideas and materials that could be adapted for use in a more peaceful setting.

With his service career now given an 'end date' he could plan ahead. *The Myth*, as she was appropriately known, would need a strong crew and, naturally, Illingworth had sought out 'men of iron' used to ocean racing in very small yachts.

Blondie was invited to crew in the 1947 Channel race and his first Fastnet race, which they won against all expectations for such a small, light-displacement vessel. For the following year's Bermuda race and double Atlantic crossing Illingworth, who could pick the cream of the ocean racing fraternity, asked Blondie to join him and, much to his (Blondie's) delight he also asked Bill King. Ken Wylie, (a Lieutenant-Colonel in the Royal Engineers who had recently been appointed to the Amphibious Warfare School at Fremington to make up the numbers of army engineers Blondie had wanted for his SCOBBS) was also chosen, for, having completed four pre-war Fastnets, his offshore experience was impressive. Taken prisoner in Crete in 1941 he had had plenty of time to design his ideal yacht while languishing in POW camps, where, coincidentally, he had considered the 30 Square Metre long before Blondie purchased *Tre Sang*.

> *Myth of Malham* was shipped across the Atlantic in the *SS Elysis* as deck cargo while we worked on her during the nine-day passage. The mast was stepped the day we arrived in New York and she was sailed up to Long Island Sound. A series of short day races were sailed as work-up and we even had time for a single-handed race in which Blondie raced against the American designer Rod Stephens in his 32 foot yacht. Stephens won.[24]

Illingworth's great obsession was the saving of weight and to this end his crews were asked to squeeze the toothpaste out of the tubes until just

[24] Author's conversation with Ken Wylie, summer 1989.

enough was left for their exact needs for the race. Winch handles had holes drilled in them and water and food were strictly rationed and apportioned in advance. Blondie's view was that he could have gone further and instead of carrying heavy plates for eating he offered to chisel out eight shallow scoops in the beautiful saloon table into which food would be ladled. At the end of the meal these scrapes would simply be wiped clean – he wasn't given the chisel!

The formal end to Blondie's Royal Marines career came just three days before the start of the Bermuda Race, and there is no doubt that the celebrations were riotous. Indeed there are still memories of Blondie singing American railroad songs into the dawn while accompanying himself on a borrowed guitar.

The race went without incident and *The Myth* crossed the line fourth in her class of fifteen and winner of the Fleming Day Trophy for yachts under forty foot in length. Although she would have done better if it had been a windward race, the conditions for which she was largely designed, John Illingworth and his crew were pleased with their efforts.

What was to be a more accurate pointer to *The Myth's* potential was not the race itself but her return across the Atlantic to Brixham in just twenty-two days with cruising sails and only six on board instead of her racing crew of eight. This crossing proved, probably better than any race could, that contrary to many opinions, speed and seaworthiness can go hand in hand if properly managed. Despite being such a small vessel it was an unremarkable journey (which was why it was, in fact, remarkable) not least of all because *The Myth* covered the 2885 miles at an average of 143 miles per day – not bad for a boat just thirty-eight foot overall. Of this return journey Blondie said:

> In the first place I think everybody was surprised when we succeeded in leaving Bermuda. Our sailing date had been post-poned from day to day whilst we strove in vain to get ourselves organized for the passage in the face of such insurmountable difficulties as swimming parties, feeding parties, drinking parties and long periods of hoggish slumber. On the personal side our morale remained high throughout the passage and we never got to the stage of finding nothing to laugh at. For this I think that three main factors were responsible: the fact that we had already shaken down together as a trained crew before we started; the decent living conditions on board; and last but not least the unfailing tact and patience of John Illingworth in command.

When, in 1980, Blondie was asked to write John Illingworth's obituary for the RNSA journal he confirmed this fulsome praise:

> John Illingworth was the best skipper that I ever sailed under. . . .
> There was never any doubt that he was in sole and absolute
> command but I never heard him raise his voice at sea or express
> any criticism of his crew. . . . By identifying himself with any
> mistake he could soothe the frayed tempers of tired men. We
> worked like the devil by day and night and remained a happy
> crew. It would be reasonable to regard John as the father of
> modern ocean-racing in Britain and he played a leading part in
> the emergence of the specialized boats and techniques that have
> long superseded the old idea of a group of cruising yachts racing
> against each other. His driving spirit and his dedicated attitude
> to the sport will be with us for a very long time.

Change the words "father of modern ocean-racing" to "founding father of modern short-handed sailing" and Blondie might have been writing his own eulogy. They were similar men, recognizing in each other those sparks of genius that can make or mar the perfectionist: in these examples of two rare characters their individual geniuses made them.

Blondie's summing up of his time crewing *The Myth* was as compli-mentary for she had given him more than sailing experience, she had also given him the seeds for deep thought on comfort and handling:

> We finished a long-drawn-out Fastnet without ever having
> lacked anything despite most of the lockers being half empty due
> to the skipper leaving behind bits of unwanted gear. We had a
> comfortable surplus of food, water, calor gas and electricity. As
> regards deck work I'm afraid I must class her as a boat that keeps
> her crew busy. This is due to her large wardrobe of headsails and
> spinnakers, but whereas I personally dislike all these things they
> are not peculiar to *The Myth* but are a familiar product of the
> rules governing the measurement of sail area.

*Tre Sang* was sold and he had gained invaluable experience with "the master" and his "busy" ship; now would come a yacht that was to launch Blondie on yet other tacks, those of writing, cruising and exploring. The next few years were to be busy years but they were not to be particularly easy years.

# CHAPTER TWELVE

## *Petula, The Tulip Major* and Jackie Lane

Throughout his life Blondie would, occasionally, keep a "biographical record" or series of "personal appreciations". Many entries, just a few words long, revolve around money and girl friends and how to make the former in sufficient quantities to acquire and then keep the latter but, containing as they do, numerous admonishments to himself to behave better or to "listen and learn" and, indeed, to be more "gay", before that delightful word became sullied by a later generation. They also show a man concerned about his private and public images. To those who knew him he need not have worried: he liked a drink – in moderation – had a keen eye for the ladies (a very keen eye for beauty) and was fascinated by the more charming aspects of their relationships with men. He discussed marriage frequently in his appreciations and would exercise, in his writing and cartoons, an enchantment with women and love, all of which suggests a shy man who found it easier to express his views on paper than face to face.

Although ahead of the time under discussion an example is a letter he was to write to the editor of a yachting magazine at the time of the Queen's Coronation Review at Spithead. He signed it "Veteran":

> As one who has languished at anchor for several days in a battle-ship at the last Coronation Review I would like to make an unusual plea on behalf of those thousands of sailors and marines who will be similarly placed in June of this year. . . . It is here that the yachtsman can once again come forward in the service of his country. . . . Two dominant characteristics of every professional seaman are a strong sense of humour and a romantic admiration for the opposite sex. My suggestion is that yacht owners should first embark as many attractive young women as can conveniently be exhibited on their decks and then sail close (remember only officers and signalmen normally have access to

binoculars) past the ships as slowly as possible. . . . Is it too much
to hope that every yachtsman in the Solent area will "do his bit"
in this deserving cause.

There are other examples of such delightful whimsy.

He felt strongly that he should not offer marriage unless he could also
offer a fiancée a civilized and work-free life. But where was the girl, even
if he had the money, and, in a civilian world, how did he meet her? Few
of his pre-war girl friends survived the war unmarried and his new life
style was not likely to attract new ones looking for serious emotional ties;
indeed, apart from the physical attractions of Blondie himself, it put
them off. A degree of social insecurity creeps into his character now that
he is alone and not in the company of his service friends amid the natural,
corporate spirit of an officers' mess.

On leaving the Corps his standing as a yachtsman held him in good
stead, but the end of his sailing with John Illingworth, coming as it did
shortly after he sold *Tre Sang*, marked the beginning of a period of
considerable self-doubt. His earned income was low, and occasionally
nil, and not helped by an inability to settle with those few jobs he did
manage to achieve. His aims were varied and butterfly in nature, oscillating between writing – a major passion (although he would sometimes
deny this) – drawing, inventing and sailing.

*Myth of Malham* ended her trans-Atlantic voyage in Brixham towards
the end of July and before the next month was out Blondie had inspected
and purchased, rather surprisingly, a yacht of considerable weight and
some complexity.

*Petula* was not suitable for ocean racing but she did offer the chance to
consolidate and broaden his experience through exploring the further
reaches of northern European waters. Although regarded otherwise by
the cruising fraternity of the late 1940s, Blondie's voyages were nothing
remarkable for they were not world-girdling nor did they have the
romance of the Victorian yachtsmen whose vessels were often run more
on the lines of men-o'-war than those of a private yacht, nor were his
cruises exotic in destination nor dramatic in length or content – but they
were different.

*Petula* came from the drawing board of, and was built by, Fife of
Fairlee in 1899. As lovely as *Tre Sang* but in a more sedate manner, she
was the beautiful, well-mannered Scottish lass to the leggy, attractive and
fresh Swede. She was a yawl, just over 41 feet long, gaff-rigged
and displacing about 18 tons. She had no wireless or aids to navigation
of any kind apart from a sextant, lead-line and log-line and, under her

previous owner, Mr William Findlay of Glasgow, had been converted from cutter rig in 1931. Supporting his earlier remarks in the yachting press[1] that gaff rig was preferable for cruising that was precisely what Blondie now intended to do.

To thoughts of experimental rigs for long-distance cruising was added ease of handling as an important factor to be considered and studied. A comfortable and fresh crew was a safe crew: from his Royal Marines' training he knew that any untrained fool can be miserable at sea and that comfort is not the privilege of the physically soft but a vital factor, when managed properly and under appropriate circumstances, in safety and efficiency. Once *Petula* was in his hands he began to devote the same energy to safe comfortable cruising as he had to winning uncomfortable ocean races, but she was not ideal for this purpose and, while enjoying her company, he was continually looking ahead. His comments for the year were short:

> Leave Corps. Overpowering urge to get away in cabin boat – something never achieved for more than a week or so. Try to buy 7 ton fishing boat. Finish with *Petula* because cheap, attractive, thoroughbred. No urge to earn money unless can achieve it cruising in *Petula*.

He took delivery of *Petula* in the Clyde and immediately sailed her south to the Solent while allowing ideas to ferment. Cruising, *per se*, he knew, would not earn money, but taking ornithologists to sea does and to test this theory he conducted a 'bird recce' in the Channel that autumn and convinced himself that here was at least one way ahead.

By the spring of 1949 he had established *Petula* as a fair, if heavy, cruising boat and readied her for his most ambitious ornithological cruise yet. While there was nothing unusual with his route from the River Hamble to the Gareloch in Scotland he planned to do so via the west coast of Ireland and the uninhabited island of Rockall where he wanted to attempt the first known landing.

At about seventy feet high, no more than eighty or so feet across its base and 160 miles west of the St Kilda group, Rockall is indeed an outpost. It is unlit[2] and has a reputation for being difficult to find, particularly in the days before yachts carried radar and GPS navigation systems, for it is 'guarded' by an area of magnetic anomaly making an

[1]  See Chapter One. *Yachting World*, 11 December, 1931.

approach in bad weather or poor visibility rather tricky. Its value as a bird sanctuary was then unknown and although heavy seas were known to break over it, some believed it to be a migratory stepping stone in calm weather. It was necessary to find out.

Apart from Tony Newing's[3] companionship for a short stretch along the British south coast, Blondie sailed single-handed – no mean feat in an eighteen ton yacht – as far as Londonderry where he was joined on 10 May, 1949, by Anthony Rainey and the ornithologist James Fisher. Rainey was appointed mate and Fisher, not in the watch-keeping roster, as cook: *Petula* had six bunks so there was plenty of space for four weeks of stores.

At 0815 on 11 May *Petula* slipped down Lough Foyle to head north-west into poor weather. Six days later and with her position confirmed by sextant at sixteen miles south-east of their destination the rock suddenly appeared dead ahead at 1400 on the 17th. Great shear-waters, an arctic skua, guillemots, puffins, kittiwakes and fulmars surrounded *Petula* with a raft of Manx shearwaters clustered together on the surface alongside. Now the crew could congratulate them-selves on being the first yacht known to have visited Rockall and although Blondie wanted to add to their satisfaction by investigating the ornithological mystery of whether or not guillemots nested, landing was out of the question in the sea that was then running. However, staring at the rock from the surface of a heavy swell, it did not take Fisher long to guess what the answer would have been had he been able to climb to the top.[4]

> No egg has been evolved which will stand up to breakers a hundred feet high. There is seldom no swell and even a low swell will send heavy spray and even green seas over the rock.

The return journey via the then un-inhabited island of St Kilda[5] reminded them of how small and lonely Rockall is in contrast even to the remoter parts of west Scotland, and especially the Gareloch where June was about to be spent in 'tropical' weather lying to an anchor while skipper and crew recharged their batteries and gave *Petula* an extensive

[2]  Attempts in recent years to maintain a light have not been wholly successful.
[3]  Then a Royal Navy Lieutenant.
[4]  Hasler papers.
[5]  The last permanent inhabitants left in 1930 – in recent years a small army team has been stationed in Village Bay to control a missile range.

midsummer refit. By July she was ready for the next phase, with an interesting observation in her log:

> I have no permanent crew but I dislike being single-handed and always do my best to entice some of my friends on board when actively cruising.

*Petula's* 1949 season was far from over with another ambitious "ornithological outing", to Sula Sgeir, Sule Skerry and Stack Skerry, places seldom, if at all, visited by yachts even now, and, with that mission accomplished, they turned for Scrabster, tucked into the north-west corner of Thurso Bay on the Pentland Firth. The three crew had included Anthony and James, again, plus Anthony Huxley, son of the noted biologist, Sir Julian Huxley.

This had been an "interesting expedition" with the line between success and failure very fine. On arriving at each island, none of which had landing places, Blondie would stay with *Petula* jilling about offshore, while one crew member landed the other two from the dinghy. The two 'experts' carried emergency rations and equipment, everyone wore a life-jacket and had learned a simple system of communicating with flags: one message, to be sent from *Petula*, read simply and dramatically: "I am leaving and will send help!" Luckily they did not have to use it.

Blondie, who had heard that roast puffin was highly recommended, sent a shopping list ashore with James who brought back one unfortunate bird from North Rona but:

> When the dish was served later that evening there was little enthusiasm.

Blondie had fallen in love with the Orkneys during his 'gun mounting' and duck shooting days at Scapa Flow and so with Gus Sillars[6] replacing the others in Scrabster they set off to renew this friendship; the longer-term aim being southern Norway where Gordon Sillars[7] and Tony Newing would join. They sailed on 21 July but due to poor weather saw little of that windswept island scenery which "he had got to know in 1938 before the hideous blight of wartime occupation descended on it for a second time". Instead they put into Lerwick in the Shetlands, "interlaced

---

[6] Lately of the RNVR.
[7] Major, Royal Marines.

with dozens of splendid voes with sheltered anchorages forming as fine a cruising ground as any in the British Isles".

Blondie was fond of cooking in his own eccentric style, with meals often designed around the peculiarities of his galleys rather than the culinary preferences of his crews. *Tre Sang's* arrangements had been primitive but functional, and on that all were agreed, while *Petula* and her layout were described by Tony Newing thus:

> The galley was right forward (presumably where the paid hand had worked in *Petula's* more affluent days) and the motion experienced by the duty cook was something I shall never forget. He played the guitar with a wonderful repertoire of American railroad songs.

Tony might have been grateful he was spared the saxophone and the two 'Georgias', but to return to cooking and its associated offshoots. Provisioning, stowing, preparation, washing up and general cleaning are all basic chores that have to be dovetailed into a yacht's watch-keeping system. To Blondie they were also areas ready for study and experiment and so with *Petula's* demands on her crew as a strong incentive it is not surprising that when he came to establish short-handed ocean racing a major aim was the development of techniques for dealing with such fundamentals in a small ship at sea.

On this trip to Norway, the first full-length cruise for which he had had to arrange a lengthy programme encumbered with these domestic details, the 'learning curve' was steep:

> I made a silly mistake to think that we could do serious cooking and its attendant washing up during our watches below. I for one was absolutely exhausted by the time we got there and I think that it was largely due to this self-imposed domestic burden.

His later comments on one log entry survives from this journey:

> Breakfast on arrival in Stravangerhaven, Norway, I see is recorded as whisky, tea, toast and marmalade – I wish I could remember what the tea was for.

Blondie liked his food and, although others did not always share his tastes, when conditions were so vile that cooking was out of the question for the sheer danger involved, all agreed that his 'Beggar's Bowl' was perfect for the occasion. The recipe for this quaint masterpiece was published a number of times and is reproduced here in case it may continue to be of value:

> Use a small pressure cooker with the lid on but the valve open. This is the only cooking container that can roll all over the cabin without loss of your dinner or equanimity. Gently boil brown rice in it with the exact amount of water which experience has told you it will absorb. Five minutes before the rice is cooked, while there is still some water left, chuck in chopped up ham, salt beef, onions, currants, nuts or any other damn thing that comes to hand. By the time it is done you may have to put on oilskins trousers. Hold the pan between your knees and eat it straight out of the pan with a spoon, holding on to the ship with the other hand. Your red wine can be allowed to swill around in the bottom of a mug in a secure fiddle. Soon the gale will seem a good deal less frightening but remember to lay off the vino before your Superman syndrome develops.

Other thoughts on food were developed in those early days.[8]

> A well-cured ham, on its bone will keep indefinitely even in hot weather, provided it is kept in fresh air all the time. Mine stand up like drunken ducks, jammed on top of a locker.
> Salt beef needs no recommendation as it played a major part in the exploration of the world. Red wine goes well with strong meaty dishes and should be poured freely into stews while cooking.
> Any form of unpolished rice is marvellous at sea and keeps for ever if kept dry.

In practice these were difficult times and rather aimless as far as money and a wife were concerned. There was a girl-friend, Jen, although her status is far from clear and all attempts to discover more have failed, but it is known that, while she obviously cared for Blondie, she did not care for his style of sailing. He needed her, physically, and was loth to let her go, but her attributes did not extend to loving *Petula*.

The seeds of the future do, though, begin to appear as his summary of this time admits that cruising in an eighteen-ton yacht did not make

[8] Culled from various drafts contained in the Hasler papers.

sense as she was "too big for cruising and too small to live in". This opening statement led, naturally to the expressed desire to develop his own yacht from the drawing board and not rely on something second-hand.

It may not have been a source of much income at this time but his first book was at least a prestigious success. In 1950 few guides existed for yachtsmen wishing to cruise European coasts. With peace, if not afflu-ence, now returned to the country, the cruising yachtsman was beginning to spread his wings, but in smaller craft without the paid hands and professional skippers of the pre-1939 days. This new generation of skipper-owners needed comprehensive, easily understood pilot books written for him (and not warships) and covering, to begin with, the nearest "foreign" coast towards which he was now heading – North Brittany. Blondie called his guide *Harbours and Anchorages of the North Brittany Coast* and explained his aims in the preface.

> This book is intended to provide the navigators of yachts and other small craft with a comprehensive guide. The main anchorages are those offering reasonable shelter and in which a small vessel can lie afloat at all states of the tide.

Blondie spelt out the dangers and pitfalls of this rock- and tide-encumbered coast in plain language, for he knew that often skippers would be delving into this book when tired, wet and cold. It had to provide the utmost peace of mind through the clarity of the writing, if not in the information it had to impart: for instance the warning about drying out in the Mont St Michel area could not be more clear to a skipper whether exhausted or alert:

> Some of the drying sand is said to be quicksand on which it is dangerous for any vessel to dry out because she may not lift on the next flood!

*Harbours and Anchorages* was published in 1951 by Robert Ross and Company in association with George G. Harrap and was impressive enough to move *The Royal Cruising Club Journal*, a publication not given to superfluous praise when reviewing pilot books, to describe it as being:

> . . . expertly written and beautifully produced that it is hard to believe it is not an official publication. . . . The usefulness of the book lies in the precise and detailed descriptions illustrated by

exceptionally clear charts . . . written in a plain, straightforward style; but there is also a fascination in the little personal touches slipped in every here and there.

Writing aside, the desire to design his own "radical cruising boat", *ab initio*, was intensifying and, although writing *Harbours and Anchorages* had taken much of his time, he always made room for sketching out the specifications of the "new boat, that would be his servant and not his master". These initial sketches were centred around one or two bench-marks: she would have all lines for hoisting, lowering, controlling and reefing the sails led to a central steering position from which the skipper need not move; she would have self-steering; she would be able to ride out a storm, if not in comfort then at least in safety and a central, circular cockpit would have a swivelling pram-hood able to be turned through 360° to keep out spray and wind and yet allow a full lookout. A serious stipulation was that this new vessel would need to keep a wife happy on long-distance ocean cruises.

In the end the design he drew would be too small for this last task although the final sail plan was near perfect for it would prevent a crew, especially a girl-friend in the early, impressionable stages of a romance, having to fight sodden canvas at forty degrees angle of heel. *Jester*, for that was to be her name, was conceived out of these ideas. As he wrote in 1952, he set out to

> evolve, for my own use, the smallest boat in which one or two people could cruise for long distances in comfort and without performing any feats of endurance . . . she was dedicated from the start to a series of experiments aimed at evolving an improved type of small sea-going sailing yacht. Specifically, I wanted a boat in which either one or two people could . . . cope with strong winds, rough water and cold weather without calling on their last reserves.

Originally, *Jester* was designed to carry a form of the Lapwing rig with which Blondie had experimented at Hammenhiel Camp on the Mark IV canoe; now the trial horse for the ocean-going Lapwing sail was, first, a Firefly dinghy lent to him for the purpose by Fairey Marine the builders, and then a canoe built for him by Vospers. These trials took place throughout 1952 at Bursledon while *Petula* was up for sale, and the moment she was gone[9] Blondie moved in with his mother at

---

[9]  See Appendix One.

Catherington. By that winter he was satisfied the Lapwing rig was right and so formal hull and sail plans were laid out on his drawing board.

*Jester* was built by Harry Feltham in Portsmouth during 1953 for £700. Of carvel-planked mahogany on oak frames with a hollow, un-stayed mast of silver spruce, she had no engine but carried a long sweep for sculling over the stern.

> Her hull up to the rail is to the lines of the Scandanavian Folkboat but I had her carvel planked instead of clinker as I don't like the latter construction in a keel boat. She measures 25 foot overall, 20 foot on the waterline, 7 foot 3 inches beam and 4 foot draft and carries a ton of iron outside. Her displacement before loading up for a cruise is about 2½ tons so it will be seen that she is of light displacement type and doesn't need much sail to drive her.

Known more properly as the Ljungstrom rig after its originator the sail plan consisted of twin mainsails on a common luff running up an un-stayed mast. By trial Blondie determined that a lack of a boom on the original meant less control over the sail so designing this double spar became the single most complicated part of *Jester's* drawings. When beating to windward or reaching across the wind the sails and twin booms would lie flat, one on the other, but when running before the wind the sails would be opened out like butterfly wings and allowed to billow either side of the mast. The whole could be reefed by simply turning the mast, thus winding in the two sails together as with a roller blind.

These experiments caught the imagination of the local and yachting press for on 20 July, 1954, the *Southern Daily Echo* carried a piece entitled, *First Details of the new rig developed by Colonel Hasler*. This theme was followed the next month by *Yachts and Yachting, Motor Boat and Yachting, Yachting Monthly* and *Yachting World*. Further afield, articles appeared in the American *Yachting* and in the *New Commonwealth Magazine*; even the *Illustrated London News* carried photographs. To Blondie this was a sign that he was a 'name' in the yachting community and if that led to commercial interest in his proposed ideas it had to be good – and blow the diffidence.

On 3 February, 1955, the Patent Office issued patent number 747200 in respect of "*Improvements in or relating to fore-and-aft sail rigs for sailing craft*", one of only three patents for which he applied. But the Lapwing rig was not just an experiment in sail design for in December of that year Blondie discussed in *Yachts and Yachting* what he called *Below Deck*

*Seamanship – an experiment in design aimed specifically at the problem of human endurance at sea,* in which he argued that among other advantages his rig led to uncluttered decks and more cabin space. As large wet bags full of superfluous sails were not needed there had to be greater comfort in the cabin of a small boat. The un-adventurous were quick to respond and in the 17 February, 1956, issue of the same magazine he was able to answer earlier correspondents and critics:

> I suggest that boats that impose an endurance test on their crews in bad weather are suitable only for short passages preferably with a nice warm hotel and an ample drying room at the far end.
>
> *Jester* is an attempt to produce a tiny boat which will enter harbour at the end of a long, hard passage in a state fit to live in. . . . Of course she is designed to steer herself and anyone who thinks steering a boat in the open sea is eternal fun hasn't done it long enough.

Although excited by the Lapwing's initial trials, he had to admit that there were shortcomings compared with the conventional, Bermudian-rigged vessels that were, by now, replacing the more traditional gaff-rigged vessels for ocean racing, and to an increasing extent, cruising as well. *Jester* was not fast to windward in light airs mainly because, with the sails 'closed', she was offering to the wind only 78 percent of the sail area of the standard sloop. With the wind abaft the beam and the sails 'open' she performed better, and, in Blondie's view "much faster than the standard sloop with a spinnaker as I think many people around the Solent will agree".

In 1954 work, and a little money, had materialized from an unexpected quarter. The film producer Irving Allen hearing of the Bordeaux Raid decided that it would make the ideal basis for an adventure film. Warwick Productions[10] concurred and help was immediately sought from the appropriate military authorities to film *Cockleshell Heroes*. The Commandant General, Royal Marines, agreed to supply drill instructors, canoeists and Eastney Barracks while the Royal Navy placed a submarine at the producer's disposal. Blondie Hasler and Dick Raikes were asked to act as military advisers to José Ferrer, the director and lead actor and,

---

[10] The British 'branch' of Columbia Pictures. Produced by Phil C Samual with Irving Allen and A.R. Broccoli as Executive Producers and Directed by José Ferrer in Cinemascope and Technicolor.

despite the almost total American involvement, the original screen play was written by the British film-writer Bryan Forbes, with Blondie's help. Columbia Pictures flew them both to Hollywood to liaise with Ferrer while "they eked out their sparse expense account at a sort of drive-in called Biff's on Sunset Boulevard".[11] But Forbes' script did not meet with the Director's approval and was largely re-written without his concurrence and with a great deal of "extraneous and fictitious material that was not to their liking".

Trevor Howard played the part of the 'regular' Second in Command of the raid to Ferrer's 'Hostilities Only' Commanding Officer, thus transposing the roles and status of Hasler and Mackinnon and for various technical reasons the location shots were taken on the River Tagus. 'On set' relations, not involving Blondie, were strained throughout and at an advanced stage he developed such strong reservations about advising on a script that only made a passing nod at the truth that he felt compelled to write to the Commandant General, Sir John Westall, to explain that José Ferrer (for whom he felt much loyalty) had fallen out with Irving Allen who was now "easing Ferrer out of the unit before filming was finished".

Dick Raikes remembers his own part in the production well:

> The script was a mass of bollocks using expressions that just weren't used but the mock-up of the inside of the submarine at Shepherds Bush studio was brilliant and slightly larger than life so that it would look the right size in the film but there was a piece of machinery that I could not identify and as they were paying me £50 to get it right I mentioned this. The director said, "Ah, you see we had a space we couldn't fill and there was something in the store that looked about the right size so we put it in". The extras had long hair and so I had all that cut off before I drilled them in what they had to do when diving. It was fun.

Blondie disapproved of the title and agonized for many hours before producing thirty-eight alternatives, not one of which had either the word 'cockleshell' or 'hero' in it – but he was overruled. Nor did he approve the ending shots and believed that the whole film lacked glamour and substance. As the film was not, strictly speaking, about his raid (for instance, there were frogmen placing the limpets) he felt at liberty to 'doctor' the ending into something even more outrageous and even

---

[11] Letter to the author dated 15 February 1989.

further from the truth. Finding a similar typewriter to that used for the original he copied, exactly, the form and style of the 'real thing' and wrote a parody of the last scenes which were then covertly inserted into the 'shooting script':

"COCKLESHELL HEROES" – SUGGESTED ENDING

EXT. RIVER – NIGHT
364.   Only one canoe is left now. CATFISH (Major Stringer and Marine Todd) drags wearily up the river. Bordeaux never seemed so far away. They stop paddling, and the canoe comes to a rest. Stringer opens the cockpit cover and starts looking for his Benzedrine tablets with a dim red torch.

INT. CANOE – NIGHT
365.   The rosy light falls on Todd's feet, which rest, one on each side, against the outside of Stringer's thighs. There is a gap between Todd's shoes and the bottom of his trousers, and the camera favours this. To our surprise we see the ankles are encased in black nylon stockings. Surely, also, the feet are too small for a Marine? Stringer hesitates, then gently pulls one trouser leg up to the knee. It is undoubtedly a girl's leg. He moistens his forefinger and runs it up and down the calf, incredulously.

EXT. "CATFISH" – NIGHT
366.   Stringer turns slowly round in his seat, his eyes full of a growing wonder. He feasts his gaze on the figure behind him.

EXT. "CATFISH" – NIGHT
367.   CLOSE-UP TODD IN CANOE
Todd is seen to be embarrassed. He – or, as we should now say, she – allows her eyelashes to droop over her blackened cheeks, but the rising and falling of the bosom tells its own story. It is JACKIE LANE!

EXT. "CATFISH" – NIGHT
368.   Stringer gulps. STRINGER (softly) Why . . . why . . . Toddy . . .

368. CONTINUED. He turns right round and removes his backrest.

## EXT. DECK OF "CATFISH" AND RIVER – NIGHT

369. CLOSE SHOT. A paddle slips unnoticed into the water, and floats away. A second later, a large splash suggests that the compass has been impatiently jettisoned.

## EXT. RIVER – NIGHT

370. The moon has laid a silver carpet on the river and "CATFISH" is floating quietly across it. (Distant music "'Some Enchanted Evening").

## EXT. "CATFISH" – NIGHT

371. Stringer has folded Toddy in his arms. They kiss, the limpets explode.

372. End title superimposed on a background of falling debris:
     "And so, their high destiny fulfilled, the Cockleshell Hero and his mate pass on towards a less turbulent river – the tideless stream of eternity".

THE END

It is difficult to know who the target was for Blondie's mockery, himself or the Producer and although this spoof ending beats James Bond in ingenuity and pre-dates him in timing, he was again overruled!

The friendship between Blondie and Ferrer lasted throughout the lifetime of each and, shortly before his own death in 1989, José Ferrer wrote:[12]

> As to Blondie, I could write a short book on him, for he was an example of what each of us can be if he wants to, and if he sets his standards and ideals high.

So deep was his embarrassment that 'his' raid should be told in a film that lionized his part in it (no matter how fictionalized it might have been made to suit the cinema-going public) that he felt unable to face the gala opening night that it was to be given.[13] Months before the World Première

---

[12] Letter to author.
[13] It was, too, the premier of a new Royal Marines march, Cockleshell Heroes, written by Lieutenant-Colonel (Sir Vivian) Dunn, Royal Marines. (See p. 387.)

at the Empire Theatre, Leicester Square, was even given a date, he explained that he would be unable to attend. With Prince Philip and Lord Mountbatten as the principle guests of honour, plus, among others, Mr Clement Attlee[14] and the Duke of Primo de Rivera, many tried to persuade him that he should be there. An added attraction, he was then told, would be Elizabeth Taylor and her husband Michael Wilding, but he remained firm, keeping any reaction to this gap in his life to himself.

At the last minute he wrote to David Astor saying that "unfortunately he had to go over to France for a couple of days so there was no chance of him getting to the première"[15] but, on hearing this, his mother, who was planning to be there, wrote a stiff letter saying that if he said he was abroad then he had better be abroad. On 16 November, 1955, and in deference to his mother's demands for honest manners, Blondie took the cross-channel packet from Dover to sit drinking in a French café until safe to return.

The film was enthusiastically received by most of the newspapers:

> "*Cockleshell Heroes* takes an honourable place in the long line of war films". *The Times.*
>
> "No ordinary film would command such an audience and this is no ordinary film. It is one which honours the Royal Marines and gives them no more honour than is their due." *The Daily Mail.*

*The Sunday Graphic* mischievously suggested that there would have to be a remake after Prince Philip had correctly pointed out to Allen and Broccoli that they had failed to give the reason for the raid, which was to sink ships that were about to sail for Japan with vital radar equipment, yet it was *Punch* that offered the most erudite review in its issue for 30 November, 1955:

> The point of the film is . . . the actual operation. . . . Yet the artificially contrived situation of antagonism between the two officers . . . is the strength of the *story*. The exploit was a heroic and impressive one – but the film account of it impresses mainly because one knows it is based on fact.

*Cockleshell Heroes* was also premiered in the United States and Canada (again without Blondie) and is still shown irregularly on BBC television.

---

[14] The previous Prime Minister.
[15] Letter dated 14 November, 1955.

Blondie's professional involvement and personal friendship with José Ferrer sparked a dormant desire to write, not casually for yachting magazines but full time and with his own illustrations which he was slowly perfecting into a cartoon style. But his brief brush with the film world as an adviser pushed him further than that and inspired him to write the synopsis for a stage play, collaborating with then little-known authoress, Rosamund Pilcher.[16]

The play, a light-hearted love story he called *The Tulip Major*, concerned a fictitious Royal Marines officer, a beautiful girl and a vibrant post-war London. While that plot was fermenting in his mind a book of his Bordeaux exploits was about to follow the film, although these two had no direct connection. The film had been the whim of an American producer but a military historian, Brigadier C.E. Lucas Phillips, OBE, MC, recognized the raid as a prime example of a Special Forces operation that needed to be objectively dissected. He wanted to delve into the mind of the leader, the training, the characters, the approach, the escape and, unlike the film, record the truth.

For commercial reasons Lucas Phillips decided to stay with the film's title: whether Blondie liked it or not, it was brief and eye catching. Lord Mountbatten wrote the foreword and *Cockleshell Heroes* was first published by Heinemann in 1956. Subsequent sales reached over 250,000.

An added snippet of interest and psychology, not in the book but raised by Blondie after its publication, is contained in a letter to Brigadier Lucas Phillips.[17] Discussing the behaviour of his men after capture he acknowledges that one was supposed to have had a premonition:

> I have been worried by the story of (his) premonition of death – more than once I have run into this and I often feel that when it is fulfilled it is not so much a case of amazing intuition, but of fatalistic resignation and losing the essential hope of survival. In other words a man who has a premonition of death does not fight for his life.

[16] Unfortunately, attempts to elicit comments or details from Rosamund Pilcher have failed. She had served in Ceylon where, one might presume, they first met although, as described in his own words, Blondie tried to keep clear of "those horrid wrens!"

[17] Dated 20 April, 1956.

It was inevitable that *Cockleshell Heroes*, the book, would be reviewed in the yachting press as well as in military journals for, as the *Yachts and Yachting* issue of 7 December, 1956, said:

> No yachtsman can really afford to miss this book because brave men in tiny craft are yachtsmen's own heroes.

And the December issue of *Yachting Monthly* made much the same point:

> It is an epic of the last war which should never be forgotten, least of all by yachtsmen who, wending their way up a strange estuary in the still of summer night, look forward to the pleasures and charms of now-free France,

while *The Yachtsman's* book reviewer wrote that winter:

> Having read the book . . . we were able to understand why the leader of the expedition found racing to windward in *Tre Sang* in a full gale a comparatively restful occupation.

But despite helping with the film and the book, there remained an acute financial problem which had come to the notice of David Astor who was becoming increasingly worried about his old colleague and believed that now he was the editor of the Sunday broadsheet, *The Observer*, he was in a position to help. On 2 May, 1956, he wrote to Admiral Mountbatten, the First Sea Lord.

> I know how much you admire Lt Col 'Blondie' Hasler. (He) is a bachelor who lives extremely modestly, sometimes in lodgings and sometimes aboard a small yacht. I believe that one reason he hesitates to get married is that he cannot afford to maintain a wife in reasonable circumstances. . . . He has a great capacity for inspiring men, particularly younger ones, and one feels that there ought to be a use for him somewhere. . . . All I wish to do is to draw your attention to his personal situation in the hope that you may know of some special way in which such a superb man can be made better use of than he is.[18]

[18] Astor papers lodged with the author.

In a second letter he wrote:

> . . . The sort of activities he engages in – such as developing this new rig for his boat – are not likely to make him rich: he has, I fear, no commercial sense.

Before acknowledging David Astor's first letter Lord Mountbatten instantly contacted the Commandant General, Royal Marines, General Sir Campbell Hardy, who confirmed what all knew:

> It has always been assumed that Blondie Hasler deliberately chose his present mode of living as being the one he found most satisfying without bothering very much about money. Very little is known about his financial state except that he draws a pension of only £445.

In September Mountbatten wrote again to Astor:

> I thought you would like to know that Campbell Hardy . . . has at last managed to get Blondie Hasler to London to talk about his future. It is true that he now realizes the need to supplement his small pension and that he has it in mind to get married. His views on employment are unusual. He wants to get as much capital possible with the probable eventual aim of farming and with this in mind is now writing a play! Except for this new departure his main interest still lies in boat design.

Just before this correspondence began Blondie's relationship with Jen reached crisis point with his desire for marriage – despite misgivings recorded in his 'appreciations' – still strong but not reciprocated. In an attempt to introduce order into his plans, if not in practice, he wrote further appraisals culminating in a major effort on 25 May.

His public life was a success, his private (as he perceived it) was less so with the main 'turning point' now the breaking up of his friendship with Jen:

1. Release from Jen means:
    a). Must start cultivating new acquaintances as fast as possible.

>   b). No longer seriously consider marrying money –
>   therefore doubly important to build up proper
>   permanent source of income . . .
> 4. What is the permanent source of income . . . ?
>    Writing, Drawing, Painting, Play and script writing,
>    Consultant, Inventor, Lecturer . . .
> 7. Time is rather short – ought to marry by 1959, really
>    (aged 45).
> 8. There is absolutely no financial future in developing boats
>    or their gear in the UK. Therefore I hereby delete it from my
>    list of activities . . .
>    . . . Don't want to become an eccentric bum. This means
>    that I shall never live in *Jester* unless actively cruising.

A week later he continued:

> Will not cruise as a pauper. It is a gentlemanly hobby and calls
> for a good deal of entertaining. Cannot therefore make long
> cruise this year. Make money instead, lay boat up if necessary,
> never again accept the burden of looking after myself unless
> actively cruising. It never pays, however broke I am, because
> ruins morale, energy, as well as taking $1/3$rd of working day. Do
> not sail *Jester* alone except for ocean passages. Get local crew or
> invite people at weekends (Females seem to work best).
>     New object for *Jester* (is to be ) ready for long cruise Spring
> 1957. Therefore (in) 1956 use her congenially as much as
> possible. She is a social asset!

But it remained a long year of doubt and insecurity for on 17
November . . .

> Playwriting main hope at present. Priority is the *Tulip Major* . . .
> I write this at lowest financial ebb – I hope the turning point.

But 1956 was not the year of his lowest financial ebb and certainly not
a marital turning point, apart from the "release from Jen", for things were
to get worse on the first front and complicated on the second. During
1954, 1955 and 1956 he had been paid for one job each year which had,
just, kept the wolf from the Hasler door.

During the first of these years he had laid up *Jester* in order to take a
six-month appointment with SD6, a Government Department aligned

with MI6 and, in some aspects, a left-over from the SOE. For this fascinating but brief period Blondie was involved in the early designs of the
Royal Marines' rubber assault craft, eventually known as the *Gemini* and
still in wide use to this day.[19] The next year he had worked with
Columbia Pictures and during the third he had helped Lucas Phillips, for
£50. With the completion of the book the last source of income dried up,
forcing him to leave the digs in which he had been living, re-commission
*Jester* and live on board: it was then that Jen left him.

However, the likelihood of a tiny income did appear as *The Tulip Major*
project became a reality, so, with the prospect of some ready cash, he
now moved ashore to the Old Rectory at nearby Bursledon and while
these lodgings were "pretty uncomfortable" they were better, from the
social point of view, than *Jester*, despite his written comments. Also in
September David Astor, realizing that no work would be forthcoming
from the military, had made an offer to Blondie that, over the years,
would provide a small and erratic supply of money.

> I am keen to persuade you to develop a specialist relationship to
> this sheet. From time to time we could well do with an article on
> some aspect of boating, boat building or boatmanship (whatever
> one should call it).

Writing for *The Observer* would lead, not entirely indirectly, to the
second most important event in his life, the single-handed trans-Atlantic
race:[20]

Rosamund Pilcher and Blondie began detailed work on *The Tulip
Major* in May, 1956, and a year later *The Dundee Courier* of 6 May, 1957,
was able to report a "forthcoming attraction":

> The Dundee Rep Programme . . . World Premier . . . *The Tulip
> Major* by Rosamund Pilcher and George Hasler. The wartime
> escapades of Major Tony Corregan of the Marines were pretty
> brisk – and from time to time even dear old Sergeant Sims found
> the pace a bit hot. But in peacetime when they get together again

---

[19] It can be parachuted fully inflated or can be inflated once in the water. It is
easily manhandled from a submarine or the back of a Land Rover and is usually
powered by a 40 HP outboard.
[20] This race, discussed in great detail later, has had many titles since its
inception to the present day. For the sake of clarity this title will be used
throughout.

even Burma pales into insignificance. With most of London on their track and a beautiful girl very much in their hair these two carry the day – and the girl – but only just. Sixteen hilarious hours in the life of the Tulip Major.

The *Daily Telegraph* also gave the play advance notice and *The Scotsman* commented:

> The Dundee Rep Theatre continues its praiseworthy policy of giving a hearing to new plays. . . . *The Tulip Major* may be placed definitely in the pigeon hole labelled light entertainment. . . . Not a momentous work but an agreeable one in which Dundee – and elsewhere given equally clever handling – has a chance of proving very good 'box office'.

The play opened at the Repertory Theatre, Nicoll Street, on 10 June, 1957. The *Dundee Courier* again:

> *The Tulip Major* brings lots of laughs . . .

The undoubted success of this play meant a great deal to Blondie, although probably less to Miss Pilcher for they parted unhappily. Under an 'appreciation' heading of 'Bright Outlook' Blondie listed the selling of the *Tulip Major* but made it clear that this depended on "Pilcher support" and that that was not forthcoming. This hurt Blondie as it was the second play he had written. The first (called *The Veteran Yachtsman*) had been for *The Observer* play competition and, although it did not win, he felt that this experience coupled to his own background allowed him to offer the 'professional' playwright ideas and plots. She, apparently through jealousy at the 'amateur's' ability, clearly thought otherwise and he was forced to re-organize his life again:

> 1st June 1957. Waiting to see if *Tulip Major* will go beyond Dundee and to get *Veteran Yachtsman* back from *Observer*? Next project to re-write *Veteran Yachtsman* . . .
> 25th June. After seeing the *TM* at Dundee, quarrel with Ros, start on *Veteran Yachtsman II* again. Best time to put on new London play is September, want to get even with Ros! Have several good new ideas.

But these plans did not last long, for two days later:

> Revert to inventing. Summer is not a good time for playwriting.

And three weeks later:

> Where now? . . . Plays still resting for the summer . . . Can't I
> potboil with short stories? It would help towards playwriting?
> Try to be unique in this as in everything. Be outlandish. Shock
> them. Make them read it twice to get the sense. Be Gay. Learn.

He wrote a third play, *The Long Voyage*, intended for adaptation into
a film script, and lodged it with José Ferrer but, as with his attempt for
*The Observer*, he heard no more. Neither scripts survive so it is not
possible to make our own judgement of how outlandish or shocking he
managed to make them.

Throughout his life it was his inventions that saved the day or made
the man and now, if not lucrative, they at least kept him occupied.

> I still fret over my many inventions awaiting sponsors, notably:
> mainsheet winch, £500 ocean racer, cabin heater, child's
> dinghy, stiff sails . . . magazine forestay. *Ferret* has failed at a cost
> of 7 weeks and about £5. Worth it, particularly for lessons learnt.

Some of these predate what are now taken for granted: the self-tailing
winch and the forestay with a sail permanently attached that could be
altered in size to suit the weather and sails made of very stiff, but
malleable material, were considered but the cloth was not then in
production although he did, successfully, achieve much the same effect
by plasticizing *Jester's* Lapwing. The *Ferret* was an ingenious method for
unblocking drains; a long flexible wire corkscrewed its way into the
obstruction which could then be pulled out, but this did not catch on,
although the original is still in use. He had the ideas but not the
marketing skills, nor (as with so many inventors) the inclination to see
them through to commercial success.

There was the occasional exception. The 'rope-winch'[21] was the
second of the three patents[22] that he lodged and the one that he regarded at the time as the most exciting. To manufacture and market this

---

[21] Patent Number 22545/58 for *Improvements in pulleys for the transmission of
power to or from cords, ropes and the like*. Dated 14 July, 1958.
[22] The third was a simple form of plotting chart for barometers.

forerunner of the present self-tailing winch he and John Chamier[23] took out a 'gentleman's agreement' on 7 June, 1958, that they would develop the Hasler Rope Wheel together, splitting any profits and development costs; but this project met an unfortunate end when a businessman they trusted 'stole' it from them. The aim had been to

> provide a rope wheel which exhibits improved power transmission at low speeds. . . . The demonstration winch has been designed as a sheet winch for sailing yachts. In particular to enable the mainsheet to be handled by the helmsman using one hand only.[24] The wheel has a deep "V" groove whose faces have angles of 20° – the width of the groove can be adjusted . . . The rope is gripped very firmly into the groove by a spring finger just before disengaging point . . .

But his finest innovation, and one that was not offered to any crooked businessman, although he had yet to experience that unhappy incident, was still gestating via various experimental forms on Ian Major's *Buttercup* and by 8 August, 1957, it had reached the top of his priority list as the Hasler Vane Gear. Originally he experimented with the trim-tab[25] system and by the end of September the trailing edge of *Jester's* rudder was fitted with this. The trim-tab was not new but he had to start with something from which he could develop his own ideas for transferring power from the water to the tiller or direct to the rudder. If the basic design showed promise, then he originally intended to lodge a provisional patent at the end of the year before asking Moody's Yard or Vospers to take over the commercial aspects. (In the end it was neither of these organizations that took on the project nor would he apply for a patent "as he did not wish to spend the rest of his life defending it".)

However, by 13 October, 1957, an offer of collaboration changed his priorities once more. They were now:

> 1. Spearfish[26] 2. Dracone. 3. Rope Winch . . . agree to work for Dracone on consulting basis at 10 guineas a day plus expenses. . . . Also resolve today to do football pools.

---

[23] Among other achievements, a yachting correspondent of international repute.
[24] For Blondie's own words on how this project failed see Appendix One.
[25] For a full description of these gears see Appendix Four.
[26] An economical, wave-piercing motor boat. See Appendix One.

In 1948 Geoffrey Nockolds, a young businessman, had kept his yacht *Juno* close to *Petula* at Crabs Corner off Moody's Yard on the Hamble, Blondie had just been elected to the Royal Cruising Club (Geoffrey was to follow four years later) and the two had kept in touch through a love of cruising. Now, in 1957, Geoffrey had "idle manufacturing capacity available" for which Blondie agreed to "send him a list of suggested projects".

28 November, 1957: Brisk. *Observer* have accepted *Mine Always Light*[27] (first comic writing). Nockolds interested in my list of projects . . . got better idea about making money. With him I am going ahead on drill guides, toasting fork, folding boat, ornithopter.

The ornithopter was a form of one-man flying machine and, as with all his ideas, it began life as a meticulous, blue-inked, mechanical drawing in a series of small exercise books. Most would agree that the simple coat-hanger had reached the end of its evolution, but not so according to Blondie who, believing that nothing was too ordinary or mundane to escape the search for improvement, attempted to design a better one. At last, in Geoffrey Nockolds, he had met someone who would, or could, take care of the manufacturing and marketing of his various ideas with the dracone a prime example.

Ever since man-handling heavy guns at Alexandria and Scapa Flow Blondie had been interested in the physics of moving weights on land. Now he was determined to move bulk liquids by sea and, in particular, oil. The super-tanker had not entered the scene and yet there was a vital need to transport oil around the world in larger and larger quantities. His idea was that dracones, long rubber sausages used as portable storage tanks for liquids, could, towed by tugs, be used to transport this cargo across the oceans. To further this basic principle Geoffrey introduced him to the National Research and Development Corporation that supports and encourages such ideas. Progress was swift and Dracone Limited took him on as a consultant for ten guineas a day – enough to allow him to devote money to his longest-term project, *Jester* and the Atlantic.

---

[27] A humorous piece about lighting fires that was so well received it was later translated into French for schools' exercises.

On paper all should have been well but a new hint of depression and social self-doubt suddenly appears on 8 January, 1958:

> Depressed. Everything going wrong . . . *Jester's* deck, the winch – I think. No sign of earning any real money except possibly from Dracone. . . . Suspect may soon ease away from inventing towards either plays, drawing or marketing one of my things . . .
>
> 10th Jan. The depression is social I think. Need a few changes of scene . . . I have alienated at least two people in this area . . . should be quieter, more modest, funnier, not so drunk. Learn to relax in people's company even when you ought to be working.

While this was not how his contemporaries saw him his personal criticism could only be cured by the acquisition of a wife and a base, and not by reassurance from his friends, notably at this time Johnnie Coke who "tried to dig him out" and galvanize him into positive action. Realizing that the lack of a permanent companion was a major factor in his inability to see his ideas through to fruition, Blondie's response was to analyse his circumstances, yet again.

> 17 May '58. Being now for first time able to keep a wife, am about to make a real effort to find one – H.J? Plan would be for wife to help set up family business (Hasler Boats Ltd – to make folding boats of all sizes) in lieu of any other insurance policy . . .
>
> 21st June '58. Have just thought seriously of marrying P but am also about to start on H.J.

But August saw him

> No longer think of marrying P or HJI or Z. Present possibilities DBS, DGB.

From which it has to be deduced that the absence of Jen, the move ashore (in fact a temporary arrangement while the money from the *Tulip Major* lasted) and the possibility of a literary career rather than one totally devoted to small boats now ensured that there were a number of girls prepared to take him more seriously. This presented him, according to his own comments, with a state of affairs for which he had no experience to deal, despite the four years during which Jen helped him to mature in such matters – an embarrassment of riches indeed.

Yet unknowingly, all for the want of a hammer, a meeting vital to his future happiness took place that summer while Blondie worked on board *Jester* as she lay to her mooring at Crabs Corner. Nearby George Naish (then the Assistant Keeper of the National Maritime Museum) was busy on his pilot cutter, *Dolphin*, being helped by his Research Assistant Susanna Fisher, the eldest of Rear-Admiral Ralph Fisher's five daughters. Unable to ignore the opportunity of meeting a pretty girl Blondie rowed across on the spurious excuse that he needed to borrow the hammer! When he had gone, sometime later and without the hammer, George remarked to Sue, "I thought he would quickly find a reason to visit!"

Sue was to appear in his 'appreciations' as a candidate for marriage (although whether or not she ever knew this remains unclear!), but not yet, for he proposed marriage to at least two other girls in the autumn, both of whom said 'no'. It must have been obvious to them, if not to Blondie, that these were proposals born of desperation rather than the love he sought:

> All prospective wives rejected me, (now) waiting for HJ without confidence.

Then on 10 January, 1959, in a move designed to spur Blondie into settling ashore, Ian Major offered him some furniture, which he took with gratitude, and began a search for a flat in order to "have his own bathroom, be able to work over meal times and entertain his friends in private". A wing of Harfields, at Curdridge, seemed suitable for the purpose, with this sudden change in domestic arrangements heralding a similar change in his fortunes and outlook:

> Dracones looking brisk so I will stay with them. No longer looking at Diana B or HJI. . . . but lurking feeling that I should revive HJI.
>
> Flat big success – gives me much pleasure, amount of housework not great. Am eating much good food with hardly any cooking. Have decided that I am far more likely to be an artist than a playwright, comparing past work in both cases.
>
> Priority for weekends.
> 1. Wife hunt. (Nothing in sight, but about to renew acquaintance with Georgie.)[28]

---

[28] Could she have been a pre-war friend who had inspired his saxophone playing?

2. Convert pram dinghy for sailing, fit Chinese lug. Object . . . is to assess by August '59 whether Lapwing or Chinese lug is better[29]
3. Have a boat in commission. Present inclination is to (enter) *Jester* for the trans-Atlantic Race.[30]

Optimism continued to creep back for on 29 March, 1959, he wrote:

Discussing plans for buying design office. . . .If I can retain £600 per annum from Dracone could soon be richer.

But he actually reverted to part-time work with Dracone Limited in order to pursue his plans for the single-handed trans-Atlantic race, *Jester's* conversion to Chinese lug rig and his embryo self-steering gear. So behind was he with all these projects that until well into 1960 he would continue to harbour doubts that he would be able to enter the race due to start that summer, yet, heedless of these delays, he now devoted time to a new occupation, and one that certainly swallowed up the hours. At the beginning of 1959 he progressed his line drawings and cartoons to a style of portrait painting in oils that met with some acclaim. However, and paradoxically, despite this artistic skill introducing him to girls in greater numbers than during his reclusive periods on board *Jester*, a form of insecurity and latent shyness continued to dominate. In May he secretly admonished himself with the words:

Personal: Impossible reputation socially, and figure of fun.

Although probably not part of his search for a wife, but with *Jester's* well-being uppermost, he confided to his notes in June and July, 1959, that he should consider

getting one or two girls to fit out *Jester* July–October and crew for me October–June. Could live at Harfields and double as secretary/chauffeuse,if two of them. Otherwise not for more than odd weekend owing to effect on local hostesses!
    Sudden avalanche of girl friends – Poll (at present in Med cruising), Cynthia (sailed . . . last Sunday) Belinda (just

[29] The relevance is discussed in the next chapters.
[30] Covered in greater detail in Chapter Thirteen.

approaching) Sue Fisher (? not answering). Possible matrimonial order: B,C,S,P. but don't know what I've got to offer first three. Must guard against tendency to 'cheese off' in middle of wooing. Remember, marriage is urgent.

And was this the Cynthia for whom he composed the following (under the pseudonym he used for many of his *Observer* pieces), a copy of which he kept among his more private papers?[31]

> With "C" by Charles Tindal.
>
> As I watch, smooth shadows trace
> A hundred women in your face.
> The agile, deep, Eurasian eyes
> Look strong, pathetic, stupid, wise.
> Beyond them, incompletely seen,
> Nun or wanton, mother, slave,
> In birth, youth, decadence, the grave.
> Each showing ugliness and grace,
> And claiming beauty in your face.

Blondie had a well developed eye for beauty, an asset he used to advantage even though 'the results' needed continual juggling in his order of preference. He perhaps did not have such a practised eye for the longer-term potential in a girl, such as love and devotion, for there is no evidence to suggest that any of his proposed fiancées saw themselves as a loving, devoted wife of his, even if he pretended to himself that he did.

Quite simply, the desire to marry was a desire for marriage before he was, in his view, too old. While all his female friends were excellent company, he knew, too, that they would not "last his pace" – and throughout his life Blondie regarded friendships as a never-ending commitment, and that particularly included marriage. His 'juggling' therefore has to be seen as a reasonably light-hearted, private way of softening the blow that the right girl had not, yet, come into his life.

> 18th Feb 1960. Girl friend order C.S.P. but not sure I can face marriage with any of these. It must be somebody who will help me in my work and with my boat as well as run a home.

[31] Neither of whom was the Cynthia who married Ian Major.

Unknown to him, of course, his future bride, who would do all these things, was, as it were, waiting in the wings and, at that moment just coming up to her 20th birthday.

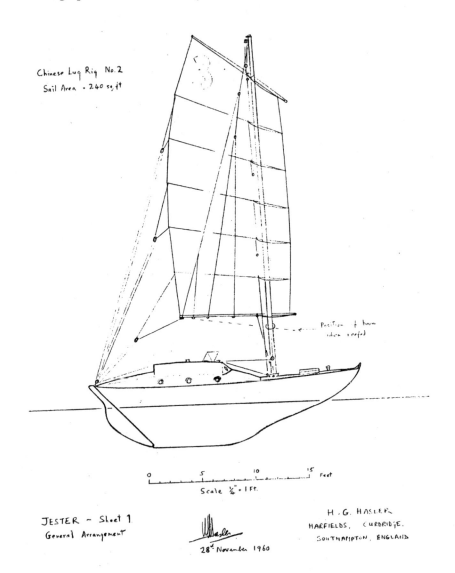

Chinese Lug Rig No. 2
Sail Area - 240 sq.ft

Position of boom
when reefed

0     5     10     15  Feet
Scale ¼" = 1 Ft.

JESTER — Sheet 1
General Arrangement

28ᵗ November 1960

H. G. HASLER.
HARFIELDS, CURBRIDGE.
SOUTHAMPTON, ENGLAND

# CHAPTER THIRTEEN

## *Jester* and *The Slocum Society*

Blondie made a number of short references to the single handed trans-Atlantic race in his 'appreciations'. While other important aspects of his life were inextricably dovetailed with this event it is sensible to study it, and *Jester's* preparation for it, in one complete, chronological movement.

To understand the gestation of the affair that was to transform many of the world's offshore racing calendars it is necessary to go back to 25 November, 1956, and that day's copy of *The Observer* in which Blondie ringed in red ink an article by Pendennis in his weekly column Table Talk. What caught the eye was a short piece under the subtitle Brave Sailors:

> Only two men I believe have sailed a boat across the Atlantic single-handed from east to west by the northern route. In 1933 Commander R.D. Graham RN (Rtd) sailed from Bantry Bay to St John's Newfoundland in twenty five days. Last August another ex-Naval officer, Lieutenant-Commander A.G. Hamilton, DSC, RN, sailed from Rhu, Dunbartonshire to Belle Isle off the northern tip of Newfoundland in twenty eight days.

The article went on to explain that Commander Hamilton had flown back to get married and that the couple would now return by steamer to take their *Vertue* class yacht, *Salmo*, by rail across to the Pacific. Peter Hamilton had served with Blondie in the SOG during the last year of the war[1] and, after his Atlantic crossing had returned, as reported, to get married. Blondie, he remembers,

> quizzed me unmercifully about the Atlantic route I had taken (which was Great Circle) and how much fog I had met and how

---

[1] See Chapter Ten.

much ice. I offered him the advice that although ice is a pest there's always a hell of a lot more open sea about than icebergs.[2]

The second point that must have fired Blondie's undeniably romantic image of a self-sufficient life afloat with a beautiful wife was contained in Pendennis's final sentence:

> Hamilton's wife . . . is a gay, slim intelligent girl who looks like making his voyaging more agreeable in the future than it has been in the past.

In two respects somebody had beaten Blondie to it! It is also interesting to speculate that supposing P or HJI or DBS or Diana B or Sue or 'Z' had said 'yes' to his bended-knee proposals then he might, too, have set off for the 'new world' and the single-handed trans-Atlantic race and those races that it spawned would not have taken place for many years.

In fact, as Blondie was to note, there had been a single-handed trans-Atlantic race in 1891, albeit from west to east and thus with the prevailing wind[3] when William A. Andrews and Josiah W. Lawlor sailed two 15ft boats from Boston to Europe. Lawlor arrived at Coverack near the Lizard after a passage of 45 days while Andrews was rescued by a passing steamer after 61 days at sea and 600 miles short of his destination.

The following account of the period prior to the 1960 single-handed trans-Atlantic Race, largely in Blondie's words, is culled from numerous drafts, letters and diaries and has been pruned of other concurrent activities in order to produce a clear run-through from conception to conclusion. There is some repetition where it is relevant to this different context:

> During the morning of 11 June, 1960, a small cannon fired three blank cartridges with an interval of exactly five minutes between each. . . . The third gun was the signal for the start of a race and within half a minute four small sailing yachts[4] each with only one man on board crossed the starting line. . . . The printed Sailing

---

[2] Letter to author, September 1996.
[3] A favourite Blondie quote; "Prevailing winds never prevail!"
[4] A fifth entry started five days after the others. Discussed later.

Instructions for the race were unusual but concise. . . . "Course. Cross the starting line from West to East. Leave the Melampus Buoy to starboard, thence to New York by any route."

In 1952 I had sold my ancient lovely, conventional 48 foot yawl *Petula* and ordered a new 25 foot boat that was destined from the start to be a floating test-bed for new ideas. Having thus condemned her, even before she was born, to a lifetime of ridicule I named her *Jester* and registered her at the port of Cowes.

The focal point of *Jester's* design is the rig and she has two complete alternative rigs both of which give unusual ease of handling. For the first seven years she carried a rig . . . based on a radical conception produced between the wars by Dr Ljungstrom, a Swedish engineer. I developed the basic idea further. The Lapwing Rig, as I call it, is supported on a hollow wooden mast of unusually large diameter built up of a number of pieces of spruce glued together. This mast is supported in roller bearings at the deck and ball bearings at the heel in such a way that it can be rotated at will by the helmsman from his position inside the cabin. It is designed to stand up by itself without the help of any wire stays or shrouds and carries a pair of twinsails that can be opened for running before the wind or closed together (so as to make, in effect, one sail of half the area) on other points of sailing. When the wind increases the sails are reefed to any required degree by rolling them up progressively on the mast after the fashion of a roller blind. To furl them, this rolling process is continued until there is no more sail left exposed.

During the winter of 1959/1960 and to provide a standard of comparison I designed a Chinese lug rig to be carried on the same mast. The Chinese lug is a fore-and aft sail and not a squaresail. It is trimmed and handled on all points of sailing just as if it were Bermudian or gaff and can claim to be the world's most easily reefed sail.

All the work of handling both these sail plans – and this is the main point of the thing – is done by the helmsman without leaving his steering position. He simply stands up on the cabin seats so that he is waist high out of the circular hatch. All the necessary ropes and winches then lie within his reach and as his body is firmly supported at the waist it is no longer necessary to observe the old seaman's advice of "One hand for yourself, one for the ship". He has both hands for the ship and can pull much harder.

To go back to 1956 when I began to wonder if there wasn't some way of encouraging other experimentally-minded yachtsmen to work towards improving small sea-going sailing yachts so that we could attack the problem from a number of different angles and compare our results by actual competition in the open sea.

A race! Of course it would have to be a race because racing is the only branch of yachting in which innovation is accepted. Nearly all improvement in yacht design have first appeared in racing yachts, and have been copied by cruising yachtsmen only after a decent interval of time has gently rinsed away the sour taint of unorthodoxy.

If it were a single-handed race it would attract plenty of publicity and would encourage a strongly competitive spirit. In order to favour the kind of development I had in mind it would have to be over a long distance with a probability of boisterous sailing conditions. A race from England to New York seemed to be the only adequate solution, for trans-Atlantic passages have a glamour of their own.

On 20 September, 1956, David Astor had written the letter suggesting the occasional article to which Blondie had agreed with the provision that his wartime rank and decorations were never used. With this contact well established, he felt easier about his proposal that would, or could, keep *The Observer* in the forefront of nautical writing. On 11 January, 1957, he wrote:

My dear David,

I have been brooding for some time on the possibility of organizing a trans-Atlantic race for single-handed sailing boats. The object of the race would be, first, to encourage the development of suitable boats, gear and technique for single-handed ocean work, and, secondly just plain sport.

As you know the Atlantic has been crossed single-handed a great many times – perhaps thirty or fifty – but usually very slowly owing to unsuitable boats and lack of a proper steering gear. I have in mind a race from Cowes to New York (probably City Island) starting July or August 1958 in order to give people a full year to develop their boats.

All entries would first have to qualify by sailing a fairly stiff course (say Cowes-Bantry and back non-stop each way). This would weed out unseaworthy entries but in any case each entry would of course be responsible for his own safety. There would obviously be some risk to life but less, in my opinion, than in the Grand National.

Is there any hope that *The Observer* would like to sponsor this race? If so, may I send you much fuller proposals for the rules, prizes etc!

I would hope to enter my own boat, and, in any case the announcement of the race might well give a boost to the development of my experimental gear neither of which has attracted much backing so far. I think it would be a thoroughly sporting and progressive event, which would attract world-wide interest and I think a good number of foreign entries.

It would also, inevitably, attract adverse criticism but I should deal with this side of things in my detailed proposals.

Or does this seem to you more a proposition for Max Aitken?[5]

In reply he received a letter dated 16 January, 1957:

Many thanks for yours about the trans-Atlantic race for single-handed sailing boats. Whether or not we ought to undertake the sponsoring of it is a question I will put up to our Manager. I rather think that he will be against it.

Before Blondie was able to reply, David wrote again:

25th January 1957. About the trans-Atlantic race our Manager definitely thinks that our Directors would not want to undertake the sponsoring of this event. Therefore there is nothing to stop you going right ahead and approaching Max Aitken.

There was less bad news:

On the possibility of our sponsoring your own entry to the race . . . our Manager is open-minded, but, naturally I have not been able to give him any idea as to what sum of money might be involved.

[5] *Express* newspapers and a "conventional" yachtsman.

But *The Observer's* Manager was not that open-minded as can be seen in extracts from two unimaginative internal memos:

> I don't really think this would do us the slightest good . . . I just don't think it would pay us an adequate dividend because a. the other papers if they reported the event would be very liable to omit any mention of our sponsorship and b. if, as he indicates, lives might be lost in the attempt to cross the Atlantic our competitors would be delighted to have the opportunity of blaming us, calling us irresponsible and claiming that we had failed to take adequate precautions to prevent such loss of life and so on . . .
>
> Just imagine the situation if one of these ships gets lost in mid-ocean . . . if you think it is kinder to let him submit his plan and then turn it down rather than reject it unseen by all means tell him to do so . . . without giving any more encouragement, however.

These arguments, un-adventurous though they were, fired Blondie to take another tack in his search for help. He even doubted, significantly and not for the last time, the need to have any sponsor at all. On 1 February he replied to David.

> . . . I think I will just go to ground with the thing for the present while I talk to sailing people about it. I don't like the idea of any commercial firm's sponsoring it . . . I would hope that the sponsor would be involved more by way of sport than the hope of favourable publicity. It is even possible that the race would best be run without an organisation, for example by somebody (me?) simply challenging all comers to race me across.

Blondie's narrative continues

> Talking to sailing people about it confirmed that most sailing clubs would scream with horror at the idea of my very unorthodox race so my thoughts turned towards the Slocum Society an 'informal brotherhood' named after Joshua Slocum, the first single-handed circumnavigator, that had been formed in 1953. Its activities were now guided by its founder and secretary

Richard Gordon McCloskey, at that time serving in the American Embassy at Lima, Peru, to whom I wrote on 26 February:

> . . . Some months ago I conceived the idea of trying to organize a race in single-handed sailing boats from Cowes to New York to start in July 1958.

He had his answer in a fortnight:

> By all means send us the proposed organisation of the race and the rules. . . . The prospect is most exciting and can be of great value if properly handled and directed.

With this light beckoning him on an excited Blondie replied quickly attaching his proposed rules:

SINGLE-HANDED TRANSATLANTIC RACE
Proposed Basic Rules – 22nd March 1957
OBJECT
1.  The object of the race is twofold: (a) sport, and (b) to encourage the development of suitable boats, gear and techniques for single-handed ocean crossing under sail.
DATE
2.  Start from Cowes on Saturday 26th July 1958 . . .
COURSE
3.  To City Island, NY, by any route, but leaving Long Island to port . . .
ENTRIES . . . may be sponsored . . .
QUALIFICATION
8.  The Standard Qualifying Course will be in two parts as follows: Part 1, from Cowes to Bantry (SW Ireland) (about 400 sea miles): Part II, from Bantry back to Cowes.
9.  Each part of this course must be sailed single-handed and without entering harbour or receiving stores or assistance. . . . They may not take shelter from bad weather . . .
12. The owner may propose any other qualifying course for his entry but this will only be accepted by the committee if:
    (a) The total course is at least 800 sea miles of open water . . .

(b) The course is likely to include a proportion of head winds and winds of gale force . . .

ELIGIBILITY OF YACHTS

13. Yachts may be of any size or type but the following restrictions will apply for the duration of the race and of the qualifying course.

14. No means of propulsion may be employed other than the force of the wind and/or the manpower of the crew.

15. Inboard engines, if fitted, must have their propellers and stern shafts removed and the stern tube plugged.

16. No outboard engine may be carried nor any form of portable assembly which could be used for propelling the boat by unauthorized means . . .

OUTSIDE ASSISTANCE

18. No physical contact may be made with other ships or boats at sea and no stores or water received from them. They may be asked for advice or information, or to report the yacht's position and condition.

19. During the race (but not during the qualification) a yacht may put in anywhere and anchor or moor for any purpose. When actually anchored or moored, other people may come on board, stores or equipment may be embarked. A yacht may not be towed into or out of harbour but may be towed from one berth to another while in harbour.

PROHIBITED EQUIPMENT

20. No form of radio transmitter may be carried. This is to prevent yachts from calling for help or reporting their position, except when within range of visual or sound signals.

RESPONSIBILITY

21. Yachts must be fully independent and capable of carrying out their own emergency repairs at sea. Any risk to life must be accepted as in other sports such as motor racing or steeplechasing. Crews have no right to expect or demand rescue operations to be launched on their behalf and the organization will NOT initiate any search or rescue action under any circumstances.

22. Full responsibility for the results of any mishap will rest with the owner or crew under ordinary processes of law. The organizers accept no responsibility towards the entrants nor towards third parties with whom the entrants may become involved . . .

The basis of these rules is in existence to this day. McCloskey wrote back on 31 March.

> I can see only one possible change that might be proposed. Instead of prohibiting auxiliary power and wireless transmitters it would be just as effective to seal them. A broken seal at the finish would automatically disqualify an entry, but not prohibit him from using them if he felt it absolutely necessary. What think ye?

Delighted with this sudden progress, Blondie sought advice on details from Alan Paul, a long-standing friend and confidant to earlier Hasler proposals and now secretary of the RORC:

> The RORC has not sealed engines or radio transmitters within my recollection. . . . There seems far less reason to seal radio transmitters as they are hardly likely to speed the progress of the competitors. The danger of allowing their use is that when the beastly thing breaks down, the Press tell the world in dramatic terms that 'Captain Slowcome' is missing and there is hell to pay.

The last sentence accorded exactly with Blondie's views. In this instance he was not concerned with 'speed of progress' nor, even, what mischief the press might invent, but if someone was to call for help and thus put another seafarer at risk then 'his race' would get the bad name he feared many would want to give it. A competitor, he felt, should sail the race at his own risk and nobody else's.

> In my world, small boats do not carry transmitters and they are always assumed to be missing unless somebody happens to be looking at them. It leads to an enviable peace of mind for everybody.

His next letter to McCloskey continued this theme:

> The question of transmitting is a difficult one and I would, if I entered, be happy to accept the fact that I should drown if I couldn't solve my own problems, but I can see that a humane organizer might have misgivings. I dread the idea of ships having to conduct rescue operations.

Six weeks later he received the letter he "was anxiously awaiting", but it was not all good news, for although the Society agreed to sponsor the race they would not be able to do so until the spring of 1960. Nevertheless if it had to be 1960 or never, so be it and his reply optimistically suggested the wording for a press release announcing that the start would be at Cowes on the last Friday before the annual regatta – in other words the end of July. Caught up with the infectious enthusiasm McCloskey agreed that it could not be too soon to start winning over what he delightfully referred to as the cynical 'piazza sailors'.

He now had an organizer who would field the press releases, distribute the rules, answer the questions, collate the entries and man the finishing line; a Starting Club was the only absentee. While he waited for the Press Releases to arrive from Lima he wrote two articles, the first for *The Observer* and the other for *Yachts and Yachting*:

> For the first time in history single-handed sailing boats are to race across the Atlantic from England to the United States. . . . The course (from Cowes to New York by any route) measures at least 3,100 miles and the leading boats are unlikely to finish in less than 35 days.

The second, much longer and more technical article for the yachting readership included two diagrams of the North Atlantic showing possible routes. It was almost exactly a year after reading Pendennis.
Thirty-six copies of the press release arrived on 18 September and read in part:

### SINGLE-HANDED TRANSATLANTIC
### RACE ORGANIZED

> The object of the race is to encourage the development of suitable boats, gear and techniques for single-handed ocean-crossing under sail. . . . Entries may be sponsored and boats need not be sailed by their owners.

In later years when the subject of sponsorship became 'an issue' Blondie could do no better than to remind people that from the very beginning he had acknowledged that, without it, the chances of success were slim, that he encouraged it from the outset is not often remembered.

The press releases were despatched to five yachting magazines, four sporting magazines, sixteen newspapers, the Press Association, the Royal

Yachting Association and five carefully selected yacht clubs. All the yachting magazines published the release but most other recipients ignored it. Blondie also sent a copy to the BBC offering his services for a public discussion on the race, and although the Corporation replied that his suggestion had been passed to the appropriate producers he heard no more.

The flood gates – for that is the effect the race has had over the years – allowing the pro- and anti-lobbies to voice their subjective views were now open. Is this racing? Is this safe? Does the skipper break the international rules for preventing collision at sea? Should they, therefore, be allowed to go? Is it legal? The arguments continue – but of even more importance – so do the races.

Blondie's preliminary work was not over for he had yet to find the yacht club to handle the starting arrangements. On 25 September he wrote to the secretary of the Island Sailing Club at Cowes "a famous and notably democratic club" and, having outlined his proposals ended with the hope that they would not give the club 'the horrors' – but they did.

Within the week he approached Mr F.G. Mitchell, the millionaire head of Mitchell Engineering, who played a considerable part in the affairs of the Royal Corinthian Yacht Club (also at Cowes) with the consequence that the Club had a reputation of sponsoring innovative events that "caused most other clubs to gasp". Mitchell was enthusiastic and suggested a meeting, but became too ill to see him. Eventually all the Club could offer was to fire a starting gun. Blondie wanted a little more than that.

Eleven months had now passed since he had written the first letter and all was going well, if slowly, but on 15 December McCloskey wrote from Peru with the first signs, to Blondie, that his race might now be 'hijacked':

> For a long time we have resisted pressure to form a sailing auxiliary to the Slocum Society but the announcement of the race brought things to a head and there was formed last month a separate but associated organization: The Slocum Society Sailing Club who will now take over responsibility for the race . . .
>
> I think the chief objection to the finish has been the selection of City Island because of the congestion in New York Harbor and the problems of Long Island Sound. . . . Another point is the fact that the finish will coincide with the beginning of the hurricane season.

Blondie was able to answer the problems raised by the newly-formed club on 13 January, 1958:

> My original draft stipulated leaving Long Island to port in order to keep boats out of the East River . . . (I don't think this is) more congested than the Solent or Land's End area and I've never really accepted the idea that the competitors will arrive in the last stages of physical endurance.
>
> I can only say that the autumn was regarded by our forefathers as the best possible time for sailing east to west by the northern route. Many of their ships were far less able to survive a hurricane than our good single-handers. Surely all offshore sailing doesn't stop on your side of the Atlantic between June and November? I think fog and ice are far more serious dangers than hurricanes. If you move the starting date I imagine it could only be to make it later, otherwise you run into the peak ice period which our forefathers dreaded in spite of having plenty of hands to keep watch.

To add delay to the 'minor irritations' over the race's destination and date, McCloskey was stricken with tuberculosis but was able to write that Bermuda had offered to host the finish. As this was not in Blondie's scheme of things he replied, in part, on 7 June, 1958:

> The question of finishing in Bermuda is interesting but not one that would appeal to me at first sight:
> - (a) It is very difficult to find, particularly for someone who has lost his longitude.
> - (b) The approach from the north is exceptionally hazardous . . .

News of the race now reached the *Washington Post* whose reporter, Mark Hanman, quoted, on 20 July, an interview he had held with McCloskey:

> "We have about 140 applications but frankly I don't believe that more than four or five boats will actually make the race. . . . It'll be, among other things, a good chance to end many an argument about the merits of a 25 footer and a 40 footer in open water . . .

A 40 foot boat will kill off its man from sheer work, a 25 footer could do the same thing from the pounding it takes. I feel that a race like this every five years will be ample."

Despite contention over the route, the destination and the starting date Blondie felt that a calm had now descended on his race with various aspects slipping slowly into place via the enthusiastic, and wholly supportive, McCloskey. In November he flew to Nigeria with Dracone Limited for a ten-day reconnaissance for future operations which was good for the coffers and thus for the continuing trials of *Jester's* new rig.

*"I should have known when I saw the self-steering gear."*

# CHAPTER FOURTEEN

## The Royal Western Yacht Club and *The Observer*

The calm, though, came to an end in December when McCloskey
forwarded to Blondie a list of objections received from a member of the
Slocum Society Sailing Club, objections that contrasted vividly with his
empirical observations and experience over the years:

> . . . The course announced for the Sailing Club's single-handed
> race is the worst possible one for a *Spray* model.[1] "Spray's track
> was projected in accordance with favourable winds and currents
> . . . common sense dictates no other course" . . .
>
> There appear to be two serious weaknesses in the race con-
> ditions as announced. First, permission to use auto-steering
> devices means that no boat without a good generator to furnish
> juice for same will have a chance. I've been with auto-pilots on
> sailboats enough to know that a man with a good one is scarcely
> single-handed . . .
>
> Second, the finish at City Island is ridiculous. After a trans-
> Atlantic passage no man is in physical and mental shape to race
> alone up that over-crowded, tide-beset, calm-plagued slot of
> Long Island Sound. . . . Why not Boston, or New London or
> Nantucket? City Island!

Blondie's reply of 8 March, 1958, was robust and based only on
personal knowledge and not subjective inexperience:

> I do not regard it as one of the objects of the race to lay out such
> a course that a *Spray* replica could win over! I don't think
> ancestor-worship should go this far and I think we should

---

[1]  Joshua Slocum's *Spray* was the vessel in which he sailed round the world
single-handed, with many stops, between 1895 and 1898.

remember that Slocum was a rebel and an innovator and that if we wish to emulate him we should be the same, not slavish imitators.

For hundreds of years, hundreds of very un-weatherly vessels regarded August as being the best month for sailing from England to North America by the northerly route. . . . Have we become cowards unable to stomach the idea of adverse weather?

In my experience the crews are more likely to be in the last stages of exhaustion during the first two days of the race than they are at the finish . . . The difficult part of the race will be getting clear of the English Channel. . . . Automatic steering does NOT involve a generator.

Meanwhile he had other problems, the seaworthiness of *Jester's* experimental Lapwing rig was a major concern with parts of it becoming highly stressed in hard weather, even in the Solent.

I wanted a sail that I could reef and furl and unreef again entirely from the steering position without having to crawl around the deck. Apart from the Lapwing rig I knew of only one rig that offered this possibility, the Chinese lug sail, one of the oldest rigs in the world. Joshua Slocum himself had chosen it for the *Liberdade*.[2] which he built with his own hands . . . and so read everything I could find. After absorbing all I could I made a scale drawing of the sail I wanted and sent it to my sailmaker . . .

The first serious entry direct to Blondie came in a letter from "a Dr David Lewis evidently practising in the east end of London", who said:

Some friends are daring enough to be interested and have asked me to enquire details.

A press notice was despatched with a note expressing the hope that 'his friends' materialized into starters but it was not difficult to guess that 'they' were the doctor himself.

Blondie spent most of that May, 1959, towing a 40 ton dracone from

[2] Three masted, 35ft junk-rigged canoe built by Slocum in 1887. His description of her in his book *Voyage of the Liberdade* reads: Her rig was the Chinese *sampan* style, which is, I consider, the most convenient boat rig in the world.

the River Tees to Flushing in Holland and then back again, a successful operation from which he returned well satisfied with his idea and its usefulness, but not so pleasing was a bombshell from the Slocum Society waiting for him in Hampshire:

NEW YORK MEETING OF THE SOCIETY

Commodore Pflieger was host . . . to members in the New York area . . . on Thursday May 21st. After considerable conviviality and an excellent dinner your secretary seized the opportunity of having a captive audience to discuss some matters of general interest to the Society . . . in brief the consensus was that the 1960 trans-Atlantic race might be better run in two legs; the first from England to the Azores and the second from the Azores to the New York area. A special bulletin will be issued on this.

John Pflieger was known to Blondie as the Commodore of the Slocum Society Sailing Club and as an hospitable American who would go to great lengths to entertain British yachtsmen but this circular made him furious and caused him to draft an immediate telegram to McCloskey.

Bewildered fatuous proposal route TA race via the Azores. Accumulated evidence suggests this route more difficult than northern or southern. If persisted with must seriously consider withdrawing support and organizing own race. Suspect proposal conceived by drunken armchair critics who have never sailed Atlantic and are not entries for race. If free dinner has this effect on members suggest such functions prohibited in Society rules. Kindly send their arguments forthwith. North Atlantic directory page five seven three Captain Boyd RN "I scarcely know of any group of islands more liable to sudden squalls, storms and changes of weather than the neighbourhood of these. No continuous fine weather may be expected at these islands until May or even later from the summer solstice to the autumnal equinox between which periods frequent long calms prevail or light baffling airs. The climate of Flores and Corvo is delightful but violent storms and sudden squalls are experienced in their vicinity at all seasons." Have persistent impression that this and previous fainthearted amendments originate from members who do not wish race to be held at all and will not enter if it is. Kindly have them assassinated and send bill to me. Hasler.

When he had finished he "jibbed at the expense of cabling all those words", so it was despatched airmail instead and replied to by Pflieger himself, who gave as good as he had received:

> June 19th 1959. The check point at the Azores was chosen because it was felt that most people wish to hit some warm weather as soon as practicable, also because it is imperative to stay out of the regular shipping lane. . . . I do not believe the Azores present more of a weather problem than any other place notwithstanding the North Atlantic Directory explanation from which you quote . . .

A contrite but still firm Blondie responded:

> 28th June 1959. I must apologize for the unbridled language of my message, even though it was half in fun, and I'm grateful to you for your soft answer. The truth is that I am considerably steamed up over what the Slocum Society is doing and not doing, about my trans-Atlantic Race . . . I must now ask the Society to re-examine its attitude towards the race.

This riposte crossed with another friendly letter from Mr Pflieger that showed him "actively trying to reconcile Blondie's views with the views of his Slocum Society advisers and suggesting Sheepshead Bay (at the eastern end of Coney Island) as a better finishing point than City Island". The correspondence continued with Blondie's reply:

> Oh hell! You are ruining my act with your amiable and civilized communications. I got your second letter today just after sending you a long and heated harangue and now I don't know what to say except thank you and will you please make allowances for the well-known crotchiness and self-importance of all inventors, innovators and other certifiable eccentrics . . . I've never been to Sheepshead Bay but have just found it on the Esso Cruising Guide! (my only available chart of the area) and it looks to me like a splendid finishing port – much better than City Island.

To the members of the Slocum Society Sailing Club this was, perhaps, all rather fun and academic, particularly as none were known to be entering the race – but to Blondie it was his future, indeed his life. After receiving two more letters from Pflieger describing further conflicting opinions he wrote on 11 July:

> The Society still shows no sign of stopping its vacillations and sticking to the rules of the race as published. So I now revert to the theme of my previous letter and have started to look for a new sponsor in this country. I would not of course wish this transfer to be made in anything other than a spirit of amicable agreement.

The start of the race now lay less than eleven months ahead with a number of factors yet unresolved. Although glad to have the race back in his own hands, as he thought at the time, Blondie recognized that the best he could hope for was another year's delay and thus a loss of impetus for his self-steering gear and his radical sail plan. But the Slocum Society did not go away that easily and were, for some months yet, to muddy what Blondie hoped were clearing waters.

As he shut one door another opened almost simultaneously by courtesy, once again, of David Astor, and *The Observer's* comparatively new Sports Editor, Chris Brasher. Brasher had taken up this post in 1957, twelve months after breaking the Olympic record for the 3,000 metres steeplechase at Melbourne but he was also a mountaineer and "lover of remote places" and recognized in Blondie a fellow Corinthian spirit. He also knew, through David, that Blondie would not put his name and reputation to anything that was unprofessionally conceived. He knew too, that he would have the support of his Editor if not the full understanding of his Managing Director, Tristan Jones. He wrote:

> I have always been fascinated by the race and so I made another attack on the Manager last week and got him to agree in principle to *The Observer* putting up some sort of trophy for the race. Is this idea acceptable to you and what sort of trophy should it be and for whom?

Blondie's reply was so immediate that it was written on his knee as he took the Poole train to join *Rob Roy*, David Tweed's handsome 9-tonner, for a fortnight's cruise on the north coast of Brittany. If not sponsorship and an organizing committee here, at least, was respectability endorsed by a paper and a Sports Editor of impeccable backgrounds:

How splendid of you to persuade your manager. . . . At the moment everything is in a state of flux including the course to be sailed and the sailing date.

Despite being the only possible entrant, Blondie now knew that 'his' race would take place, for the trophy gave it substance, and even if there was no yacht club to organize the start nobody could stop the entries (if they materialized) crossing the Atlantic *from* wherever they might, collectively, choose to start *to* wherever they might collectively choose to finish. It was 'on' and even his Chinese lug-sail trials, as though sensing the significance of the occasion, convinced him that it was precisely the rig for which he was seeking. A letter from Bruce Robinson, an advertising executive on Madison Avenue who was also an active member of the Slocum Society, sealed his optimism.

It seems that at a meeting of the Slocum Society in June it was decided that there should be a stop-over in the Azores. . . . I say: to hell with the commercial skippers and believe that . . . the contestants should be allowed to leave Cowes and sail any way he damn well chooses to New York. If he wants to skirt the Labrador coast it's his business – if he wishes to sail to New York via the Azores and Bermuda that too is his business. But a rule that he must go via the Azores seems to break all purposes of the freedom of the race itself.

Now I've said my piece and feel better for it. I might add that since you have been the prime mover of the race from the English end of things and since there are more entrants from the Cowes end, your rules should prevail. Yours sincerely, Bruce Robinson.

Blondie replied thanking Robinson for his whole-hearted and refreshing response and ended by saying that, while he was trying to get a London newspaper to take it on, offer prizes and set up the publicity, he still hoped that the Slocum Society would play a useful part in the finishing arrangements.

But the Slocum Society remained in fighting mood and in the September, 1959, issue of the *Spray* criticized Blondie, the only entrant:

Commodore Pflieger is knocking himself out working on the trans-Atlantic race. We hope by the next issue to have a full report. We are not entering the race which makes any comment of ours uncalled for and ungracious. Having said that we will make an uncalled for and ungracious comment: With darn few exceptions, entrants[3] want the race tailored specifically for them.

What the author meant was, there were no American, nor Slocum Society Sailing Club members entering because it was not tailored for them.

Nor had John Pflieger given up with his Society's involvement and continued to despatch useful but muddling comments, forcing Blondie to answer the latest batch on 16 September:

> I am grateful to you for trying to retain at least part of the race in its original form, but I am very much against trying to start it anywhere near as early as May 21st, for various reasons: (a) people would have to sail the qualifying course in April which is nearly as bleak over here as it is in Long Island Sound. (b) In the North Atlantic the ice limit comes furthest south in June while July is the worst month for fog (USCG Pilot charts). It really is true that in the days of sail August was regarded as the best month for sailing from England to the USA. They had hurricanes in those days too but they realized that the risk of running into the dangerous part of a hurricane is remote, whereas ice, fog and headwinds are with us always. A good boat, big or small, will survive a hurricane but not collision with ice.

Then, out of the blue, towards the end of September, the first fully-qualified and firm entrant made himself known to Blondie. The 'friends' that David Lewis had described as being 'interested' turned out, as predicted, to be the doctor himself:

> I eventually wandered off to Norway in *Cardinal Vertue*[4] without having received the rules for the qualifying event. I have just heard that they have accepted Burnham-on-Crouch to Stavanger and back single-handed as a qualifying sail so with trepidation I now find myself entered on this thing next year.

---

[3] There was only one – and the race had been his idea! Blondie had every intention of entering for the same reason he gave to Lord Mountbatten about leading the raid of Bordeaux.

[4] A five-ton cutter of the same overall dimensions as *Jester* but heavier and carrying more sail.

On 24 September, 1959, Blondie lunched with Chris Brasher and the News Editor of *The Observer*, Michael Davie. The newspaper now felt that it might be able to sponsor the race, providing the actual control could be placed in the hands of a responsible yacht club as the newspaper was "not technically equipped to do so itself". In order to justify the financial aspects the paper would need access to exclusive reports from each entrant while the race was in progress: a request that raised two problems – how to persuade all entrants, especially those from abroad, to sign their exclusive rights to *The Observer* and how to get radio messages back from small boats in mid-Atlantic – especially, as Blondie was obliged to point out, with boats, including his, not likely to possess any way of generating electricity.

But these were small problems of detail that could be addressed over the coming months; the real delight was that this was progress which would encourage the right yacht club to work in association with *The Observer*.

In the meantime Blondie met his only fellow competitor for the first time when they found that they agreed on almost everything, even a compromise start date of 11 June, which they relayed to Pflieger. Blondie was much taken by the doctor and found him to be

> A small, muscular fellow with a passion for boats, hard exercise and adventure and a very engaging way of protesting that he is nothing but an ignorant fumbler living in a permanent state of terror. Nothing could have been further from the truth. He seemed to me to be the sort of man we wanted. . . . What we had on our hands was somebody who was going to sail that damned race if it killed him. From this time on, I knew that the race was really going to happen.

By good fortune, that year's October issue of *Yachting Monthly* contained a description and photograph of the 25 ft yacht *Eira* in which Valentine Howells had just sailed single-handed from Cork to Corunna in 5½ days and back to South Wales in 7½ days. Two aspects particularly caught Blondie's eye: the yacht was a Scandinavian 'Folkboat' which meant she was more or less a sister ship of *Jester* and she had been fitted with a wind-vane self-steering gear which "worked perfectly". Blondie wrote to Mr Howells at once:

> Congratulations! Is there any hope that you will enter for the single-handed trans-Atlantic race?

At about this time Hugh Somerville, the editor of *The Yachtsman*, passed on a letter from "a Mr Francis Chichester" enquiring about a race which had come to his notice two years before through Blondie's statement pinned to the Royal Ocean Racing Club's notice board.[5] Chichester had written:

> May I ask you if you have any news of the proposed solo race to New York in 1960? This seems to me a most sporting event but when first proposed there were two qualifying requirements which seemed unreasonable.
>
> Each entrant to qualify for the race must first sail single-handed to Ireland and back from Plymouth. . . . It would be easier and less hazardous to sail to New York. . . . The second condition is that an auxiliary engine must be removed before the start of the race. This seems not only an unnecessary expense but the elimination of a possible aid to safety.

Blondie, who had not met Chichester, but knew "vaguely of him as a map and navigation specialist" was unimpressed and told Somerville why:

> Publish Chichester's letter if you like but it sounds half-witted to me. If he had read the rules which were published in 1957 he would know that an owner may propose to sail any qualifying course he likes in any part of the world provided that it offers a real test of the ability of the man and his boat. Engines may be carried but will be sealed. Any one who wants to use one "as a possible aid to safety" may therefore do so and give up the race.

On 15 October Blondie received a reply from Valentine Howells which thrilled him for he now had three entries and that really did mean a race and if the worst came to the worst they would start themselves and let the publicity look after itself, which, given the nature of the event and the ghoulish inquisitiveness of the media, it inevitably would. Val Howells' letter included a photograph of "yours truly" who, as Blondie wrote in his diaries, "appeared to be a gigantic fellow with a large black beard". On the same day Francis Chichester also wrote with more good news:

[5] Where, according to Blondie, the secretary was kept occupied rubbing out the "proliferation of unsolicited, usually adverse, comments".

"A fourth!" Blondie commented, but in the same mail was another letter from Pflieger which was to precipitate a final severance from the Slocum Society:

> At our last meeting . . . the rules were very much altered. . . . This will be more of a contest than a race and anything goes including the use of an engine. . . . Moreover departure time will be at the convenience of the participant any time during 1960 and arrival limited to that year.

For the calm-mannered Blondie this was the last straw. He received the amended Slocum Society rules but "hardly bothered to read them as he felt that nobody was interested in taking part in entering a cruising competition" so, with support from all the probable entrants, he decided to run the race himself and if he could find a supporting yacht club so much the better. On 21 November he wrote to Chris Brasher lamenting the manner in which 'his' race had nearly been hijacked into a lukewarm contest with the use of an engine almost mandatory!

Francis Chichester, the fourth declared entrant, now took a positive role in the race organization; this was not totally altruistic for he was known to be mildly jealous of Blondie's dream (he also expressed a latent desire "to be more like Blondie Hasler")[6] and wished to be part of it. Blondie, generous in his gratitude, wrote later:

> He took a great deal off my shoulders when he volunteered to handle all the secretarial work from his office in London which was close alongside the RORC.

The founding of the race has often been ascribed to Francis Chichester and, while he did help Blondie immensely, he played no part in the original idea nor the framing of the rules.

With the race approaching an even keel Blondie wrote to David Astor expressing his loyalty and a barely-disguised request for more substantial support than the trophy – grateful though he certainly was for this token of faith in the project – as rumours were rife that another, unnamed, sponsor was preparing to put up a "massive prize". Although embarrassed at this apparently "churlish" response to *The Observer's* already generous offer of a trophy, he was worried that, by default, the whole race could become the property of another. As he put it:

---

[6]  Conversation between the author and Mike Richey, spring 1996.

> I know that you will understand it is my sincere, personal hope
> that the name at the masthead may indeed prove to be *The
> Observer's* and not *Threadgold's Thorogrip Garterette's*.

David's view was that if a better offer of support came from elsewhere
he would not be put out, but, as it turned out, there were no further bids
in the pipeline and on 6 December *The Observer* agreed to accept the
responsibility as backers of the race and not just the donators of a trophy.
It was the start of a most harmonious relationship that continued many
years and which was to encompass yet more Hasler ideas.

There was still no organizing yacht club and, with such a sponsor as
*The Observer* Blondie felt that he owed it to them to find one, whereas
had there been no sponsor he and his fellow competitors would simply
have sailed west from a mutually agreed port. He now approached the
Royal Yachting Association and the Royal Ocean Racing Club for
advice. The RYA could offer little help, then,[7] while the RORC
reminded Blondie that they used the Royal Western Yacht
Club's premises in Plymouth to host the end of their Fastnet races and
knew them to be a forward-thinking club that might provide the professional backing he sought. As a start from Plymouth would cut the
difficult, initial down-channel passage considerably, it was an attractive
proposition which Blondie took up with relish.

Chichester was invited to write direct to the yacht club's secretary, Mr
George Everitt, while Blondie wrote for 'agreement in principle' to
the Vice-Commodore, Lord Morley. By tradition, the Royal
Western Yacht Club did not have a 'working' Commodore (then Sir
Winston Churchill) nor, in practice, a 'working' Vice-Commodore,[8] the
day-to-day business being conducted by the Rear-Commodore,
Lieutenant-Colonel Jack Odling-Smee to whom Lord Morley forwarded
Blondie's request.

Once the letters to the RWYC had been received, Chris Brasher
convened a meeting in Plymouth before taking with him by train to the
West Country, Blondie, Francis and *The Observer's* Promotions
Manager, Lindley Abbatt. During this 'vital' journey all agreed that they
were about to face the last opportunity they had to give the race the
backing it needed: all accepted that if the Royal Western could not

---

[7] Later, when the race came under attack from the "nannies" the RYA's
support was to be invaluable. See Appendix Two.
[8] All posts are now held by "working" flag officers.

handle the race then it would revert to "nothing more than a personal challenge between one or two people".[9]

They need not have fretted, for the RWYC and, more than any other individual, Jack Odling-Smee, took to the idea as a dolphin to the ocean. Blondie's proposals could not have fallen on more receptive shoulders and, in Odling-Smee, he found a man of immense strength of character, foresight and courage in the face of what many would come to regard with increasing tempo as "a crazy hazard that would produce a public outcry if yachts disappeared sending the gallant sons of Old England to their watery deaths".[10] Blondie and Jack shared a similar outlook on life and the "nannies of the cotton wool society" that try to dominate it. David Astor was delighted:

> In Jack Odling-Smee, Blondie found the perfect ally; the same dislike of rules – a very kindred spirit.

But, like them or not, there had to be some 'ground rules' and as soon as these were established and the Royal Western had agreed that *The Observer*-sponsored single-handed trans-Atlantic race was a worthwhile project to support, a sub-committee was formed of Lieutenant-Colonel Jack Odling-Smee, Commander Robin Gardiner, Commander Philip Yonge (then the Queen's Harbour Master for Plymouth), Dr Neil Beaton and Mr Cecil Roberts, all highly successful, but conventional, ocean-going yacht skippers and a team most likely to ensure smooth running up to the start: after that it would be up to nature, the competitors and their yachts to see the enterprise through safely.

*The Chronicles of the Royal Western Yacht Club*[11] record some of these events:

> After meetings with Hasler, Chichester and *The Observer* the Rules and general conditions for the single-handed trans-Atlantic race were agreed. *The Observer* gave up their exclusive rights for publicity and there were to be no money prizes. In the USA the Slocum Society and Bruce Robinson made the arrangements for the finish.

[9] Letter to the author from Chris Brasher dated 13 December, 1996.
[10] Paraphrased from Chichester's book, *Alone Across the Atlantic*. George Allen and Unwin Ltd, 1961.
[11] Compiled by the late Captain T.W.B. Shaw, DSC, Royal Navy and produced privately for members in 1984. Subsequently Shaw was to be the sailing secretary responsible for the race.

There were still many details to be sorted out: *The Observer* had to protect itself commercially from bad publicity if things were to go wrong, the Royal Western Yacht Club needed to establish the safety rules, the starting procedures and, in conjunction with the sponsor, the prizes, and the competitors needed to prepare for the gruelling crossing of three thousand miles of notorious waters. To tackle their own problem *The Observer* decided not to sponsor the race directly but instead to form a sponsoring committee of national names. This decision, however, met with cynicism from Blondie who found it:

> Hard to visualize Prince Philip, Mountbatten, Sir John Hunt, the Bishop of Norwich or even Lancelot Fleming lending their names to negotiations of publishing rights.[12]

The committee was never formed and the newspaper reverted, with its fingers crossed, to the role of sponsor.

By now everything was as in place as it could be: there were enough entries to make a race of it; a sponsor had put up a trophy and was accepting the responsibility and all the risks that that implied; the Slocum Society had dropped any pretence of influence but had agreed to organize the finish at Sheepshead Bay, New York;[13] a prestigious yacht club had taken over the secretarial duties, organizing and starting procedures; Bruce Robinson had arranged for radio transmitters to be loaned[14] and the race even had a name, *The Observer* single-handed trans-Atlantic race or, eventually, OSTAR for short.[15]

[12] Before his views prevailed, Blondie asked Mike Richey to sit on the committee as they "wanted one or two practical seaman as well". Letter to Richey dated 21 January 1960.

[13] From a letter to the author from Chris Brasher dated 13 December, 1996: "In the event I and other members of the British Press had to take things in hand in New York rather than leave it in the hands of what we considered to be 'old dodderers'."

[14] Mr E.C.B. Lee, then secretary of the Naval Lifesaving Committee recalls in a letter to the author dated 22 August, 1996, that the RWYC decided that all yachts should have pyrotechnics on board. He supplied them just before the start and states: "When Blondie returned from America he called at my office in Bath and returned the flares. I had not asked for them back and none of the others returned theirs".

[15] There is a little doubt over when it was actually first named OSTAR. *The Observer's* first proposal on 6 February was The Atlantic Single-handed Yacht Race. At that time the paper was anxious not to have its name directly linked to the race for fear of ridicule if it was a disaster. Hence the proposed forming of the Sponsoring Committee.

No account of these final days would be complete without mention of the "half-crown bet"[16] which Chichester mentions in his books *Alone Across the Atlantic* and *The Lonely Sea and the Sky*.[17] His own version has it that while the Royal Western Yacht Club were deciding whether or not to be involved he offered Blondie a half-crown to race him across regardless, thus implying that he instigated the whole thing by making this bet. He makes no mention of the other competitors already entered nor the fact that Blondie, Lewis and Howells had, before Chichester's entry, decided they would sail to America whether officially sent on their way or not. In truth all four competitors agreed to put in a half-crown and race for the purse. This eventually spawned the delightfully symbolic Half-Crown Club to which every finisher is entitled to membership.

Let an edited version of the Royal Western Yacht Club's own *Chronicles* tell the final pre-race story:

> Competitors and Bruce Robinson, (representing the Slocum Society) were dined in the club on 9th June and the race started at 1000 hrs on the 11th from the RSWYC line. Only four started.[18] *Jester* with Blondie Hasler, *Cardinal Vertue* with David Lewis, *Eira* with Val Howells, *Gipsy Moth III* with Francis Chichester. *Cap Horn* with Jean Lacombe started three days late, the trimaran *Nimble* with Arthur Piver did not start as Piver was recalled to the USA on business, *Blue Haze* with R.M. Ellison was not ready and *Sayonara* with W. Karminski was damaged in transit.

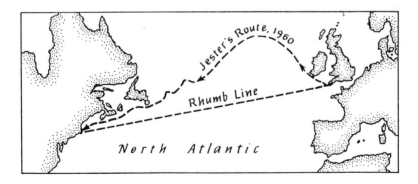

---

[16] Two shillings and sixpence or, today, 12½ pennies.
[17] George Allen and Unwin, 1961, and Hodder and Stoughton, 1964, respectively.
[18] Here, in the order in which they entered.

# CHAPTER FIFTEEN

## *Jester* and Atlantic

On Sunday 6 January, 1957, Blondie had written an article for *The Observer* headed "Building a Boat" and prefaced his piece with this rhyme:

> I dared to think – I dared to say –
> That I could build a boat.
> And many others thought the same,
> But questioned – would it float?

The sailing world knew that *Jester* floated, but could she race the Atlantic competitively? By the very nature of the event there were no witnesses to Blondie's part in the race: no anecdotes, no third hand gossip of what happened between Plymouth Sound and Sheepshead Bay. What does exist, though, is his diary, or 'social' log, and with this to hand it would be wrong to tell of the race other than through his own words. He kept a separate navigational log, of course, but to quote from that might be muddling. On 10 June, 1960, the day before the start, he wrote:

> Worrying, and stowing and shuffling mountains of equipment half of which has been thrust and stuffed at me during the previous day: a wheelbarrow full of unidentifiable emergency boxes of survival rations: a joke survival ration pack of a bottle of gin and a miniature bottle of Vermouth presented by a Plymouth gin maker. I nearly threw that one back on the wall before I realized what was in it: *Jester* was getting lower and lower in the water till she felt like an iceberg and hardly moved under me when I walked on her.

Dawn on the morning of the start was recorded as

> wild and windswept, promising a hard beat to windward and sea-sickness.

Later in the day he continued:

> Bang! We're away. Another load lifted – nothing to do but sail the course now – if that flaming cinema photographer would take his launch out of my daylight. The launch goes full astern neatly. I remember that Plymouth was breeding good seamen long before Drake, and these boats are being handled by Plymouth seamen and not by the photographers hanging over them like grapes out of a fruit-basket.
>
> I mustn't look at my friends escorting me silently at a discreet distance in their yachts and launches as I weep rather easily and might hit the Melampus buoy if I start blubbing now . . . but I do wish they would stop being so damned kind to me just for five minutes then perhaps I shouldn't have this trouble – let me see, where did I stow Nancy's[1] eggs, and all those strawberries: for heaven's sake how am I ever going to eat them all, if I'm seasick!
>
> Oh stop fussing! We're getting a clearer wind now and *Jester* lies down a little and starts throwing seawater over herself – splashes of it come in through the side hatches because I haven't finished the lashing-down arrangements. It will flush out the bilges even if it doesn't do the carrots much good on the way in.

Blondie's plan was simple:[2]

> The shortest sailing route is the northern route or great circle route which loops up from Land's End to 51°N; 25°W, then down close to Cape Race, Newfoundland, and so down to New York from the east-north-east. This route measures about 3,000 miles but passes through a large area, covering the Grand Banks, in which there is certain to be a lot of fog and which may well in July still harbour a good many icebergs.
>
> My own reading on the subject, much of it from books written in the great days of sail, suggested that a high northern route –

---

[1]  Nancy Odling-Smee, Jack's effervescent wife.
[2]  Taken from various drafts in the Hasler papers.

much higher than the great circle – tended to give fewer gales, a smaller proportion of headwinds and a less adverse current. Sailing ships from Scotland usually arrived in Boston or New York in faster time than ships from the English Channel and it was quite common for a ship leaving the Thames to go north about through the Pentland Firth if the wind was westerly. It may, I hope, be true that *Jester* is inherently better to windward than a square rigger.

He therefore planned a course that led him close past the south-west corner of Ireland – the Fastnet Rock and Mizen Head – before curving up as far as 55°N at 30°W but, in the event, allowed himself to be pushed about 300 miles even further north.
Throughout the following weeks of this northerly parabola *Jester's* log reads at various stages:

Eighty days worth of food and water for one gentleman in reduced circumstances – she feels as heavy as lead and I will take a long time to eat her up to a reasonable waterline again. . . . I look at the sail, my delicious Chinese lug-rig that I tried out for the first time half-scale on a pram dinghy nine months ago and have been in love with ever since. Is it really capable of crossing the Atlantic? I've never even crossed the Channel with it: never had it out in open water: never weathered a gale: whatever happened to all those exhausting trials that used to be bracketed over a period of several months – my master programme? I know the answer because it's the old answer; I took so long to design, brood over, organize, make and fiddle with it there wasn't any time left to try it out. But this doesn't worry me, work is more fun if you have a gamble on your guesses: I'm not staking anything I can't afford to lose . . .[3]
Those long sail battens are bending like fishing rods already; I expect they are too thin and will break – so what! There's a complete spare set in the fo'cs'le and as for spare timber: "What on earth's all that wood and stuff for?" said the reporter that

[3] Of all the competitors he in particular had not given himself time to complete a qualifying cruise, not, in the end, required by his own committee. This also highlights a problem that he recognized as a life-long failing in disguise – too much preparation.

peered down my fore-hatch at Plymouth. He saw only a small part of it . . . Sail damage? I am carrying a spare terylene main-sail – never yet set – and a lot of repair gear. Rope? Over one hundred percent spare of everything and I'm damned if that famous manufacturer didn't give it to me for nothing – some of these firms are nearly as bad as my friends!

That un-stayed mast that seems to wring sharp cries of alarm from seasoned boatmen. I think it is the strongest thing in the ship, much stronger than I need but if that guess fails me and the whole rhubarb collapses over the side I rub my hands in odious self-congratulation and emerge from the fo'cs'le with two long spars already fitted up as a bipod jury mast and the sweetest little jury sail you ever saw. No, I don't think I can win the race with it but the whole episode would be technically satisfying . . .

One by one our escorts have dropped away and now we are passing the Eddystone and there are none left – just the four of us strung out in long procession and I'm at the back of it.

Above everything I want this race to be a success; to become a regular and recognized event. I believe that the design of small sea-going sailing boats is still in its infancy. This is the best way of encouraging it to grow up. I know that there are many yachtsmen who are set against the whole idea and I can under-stand their point of view and I think of them back there waiting to be proved right: they can go on waiting while I look up at my own un-stayed mast twitching away like a turning fork as she pitches into the Channel sea. Oh well! I suppose this is the quickest way to learn . . .

I did feel a little squeamish but I have not yet been sick: no sea-sick pills; no laxative pills; no other damned pills – no point in owning a beautiful self-compensating machine if you are going to start throwing spanners into the control system. All it wants from me is no food until it's hungry, no drink until it's thirsty and above all I think it wants me to lie down and stop fussing – peering anxiously around when there is absolutely nothing to see and only slightly more than nothing to worry about – so I lie down with a rather faint smile . . .

The last view of Europe, the Bull Rock off the south-west coast of Ireland, with the lighthouse on its top still lost in the fog. It is an old friend as I was here eleven years ago in *Petula* with an Irish ornithologist . . .

We are now at 56°N, in mid-Atlantic, in a very boring gale that has been blowing for three days and shows no sign of stopping. If I were cruising I should be comfortably hove-to. As things are I am driving the poor little thing into a filthy, breaking sea with four reefs down. I suppose it is natural under these circumstances for me to talk to her and encourage her but I notice I am now addressing her as "darling" which is a habit I may have to eradicate when I start sailing with a crew again. I have turned the hood so that its open side faces forward and I stand with a full belly and a glass of wine in my hand revelling in the way she goes. This is what I came for . . .

The nearest land, Greenland, two hundred and eighty miles away, and it feels like it. I get out my banjo-ukelele and improvise a song entitled "Meet me tonight in Greenland". This does a great deal for me, exercises the voice without making me appear (at any rate to myself) to be insane; satisfies the need for music and makes me giggle at my own jokes, which are, for the most part, indescribably weak . . .

Sea birds, the only living thing I have to look at, and I watch them for hours. Few species are truly oceanic and once I get fifty miles offshore there are just fulmars, petrels, shearwaters and the occasional skua. Fulmars are so pretty with their soft, dark eyes, that I regard them all as girls. Gannets, left behind long ago on the Irish coast but expected to re-appear on the Grand Banks, look like minor civil servants with their spectacles jammed firmly on their noses. If I were a gentleman gannet I should make love to a fulmar and there would be hell to pay in the Gannet Conservative Association . . .

For the first four weeks I've felt as if I wanted to be quite cut off from the world while I get on with the job. Now I gradually begin to look towards my return and I sit down at a heavily sloping table to write a letter. *Jester* is pitching and my handwriting is wildly erratic she will almost certainly deduce that I am round the bend.

A large part of the thinking behind *Jester's* design was to give him time to enjoy life without having permanently to be changing into oilskins to work on the upper deck: his guiding maxim had always been that a relaxed and rested crew is a safe and efficient crew. Writing letters and his 'social' diary were part of that relaxation and one such gives a personal insight into his way of life alone at sea:

My dear Dodie . . .[4] all this to both of you of course and I think of you often when I am drinking your delicious wine. Opened the first bottle of Côte du Rhône 1955 on the 29th to celebrate having successfully spoken a charming steamer *The Southern Prince* on a foggy day when the nearest land was Greenland only 300 miles away, and it felt like it. The wine did noble work. . . . I have learnt an awful lot about Chinese rigs and the self-steering gear, which have worked surprising well. . . . I am now only 80 miles from Cape Race, Newfoundland and have just passed close north of the Virgin rocks – or over them. These rocks are the highest part of the Grand Banks with a least depth of three fathoms so need not be avoided by five tonners unless the weather is bad.

I am quite unwashed and have a red beard speckled with what is known in America as 'banker's grey'. You buy it in a bottle to make yourself look like a man of distinction! But mine is natural and quite undistinguished.

His log continued:

I feel absolutely fresh and only faintly unwilling to plunge back into civilization. My experimental boat has done better than I would have dared to have hoped. My head is full of wonderful bits of design for my next boat, for *Jester* is only a beginning – a timid step forwards in a new direction. Two broken sail battens on the way and that seems to be about all the damage. I've never had to go on deck in an emergency or in bad weather. The wind vane steering gear has become a part of me – something I shall never again sail without even if it is only from the Hamble to Beaulieu for the weekend.

The approaches to New York have now accepted all the worn, torn, ancient, friendly, warm clothes that I have been wearing in the high latitudes and I felt an absurd little pang as they went over the side. There's half a loaf of the world's best bread left in the food locker. I baked it myself yesterday starting with wheat-grain and grinding it in a coffee grinder, making it ferment with sea water (which happens to have just the right amount of salt) and dried yeast and baking it in the bottom half of a pressure

[4] Dodie Wallis, an old friend whose daughter, Belinda Martin, would be a godmother to Dinah Hasler.

cooker with a biscuit tin lid covering the top. There were three of Nancy's eggs left this morning and one of them for the first time was bad, the other two were delicious . . .

Now I can see the Ambrose light ahead and *Jester* sees it too and picks up half a knot. I've washed, shaved and put on clean clothes. If I stopped and think about it I would get that uneasy feeling that everything is too perfect to last. As things are I sit down and write in the log, "Light vessel fine on the port bow – distant one mile", I then light the stove to make a cup of Elizabeth's Lapsang Souchong – there happens to be one very small piece of lemon left!

Blondie arrived in Sheepshead Bay after 48 days, 12 hours and 2 minutes, second only to Chichester (40.12.30) in the much larger *Gipsy Moth III*; but the winner had paid the penalty of near exhaustion by driving his boat down the rhumb line for forty days with numerous sail changes and reefs, all of which required long hours soaked on a sloping and slippery deck. There was no doubt in the minds of those who saw the competitors arrive that Blondie had won in terms of effort expended and technical development – the prime aims of the race. Next behind Blondie was David Lewis after fifty-six days along the great circle route, followed by Val Howells in sixty-three days, then Jean Lacombe in seventy-four days, both of whom had followed southerly routes.

David Lewis had had an interesting race for he lost his mast shortly after the start but thanks to fine work by Mashfords (renowned boatbuilders at Cremyll) he was able to restart after only a two-day delay with a new one. As Blondie was to comment, "Lewis may well have been the only skipper ever to appear in an ocean racing prize list having been dismasted three thousand miles short of the finishing line".

To all went the accolade of having successfully pioneered a form of ocean racing that was to increase in popularity more than a thousand-fold. Without their adventurous and courageous spirit this most exacting, exhilarating and pure of sports might have been still-born at the outset, or, at best, been delayed for years until a sceptical press and yachting public (and there were plenty of both on either side of the Atlantic) had been more slowly weaned to such contests. Blondie took no portion of the praise, believing that if it had not been for the other competitors taking up his challenge he would have gone down in history as just another single-handed eccentric sailing for the new world.

The race had been a success with no casualties or serious damage for which much praise must be laid at the doors of *The Observer* and the Royal Western Yacht Club and, respectively, Chris Brasher and Jack Odling-Smee. Although it was the competitors who undertook the ordeal these two august bodies took considerable commercial, financial and moral risks in playing their various parts. Although the race would have occurred without them, its reputation as an international event that should now be taken seriously was due to their calm, professional approach and guidance. Benchmarks that remain still.

Blondie was quick to praise Chichester: others, though, believed that his own performance in such a small boat and without at any time becoming exhausted, itself a danger every bit as destructive as bad weather, was the greater achievement. He ended one article on the race with these words:

> I cannot close without paying tribute to Francis Chichester's superb performance in winning the race in a 38 foot conventional ocean-racer that might well have proved too much of a handful for a younger and more heavily built man.

But it required a third party, a non-competitor, to sum up the race and this was left to Chris Brasher, the man who had had so much to do with getting the thing under way:

> To the second man in any race goes little glory. But to Blondie Hasler who passed the Ambrose Lightship off New York . . . to become the second man to finish in the single-handed trans-Atlantic race, will go immense satisfaction. To a man who has had his share of glory during the war this is a greater reward. . . .
> If this race had been a race run on handicap lines (Hasler himself insisted that there should be no handicaps because of the impossibility of rating new and unconventional designs) he would undoubtedly have won it . . .
> But he also came to prove his theories which, as he sat and talked cheerfully, happily and quietly as *Jester* rode to the wash of passing liners in New York harbour last night seemed to be finally and completely proved. In ten, maybe twenty years – for yachtsman are a conservative breed – the present idea of what a yacht should look like will be outmoded and the crowded rivers and new marinas will be filled with '*Jesters*'. And Blondie Hasler

will have proved that it is possible to take the chores out of sailing.

The marinas did not fill up with *Jesters* (although there was a marked increase in the number of 'junk' rigs that did appear and similarly-sized vessels would now attempt long ocean voyages) but they did fill up with self-steering gears to take much of the tedium out of sailing short-handed, not, as Blondie was always at pains to point out, to allow more time below but more time to attend to the welfare and safety of the vessel as well as keeping a proper lookout.

But the success of this first (but not, as it would turn out, the most controversial) race can also be measured by the fact that it remains the only one to date with a one hundred percent success rate: five yachts crossed the starting line and five finished. Never again would such a statistic be recorded, yet it is interesting to note that four out of the original five entries would now be banned for being shorter than the minimum length many in the 1990s feel is sensible! This view has yet to prevail but it surely exists.

The moment his race had finished Blondie was thinking of the future and used the return journey to marshal his thoughts. He sailed from Sheepshead Bay at 1900 on 24 August to make slow time into the middle of the Gulf Stream, the 'alleged' axis of which he reached in 38° 21"N; 66° 57"W during the evening of 30 August, six days out at a daily average of only 63 nautical miles. This was followed by a fast three weeks along the great circle route towards the western approaches until 270 miles from the Bishop Rock by when he was averaging 95 miles per day with a best day's run of a remarkable (for her waterline length) 145 miles.

The wind now turned into the east to slow his average to 86 miles per day over the 3225 miles compared with the outward journey of 71 miles, an elapsed time 37 days and 9 hours to Plymouth. He passed the Needles at 0400 on 2 October.

Now it was all over the 'opposition' felt they could give tongue to their reservations, although without any disasters their guns were well spiked. But there were public comments and one that has dogged the sport ever since is that of keeping a safe lookout at sea when single-handed.[5] A fundamental of sailing thus, Blondie argued, is the ability to sleep when safe to do so and, although written some time after this first race, it is useful to read his views:

[5]  See Appendix Six.

I have made some long single-handed passages in small boats and have deliberately developed the habit of catnapping by which I mean sleeping or dozing very frequently and for very short periods at a time. We sometimes read of single-handed voyagers with efficient self-steering gears who take a pride in working a 'shore routine' when at sea putting on their pyjamas and going to bed. . . . Such a routine is obviously . . . un-seamanlike and inefficient even in mid-ocean. . . . In my opinion a single-hander should aim at never sleeping for more than half an hour at a time, usually much less. Given adequate self-steering, the art of single-handing is the art of catnapping. . . . A useful piece of single-hander's equipment is a clockwork kitchen timer that can be set to ring its bell after any selected number of minutes . . . (this) removes the worry about not waking up and thereby induces relaxed sleep. I commonly set mine for a maximum of 30 minutes when offshore . . . but in ice and fog or shipping lanes it sometimes gets set for as little as two minutes. Two priceless minutes in which your brain switches off and re-charges itself in a way that may not yet be properly understood. . . . Just occasionally, such as when negotiating ice and fog simul-taneously, even two minutes . . . may be too risky. In that case I try to make myself fairly comfortable on watch with warm clothes, a cushion and a flask of coffee – but not any food and for God's sake not any alcohol. Booze is for celebrating the easy times not for coping with problems. False courage is dangerous and the sense of having a charmed life has often been the prelude to losing it.

When stuck on watch in this way I cultivate the five-second catnap. The watchkeeper's position will not be suitable for real sleep so when he nods off he will wake up with a start but not, I hope, with any sense of guilt. Each 'start' activates his brain and his conscience into having a good look around. Each five-second catnap puts a small charge back into his battery and after a few hours of it the catnaps themselves may become unnecessary. . . . I have arrived back in the English Channel from the United States and . . . seemed to have stored up so much reserve energy that I needed no sleep at all for the last 24 hours and was able to enjoy every moment of sailing close past all my old familiar headlands.[6]

---

[6]   Draft article among Hasler papers.

Perhaps the last words on this first race should go to Commander Lloyd Foster, once Secretary, then Commodore of the Royal Western Yacht Club and author of *OSTAR*:[7]

> I can see no way in which the (single-handed trans-Atlantic race) could have remained as it started, a nice gentlemanly, amateur affair. Nor do I believe it would have been in anyone's interest that it should . . .
>
> The first race was the only one in which there were no multi-hulled yachts. No one knew where anyone was during the first race although each yacht had been fitted with a radio trans-mitter. Blondie Hasler always hated radios in yachts and, after the first race . . . he said: "This race amply confirmed my previous views on wireless transmitters! Please don't ever do anything to make these damn things compulsory!" . . . one of the reasons Blondie was against yachts having radios was that he feared that if they got into difficulties they would send out distress signals and cause a lot of trouble! He said; "It would be more seemly for the entrant to drown like a gentleman." . . . No race organizer today could even think of denying the competitors the wherewithal to summon help, although there is an argument that yachts would be more seaworthy if they were unable to do so.

The race committee always valued Blondie's opinions: on the question of multi-hulls in the next race he replied in August 1963:

> I would agree with anyone who said that multi-hull yachts have not yet proved that they can be driven to windward across the North Atlantic whether single-handed or not. Nevertheless, the lesson of history is that boats which are considered un-seaworthy by the 'expert' of today will be proved seaworthy, or will be developed into something seaworthy tomorrow. Conversely many craft thought to be seaworthy in the past would, rightly, be thought unseaworthy today.

Multi-hulls were allowed to enter for the next race in 1964, but the RWYC reserved the right to refuse any yacht they thought unsuitable.

---

[7] The standard reference work on the race. Published in 1989 by Haynes Publishing Group.

Writing in the January, 1964, issue of *Yachts and Yachting*, prior to that race, Blondie said:

> All who are interested in the development of new types of sailing yacht will welcome the decision of the RWYC to accept multi-hulled craft as entrants in the (next single-handed trans-Atlantic race). I now hope that one or two modern cruising catamarans and trimarans will accept the challenge if only in order to silence those critics who believe that such craft are incapable of making an efficient passage to windward across the North Atlantic.

Two catamarans and one trimaran did take up the 'offer' and all would finish safely, although not among the leaders. Much to Blondie's delight the first multi-hull into Newport, Rhode Island, was to be a catamaran sailed by David Lewis.

# CHAPTER SIXTEEN

## Miss Fisher and *Dum Dum*

During the uneventful west-east journey and with his ideas proven 'in action' Blondie was able to analyse the results for the future:

> September 1960: Blowing back from New York . . . I am thinking about a new boat. *Jester* was designed for cruising not racing and although her Chinese rig is incomparable for safety and east of handling it will not go to windward really well and her hull is too short to develop a high maximum speed. If I am going to enter for these races I need a much longer boat with a Bermudian rig and I shall just have to swallow the extra work and discomfort.
>
> I love outlandish experiments and any new boat will have to be as unlike a normal boat as I dare make it. Being different just for the sake of being different is a good experimental philosophy and cussedness rather than necessity is the true mother of invention. So I start sketching a very long, thin hull with rectangular sections and twin ballasted keels.

Back on dry land he resumed his periodical 'appreciations' in the thin blue-blacked, loose-leafed book kept for the purpose and in December was able to sum up the year:

> A good year. Single-handed trans-Atlantic race has boosted my reputation. Not certain about putting *Jester* in the Boat Show is worth the effort and time but she is there. Design and consultancy work is increasing – entirely in Chinese rigs and vane-gears so far. Have resolve to resume drawing with felt pen quarto size for framing. Keep saying that an artist is what I want to be. The £500 ocean racer grows in my mind but am not sure how to finance her.

C.S.B.P. C getting serious.
Jura very profitable last spring – still going on.

From which it is easy to deduce that *plus ça change, plus c'est la même chose* would be an accurate description of Blondie's life on his return. He now wanted to draw for a living; he decided to race again and give up cruising; he needed to be involved with Dracone for an income; he had to continue inventing for peace of mind; he had made some money through his Jura surveys with a promise of more to come[1] and the same four girl-friends continued to be juggled in order of preference for marriage – although there is still no evidence to suggest that they knew this!

With mixed feelings Blondie had allowed *Jester* to appear in the pool at the 1961 London International Boat Show for his main concern, made only half in jest, was that she would sink in front of thousands of spectators, and, while she and her rig attracted the crowds it was the steering-gear that provoked the majority interest for serious yachtsmen. Although fitted with a trim-tab system which was simple, efficient and cheap it could only be set on certain rudders and, if damaged, was difficult to repair in mid-ocean, and that usually requiring a dive over the side. Ideas for harnessing the waterflow past the stern to power the rudder via the tiller had been forming in Blondie's mind but they were not yet ready for display.

Money remained at the heart of his problems, so to finance his immediate future *Jester* was "put up for sail (sic) in April, 1961, available July" – but in reality she was still needed as a trials horse and, with no potential purchasers, he kept her for the first "very promising" practical experiments of the "bottom end of the new steering gear", the servo-blade itself.[2]

By chance Blondie met John Lewis at the Boat Show who had already designed two 10-rater sailing models with twin keels both of which were fast in hard weather but rather dead in light airs. Only interested in heavy weather for his £500 ocean racer he took a closer look and, believing that here might be the germ of an idea, pooled his ideas with John and brought in Ian Major. After much backing and filling they built three seven-foot sailing models carrying identical rigs: a round-bilged single-keeler, a round-bilged twin-keeler and a rectangular-sectioned twin-keeler that Blondie named *Dum Dum*.

*Jester*, being a drain on his time and money had to go again, and so in

---

[1.] See Appendix One.
[2.] See Appendix Four for working drawings of both types.

May was, at last, painted prior to being advertised for the second time,[3] but again, with no takers, she was taken off the market and lent instead to Susanna Fisher and May McGuire for a channel cruise.

There was, though, another adventure waiting in the wings of his mind, and the second single-handed trans-Atlantic race planned for 1964 was also getting closer.

> 6 June 1961. Have just cancelled advert in *Yachting Monthly* (selling *Jester*) because last week hatched scheme for Loch Ness Patrol and hope to get sponsored and to take part . . . I have too many projects but feel I have to cast my net wide as so few of them take. Am so broke that must potboil for a bit. C project recovering slightly from dangerous rivalry of R.T.

In July Blondie was asked to be godfather to David and Bridget Astor's daughter Nancy which pleased him immensely while in August an even more important source of satisfaction occurred on the 30th with the arrival, as 'assistant', of Susanna Fisher's twenty-year-old sister, Bridget. Susanna had been asked if she would help with an expedition to Loch Ness due to start with a preliminary 'recce' in September, but, happy with her job at the National Maritime Museum, had declined with the words, "No, but I do have a sister who is free."

Bridget was the third of Ursula and Ralph Fisher's five daughters. Attractive, witty, calm and effortlessly efficient, she was already a well-experienced yachtswoman and, with little inkling of what the Loch Ness Patrol was all about except that it involved sailing, quickly said yes.

Blondie's literary relationship with *The Observer* was gaining in strength and if it did not produce a significant income it did prevent his pension from being swallowed up in the pursuit of new ideas. Now the paper agreed to sponsor both Loch Ness and the design of *Dum Dum* for the next single-handed trans-Atlantic race. This upward slope of his finances' roller-coaster progress merited bullish comments in his 'appreciations'.

> 30 Oct 61. Much more flourishing. Loch Ness Patrol going strong with small retainer and expenses . . . Bridget Fisher coming down again to resume work as incomparable assistant. Other jobs under way . . . Chinese rigs. Designing production

---

[3.] Extract from an advertisement in *Yachts and Yachting* for 5 May, 1961: "For £1500. Owner proceeding to more radical design".

prototype of Hasler Vane Gear, Vospers have withdrawn (their support) and (so I) aim to make and sell six sets this winter, God knows how. Ian may want me in the West Indies for a month . . . *Jester* has done 10 days recce on Loch Ness, now laid up in Inverness. View of C. is now calmer but I still want to marry her.

Ian Major was as good as his word and on 15 December Blondie flew to St. Thomas in the Virgin Islands where he spent an idyllic month conducting a private survey of Mangrove Lagoon. On returning to the United Kingdom he found, rather to his chagrin, that C had succumbed to the "dangerous rivalry" and was now engaged to R.T. On 18 January Bridget Fisher re-joined as assistant:

1 Mar 1962 and the better times seemed to be continuing. Active, happy but have bitten off more than I can chew. Have just got over the hump of organizing production of 12 pendulum-servo models (HV/1 gear).
    Bridget working whole-time otherwise life would be quite impossible. Recently decided must own cottage to have stable base for operations plus workshops, office, stock room incorporated . . . *Dum Dum* must be built next year to be ready for single-handed trans-Atlantic race in 1964?

His pessimism over vane gear sales was unfounded, but as a revolutionary idea it would take a brave few to force open the floodgates: Lord Strathcona, Bernard Ellis, Geoffrey Nockolds, Paul Dacre, and Messrs le Blanc Smith, Bohemer, Schendorf and Forsyth all ordered gears, but production beyond these first eight now had to stop for a monster: the Loch Ness Patrol was to be a wonderful piece of whimsy that he took very seriously.

# CHAPTER SEVENTEEN

## Bridget and Loch Ness, *Jester* and Mock-Monsters

There was nothing unusual about Blondie's desire to seek out the family of monsters that are believed to inhabit Britain's largest freshwater lake, for it was entirely in keeping with his love of outlandish experiments. Conscious of being ridiculed, he knew, too, that his reputation as a man of serious, if humorous, intent would lend his latest exploit the desired portion of *gravitas*.

Having hatched his plot in June, 1961, and completed his preliminary, academic researches during early summer he was clear on two points: first, he believed that there must be an elusive animal of some, probably unknown, species living in the loch and, second, he would need outside help to bring his search for it to fruition. Once again he had turned to the newspaper that, so often, placed faith in what others would regard as way-out ideas.

Loch Lomond has the largest surface area of any freshwater 'lake' in Britain, but Loch Ness, one of the Caledonian Canal's chain of lochs linking Inverness and Fort William, holds the greatest volume of water. Indeed Loch Ness contains more freshwater than the total of all lakes and reservoirs in England and Wales and yet, while it has been of fascination to man for centuries, it would not be until 1992 that its depths were surveyed with anything more modern than Sir John Murrey's[1] lead weight and piano wire measurements of 1903. As the Royal Geographical Society's Magazine was to state:

> It is potentially one of the most interesting freshwater laboratories in Britain and yet, until 1992, little detailed research had been carried out in its waters . . . It is (also) the destination for generations of sleuths, crackpots and publicity seekers. But not

---

[1.] A pioneering oceanographer of the era.

a place where most reputable scientists have wished to be seen, for fear that it might be thought they were looking for (or, even worse, that they believed in) you know what . . .:[2]

Although written over thirty years after Blondie's patrol these comments are as relevant to 1997 as they were for 1962 and it was against that background of scientific scepticism that he had sought sponsorship. The first points on which any potential supporter needed to satisfy himself was whether Blondie was a sleuth, crackpot or a publicity seeker. He was certainly regarded as eccentric and, perhaps, unusual, but his projects – no matter how out-of-the-ordinary – contained elements of possibility and, so far, had all reached some form of successful fruition: a powerful argument in his favour, even if this latest one involved the search for a monster whose fame relied, almost solely, on its ability never to be seen in any constant or recognizable shape.

Blondie opened his case in an *Observer* article by discussing the "sounds emitted by the Bottlenose Dolphin", and believing that the monster might also communicate in that way, argued that *Jester*, as a silent, mobile search-station able to listen as well as look, would offer the best chance of positive identification. Her specialist qualities for such work included her size and lack of engine. She was small enough and quiet enough not to frighten the monster away.

Blondie's suggestion was, predictably, supported within the newspaper by David Astor and actively campaigned by Chris Brasher but was treated with his customary scepticism by Tristan Jones, who, on 14 June, 1961, felt that he "could not react usefully to this scheme without having some notion of the money to be involved". He was unclear, too, whether the object was to disprove theories of vegetation and marsh gas or to actually find the monster: the former aim, in his view, "was useless" and as for the latter, he "doubted if it was possible to prove the monster's existence without a net – and for that you needed a trawler".

But Jones was not the only one to be cautious, as the paper's science correspondent, John Davy, demonstrated in a long memo to David Astor:

Before we decide about Colonel Hasler's proposal I suggest a meeting at the office attended by Hasler . . . Richard Fitter[3] . . .

---

[2] Nicholas Witchell's report on *Project Urquhart; May 1994.*
[3] R.S.R. Fitter, noted naturalist, lately editor of *The Countryman* and then Nature Correspondent of *The Observer.*

> We should ask Dr Tucker to bring to this meeting a precise
> account of what experiments should be made . . . It is absolutely
> essential to have the complete co-operation of Tucker for there
> are many distinguished scientists who do not consider the
> Monster even remotely respectable and they will continue to
> oppose it. Dr Tucker is under a cloud and has made himself very
> unpopular with a number of scientists by nagging about the
> Monster for the past eighteen months. He is an extremely good
> scientist. I think Hasler has probably under-estimated the tech-
> nical complexities involved.

Blondie had not under-estimated the technical complexities involved,
but others, as with his original ideas for the trans-Atlantic race, were
reading too much into the project. Now there was a danger of the whole
exercise being placed in jeopardy by an overload of scientists and their
complicated experiments that, he believed, would only put the monster
off. He was proposing, in military parlance, a series of standing, observation, listening and (here he parted company with military operations!)
'feeling patrols': passive rather than active.

To meet these aims the operation would be equipped with nothing
more sophisticated nor intimidating than a collection of cameras,
binoculars, passive underwater listening devices, a wooden pole whose
outboard end would be 'armed' with tallow or plasticine in the manner
of a traditional sounding lead (to obtain an impression of the monster's
skin texture) and masses of patience and humour.

Blondie's feasibility study finally satisfied Tristan Jones and, after discussions on syndication rights on 19 August, the way was clear to sail
*Jester* for Inverness at the beginning of September. This was also a good
testing cruise for the new pendulum-servo steering gear especially as it
coincided, unplanned, with what he was to refer to for the rest of his life
as "the great gale".

On 16 September, off the east coast of Scotland, he was hit by the
heaviest seas that he was ever to meet. It was not that they were huge in
the Cape Horn sense, but they were dramatically short and steep and at
one point threw *Jester* bodily to leeward with such force that a hole large
enough for Blondie to crawl through was punched in her coach-roof.
Blondie's standard reply to any setback would begin, "Ah good, now I
know," and on this occasion was followed by, "the steering gear can
survive such a vicious knockdown but the coach-roof needs to be
strengthened." He was greatly encouraged. Yet more good came out of
this near tragedy through his enquiries for help for the reconnaissance

patrol when Guy Goodbody, a local resident who carried out the repairs, introduced him to a man who would become his lifelong working partner and with whom he would develop more ideas for yacht designs.

Jock McLeod,[4] recently invalided from the Seaforth Highlanders as a Major, lived nearby and, although due to sail with Peter and Ann Pye[5] on a cruise to Brazil and back starting in May '62, was certainly available for the recce if not the main patrol. He agreed to crew *Jester* for a fort-night on Loch Ness during which time "Bridget came up as Blondie's new found assistance . . . and we had a very entertaining time!" Jock's fascination with the Chinese rig on *Jester* and her experimental vane gear (plus an admiration for Bridget,[6] who was much closer in age to him than to Blondie, who anyway was telling his diary that he wanted to marry "C") sealed the friendship!

On completing the reconnaissance *Jester* was laid up in Inverness for the winter while Blondie headed for the more salubrious weather of the West Indies and the month's survey of Mangrove Lagoon. The rest of his time was devoted to building the first batch of vane gears, researching all known sightings of the Loch Ness monster and following these up with interviews and correspondence.

He was, though, not alone: a team from Cambridge University was planning a scientific monster hunt that summer, causing *The Observer* to believe that they might be backing the wrong expedition. Not wishing to support two operations (but wishing, for commercial reasons, to hedge its bets) the paper, with canny foresight, gave the undergraduates a £500 grant from the 'Hasler Expedition', ostensibly in return for their co-oper-ation.

Having delivered the first vane gears in the spring of 1962, Blondie and his team were free to move[7] to Dochfour Lodge pier on the north bank of the Loch near Kirkton where they established their first base camp on 25 May. Six days later he wrote a preliminary situation report to David Astor which contains the interesting background to one or two comments made earlier, for which, at the time, there had been little explanation:

[4.] With a similar sense of humour he had, too, been educated at Wellington College, although some years after Blondie.
[5.] A celebrated husband and wife ocean-cruising/exploring team in their gaff-cutter *Moonraker* (preserved in the Exeter Maritime Museum).
[6.] Conversation with Mrs Rachel Lambert, January 1997.
[7.] Fifty-eight people had volunteered to join the patrol but this was pared down considerably.

Although the odds against us are longish, the monster situation is brisk . . . Two first-class sightings: both saw it steaming along at very close range, one last August and one three weeks ago. There really is no doubt that the Loch contains at least one large aquatic animal and that it is of a kind unknown to zoology.

I should also like you to consider . . . the extraordinary back ground situation which is to me a classic example of evidence in conflict with dogma. To try to sum it up:

1. A steady flow of eyewitnesses insist that there is at least one large unknown animal in the Loch and I do not think that any intelligent person who has interviewed these witnesses has ever doubted the fact.

2. The zoological establishment say that no such animal can possibly exist and that therefore it does not . . . But some of them will tell you, in private, "Yes, of course there is something there, but I don't know what it is".

3. The case of Dr Denys Tucker has further widened the gap . . . he has been the spearhead of the current revival of interest in the animal and has personally inspired me. If we achieve anything, he deserves full credit for his scientific courage . . .

4. Loch Ness has had one or two well-publicized hoaxes, and in the same category I place the writings of Dr Maurice Burton – an unscrupulous ex-zoologist who makes a steady income out of writing an interminable series of different "explanations" of the monster.

5. All this has resulted in the subject being treated flippantly by most newspapers and by the BBC . . .

It seems to me to be a situation in which *The Observer* can play an important role in the restoration of good feeling and scientific sanity.

It is now necessary to go forward to his final report to understand Blondie's initial thoughts on his patrol; under the heading, *Jester in Search of the Joker* he was to write:

The case for a large aquatic animal in Loch Ness rests on the evidence of a small number of people who have seen it at close range under conditions that leave no room for any alternative explanation. R.T. Gould christened it 'X',[8] the local people call it '*Nessie*', and their forefathers called it *Niseag* or the *Water Horse*.

Those of us who accept the evidence for its existence are still left guessing whether it is mammal, reptile, amphibian, or even fish; whether there is a viable colony; how it eats, breathes and breeds; whether it visits the deeps of the loch (down to 750 feet) or lives wholly in the upper layers; what senses it employs to navigate and feed under water; and what causes it to make its rare appearances on the surface.

Richard Fitter had studied the Loch Ness Monster from an academic view and, being 'a believer', was less inclined to scepticism than some. His view[9] held that Maurice Burton was indeed a cynic who believed that most people "could not tell an otter or a red deer from a monster at two hundred and fifty paces". Fitter's counter-argument ran that, while it was true that many observers were indeed untrained in the art, most were locals who could tell the difference very easily. Of course there had been freak sightings and hoaxes but "many people who have seen it are firmly convinced that it exists, while many who have not are equally as determined in the opposite view". Fitter continued:

> What are we to make of a phenomenon which some say is merely meteorological, a gust of wind on the surface of the Loch; others claim it to be a jet-propelled mass of rotting vegetation; and yet others have suggested it to be a whole zoo-full of animals: shark, eel, whale, sturgeon, squid, crocodile, ribbon-fish, seal, walrus, sea-lion, sea-leopard, sea-elephant, otter, red deer, *plesiosaurus*?

Finally, Fitter brought sense to the arguments by declaring:

> But the real fascination of Nessie remains his capacity to split people into believers, sceptics and unbelievers, the light he throws on man's tendency passionately to take sides in a matter of pure intellectual speculation. So the inexorable human inquisitiveness drives us on to find out what, if anything, there is

[8.] The name by which the monster was known throughout the patrol. Blondie never used the term, "Nessie".
[9.] *Punch* magazine 1 August, 1962.

in Loch Ness . . . In recent years (several) expeditions have at least succeeded in establishing that there are enough fish in the Loch for a large aquatic animal to feed on . . . There is now even a body in existence specifically devoted to tackling the problem, the Bureau for Investigating the Loch Ness Phenomena . . . its directors are . . . Peter Scott[10] and myself.

Blondie planned that *Jester* would stay 'on patrol' throughout the eight-week search, coming to the shore only to change crews at eight o'clock each morning. During the early phases she would be hove-to in one of many pre-determined square-mile sectors for a twenty-four hour period and then move on to the next sector with the new crew. For each daylight period the three-man crew would divide their duties with one on watch, one asleep (but dressed ready for instant action) and one off duty. By night two crew would be on watch, one armed with a flash camera and the other an Aldis lamp in order to "dazzle 'X' should he come to the surface to investigate this silent and slow-moving surface object".

*Jester* also carried an underwater hydrophone that could be lowered to about 80 feet. On board there was the plasticine-armed rod for impression-taking and later on they would improvise a waterproof, square "look-box" about six feet long with plain glass at the bottom end by which they could peer into the depths as far as seventeen feet.

Orders for the on-board crew were military in style, detailed and well rehearsed under Blondie's light-hearted but serious guidance – for instance:

> If eddies and/or hump tips appear at close range and are more or less stationary then 'Close Range Action' will be ordered.

These 'action stations' were to be initiated verbally without pressing any alarm buzzers that might frighten 'X' and on this order the helmsman was to make a running commentary into a tape recorder while the following procedures were followed:

> Procedure One. Lying Off. If lumps are over 12" high and over 3' long obviously use feeling pole. Keep *Jester* about 40' distant and pan cine slowly to and fro the whole length of humps and

---

[10] The internationally renowned naturalist – later Sir Peter, and perpetrator himself of an elaborate intellectual hoax!

wash. If head and neck appear, concentrate on it. Feeler[11] lies flat on deck to clear the field of view.

Procedure Two. If humps are very small or absent, helmsman, guided by signals from feeler tries to get *Jester* sailing alongside X at same speed and parallel at about 10' distant. Feeler ensure that plasticine pod has smooth surface. First impression: plant armed end of pole firmly against X's body. Press with about 30 pounds. Note angle and depth of pole then withdraw and reverse pole using plane end for all future feeling.

Feel for length and probe *very gently* at right angles to X's body to establish length in relation to eddies or humps. Call out pole depth, angles and position in relation to eddies or humps. eg. "45 degrees, 5 feet to right of right hand eddies".

Belly Rub. From a slightly greater distance, rub side and lie pole very gently along underside of body to establish flippers, etc. Cine photographer focus down and expose three second take of the feeler and his pole every time he makes contact. It is desirable to avoid *Jester's* keel touching X but better to risk this than to fail to get a *first impression* which could be of primary importance.

The patrol started with hectic preparations all around *Jester* as she lay alongside Dochfour Lodge pier on 3 June to where, the day before, Bridget Fisher and Blondie had brought her up though the five locks from Muirtown Basin. Here they were met by Adrian Martienson with "an ancient towing vehicle" in the form of a 1939 Ford V8 car for towing the expedition's two caravans down the Loch's shore in stages.

Later that day Geoffrey and Sheila Brookes arrived in their mini-van crammed with high- and low-frequency underwater listening sets and much of the camping gear. The Dochfour Estate's Resident Engineer was so worried the pier might collapse that he came to warn them that evening of its limited load-bearing capacity, but it took the strain magnificently and by sunset the temporary helpers had gone, leaving a team of seven: Blondie, Bridget, Geoffrey and Sheila, Molly Eady, Adrian Martienson and Peter Keene.

At 1030 on Monday 4 June, powered by an outboard engine, *Jester* left the groaning pier towing one canoe and a dinghy: the weather was calm, sunny and warm. Blondie, accompanied by Geoffrey and Molly, formed

---

[11.] The crewman with the plasticine-armed pole.

the first sortie, while the others shopped and moved the mobile base-camp to a lay-by further down the shore. Ten minutes later *Jester* left Loch Dochfour to enter a flat-calm Loch Ness. The weather was perfect for monsters, as, during his tabulated excursions to the surface, 'X' has usually preferred a mirror-like surface – but these conditions were not to last.

> 1115 On station . . . Brookes testing LF listening gear and writing out layman's instruction for operating it. Rather too much background noise – unexplained tapping noise (like halyards slatting against mast) received for short time near Tor Point. Later: allowed hydrophone (unintentionally) to touch bottom. No apparent damage – morse radio signal came through on it periodically.

Lessons were learned quickly: by 1300 it had been decided that towing two small craft was conducive neither to quick manoeuvres nor speed under sail in light airs so from now onwards *Jester* would rely on a single, large sweep for auxiliary propulsion.

Those first days of steadily deteriorating weather were spent mainly on equipment trials and settling down rather than in observation, but morale remained high especially after a meeting with a Mr Gourley of Gourock who had "had a good sighting in 1937 at this place".

> For the first month we had more than our share of fresh winds, and rough water reduced our chances of seeing anything on the surface as well as producing background 'water noise' that interfered with our listening.
>
> The routine was pretty strenuous and fatigue was one of our problems. Some people could keep at it indefinitely and remain efficient; others needed a rest after one patrol, but seldom got it.

By 24 June, and after 20 days of non-stop work on the Loch, *Jester* reached Fort Augustus:

> So far we had no results except doubtful clickings and I now planned a return sweep up the Loch with the emphasis on LF listening . . . At the same time . . . we developed a technique for using our 10 foot plywood dinghy for both LF and eeling.
>
> We had started off with the idea that 'X' probably feeds on eels but after laying the deep eel line in over 700 feet a good number

of times (it took over two hours to haul the first one to the surface) and finding the bait generally intact I began to feel that there are probably no eels or any other fish life in the deep water and that there would seem to be no reason for 'X' to go deep either . . .

Over these four weeks it gradually became clear to Blondie that not only was Bridget an efficient companion but she was totally in sympathy with his philosophy, whether it concerned monsters, vane gears, cooking or yacht management: she was also one of the most tireless in watch-keeping. He had, quite simply, fallen in love with her. On neither side was it love at first sight: for her part Bridget found Blondie stimulating and exciting company, never letting boredom or signs of frustration enter his life. So close were they in their views on the job in hand, for which a marked sense of humour was essential, that the age difference between them did not enter any equation, consciously or sub-consciously: she was experienced beyond her years as a yachtswoman in her own right and he did not take life as seriously as others of his age and experience might have done. Work was serious but that did not mean it had to be approached in any blimpish or stressful way. That they made a marvel-lous, compatible team was obvious to all members of the expedition and by 28 June even Blondie could not avoid combining his admiration for Bridget as a member of the team with his now total attraction for her as companion. As a result of considerable thought therefore, he was able that day to make a single-line statement in his private diary:

HGH first proposed to BMLF.

No mention is made in the Loch Ness Patrol log although the day's entry (including the fact that Blondie had a bath for the first time since the patrol started)[12] is recorded in red biro. Clearly he was politely refused, for it is not for another three years that BMLF's initials appear in the diary – and for the same reason. Equally clear, by the use of the word 'first', was Blondie's view that he would persist! This event also marked, most significantly, the end of the self-analysis that had been the main purpose of his irregular 'appreciations' begun in 1956: no other girl's initials were to appear again in his notes and, apart from one or two factual observations most involving 'inventions', the entries themselves now begin to peter out until the blue, loose-leaved book is 'closed' on

---

[12.] Before or after the proposal is not stated.

6 January, 1963; its need as a form of catharsis having run its distance and done its duty.

As if to balance this private disappointment the next day's entry records (in blue biro once again) events of immense corporate excitement. Tabulated in a combined report headed, *Report of Sighting of Unidentified Object on the 29th June 1962*, two unemotional and balanced men, Max Barton (a Squadron Leader in the RAF who had now joined the team) and Dave Dunn (of Birmingham University's Electrical Engineering Department, another new arrival) speak of their experience. They were sharing the morning watch in *Jester*, drifting in the very light weather with the high-frequency hydrophone lowered to eighty feet when, according to Dunn:

> About 0530 we were ½ a mile SW of the camp when a gentle breeze sprang up from the north and slowly spread across the loch giving a ripple of about ½". I saw a ripple about twenty yards astern – such as might be left by a fish just poking the surface . . . Barton was on the fore-deck and as we drew closer he saw that the "ripple" was in fact two distinct ripples separated by about eight to ten feet whirling in opposite directions. He photographed them. Meanwhile they moved off towards the north-east at about ½–1 knot and I manoeuvred under Barton's instructions. We managed to circle them completely while Barton took some more photographs with his own camera. We were within eight feet of them and saw their height, peak to trough was about 1". Barton suggested they could have been made by a creature using two flippers to keep itself relatively stationary in the water. After about ten minutes we lost sight of them as they drifted out into the Loch.
>
> There did not appear to be any wind on the surface which could account for these whirls. All the time they were in sight the high frequency gear was in operation plus a tape recorder. Five minutes later we heard some distinct 'clicks' totally unlike the atmospheric crackle previously heard, were more like a typewriter, varying randomly with time – or so it appeared – a few odd clicks and then a few more rapid ones. I made a search through the three frequency channels – 30, 50 and 70 Kc/s and found that the sounds came through best on the 30 Kc/s channel and so recordings were done using this channel. The sounds lasted for about ten minutes. About ten minutes later we heard the clicks again. This time they seemed to get fainter but this

may have been my imagination. No recording of the second set of clicks was made . . .

Surely, they believed, it could not be a coincidence when just three hours later and about a mile away, while almost becalmed in the mouth of Urquhart Bay, the new team of Peter Ogilvy-Wedderburn,[13] Albert Trainor and Peter Hewett also witnessed a similar phenomenon as a further extract from *Jester's* log, written by Peter Ogilvy-Wedderburn, describes:

> 1000. Tacking across Urquhart Bay with just enough wind and heading for middle of Loch. 1100 Hydrophone lowered to 200 feet with 5 x ½lb weights. 1105. Peter Hewett saw two whirlpools similar to those described by last watch. Dist. about 50". Saw two black objects just awash at whirlpools when 3rd smaller whirlpool appeared in triangle with others and about 10–12 feet away. First two sightings 8–10 feet apart. Six photographs taken between 50 and 25 feet with appropriate range settings. Nothing heard at any time on hydrophone. Wind SW force 0 – 1. Slight ripple, 9/10 cloud, vis good. Owing to excitement tape record not taken.
>
> 1142. More odd ripples followed by black bumps, first 1, then 2, then 3 more; difficult to judge distance apart but about the same as last time. Bumps and ripples disappeared at 1146. Still nothing on hydrophone. 1315. More ripples. Tape recorded and photograph taken.

Although both the 'Barton' and 'Ogilvy-Wedderburn' eddies were photographed, the images were too indistinct for reproduction in a newspaper, yet the originals do show the Loch's disturbed surface as described by the crew members in their logs and on the tape recorder running at the time. On the subject of photographs (without which, he knew, there would be continued disbelief) Blondie commented:

> We are once again up against the fact that the human eye, particularly when helped by 7 x 50 binoculars, is a very much better optical instrument than any hand-held camera.

[13.] An interesting friend of Blondie's: Commander Sir Peter Ogilvy-Wedderburn Bt RN (Rtd) had been educated at the Nautical College, Pangbourne, was the 12th baronet and listed 'Loch Ness Monster hunting' among his interests in *Who's Who*.

The patrol was exhilarated by these sightings: if nothing else was ever seen or heard the long hours in relentless pursuit of a quarry that called all the shots would have been worth everything: faith in 'X's' existence, no matter what actual form it might take, had been vindicated. Meanwhile Blondie summarized a list of the relevant points from the two sightings:

> The first sighting: The whirls were a fixed distance apart and stayed that distance apart even when moving through the water. The whirls rotated in opposite directions, causing a ripple of about 1" from peak to trough. The whirls could be seen at a distance of up to forty yards since the rest of the Loch was calm with ripples not exceeding ¼" peak to trough. The motion of the whirls could not be attributed to the wind or water currents since they moved in opposite directions to the rest of the water and only two were seen although a search of the entire stretch of water was made.
>
> Five minutes after the (first) whirls were last seen clicks were heard on the high frequency listening set. These clicks were very distinct . . . No clicks were heard when the whirls were present. The clicks and whirls are not necessarily related.
>
> The second sighting: Eddies were rotating, depressed in the middle about ½" below the waterline. Could not have been gas or liquid rising to the surface . . . At no time did O-G see any wake from any hump. *Jester* just had steerage way throughout . . . Consider eddies had been freshly formed. Skin texture appeared to be smooth, like rubber.
>
> Justification of my technique: eddies and hump tips can only be seen at short range and remain sufficiently stationary for *Jester* to overtake at 1 knot. Doubt if shore, motor boat, rowing boat or canoe could do it . . . Now seems possible that X is detecting by echo location – hence the clicks and approaching *Jester* when she is almost stationary. Curiosity? Policy is to make friends by remaining still and quiet and not touching it. Technique must now include underwater photography (still and ciné), under-water periscope or 'look-box' or perspex underwater planks in *Jester*, low down at foot of mast.

Of these last suggestions there was time to construct only the 'look-box' but "morale was much restored by these sightings with plans for the remainder of the patrol now modified to take account of these experiences".

Throughout the weeks they were troubled by what were nicknamed 'mock-monsters' taking many forms, as this extract for the log of Sunday 8 July highlights:

> 2000. Molly comes up from watch below, sees mock-monster through binoculars, says, "What's that?" John Taylor, "It's a stem of a hollyhock floating – we have already investigated and logged it." Molly (a professional gardener) says: "Can't be hollyhock at this time of year!" (Investigates again, pronounces it to be a lupin.) All crew agree that in calm, very small floating objects look huge in binoculars. *Jester* returns with half a dozen mock-monsters – driftwood, cans etc.

Once, all was brought to a lengthy halt while they closed to investigate, with great stealth and caution, a water-logged mattress!

Although Blondie was convinced that what they had seen earlier could not be explained by any normal activity, he was unable to take even these impeccable sightings at face value and so established a series of trials to see if the eddies and whirls could be replicated by "artificial" means:

> On July 26 when I was patrol captain we again sighted small disturbances astern, but I established by trial that I could create similar eddies with *Jester's* own manoeuvring and I do not 'claim' this encounter. The eddies observed on June 29 can not be explained in this way, since they persisted very much longer and some of them were not in *Jester's* track.
>
> These appearances suggest the presence of a large animal swimming or floating lazily just below the surface and the small black lumps were the extreme upper parts of it. This interpretation will hardly appeal to the anti-monster school, and I would agree that we must be on our guard mistaking fish for X. But, equally, we must be on our guard against mistaking X for fish and these cannot have been fish because fish do not appear in this way and would not, in any case, have surfaced together, remained in a fixed formation for so long and submerged together.

On 30 July *Jester* came alongside for the last time. There had been much interest, scientific and tourist, including an unannounced visit on 17 July by two Americans who inquired "if this was the American expedition led by Colonel Hasler"; they went on their way assured that it was, in fact, "a thoroughly British performance looking for a very Scottish monster".

With considerable justification Blondie's summing-up was positive:

> We still firmly believe in the elusive X and among the many
> friends we made around the Loch we found a general desire for
> the animal's existence to be proved and accepted. A good
> number have either seen it themselves or know someone who has
> and I think they get a bit tired of being laughed at.
>
> We came away having failed to achieve our primary object and
> with a fresh respect for X's powers of concealment. But I think
> we took the first steps along a new path that may enable future
> expeditions to achieve leisurely, close-range encounters.

As his experience had increased, Blondie became more able to define
thoughts for the future and, as a direct result of the sightings of 29 July,
decided, particularly, that:

> It might be possible to sail *Jester* over the animal and to achieve
> physical contact either by grounding or by touching it with a
> sounding rod. I will not, however, allow this to be done, as it
> might well be intimidating. My highest hope is that the animal
> will come to regard *Jester* as a harmless and congenial
> companion.
>
> I do not therefore intend ever to do anything to disturb it or
> to try to make it come out higher on the surface. With luck it
> may do this of its own accord. Failing that our best plan seems
> to me to attempt underwater photography and observation while
> *Jester* is close to it.

In Blondie the monster had acquired a sympathetic, humane admirer
who would rather play the passive role than upset 'X's' long vigil of his
vast and ancient domain, views that he expounded in *The Observer* on 19
August, 1962:

> I begin to feel that there may be more chance of getting within
> thirty feet of X underwater than within a mile of it on the surface.
> Therefore if I were planning another expedition I would put the
> emphasis on underwater observation.
>
> In mid-loch I would use a sailing boat similar to *Jester* but with
> transparent panels in her bottom planking at the bow and stern
> just under water. She would be on the Loch over a much longer
> period but would patrol only in quiet weather.

By the shore I would try to find, by further long-lining, a really good eel location in twenty to thirty foot of water and would then put down a permanent observation chamber with an air and access trunk leading up to the beach. Both the boat and the chamber would use underwater listening, would experiment with different lures hung within their field of vision and would have underwater lighting ready.

The expeditions had been joined, briefly, by Professor William Hawthorne[14] who offered useful advice that backed up Blondie's views, for he too believed that future searches should concentrate on luring X closer by using lights, underwater and on the surface, mimicking the noises recorded by the Loch Ness Patrol and even by towing a dummy monster made from a dracone fitted with flippers and air-filled humps. But for this patrol time had run out and so with sadness it broke up as planned and on time, allowing everyone to return to their less esoteric duties and pastimes. All had found it a wonderful form of escapism, encompassed within a deep vein of serious intent, not one member of the patrol came away unconvinced of the presence of something unsolved lurking in Loch Ness's depths. It was not, though, the end of Blondie's involvement with Loch Ness's "Water Horse" for he would continue through his life to help and advise others who took up 'X's' challenge.

David Astor, aware that Blondie might have felt that the expedition had not been a success and that he would, as he had in the Royal Marines, blame himself for 'X's' lack of co-operation, put his mind at rest:

> How sorry I am for you and your colleagues that you have not actually sighted the brute beyond all question. Please don't feel that anybody here is anything but delighted that you will at least be giving us a good mystery story and enhancing our reputation as a paper with serious scientific outlook. Don't imagine we are disappointed – how could we possibly have expected more?

He may not have found what he was looking for beneath the surface of the Scottish loch, but above Blondie had fallen for a girl who could match him in humour, love of adventure and desire to research through

[14.] Later Professor Sir William Hawthorne, Kt, CBE, FRS, MA, ScD, FIMechE, FRAeS, then, *inter alia*, Professor of Applied Thermodynamics, University of Cambridge. See also Appendix Five.

practical experiment. She was more than his equal at business matters though, for at the patrol's end Bridget sold their second-hand Elsans to the Army for a profit – and that takes genius!

Blondie did not want to lose her (there was certainly work enough for two waiting back at Curdridge) but Bridget's sailing was not over as she stayed in Scotland to join her father for a cruise to the Mediterranean. In December Blondie wrote a testimonial acknowledging, in effect, that others might have call on Miss Fisher's talents if not her affections:

> TO WHOM IT MAY CONCERN
> The bearer, Miss Bridget Fisher, has worked as my assistant for a year, both in business here and on the Loch Ness expedition last summer. I would gladly employ her again.
> She is remarkably energetic, conscientious and painfully honest. She is willing, and able, to take responsibility. She can type, do scale drawings and is good at practical work of any kind.
> Believed to be one of the most seaworthy girls in England, she has handled and maintained boats all her life.
> I can strongly recommend her for any job to do with boats or the Boat Show. HGH.

Bridget never needed to show this letter to a potential employer.

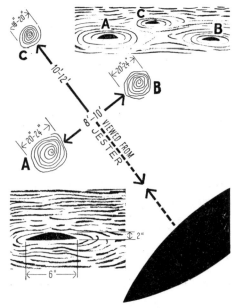

**Eddies and humps seen on June 29.**

# CHAPTER EIGHTEEN

## Jazz in Newport

Towards the end of his memo on 29 June, 1961, supporting the Loch Ness Patrol Christopher Brasher had continued with comments on the next trans-Atlantic Race, tentatively pencilled in to *The Observer* diary for 1964. It was feared that those who ignored the 1960 race suspecting (or even hoping for) a disaster now realized that it worked rather well and wanted to get in on the act, to influence and take their share of the credit for future successes. Brasher insisted that the main trophy should still be financed by *The Observer* (for no one could take away the kudos of having had the courage to be in at the beginning) but that options on stories should be restricted. Although a little unclear what Blondie's actual plans were he preferred a direct sponsorship of one of two possibilities that he knew Blondie was considering – a seventy-foot canoe with five masts or the smallest and cheapest boat that was practical.[1]

In an internal memo Lindley Abbot also expressed concern that others now wished to put up considerably more money, a grander trophy and hinted that 'they' might wish to steal Blondie; having made that point, he correctly forecast that the Royal Western Yacht Club would retain its original loyalty and suggested that the paper should do likewise and support the 'father of the race' with the smallest and cheapest boat. He didn't, though, dismiss Blondie's alternative steed out of hand - "acknowledging that the seventy foot canoe sounds to have terrific possibilities".

But *Jester* was not entirely forgotten and on 18 October he sailed her south from Inverness, taking a leisurely but boisterous two weeks to reach her Hamble moorings.

Now to the smallest boat for the trans-Atlantic: on 1 September sea trials of *Dum Dum's* Mark I model were conducted at Birkenhead

---

[1] The £500 ocean racer for which *Dum Dum*, then *Tum Tum*, would be the models, and finally *Cum Cum* would be the half-sized prototype.

successfully enough to encourage the design of *Tum Tum*. More trials and comparisons took place in the relatively sheltered waters of Gosport on 1 December, 1962, in preparation for the Solent's more open waters the next day.

While these trials were progressing satisfactorily, the vane gear was also forging ahead despite one or two 'bugs', but it had already proved that "it was possible to sell at a profit" and so to make it even easier and cheaper to produce a number of parts were made common to both the trim-tab and pendulum-servo versions. With these projects, and a few commissions for Chinese Rigs, in the pipeline,[2] a new confidence entered his life, especially when Bridget came south to work at the Boat Show during the first week of 1963 and on *Jester* at the week ends. She 're-joined' at the beginning of a year of changing fortunes centred around a 'floating breakwater'[3] and the design of *Cum Cum* which in effect, was to be a smaller, prototype version of the projected vessel for the trans-Atlantic race. Jock McLeod also joined the team:

> By my return in 1963 he'd production of the component parts of his pendulum steering gear under way, with different firms producing different parts. We put them together and produced individual drawings to show the client how to fit the completed gear to his boat.

Meanwhile Blondie's confidence manifested itself in the purchase of The Old Forge (also at Curdridge) and by 23 November, 1963, progress was speeding up:

> Out of *Tum Tum* I design *Cum Cum* a 22 foot dayboat which becomes the prototype of the Stanley 22 class and sail her first trials round a deserted Solent in November. She goes rather well.

The design for this new range of boats was first shown at the London Boat Show in January, 1964, by the manufacturing sponsors, Stanley

---

[2.] One was a junk-rigged schooner, *Ilala*, designed and built for a woman owner who intended to sail to the West Indies with her family. The cruise was abandoned in southern Europe and the yacht bought by Mike Ellison for the second single-handed trans-Atlantic race.

[3.] On 22 December, 1962, he had submitted the first proposals to the National Research and Development Corporation of what he considered "his biggest thing yet". See Chapter Twenty-One and Appendix Five.

Works, a power tool company. Described as being "easy for amateurs to construct", the drawings were praised in *Motor Boat and Yachting* of 6 March, 1964, under the heading of *The Shape of Things to Come*:

> The Stanley 22, a two-man keel boat is impressive, if not to say strange . . . The design was commissioned from HG Hasler, by now well-known for a relentlessly logical approach to sailing problems which is quite undeterred by tradition. Costs, including sails, is in the region of £150 . . . While developing the boat the designer has been thinking in terms of an offshore racer on similar principles, a cabin boat 44 foot overall and 8 foot in beam and yet costing only £1500. A successful boat at such a price could attract hundreds to ocean racing.

But the 'grown up' design was nowhere near ready for the single-handed trans-Atlantic race so *Jester* was entered for this second contest, a decision Blondie announced to David Astor on 14 April, 1964, just five weeks before the start:

> I am going to enter the single-handed trans-Atlantic race in *Jester* after all, but have absolutely no hope of getting a place this time. But I may get a holiday which would be nice, and sleep whenever I feel like it.

With that he prepared her for the race and sailed to Plymouth. But one problem that his ingenuity had been unable to resolve satisfactorily still troubled Blondie: what tie to wear in the various yacht clubs of which he was a member. He did not wish to fall foul of the etiquette of such matters, yet he did not want to clutter up *Jester's* limited stowage. Quite suddenly, and much to his amused delight, the problem was solved after he invited on board three members of South Devon's *Jesters Rugby Football Club*, to thank them for their help with the pre-race administration. One of them, suggested Graham Adam,[4] should donate his *Jester's* tie which, somewhat obviously, sported the appropriate symbol. It was gratefully received with much laughter. Now the yacht had her very own tie and Blondie was never embarrassed again.

Fifteen starters came to the line in Plymouth at nine o'clock on the morning of 23 May, 1964, and of those fifteen all were British but for one Australian, two French and a Dane. There were still no Americans.

---

[4.] Later a member of the race committee and the Royal Cruising Club.

On the European side of the Atlantic the race was being taken very seriously and particularly by the French. Indeed it was to be the entry in this race of a young French naval lieutenant that led, via various milestones, to short-handed, long distance marathons achieving a popularity that has never waned.[5] Blondie's dismissal of the conventional rating rules (with their complicated handicapping systems and strict observance of design criteria that stilted speed and real innovation) was now to lead, directly, to France adopting high-speed trans-ocean racing as her new national sport.

It can also be argued that, had France not taken her new sporting super-stars to heart, then single-handed ocean racing would have remained just another eccentric oddity practised by an enthusiastic few. In French yachting circles Blondie's name is still revered, nor has he ever been forgotten in Bordeaux, for it was he that gave the country her modern sporting heroes.

The rules for the second race were not changed significantly, with, in Blondie's words, "independence at sea remaining the utmost priority":

> Yachts must be fully . . . capable of carrying out their own repairs at sea. (Skippers) have no right to expect, or demand, rescue operations to be launched on their behalf.

Before the race, though, he felt moved to counter comments that had been made without foundation and certainly without knowledge. Under the heading, *Is It Sane?* he wrote:

> When we organised the first race we hoped to encourage the development of boats that were not only seaworthy, fast and weatherly but also comfortable and exceptionally easy to handle.
>
> This year will give us more interesting comparisons. Multi-hulled boats are admissible and David Lewis has entered his 40-foot ballasted catamaran. It would be nice to see a big un-ballasted trimaran joining in if only in the hope of silencing those wicked critics who whisper that such craft have so far only crossed oceans by blowing downwind at modest speeds and are no good at serious windward work in rough water. It would be useful to find out the truth.
>
> The average size of boat will be larger this time, and several will carry fairly sophisticated vane gears whose performance will

[5]. See Appendix Two.

be watched with interest and – at least by me as I make the damned things – with anxiety, until they have shown the ability to survive a long dose of North Atlantic.

There are no signs of a successful solution to the rig problem. *Jester's* Chinese lug is very fast off the wind and exceptionally easy to handle at all times, but I have not yet been able to make it go to windward against a Bermudian sloop rig. What we are all waiting for is a sloop that can be progressively furled all the way from full sail to bare poles without crawling round the deck and without ever changing sails. We seem to be as far away from it as ever.

The last enemy, and one we may never conquer, is the crazy motion of a small yacht in heavy weather. In a buoyant five tonner the act of lifting safely over breaking waves is achieved only by a series of swoops and jerks that can reduce living on board to a question of survival . . . After the last race I bought some drinking tubes as used by invalids which at least make it possible to drink hot soup from a mug without throwing it all over your face. What seems needed now is a sort of dentist's chair below decks in which you can cook, eat, navigate, read and even sleep with your whole body supported against the motion and all your muscles relaxed. But this might interfere with what is undoubtably the world's most efficient slimming treatment.[6]

He started his 'social' log of this race with a few comments:

. . . On paper *Jester* is one of the slowest boats in the race . . . fitted with the pendulum servo wind vane steering gear which I have originated and developed since the last race. Variations on this gear have also been fitted to five other entrants (*Lively Lady, Ericht 2, Akka, Ilala, Tammy Norie*) but it has not yet proved itself in an ocean crossing . . .

My other eccentricities arise largely from a love of discarding things that are often thought to be essential. This year I am not carrying a barometer thus finally (I hope) killing the dreaded weather forecast which is nearly always inaccurate and has destroyed my morale too often in the past. Weather forecasting has little value in a boat that is fully seaworthy and which can be reefed or un-reefed in less than a minute. The lack of a radio

[6.] On the return journey he built one.

receiver means that my longitude calculations rely solely on the accuracy of my chronometer. Every four seconds of error will put my position nearly a mile wrong and I may be as much as 40 days at sea without any means of checking longitude. Therefore instead of a chronometer I carry three or four good watches which have been accurately rated before I leave England. I must remember to wind them daily.

I feed well without using much tinned food . . . The bread should last at least three weeks before I turn to lifeboat biscuits.[7] It is embarrassing to have so many kind people giving me so many things – particularly if I decide to give up the race off the Eddystone and sail home[8].

At sea, anything resembling luxury takes on a new value and I deeply love a glass of gin every evening, red wine for lunch and dinner and a post-prandial delight known as Feg's Mudge.[9] A battery tape recorder will play my favourite jazz records in any weather and I am taking a clarinet just in case I feel persistent enough to learn how to play it. I would have preferred a trombone but there seems to be no room for the slide – no part of *Jester* corresponds to the New Orleans tailgate.

23 May 1964 – 0800 BST: *Jester*, more or less ready for the start, is moored in the Millbay Docks alongside *Juno*[10] and *Redlapper*.[11] On board them are Geoff and Sue Nockolds . . . Jock and Bridget . . .

0900 Gun. Not a very good start but the competition is not strong and I think I am second boat over . . . then the lovely French *Pen Duick* carrying a large red spinnaker goes past me to leeward off Rame Head . . .

1100 Vis closes in, steady rain. I am snug under the pram hood of my control hatch and pity all the other competitors out in the rain in their oilskins. I wash down my seasick pills with a glass of gin to celebrate having started.

The log continues across the Atlantic with little to report except the occasional request to passing ships for his position to be reported to Lloyd's of London.

---

[7] A passion which he and Bridget would eventually market.
[8] Always a worry and why he spurned personal sponsorship.
[9] A popular concoction from Bridget's younger sister Margaret.
[10] Geoffrey Nockold's beautiful forty-three-year-old gaff cutter.
[11] Major General Bill and Rachel Lambert.

A basking shark (I think) breached right out of the water 50 yards on my starboard bow and fell back in with a huge splash. Only a few months ago I was denying that they ever did this . . . 25th May . . . 0605. I am passed by an RAF Shackleton flying round me at a few hundred feet. My radar reflector is still hoisted and I wonder if he can see it from the little dustbin underneath his fuselage – that is if I am right in believing that it contains radar and not just gash.

Blondie's custom was to write a résumé at the end of each week in addition to his daily 'social' log: the end of the first week at sea tells of fine weather, fresh food (including strawberries and cream) optimism and the carefree life that he sought:

30 May. Fired with enthusiasm and a sunny evening I increase to full sail. The mast bends as she rolls in a way that I find alarming but until we break one of these un-stayed masts we shall never know how much we've got in reserve[12] Yesterday and today I have heard aircraft noises more than once and a long way overhead . . . One of my nightmares is that one of these damned things will have to ditch, will see me alone in the sea and will make a faultless emergency landing alongside me and present me, before it sinks, with rubber dinghies containing about 19 passengers and several air hostesses. All I need is one air hostess.
    . . . I've just been using Plymouth Gin to top up one of my compasses to get a bubble out of it. During the war I once served with a naval unit that succeeded in indenting for a bottle of gin regularly for this purpose . . .
    A liner passed close by . . . I celebrate this happy encounter with a glass of . . . whisky and with a few tracks of Clarence Williams' Jug and Washboard Band recorded 31 years ago . . . I learnt yesterday that it is not advisable to let Williams blow his jug when I am trying to count seconds against a sun-sight. The seconds get sort of syncopated . . .
    A gala dinner to celebrate having crossed 30°W (regarded as halfway) and having spoken a ship. I started by getting hold of the enormous York ham which usually sits on the sideboard locker wrapped up in its cloth like a mummified penguin . . . This I eat with a glass of Pug Wallis's 1959 Medoc followed by

---

[12.] Another case of "Ah, good. Now we know how far it will bend!"

bananas and cream and double rations of Feg's Mudge and chocolate . . . I play one track of my taped music at a time and it is doing me a lot more for me than a wireless set would. For the past two days I have been trying to start learning the clarinet but very few notes would come out and now I've fitted a new reed I can almost blow a scale. The noise is deafening inside *Jester*'s cabin.

His summary for the second week, 30 May to 6th June, read:

This has been a fantastic week . . . I am now 7½ days ahead of my 1960 position . . . For at least a week I shall be crossing the area in which icebergs (and unfortunately fog) may be met with. For *Jester* it is perhaps not so much the big berg as the small growler that I fear. And I do fear them . . . Part of the attraction of sailing consists in coping with ordinary, wholesome fear as in many other sports such as rock-climbing – so here we go. If I had a wireless I could probably get the ice reports which would tell me where the most southerly ice is. But this would be rather like climbing a mountain by helicopter . . .

8th June . . . During the night I have crossed the parallel of 50°N which is the latitude of the Lizard so that my loop to the north is now completed. Now we head for some sun and warmth which I look forward to. However, as the sun goes down it gets cold and while I am enjoying a glass of Norman Tailyour's brandy I change into serge trousers, long seaboot stockings and seaboots so that I look like a trademark for sardines . . .

9th June . . . 9 miles to the west of my estimated position the Pilot Chart has a wriggly red line on labelled 'Maximum Ice Limit' meaning pack ice as opposed to isolated bergs. I think this may be a fairly severe year for ice so I am now steering south for a bit so that I shall at least skirt 'Maximum Ice Limit', although still of course in the heart of the iceberg zone . . . My courage is weak at 0600 and I put the worst interpretation on everything . . . Now, having breakfasted off a large pot of porridge I feel braver . . . Decided to ignore ice until I actually see some . . .

10 June. 0700 (local) Aha! At last – an iceberg distant at east 4 miles. Two conical peaks, marvellously white. I am thrilled – it is the first berg I've ever seen at sea. 0915. Becalmed, bright blue sea. My iceberg which is still at least 4 miles away looks

totally beautiful – the same pure white and blue shadows, sort of cardboard beauty as a peak in the Alps but breathtaking when it rises out of a blue sea . . . 1145. I heard noises like quarry blasting coming from my iceberg and was just in time to see it completing a capsize with great splashings from the side that was going under and a whole fresh chunk hauled streaming out of the sea on the other side. It is now no longer visible as two conical peaks but as a sort of sphinx shape. I guess that its waterline is just below my horizon, say 3 miles away, and I've just taken a sextant angle of its height . . . which would make it about 120 feet high.

1430. Sail past my iceberg about 300 yards to windward of it . . . Just as the textbooks say, the sea to leeward of the berg is littered with growlers and ice rubbish which is all driven by wind and wave whereas the berg is affected only by current. I made a point sailing close to the berg and to one of the growlers to assess whether one could reasonably hope to hear the waves breaking on them in time to give warning at night or in fog. It seemed to me that I would not hear them, at any rate under these calm conditions, so it looks as if there is no substitute for a good lookout . . . This is . . . the heart of the iceberg zone so I shall be glad when I am out of it. It is difficult for a single-hander with a normal nervous system to get enough sleep around here.

12th June. As I approach land the dominant navigational problem is the possible error in my calculated longitude due to the error in my assumed Greenwich Mean Time as taken from my rated watches. This morning with a clear head after lots of sleep I have been sorting this out. First I establish, by considering the basic principles, that if my assumed GMT is fast, my calculated positions will all be too far WEST of my true position, by an amount equal to one minute of longitude for every 4 seconds of time. In these latitudes one minute of longitude is about ¾ of a nautical mile. I then consider the performance relative to each other of the four rated watches which I am using and discard two of them as being obviously variable and unreliable. The remaining two (watch D and watch A) put up a fine performance for the first two weeks when they agreed to within one second but the last week of cold weather has now caused them to disagree by 50 seconds with watch A being the faster. If this discrepancy continues I shall use watch A instead of watch D as I approach land but will still allow for the possibility that watch

A may be slow. Given reasonable sights I shall know my latitude exactly irrespective of any error in time and can run up my latitude to the landfall.

And his summary for 6–13 June read:

> I am now 13 days ahead of my 1960 position . . . The problem is the notorious Sable Island that has wrecked hundreds of ships. My favourite authority, Captain Charles Hare, RN, who by 1846 had crossed the Atlantic one hundred and eleven times under sail, calls it "a place that cannot be too much dreaded" and begs me not to try to pass to the north of it . . .

Exact time and thus longitude troubled him, and caused hours of re-working sights from his different watches with their various and uncertifiable errors.

> 20th June . . . At 1000 today watch D suggests that watch A has gained 107 seconds. Watch A suggests that watch D has lost 107 seconds. Allowing a maximum possible error of 60 seconds outside these and continuing to navigate by watch D I can now put down an extreme position.

And having done so he could sum up the forth week, 13–20 June, thus:

> Compared with my rakc's progress of the first three weeks this has been exasperating. But it has been rather a tense week having to fight past Sable Island in strong winds and lousy visibility with an unknown error in longitude.

. . . which was a combination of three of the most feared aspects of sailing.

> I am now only 430 miles from the finish but unless these cursed head winds let up I shall still be at sea a week from now.
>     21 June. Steamer siren quite close – vis 300 yards. I blow my ex-Greek railways foghorn which makes a noise like a child's trumpet in reply to each blast of her baritone sax . . . To hell with *single-handed* ocean racing . . .
>     22 June. The bananas (with cream and sugar) have lasted well. I've only had to throw away one end of a few of them. It is

peaceful tonight and I am enjoying it. I am full of good food and drink. The swell has largely died away. *Jester* slides along close-hauled at half a knot under her woolly moon with the rig making Chinese creakings . . . inside the cabin Humphrey Lyttelton and Buck Clayton are playing their slow blues '*Fondu Head*' with marvellous delicacy but . . . alas my poor sun sights. First sun but no horizon, then horizon but no sun, now no sun, no horizon. Vis ½ a cable.

Shipping in poor visibility alarmed him and even had him blowing his foghorn at what turned out to be a high-flying aircraft making a noise similar to an approaching ship's bow-wave! Throughout the log Blondie records speaking to ships that had no command of the English language nor, sometimes, any understanding of the internationally agreed procedures for signalling at sea. One such was the ship with two names; *HEBA* on the bow and *NEVA* on the bridge.[13] Eventually, having been hailed by the captain through a megaphone that "He no understand", the *Heba* or *Neva* hoisted a two-letter flag signal. It was then Blondie's turn to be found wanting, for he possessed no flags nor signal book. The only specimens given in his Nautical Almanac were:

"What is the best time to cross the bar?", "You should keep a look out for mines", "What is the weather forecast?" and "I am adjusting my compasses". None of these was Echo Lima.

The final week, 20 –27 June, was summed up thus:

Last Saturday I complained of an exasperatingly slow week but words fail me in describing this one . . . 268 miles made good.

28th June. Woken out of a deep sleep by a steamer siren quite close. Shot out of the hatch to find visibility 20 yards at sea level. Having lowered the reflector at dawn I now hold it over my head with one hand while I blow my horn with the other. Luckily nobody sees how absurd I look. I am converging onto the main (inward) New York shipping lane now about 8 miles south of me and although I can't yet see any ships there is a continuous low rumble from that direction rather like the Kingston By-Pass.

[13.] Blondie did not appreciate that a Russian V is an English B and an English N is a Russian H!

1740 GMT 1240 (local). Yes, I have just confirmed that the light vessel is now 3 miles away fine on the starboard bow . . . I take another sun sight to get an accurate check on my watches then go down and start the post-mortem on my longitude. The light ship appeared *ages* before I expected it and now establish that it was in fact 2½ miles east of my point E and my calculated longitude was 38 miles too far east. In other words my watch A which I thought was probably just over 2 minutes fast was in fact over a minute slow while watch D, on which I was navigating, was 3 minutes 15 seconds slower than its rated error . . . I was damned lucky not to miss the lightship altogether and not to get myself disqualified through having passed the wrong side of it . . .

My luck included . . . a morning star fix and sun sights later, and it was a heaven-sent timing just as I was getting a meridian altitude to give me an exact latitude.

This is the climax of the passage and I drink a glass of whisky to the Nantucket Light Vessel and mutter private terms of endearment to my little boat which always looks after me so well. From the tape recorder, rather louder than is necessary, Eddie Condon, Pee Wee Russell and their inspired associates are taking the bones out of *Madame Dynamite*. The fact that the wind is dying again doesn't seem to matter.

30 June. No land sighted yet but *Jester* must be smelling the finish – charging along at 5 knots through a smooth sea. If Bill were here he would say that those Newport girls have got hold of the tow rope . . . This is rather tense – my dead reckoning is getting close to the finish and there is a danger of hitting the beach without seeing any lights . . . suddenly the fog clears and there is the Brenton Reef Light . . . and all the other bloody lights I've been longing for . . . she is reaching for the finish . . . some more cleaning including heaving over the side my remaining loaves of stale (but edible) bread and all the old, torn, dirty, warm clothes that have been such good friends to me in the high latitudes. Rest in peace.[14]

The wind is hardening, the mast and sail-battens are bending like fishing rods and I ought to reef but can't bring myself to do it. I don't think *Jester* wants me to with the actual street lights of Newport visible ahead. She is at full gallop and I give her her

---

[14.] The first race's dirty clothes had also been offered to Neptune at this spot.

head. I can see the dark outline of the actual land – the first since Land's End . . . She roars over the line as I take the time. 07.07.15 by watch D; subtract 02.21 fast equals 07.04.54 GMT. Total elapsed time 37 days, 22 hours 4 minutes and 54 seconds if anybody cares.

. . . Suddenly notice that the onions have developed a strong smell . . . so I ditch the remaining 6 lbs and hope they won't float up on Bailey's Beach.

0400 (local) there is only one empty pontoon just astern of *Gipsy Moth* and *Jester* takes herself in under sail like a perfect lady . . . The sun is already hot but there is no sign of life anywhere which suits me well because I have to spend an hour stowing everything neatly so that she can look proud of herself. And so – at least to me – she does.

The thrill to Blondie was not his own safe arrival but that the race had been won by a Frenchman, and even this good news was surpassed by the excitement that Tabarly had done so in a boat specially built. His praise was fulsome:

30 June . . . Eric has won in the superlative time of 27 days – I am delighted because he is French and because his boat is the first to have been designed especially for this race. This is what I always hoped would happen. Val Howells third after twice having to return to harbour for rig repairs with Alec Rose fourth and then *Jester*.

Val and Alec are using my latest vane steering gear and it is a huge relief to learn that it works without its daddy – probably works better in fact when it hasn't got Fusspot fiddling with it.

*Frenchman Supreme in Anglo-Saxon Ocean* screamed the *Paris Match* but it was only after it had been pointed out to General de Gaulle that the "British Race" had been won by a French naval lieutenant that he and his government took any notice of the event at all. From this moment on, as they say, the rest is French sporting history – and continues to be so.

Despite slipping to fifth place it had been another personal success for Blondie, for his steering gear and for the race itself as an international event. Fifteen yachts had started from Plymouth and fourteen had finished in Newport, the only retirement being *Tammie Norrie* who eventually completed the course anyway.

Blondie would have returned to the Hamble almost immediately but there was a pull from another love:

> I prepare for a few days in Newport before sailing home. And now I hear that the Newport Jazz Festival starts on Thursday with enough great jazz players to make me dizzy. I shall be there . . . Then just step back into *Jester* and sail home to Bursledon.

And with that his log for the second single-handed trans-Atlantic race ends. The occasional frustration (usually with his own performance) had been recorded and rude comments about the weather were sometimes forced onto the pages but otherwise it was a relaxed account of life at sea in a well-found vessel, skippered by a self-reliant and experienced skipper revelling in plenty of fresh food, good wine, good and bad music (the bad was the 'home-made' variety) and the fact that the oilskins and sea-boots had remained in their stowage for all but a few hours. True to his belief in what it was all about, Blondie had arrived considerably fresher than when he had started.

Although not the last word on the race – those come later – *Punch* could not avoid a light-hearted dig at the expense of *The Observer* and the *New Yorker* in its 12 August issue:

> For many, the wind went out of the story when the Frenchman, Tabarly, romped home in twenty-seven days; but the last-across competitor, an invisible and inaudible Dane, lay on the *Observer's* conscience for sixty-one days . . . But *The Observer* stayed faithful to its epic. A week after the Dane tied up, it gave a page of extracts from the log of Colonel H.G. Hasler, who was fifth across; good salty stuff, all about damn great whales coming up and blowing like steam engines, and the gallant navigator blasting his ex-Greek Railways foghorn at insolent steamers. The Colonel took with him a year's supply of the *New Yorker*, which he hadn't time to read, and strewed them across the Atlantic. We've all wondered how to catch up with the *New Yorker*.

The return journey, begun on 6 July, was for the most part also without notable incident, but he enjoyed it so much that even the dull days were made to sound fun and it would be a pity not to record some of them just because they lacked drama.

1055 (GMT). Push off from the pontoon under full sail and manage to slide out without sinking the 12 metre *American Eagle*. Bill Howell is there with a hangover, which does not surprise me as he was making more noise than the Jimmy Smith Trio at the Jazz Festival last night.

Scarcely a day passed without some mention of the flora usually attached to the hull or fauna playing 'chicken' under or across *Jester*'s bows and threatening the servo-blade towards which he felt a maternal instinct:

10th July. The first Portuguese Man o' War goes by 'sailing' on a reach with its inflated bladder looking like a large, transparent Cornish pasty in various bright, obscene shades of mauve . . . 13th July. A naked lunch but sitting with no clothes on I enjoy a dressed salad . . . Then cleared out the vegetable locker . . . The carrots in plastic bags, imported from the USA and brought to Dartmouth, Devon, are beginning to rot at the ends so I take them out of their bags, trim and scrub them and stow them where the air can get at them. They are now on their 3rd transatlantic crossing.

On 5 August home was not far over the horizon:

0800. Grey sea – overcast . . . Everything seems English this morning, including the force 4 breeze, which has a solid feel about it unlike these namby-pamby foreign winds.

. . . and two days later he made a perfect landfall on the Bishop Rock lighthouse off the Isles of Scilly. The Atlantic had given him an easy passage, a great deal of which was due to his and *Jester*'s ability, but, as is so often the case, the worst fright came within sight of land. He had closed to within one and a half miles of the Lizard's signal station to make a signal by light.

"British yacht *Jester* from USA to Southampton. Please report my position to Lloyd's" . . . As soon as I had finished sending the message I ran into the worst overfall I've ever been through and I dared not gybe to escape to seaward because the wind had freshened. So I spent a hectic half hour fighting through against the ebb, helping the vane gear by hand. Once or twice I thought she might roll or pitch-pole but she behaved perfectly.

After the relative peace of the ocean it was a rude reminder that the sea, if it so chooses, will always have the last word. He blamed himself and the Channel forgave him this brief moment of inattention by allowing him to finish the voyage peacefully:

> 8th August 1964. As there is no point in trying to fight my way up the Solent in the dark against a spring ebb I am standing into Bournemouth Bay to have dinner and get some sleep . . . Have ditched all the clothes I was wearing this morning . . .

At midnight he was hove-to cooking a double ration of curry and by 0715 the next morning was becalmed off Lymington:

> Drifting up the Solent stern first. 1030. Reaching and running up the river (Hamble) with the flood with lots of people waving and being nice. 1130. Pick up my mooring at Moody's. Jock and Geoff (Brookes) are on the pier having just come back . . . from trying to meet me in the West Solent. Bridget and Sheila are telephoned and we all gossip and eat lunch while waiting for the customs. It seems to me to be a marvellous home-coming.

Now that it was all over for the second, and in many respects the most significant, time, Blondie was able to write about the self-reliance of the competitors and their ability to overcome setbacks. He preferred to praise genuine 'effort against odds' and was never impressed by feats of endurance for their own sake, not that there were any in this race nor had there been in the first; to his relief it had not so far attracted that type of yachtsmen:

> We can look back on the second single-handed trans-Atlantic race and see what we learned. Once again every competitor proved well able to look after himself, even those who had put back into harbour for repairs. There were two catamarans and a trimaran competing for the honour of being the first such craft to cross the Atlantic from East to West. The trimaran *Folatre*,[15] though last of the three to finish, finally sailed direct from Plymouth to Newport in under 35 days which would have given her fourth place if she had been able to do it first time.

[15.] Sailed by Derek Kelsall.

Many people (including me, dash it) may still doubt the ability of the multi-huller to cope with the ultimate (and very rare) hazard in which a rogue wave picks you up to a great height and then crashes bodily, throwing the boat, perhaps upside down, into a trough of water that feels like concrete . . . With further development a multi-huller may possibly be able to win although my own guess is that the single-huller, given comparable development, will always do better in hard going and rough water . . .[16]

We were all surprised, if not dismayed, by the size and erratic behaviour of the spectator fleet that turned out for the start and *Akka's* infuriating collision may at least underline the need for some spectator control in the future. It will not be easy but to the combination of the Royal Western and the Royal Navy all things are possible.[17]

As to the future, there are signs that the race may begin to attract a type of competitor who regards it (quite wrongly) as a test of courage rather than skill and it may be that the qualification for entry should now be stiffened, perhaps back to the original idea whereby each entrant and his boat had to qualify by making a long single-handed passage together. If it did nothing else, this might reduce the number of gear failures during the race but it should also relieve the club of much of their responsibility for assessing the competence of the crews.[18]

Later, when entrants began to attract sponsorship, in some cases millions of pounds each, he believed that the 'spirit' of the race remained intact, but he would still feel the need to defend it. The race, with its spin-offs such as steering gears and the proliferation of short-handed and fully crewed marathons across the Atlantic, Pacific and around the world that

[16.] His prediction was partially correct. Single-hulled boats continued to win but as multi-hull design developed it would take larger and larger mono-hulls to keep up with them. Eventually they became almost unbeatable length for length – but continue on a knife-edge at speed in heavy weather.

[17.] In the future Royal Marines were to man the *Gemini* fast rubber assault craft – he had been called back to SD6 to advise on their design – to act as marshals. Impressively handled, they would have 'Royal Marines' stencilled in large letters down their sides but in case of an embarrassing capsize in front of the television and public, and much to Blondie's amusement, they also had 'Parachute Regiment' painted on their bottoms!

[18.] Hasler papers.

it was to spawn, has often been regarded as Blondie's greatest achievement and with this view it would be difficult to argue.

> How can you enjoy racing if you've no chance of winning? Three answers occur to me. First, a good sportsman can enjoy playing tennis against a champion even if he never wins a point, because he enjoys playing tennis and enjoys testing himself against a brilliant performer. It is the *champion* who is more likely to be dissatisfied with the game. Secondly, the competitors in this race are together in Plymouth for a week before the start, and will soon seek out the boats whose performance will be comparable with their own. *These* are the boats they are racing against, and these are the skippers they will get together with at Newport after the finish. Thirdly, the mere achievement of sailing single-handed from east to west across the North Atlantic is in itself enough to satisfy most people's ambitions. The race is not only against the other competitors but against the great evil sea itself . . . and there are crumbs of comfort for everyone . . .
>
> People sometimes ask me if I approve of the way in which the race has developed, hoping (I think) to get a negative answer. If so, they are disappointed. It is true that the race is now a very different affair, with a number of huge boats built to win it, many of them fully sponsored by commercial firms and sailed by men who could reasonably be called professionals. These boats appeal to the media, but do not necessarily excite any great interest amongst the other competitors. The great majority of entrants are still un-sponsored amateurs sailing the race just for the thrill of doing it rather than with any appreciable chance of winning an award. As long as this continues to be true, I shall feel that the spirit of the race is unimpaired.

And finally:

> If we can keep everything on the rails I think the single-handed trans-Atlantic race will develop into a legitimate and respected branch of yacht racing and some of the technical lessons learnt from it will soon begin to benefit cruising and ocean racing yachtsmen everywhere.

He was right.

# CHAPTER NINETEEN

## *Sumner*, **Marriage and Barra.**

Safely back at home both *Jester* and Blondie looked, as it were, to their respective futures. *Jester* needed to be replaced by the £500 ocean racer, still in half-size form, and his next sailing project (not entirely un-connected) required impetus from a new 'godfather'. There was also the floating breakwater, Blondie's ingenious device for breaking down heavy seas now showing encouraging results with the National Research and Development Corporation.

*Jester's* fate was sealed by advertisements appearing in *The Observer* for 23 August, 1964, and *The Times* of the 21st:

> Magic carpet. *Jester*, world's most efficient 25 foot ocean-crossing sailing boat for one or two people. £1600 in commission. Box . . .

It was a sad moment but with the excitement of the new craft and a new race in which to test her there was much to plan, leaving little time for remorse. *Jester* did not sell immediately but on 23 November the design team of Illingworth and Primrose carried out a Purchase Survey for Michael Richey,[1] which event marked the beginning of a friendship for him that lasted until Blondie's death in 1987 and *Jester's* loss at sea during an Atlantic crossing the following year.

Mike Richey was the ideal man to take on responsibility for this wonderful little boat for he came to love and cherish her even more, if that were possible, than her creator. Mike is a remarkable navigator, a fact that was to be proved by this partnership over many thousands of interesting miles. In fact he had missed the newspaper advertisements

---

[1.] Interestingly, Mike Richey had been trained for service with the Combined Operations Pilotage Parties and posted to Ceylon but the war's end prevented this.

and only read of the sale on the RORC notice-board; initially uninterested, he was induced to buy her by Francis Chichester. Mike's memory of those days are clear:

> When I bought the boat in 1964 I inherited a book of notes relating to her construction and was amazed at the thought that had been given to every detail: the size of a biscuit tin, the dimensions of a chart, the weight of an anchor were all recorded with meticulous precision. *Jester* was far from a shot in the dark. She was characteristic of Blondie's thoughtful and measured approach to such matters . . . Angus Primrose would say that she represented the only radical advance in yacht design this century. It is a bold claim and much of what seemed unusual thirty years ago – the un-stayed mast, the full enclosure, the ability to handle the boat from a single position – has gained wider acceptance. But the boat remains a tribute to her designer's originality of mind and his capacity to get to the heart of a problem.[2]

She will remain among the 'greats' of this century's sailing vessels.

The next sailing project that was looking for a 'godfather' was the Round Britain Race. In October he 'initiated' what he then called the British Isles Circuit Race for two-handed yachts with a simple aim that owed much to its earlier cousin:

> The race is a sporting event to encourage the development of suitable boats, gear, supplies and techniques for efficient short-handed cruising under sail and also to test the speed and seaworthiness of widely differing types of boats by enabling them to race against each other on equal terms.

Many would come to regard this race as a sterner test of boats and crews than the trans-Atlantic for there are a few fundamental differences: the shorter, two thousand mile course is seldom far from land and passes through some of the world's busiest waterways with notorious tides and winds adding to the test; there are four compulsory stops each of forty-eight hours and it is sailed by a crew of two which, while obviously making for some ease of handling, produces its own problems, often

---

[2.] Letter to the author from Mike Richey, 1 April, 1996.

psychological. Indeed the test of crews' relationships was to become a vital factor in the race and a well-studied phenomenon.

To sail single-handed round Britain was clearly not sensible, nor was it considered a particularly good idea to sail nonstop, although initially some skippers felt that that is what should have been required. While perfectly possible of course, Blondie's view was that it would be "more fun" if, within the overall race, a number of unequal-length legs imposed their different tests of navigation and pilotage. These compulsory ports of call stops have changed only twice: in 1966 they were Crosshaven in southern Ireland, Castlebay in Barra in the outer Hebrides, Lerwick in the Shetlands and, for the first race, Harwich in East Anglia. The second race used Lowestoft as the final stop but in 1993 this was replaced, due to sponsorship pressure, by Hartlepool.[3] In 1998 it is again Lowestoft. The race, which has always started and ended in Plymouth, takes the yachts clockwise round every outlying rock or island of the British Isles except Rockall and the Channel Islands.

As with the trans-Atlantic race there were critics in advance, most of whom, as before, had no intention of entering and for whom adventure and empirical experiments remained dangerous pastimes from which those who took part should be saved. Blondie's answer to these unexciting people was robust and down-to-earth:

> The only reliable judge of seaworthiness is the sea itself and the seaworthiness of an individual boat depends to a large extent on how she is handled. To exclude a boat on a questionable point of opinion is not usual in yacht racing, creates instant bad feeling and leaves the opinion unproven. To allow the sea to eliminate a design is fair, unanswerable and a useful contribution to the science of seafaring. One of the main points of our races is to allow experimenters a free rein and to learn something from the results.[4]

The race was conceived in identical letters sent on the same day to *The Observer* and Colonel Jack Odling-Smee of the Royal Western Yacht Club. *The Observer* accepted responsibility for the trophies and press relations – again taking the strain and expense of such matters – with the yacht club handling the practicalities of the race itself. There was,

[3] Hartlepool Development Corporation were the prime (and highly successful) sponsors of this race.
[4] Hasler papers.

though, to be an understandable addition, for the 'once-a-week' *Observer* needed to involve a daily newspaper. With yachts racing around the British Isles news would, or should, come in daily, thus ensuring that a Sunday broadsheet would always be out-of-date. To avoid this Blondie suggested that competitors be required to fill in daily pre-printed logs to be handed to race officials at the various stops.[5] Meanwhile, the co-sponsor that *The Observer* had in mind was Sir Max Aitken, Chairman of Beaverbrook Newspapers and a renowned yachtsman. David wrote to him on 16 December, 1964:

> We have accepted an invitation to sponsor another major yachting event and are free to invite any other newspaper of our choice to act as co-sponsors. We see the *Daily Express* as the ideal partner in the exercise.

By 4 January, 1965, Tristan Jones had begun to realize the benefits to his newspaper of such races, but, while agreeing to the latest, did still try to insert a number of alterations to the rules, including a start in 1965: Blondie retained a firm and practical view:

> The Royal Western does not want to handle it in a Fastnet Race year (every odd year) nor, of course, in a trans-Atlantic race year (every fourth year, even year)[6] and that virtually fixes the race as being every fourth year starting in 1966.

Seeing the sense of this and other contested points, Tristan Jones contacted Tom Blackburn at the *Daily Express*:

> I have now heard from Blondie Hasler and attach two copies of his letter . . . Would you and Sir Max be free to lunch with Blondie, David Astor and myself.

They were free: the details were agreed and preparations made for the first Observer and Daily Express Two-Handed Round Britain Sailing Race[7] to start on 2 July, 1966. On 10 March, 1966, Blondie was interviewed by Crab Searl of the *Yachting and Boating Weekly* at which he explained the ethos of the race and its aims.

---

[5.] This requirement was dropped for the third and subsequent races.
[6.] Not least of all because it was hoped that the list of competitors would include those who wished to do both.
[7.] Later to be renamed The Round Britain and Ireland Race – reflecting the course rather more accurately.

It would be, he explained, a greater test than the trans-Atlantic for the pilotage would be more difficult and the chances of shipwreck much greater when rounding, for example, the unlit St Kilda group of islands west of the Outer Hebrides. Bad weather, he said, is always much more difficult to cope with in coastal waters and particularly on a lee shore, which is why he chose the specified ports; all had reasonably easy entrances at any state of tide and were well lit and 'usable' in an onshore gale. Separately Blondie noted that:

> Orthodox Royal Ocean Racing Club ocean racing is really just an extension of round-the-buoys racing. The idea is that as many men as possible should do a lot of hard and uncomfortable work, get thoroughly soaked and then come into harbour to hot baths, wives, and pots of drink. The single-handed trans-Atlantic and Round Britain Races are trying to achieve the opposite – the art of sailing fast round the ocean *without* excessive discomfort or exertion. A good seaman can overcome almost anything, but he has a better chance if he can reduce his physical effort.

Much to Blondie's dismay there was to be a cash prize of £1000. Tristan Jones had not given in on this, but it did not last beyond the first race for which he was grateful as, in his firmly announced opinion, "prize money tends to destroy the good feeling between the winner and the other competitors".

Prizes 'in kind', more universally acceptable to the competitors, would eventually be offered by various commercial organisations, dominated, (significantly, when considering the men and women to whom these races tend to appeal) by the tobacco and alcohol industries. There was no prize for the first leg but for the second that ended in Barra, John Player and Sons (tobacco) put one up, as did John Dewar and sons (whisky) for the leg ending at Lerwick; Tollemache and Cobbold Breweries gave one for the leg ending at Harwich, and Coates and Company (Plymouth Gin) for the final one back into Plymouth.

A pre-race qualifying cruise had been re-introduced for the trans-Atlantic race but, despite Blondie's views, it was not required for the first Round Britain:[8]

> I'm sorry that it hasn't been possible for the Round Britain Race because the course can be fairly hazardous in places and if

---

[8.] It is now.

anything goes wrong and rescue services have to be called out it gives the whole of ocean racing – or cruising – a bad name.

The race was announced in April, 1965, making it clear that multi-hulled craft were encouraged. Ten out of the sixteen starters were to be 'multis' which was pleasing, for Blondie had yet to be convinced of their performance, especially to windward in a blow when compared with a well-found, single-hulled yacht. Now he would soon know the answer. None in the previous single-handed trans-Atlantic race had gained honours, nor particularly creditable performances, so they remained an unproven concept for ocean racing; but he did want them tested.

While all this excited Blondie a more significant event occurred that was to bring the final happiness that had eluded him for so long. On 23 April, St George's Day, 1965, at the age of fifty-one and nearly three years after his first attempt, Blondie proposed to Bridget Fisher: the answer this time was a firm 'yes'. They had celebrated her twenty-fifth birthday three days before.

Blondie's greatest worry was over at last and for Bridget, who had been working for him frequently but not continually over the previous three years, she was as sure as he that they were doing the right thing. Nor had there ever been much doubt in her determined mind. It was just that, during the Loch Ness Patrol, twenty had been a little too young, no matter how great or small the actual age difference. Now, well into her third decade and knowing Blondie so much better, she knew, too, that it was sensible. Blondie wrote at once, and with some trepidation, to Ralph Fisher asking for Bridget's hand, but he need not have fretted, for, although perhaps a little surprised, the Admiral gave his whole-hearted and immediate consent.

The engagement was made public on 1 July and approved absolutely by their friends, some of whom felt considerable jealousy for Blondie's good fortune: Bridget was indeed vivacious, intelligent, determined, nautically wise and with her very own sense of humour.

Quite frankly they were an ideal match and, as this had been obvious from their first meeting, it was a marriage encouraged and supported by all who knew them.[9] David Astor's reaction was to offer Tarbert Lodge for the honeymoon, plus the use of a motor launch, both of which Blondie accepted with enthusiasm, although he did surprise his host by suggesting that part of the holiday would be spent in a tent on the shores of the Loch.

---

[9.] Numerous unsolicited comments to the author.

The wedding was planned for 30 October, 1965, at Aberfoyle where a marquee was erected in the grounds of Admiral and Mrs Fisher's house, Dalnacreoch, at Gartmore, Stirling. On Blondie's part there was one final worry and that was his inability to kneel for any time – as Jock McLeod, the Best Man, recalls:

> Before the wedding Blondie knew that kneeling was an agony to him. He started practising to try and increase the toleration time so that he would not have to leap to his feet in the middle of the blessing! I often found him kneeling near his drawing board with a stopwatch in his hand trying to increase the time each day!

Blondie, who felt guilty about a 'free honeymoon', had arranged for a flight south that evening to London and the Savoy Hotel from where, two nights later, they took the train and steamer to Islay and Jura. On their return home to Hampshire Bridget moved into the house from the caravan in the Old Forge's garden[10] where, as assistant, she had had her bedroom.

> Now that she was 'Mrs Hasler' it was considered perfectly proper for her to move into the main house! To prevent over-crowding, I moved from the Old Forge to a small rented cottage at Upham nearby and commuted each morning.[11]

In June, 1965, between the announcement of their engagement and the wedding, Blondie had started designing *Sumner*,[12] the largest version of the £500 ocean racer and the natural progenitor of *Dum Dum, Tum Tum* and, penultimately, *Cum Cum*.

---

[10.] To where, in March, 1966, a letter was addressed in error to: HG Hasler, the Old Forget . . . His 'formal' reply to MS Gibb (dated 1st April) – his friend Mike Gibb – began: "Dear Sir, Whilst I realize that in the rough and tumble of business life there is little place for the civilities to which my partner and I have been accustomed in the Services, I had hoped – apparently in vain – that our mutual relationship would not degenerate into personal vituperation. I am not for one moment denying that the first flush of my youth may be over, or that my powers of mental retention may not have diminished somewhat, but if you have criticisms to make along these lines I feel that you could have chosen a more tactful way of expressing them . . ."

[11.] Letter from Jock McLeod to the author.

[12.] Blondie named her "after Captain Thomas H. Sumner, an ordinary American shipmaster who gained his place among the great empiricists in 1837 by discovering the position line system of astro-navigation".

1965. The largest drawing board is set up and I wrestle with the proportions of the new boat. Guesswork, guesswork. She emerges from the drawings at 46 feet long and 6 foot 9 inches beam. In section her sides are vertical and completely flat throughout her length. Twin wooden fins project downwards vertically from each side amidships and have cast iron ballast bolted to their lower ends. The hull proper draws only 10 inches of water at 3½ tons total displacement and the fins draw 4 foot when she is upright and about 4 foot 9 inches when well heeled. She has a dinghy-type rudder with lifting blade so that I can experiment with hydrodynamic balance in relation to the wind-vane steering gear. The freeboard of the hull is moderate forward but very low aft and I have to give her a high coach roof also of rectangular section in order to get the 5 feet of headroom that I need. Manual steering will be from two circular hatches amidships as in *Jester* and two further hatches by the mast are for sail handling.

I am trying to modify the gear of her Bermudian sloop rig so that all sail handling can be done from these hatches without going out on deck, but am not sure that I can solve the problem. The light alloy mast is stepped on top of the coach roof and surrounded by self-draining sail bins accessible through five sliding hatches in the deck.

Now it unexpectedly transpires that I am going to get married before the end of the year. This seems the hell of a way to start a marriage, being obsessed with a hair-brained project whose only certain result is poverty. I think I might chuck it, only she won't let me.

He was right, for Bridget was made of stern stuff and the project continued uninterrupted.

The boat is laid down, upside down, in Don Fuller's little yard in September, in a polythene-covered shed two miles from the sea in Sussex. The frames, of pine and plywood, are set up upside down, the spruce longitudinals run between them and the skin of thick marine plywood glued and screwed to the bottom and topsides . . .

February 1966. Now at the weekends many helpers work away at the dreaded Foam – we are cutting up large quantities of rigid PVC foam and gluing it to the inside of the plywood panels of the bottom and topsides.[13] This is supposed to do three things: to provide emergency buoyancy so that she does not sink even if fully flooded; to stiffen the plywood panels against flexing as she pounds into waves; and to enable the bilge water to collect into narrow waterways from which it can be pumped instead of dispersing all over the flat bottom. By gluing and screwing a plywood sole down on top of the foam we have a form of sandwich construction which is nice theoretically but may not stand up to actual service. As we drive over to the yard for another week-end of amateur labour I recite my full list of qualms:

1.   She will float a long way below her designed water-line.
2.   She will be tender.
3.   The angle at which I have set the fins (they have toe-in like a car's wheels) will prove too much and the induced drag will make her slow.
4.   She will pound so violently in a head sea that the hull will be damaged.
5.   When running before a steep following sea she will continually stuff her long bow under the wave in front – a tendency shown by all long narrow boats.
6.   The separate rudder will stall at speed and she will get out of control.
7.   Or else it will break off leaving us rudderless.[14]
8.   All the foam will break up and become unstuck from the plywood panels.
9.   The mast, which is designed to be bendy, will bend beyond the point of no return.
10. We will find it impossible to handle and reef the big mainsail in the way I have planned.

Bridget has already renamed her *The Sumnerine*.

7th May and with the race due to start in under two months on the 2nd July we are going to move her (only a fortnight late) . . . She is sitting on a cradle in the form of a sled . . . and can be slid or spun in any direction . . . Long ago, in the Marines, I used

[13.] Itself one of the radical innovations used in her design and construction – later used by commercial boat-building companies.
[14.] The only one of his pessimistic "qualms" to come true.

to mount 6-in guns by such archaic means . . . By late afternoon we leave her forlornly in the middle of rural Sussex.

9th May. With a 5–ton mobile crane, a tractor and an enormous rusty bomb trailer left over from the war . . . we proceed like a funeral procession the two miles to Bosham quay, where she is run down on to the hard, dry bed of the creek at low water . . . Worries about leaks and flotation prevent me from eating lunch . . . she is almost afloat and doesn't seem to be leaking much so we hastily fish out a bottle of Perquita and get into the rubber dinghy. As she floats, Bridget pulverises the bottle against her stem. "I name you *Sumner*. May the wind and the waves be kind to you, and may you always be a lucky ship." She explains afterwards that she didn't mean the wind and waves had to be *calm* (she hates calms) but just that, however rough, they had to be *kind*. I know exactly what she means.

12th May. We slip our moorings at Bosham and sail placidly round the 25 miles to our home moorings on the Hamble. She seems to handle well and pleases me by spinning through the wind very fast when short-tacking in narrow waters.

13th May. We take her out into the Solent with a launch in attendance to get some photographs. There is a good southerly breeze and she is hard-pressed in the puffs under full sail. She feels as if I have somewhat over-rigged her but she steadies up and 'finds her bearings' at about 35 degrees of heel, with the lee rail just touching the water and the windward ballast keel just breaking the surface. She seems to go like smoke and the launch can't keep up with her.

She came up to expectations during those early, and rushed, trials but there were a number of innovative ideas that would need the test of the Round Britain race before they could be called successful. One was the reefing system that, although not recognized as such, was the forerunner of what is now known as slab reefing, itself a derivative of point-reefing.

Blondie, Bridget and *Sumner*, plus fifteen other entries, did make the start line in Plymouth Sound on 2 July, 1966, for the race that was to influence yet more short-handed marathons, and some fully-crewed versions.

Of the sixteen entrants ten were multi-hulled, these divided between four catamarans, five trimarans and a 'double-outrigger'. The trimaran *Toria*, launched just three weeks before the race was skippered by her designer Derek Kelsall who had sailed the trimaran *Folatre* in the previous trans-Atlantic race. Derek knew what he was doing and fellow competitors had every reason to be wary of his likely performance. These were the earliest days of offshore multi-hull seamanship and "the chase was on" – as Christopher Brasher, writing in *The Observer*, commented:

> "We don't wish (the catamarans and trimarans) ill luck but we just want it to blow hard enough for them to break up". It was, of course, a conventional yachtsman talking about the most fascinating aspect of the Round Britain Race – the battle between the single-hulled and the multi-hulled boats . . . There is no doubt that (they) are the fastest boats in the race but will they stay the course? Can they be driven fast for 2,000 miles in some of the most treacherous waters in the world without breaking up? I like the chances of Derek Kelsall's *Toria* and then there's the rank outsider – Blondie Hasler's *Sumner*. Nobody, not even Blondie, knows how fast she is.

But *Sumner's* part in the race was not to be as long-lived as Blondie and Bridget hoped. During the first leg she held her own *en route* to Crosshaven and had even overtaken two of the fancied single-hullers in slow weather which pleased her crew immensely, especially as they regarded her as a heavy-weather boat.

Writing from Crosshaven for *The Observer*'s 10 July edition Blondie commented:

> On this first leg the multi-hullers showed up better than the single-hullers and the trimarans better than the catamarans. *Toria* the winning trimaran, for this leg, averaged about 4.77 knots . . .
>
> In *Sumner* Bridget and I had a painless sail and are not the only ones who are waiting anxiously to see how we make out when it blows up hard and lumpy and we wish we were at home in the garden.

He was soon to find out and in *The Observer* for 17 July was forced to write from Barra:

> I'm afraid that *Sumner* is out of the race. On Wednesday at 2.15 am Bridget and I weighed anchor at Castle Bay, Barra, in the dark and started out to sail the third leg of the course (a 420-mile

stretch round St Kilda and up to the Shetlands) with a weather forecast of gale Force 8 to check any undue exuberance.

By 8 am. we were on our way out to St Kilda getting our teeth into a hard thrash dead to windward in Force 5 to 6 under small mainsail and storm jib, with the boat going well and climbing the seas like a duck. At 1130 am with the wind hardening and the boat 20 miles off-shore there was a sharp crack from aft as the lower rudder gudgeon (the bearing on which it turns) carried away, leaving the whole of our variable-sweep rudder banging and twisting around on its upper gudgeon and the boat unsteerable.

In the course of an hour or so we managed to get the rudder in on deck without losing any fingers but much of the metalwork was twisted to hell and there was nothing we could do to repair it at sea. So we dug out some timber, brass strips and bolts from the forecastle and made up a small but serviceable jury rudder to hang on the original pintle.

By this time it was blowing Force 7 or 8 and we knew we had to stand even further off-shore for safety . . . So it was 7.30 on Thursday morning before we anchored again in Castle Bay feeling a perverse satisfaction at having successfully exercised some of the precepts of the Manual of Seamanship. Now Mr McNeil, the lifeboat mechanic is devoting most of his day to welding up a temporary rudder gudgeon from bits of scrap steel in his back-yard, doing a great job with quite inadequate resources . . . A boat without a rudder is not funny and next time it might happen somewhere with less sea room. So we feel we have to take *Sumner* out of the race and cruise her back to the Solent where I can do a serious redesign of the rudder hangings.

Showing up weaknesses of this sort is one of the objects of the race and in 750 miles of vigorous sailing we have given the totally unorthodox *Sumner* a very good testing and have been increasingly pleased by the way she behaves at sea.

Although out of the race, Blondie kept a close eye on individual performances and overall results. What pleased him particularly was the number of designers and inventors who had shown a professional interest in the race, which was more than was the case, so far, for the trans-Atlantic. Already mentioned was Derek Kelsall, but there was also Rod Macalpine-Downie in *Mirrorcat*, Eric Wills of *Startled Faun* who

described himself as a 'reticent inventor' and James Warram of the enig-
matically-described 'double-outrigger', *Tiki Roa,* but who, being more
interested in developing his own version of the Polynesian craft with
which he was fascinated, was really not among the main stream of fast
craft designers. Don Robertson of *Snow Goose* saw himself as "always
designing, always experimenting" – with excellent results: these were all
men after Blondie's heart.

Due to its perpetual proximity to the British mainland and the
enforced forty-eight-hour stops when the press could refresh themselves
with instant news, many contemporary reports were written. One[15]
describes the scene in Barra:

> After four or five hard days at sea a couple of nights ashore even
> in some little grey Hebridean Hotel are not to be sneezed at.
> Only diehards like Colonel Blondie Hasler who don't really see
> why 'ashore' was invented anyway, preferred to stick in the old
> bunk out in the anchorage. (He was, after all, on his honeymoon
> – or near enough!)[16]
>
> Blondie Hasler of *Sumner* promised to be the master carpenter
> of the race. The sound of hammering emerging from the hatch-
> ways in harbour and afloat had spread the rumour that he was
> secretly converting his single-hull into a trimaran on the way
> round just to surprise us at Plymouth. As it was, his rigging of a
> jury rudder in a Force 7 wind off the Hebrides must have been
> a feat even for him.

Bridget was the first woman to take part in any of these races and as such
deserves her full share of glory, though not, sadly, crowned by a finish in
Plymouth, but certainly enhanced by the manner of *Sumner's* retirement.
Praise for another aspect of her ability came from the journal of the Royal
Naval Sailing Association in which one competitor wrote of his stop in
Barra:

> Any thoughts of being roughy, toughy sailormen were shattered
> by the sight of the charming Mrs Hasler doing her shopping so
> cheerful and smiling.

[15.] Roy Perrott.
[16.] The next few races had a 'no sleeping ashore' rule! – which tended to be
abused in the most amusing and inventive ways. Ostensibly this was to
encourage sensible on board accommodation.

The race was an astounding success. Ten of the sixteen made it back to Plymouth still racing and of those that had had to retire only two did so because of damage, a remarkable testament to the preparation of the boats and the standard of the crews, along with the unceasing vigilance of the RWYC Race Committee before the days of a compulsory qualifying race.

The tabulated results were the first signs that multi-hulls were here to stay as serious ocean-voyaging craft, for not one of the first six to finish were single-hulled yachts: the 40-foot trimaran *Toria* romping home, untroubled, in 19 days, 17 hours and 23 minutes.

The last words on this race go to Blondie writing in *The Observer* of 7 August, 1965:

> British yachtsmen often feel, perhaps with some truth, that our coastal waters provide fiercer and less predictable sailing conditions than the coasts of any other yachting countries. Any boat that can consistently make good passages through this watery maze of gales, tides, cold rain, steep seas and low visibility has proved herself and her crew to be seaworthy at least.
>
> Just now a lot of British yachtsmen, including myself, are reluctantly having to adopt a much more respectful attitude towards unbalanced, multi-hulled sailing yachts in the light of the astonishing results of this year's Round-Britain Race which concluded last Monday with the arrival of the last survivor at Plymouth, still 12 days inside the time limit.
>
> In our unorthodox single-huller *Sumner* my wife Bridget and I were happy enough in hard weather and though we were getting along quite well until we carried away our rudder by the beginning of the third leg we were no longer saying to each other every time it blew: "Keep an eye open for a couple of whales in company – they may be a catamaran upside down."
>
> The 1966 Round Britain Race has been a distinct success. Nobody called out the lifeboat and all competitors with structural or rigging trouble got themselves back into harbour unaided. Above all the race will remain a milestone in the struggle of the multi-hullers towards acceptance and seems possible that the next single-handed trans-Atlantic race in 1968 will be dominated by them – depending largely, I think, on how successfully they can be made to steer themselves with a wind-vane steering gear.
>
> Fast multis, like ice yachts, play hell with their own Apparent

Wind direction when they accelerate and I don't think we yet know how to make a vane steer them properly. There will be plenty of incentive to find out.

They did find out and his prediction was nearly correct; it just took a little longer than he expected. Mono-hull yachts were to come first and second in the next trans-Atlantic race but they had to be seventeen and ten feet longer, respectively, than the first multi-hull.

As for the next Round Britain race in 1970 it, too, was to be won by a mono-hull but she had to be seventy feet to beat a thirty-six foot catamaran into second place.[17] The day of the 'tris and cats' was to come, but not quite yet, and even then it was to be a far from painless exercise.[18]

However, for Blondie, who was not to take part again in any of his races, the satisfaction from 'inventing' it all was complete.

"I'm sorry mate. It's a single-handed race."

[17] Don Robertson's catamaran *Snow Goose* (which had also come second in 1966, crewed on each occasion by David Cooksey, later Sir David). The winners in the seventy foot monohull were Robin Knox-Johnston (later Sir Robin) and Leslie Williams.
[18] For more information on subsequent races see Appendix Two and Lloyd Foster's *Ostar*.

# CHAPTER TWENTY

## *Peanut, Mizpah, Pilmer* and the Doomsday Project

To continue with Blondie's life away from the single and two-handed races it is necessary to introduce Michael Gibb of M.S. Gibb Limited. Mike was a staunch friend with the commercial courage to back the unknown quantity of a steering gear (itself still a radical departure for the conventionally minded) designed and proved by one man. With the contract to manufacture and market the various steering gears Gibb also offered Blondie a contract to illustrate the advertisements in the yachting press. These simple line sketches usually depicted some unfortunate female crew protesting that her skipper was always lashed to the helm while she craved attention, the inference being that a Hasler Self Steering Gear would put some fun (and the man?) back into her life.

1966 was a successful year. The first memorial had been dedicated to the memory of his Royal Marines lost during the raid on Bordeaux; he was happily married; the floating breakwater was under the wing of the National Research and Development Corporation; he had a business partner, his two races were being discussed as blueprints for longer events and M.S. Gibbs sold no less than fifty steering gears, but like the true inventor, the invention was all, marketing was left to others almost on a take-it-or leave-it basis, and in some respects the same was so with his races. He maintained great interest and was always consulted but never again took part.

The Hasler Breakwater, considered by Blondie to have had the greatest commercial potential of any invention with which he was involved, came to public prominence in August, 1969, when, that month the NRDC (and two supporters in particular – Tom Coombes and Gordon Rollinson) wrote the following in a glossy, four-page illustrated handout:

> The structure will provide good protection against wind-driven waves for drilling rigs, dredgers, floating cranes, yacht marinas,

etc. It could readily be towed to a new location and will be suitable for conditions varying from deep water to drying beaches.

A number of models were built, with many of the experiments taking place at Vosper's Yard, allowing Blondie to settle, finally, for a catamaran design with one long, wide hull to windward and a smaller, thinner one to leeward. With this principle proving to be the most efficient, a large working model was built and moored in the Solent and used for demonstrations.[1]

During these studies Blondie deduced that if energy was being absorbed or 'killed' then it should be put to some useful purpose, an idea that led to the design of the Wave Energy Pump, or WEP, for generating electricity: this, too, was taken up by the NRDC. A small model managed to pump limited amounts of water, but after months of trials and re-designs, it was concluded that the energy extracted would never be enough to warrant further work.[2]

Many more projects, or the ideas for projects, floated through Blondie's imagination and into mechanical drawings roughed out in blue ink in small notebooks. Some were brilliant in their inventiveness and some simply old-established ideas that were given the Blondie scrutiny and a new look.[3] A tiny selection includes a soap-cart for children that leaned into the corner; canoes propelled by a fish-tail device; the plasticizing of sails[4] which he used on the Lapwing rig and, alarmingly, the 'ornithopter'. His thoughts, literally, knew no bounds and were by no means confined to matters nautical.

He would turn to *The Observer* for inspiration and, where necessary, help. It was not so much that he thought they would, or could, assist, but he harboured a great loyalty to the newspaper that had set some of his most enduring inventions in motion; in their turn *The Observer* showed initial interest in the idea of *Observer Boats Limited* about which Blondie wrote:

> It is proposed that (we) should launch *Observer Boats* as a new promotion. This would involve setting up a small company . . . whose major or sole shareholder would be *The Observer*.

[1] See Chapter Twenty One and Appendix Five.
[2] Letter to the author from Jock McLeod.
[3] See Appendix One.
[4] To give a smoother air flow over the woven material – pre-dating modern concepts.

The first boat he had in mind was already in prototype form as the *Peanut,* a small, glass-fibre, unsinkable, child's rowing dinghy. For this he had enlisted the help of Ted Goacher with his expertise in plastic technology and who "shares with me, by private agreement, any design royalties".

The *Daily Mirror* was enjoying well deserved success with their Mirror sailing dinghy and Blondie's view was that *The Observer* could do the same with a wider range of boats. David Astor, of course, was interested and read the 'Advantages' paragraph of the business plan with enthusiasm. It was an imaginative idea, well considered and presented, but, as with previous suggestions, this one fell across the desk of Tristan Jones who, on 4 December, 1971, found reasons for rejecting the project. The first, with which Blondie could not argue, was that *The Observer* was not a manufacturing company and could not have money tied up in stock, but the second was less understandable, coming, as it did, from someone with limited knowledge of the sea. David forwarded Jones's minute to Blondie for his comments:

> It is inviting disaster to make tiny boats for children "aged between 1 and 14". There are scores of imbecile parents who will happily buy such a thing to please a child, not realizing that unless they also have a separate boat of their own at the beach, they will be quite helpless if a breeze or a current starts to drive their 4 year old away from the shore.

Jones's views would have been received more sympathetically if he had said "Yes, and now design the boats for the parents which *The Observer* will also market" – but he hadn't.

Blondie was concerned but not so much with the dismissal of his proven idea as for the second reason for it and replied on 15 December:

> Your objection seems extraordinary. Surely a seaworthy child's dinghy is far less dangerous than the inflated rubber horses and floats that set out in shoals on unplanned Channel crossings every time it blows offshore in summer? And also, for that matter, far safer than a child's bicycle, which is one of the quickest ways of getting a child under the wheels of a lorry? But you can probably point out that you aren't offering rubber horses or children's bicycles either!

It was *The Observer's* loss for not only did the *Peanut* prove to be a success but Blondie moved up in size to design small, junk-rigged vessels for the cheaper end of the market.

With two years *Peanut* was selling well at £33 (plus comprehensive instructions and a guide written by Blondie headed *Advice to Parents*) and had been the subject of an enthusiastic review sub-titled *A Waterbaby's Dreamboat* in *Yachting Monthly*, a magazine devoted to safety.[5] Being light but rigid, as all who venture afloat know, makes a dinghy more easy to handle with less muscle power required than for a comparable-size rubber equivalent with heavy drag and poor directional stability. With no sense of sour grapes Blondie later reported to David Astor in May, 1973, that the "midget dinghy for children" was well into production by a company called, naturally, *Peanut Boats*.

> The boat seems to be unique and is already starting to create a
> new generation of waterbabies who learn to row soon after they
> can walk and just as instinctively.

Another design was in answer to an American who wanted a "midget version" of *Jester*. Initially believing that the project was impracticable, he started by drawing a figure of a six-foot, two-inch tall man in "the best positions for steering, cooking, eating, sleeping, chartwork, lookout, taking astro sights and sail handling with the boat both upright and heeled" and then designed the hull around these dimensions – the result was *Loner*: with built-in water catchment areas and other radical innovations forced upon her because of her size she was a prime example of lateral thinking.

By the end of 1973 Blondie had developed new thoughts along what he called 'alternative technology' lines which he presented to *The Observer* in a short paper listing areas of concern where such technology should be applied. This, he revealed in a letter to David, was no sudden revelation as for years he had been worrying how he could assist the ecology debate.

Doomsday Projects
*The Observer* is sounding many warning noises about the
economy, but I see few signs of anybody taking practical steps to
ease the pain of a contracting economy. Would you feel that the

---

[5.] See also Tom Cunliffe's "Lessons learned in *Peanut* are for life". *Yachting Monthly*, July, 1990.

paper could do something more positive and I would hope more news-worthy by sponsoring selected 'Doomsday Projects' whose object is "to prepare and demonstrate pilot schemes aimed at maintaining a satisfying way of life without the use of fossil fuels"?

Being at home with the elements, he felt that we should all come to terms with the natural world and 'join it not destroy it'. As sustainable living was the key, his core points for 'environmentally friendly living' were tabulated for the newspaper's readers to consider:

1. A Doomsday garden – family survival off a small plot of land, treating food as an essential fuel rather than as a sensual pleasure.
2. The preservation of food without canning or refrigeration.
3. The collection and use of rainwater off your roof.
4. Use of wind and water power on a local scale.
5. Grinding wheat by hand. Traditional bread ovens.
6. Charcoal burning, uses of coal.
7. Return of draught horses, carts and carriages.
8. Revival of barge traffic on inland waterways and estuaries.
9. Revival of sailing passenger, cargo and fishing vessels.
10. Revival of village crafts such as blacksmith, cooper, wheel wright, tanner and so on.

Naturally, he ended the paper by emphasizing that he was suggesting nothing he was not prepared to experience himself:

My own starting points include trying to revive the village forge at this address, and doing a short course in blacksmithery!

Another environmentally-friendly project took shape on his drawing board. Believing that landing craft were vital for inter-island work and aware of the average winds among Scotland's western isles, plans for such a craft evolved which sported two masts down one side of the well-deck and, instead of an engine room, space for a tractor to back into the stern section so that it could, on those rare, windless days, couple its power take-off shaft to a propeller (which, with a skeg, would be retractable). Once the vessel had reached its destination the tractor would be landed to continue its work or to help offload or load.

Complementing all this was an increasing desire to escape the

crowded, urban life of southern England and head north, even as far as
the Shetlands. David was approached:

> Would you have any interest in farming a small corner of Loch
> Tarbert, Jura? The most probable type of installation would
> consist of moored floating cages for rainbow trout or plaice or
> moored rafts for rope culture of molluscs . . . Shore facilities
> could be minimal, or even nil, if a small vessel is moored as a
> base for operations.
>
> The only hope of getting fish on to the ordinary person's menu
> is one day going to be to farm it. In essence, the proposed fish
> farm involves installing fairly expensive fish cages but once this
> has been done they are supposed to last for ever with no more
> maintenance than can be done by one man working by himself
> . . . In other words I see it as a crofting system, rather than a
> factory.

He was not, of course, talking about salmon but of everyday fish. He
continued:

> It so happens that I am now in the middle of evolving a proposal
> for a new kind of floating fish cage which is intended to over-
> come the problems which have beset fish cages in the past, and
> there is no point in my doing anything else about fish farming
> until I have got a reaction from the NRDC about this particular
> device – the ROFFEC or Rotary Floating Fish Cage.

Far from regarding these latest suggestions as a bore for a busy newspaper, *The Observer* took all his ideas seriously with the science
correspondent, now Nigel Hawkes, being invited to give Blondie 'cause
for optimism' by telling him that his "highly interesting thoughts would
be met with an equally positive response by the newspaper". Indeed,
instead of attempting to stem the flow of ideas from the Old Forge, David
actively encouraged them.

> I very much enjoy getting this flow of ideas from you. I hope that
> this may mean that you are not departing in the near future to
> the Orkneys or Shetlands.

But in the end the Doomsday projects did not find favour with Hawkes
who believed that a great deal was already being done in that field. The

market, he considered, was saturated, although it was put to Blondie that he might like to take up his theories with more specialized journals. Nevertheless, and unknown to Blondie, David was to continue the theme with Nigel Hawkes in 1974:

> His mind is still working on ways to beat what the future may hold . . . His general belief is that there are more people writing books about doom than there are people carrying out practical experiments in making do without fossil fuels etc – chiefly for the reason that it is so difficult to make these experiments success-fully. I won't try to outline his numerous ideas but it seemed to me that we might have made a mistake in discouraging him from doing some work for us in this field.

In the end Blondie grew to the view that perhaps "the need for the return of large numbers of draught horses, barges and commercial sailing vessels is a little bit further away than it seemed then".

Little changed with marriage until May, 1967, when the Old Forge's attic was converted into a nursery in preparation for the birth, on 15 July in Winchester Hospital, of Dinah Lindsay Hasler with Thomas Arthur Hasler following on 17 December, 1969. Independent and single-minded, Bridget chose a home-birth for the second child.

In 1969 Jock's mother died, leaving an empty house in Scotland to which he now moved, having agreed with Blondie to split the business into two halves: Jock would continue to advise clients on how to convert their yachts while Blondie concentrated on vane gears and one-off special Chinese rigs. This was also the proliferation era for single-handed round the world attempts which first included just one stop and when that had been done twice (by Francis Chichester and Alec Rose) there were no stops. But events closer to home kept him busy and it was the entry of the fifty-foot, twenty-three ton yawl, *Speedwell of Cremyll* in the 1970 round-Britain[6] race that gave him the opportunity to develop his most powerful steering gear so far. Up to then vessels fitted with his vane-gears had either been small or they had been designed to be sailed by one man with a corresponding ease of handling for wind-vane equip-ment, let alone the human crew. *Speedwell* was large, heavy, designed to be raced by a crew of eight and, of design importance, possessed a mizzen boom proud of the stern by some feet; she also had wheel steering.

Then, on 19 January, 1971, Blondie's mother, the indomitable Annie,

[6]. Sailed by Ewen Tailyour and Roger Dillon – both Royal Marines officers.

collapsed at her home in Catherington and died a week later on the 26th. Blondie and John had been devoted to her, never failing to appreciate the sacrifices to which she had willingly subjected herself to ensure that her sons succeeded, through humility, example and impeccable behaviour towards others. Her pragmatic, understanding attitude towards two independent and adventurous young boys had remained an often-remembered example to them both throughout their very different lives. She had forged their characters and John and George had both recognized their debt by bestowing life-long love and support.

Although still sailing *Sumner*, Blondie's desire to experiment was not satisfied and in January, 1972, he flew to the Shetlands to buy an elderly, gutted-out, wooden fishing vessel called *Mizpah*. In October of that year he explained why in a letter to Bruce Jones of the White Fish Authority in Lissiemouth:

> She is a 34 foot Fifie (or Baldie) built in 1919 at Banff as a lugger without auxiliary engine a lug mainsail and mizzen . . . I intend to re-rig her . . . have a coach roof built over her hold and use her as a family cruising boat and for carrying my own freight, eg building materials, if we were to buy somewhere to live in a remote part of Scotland.

What had intrigued him was the possibility of fitting her with a dipping-lug rig which he knew from studying similar French craft of the Brittany coast had remarkable windward performance. Geoffrey Nockolds was not so convinced and laid various bets that his gaff cutter, *Juno*, would trounce the northern, re-rigged upstart. But there was still loyalty to old ideas and that summer *Sumner* was fitted, successfully, with a Chinese lugsail.

Although Blondie was able to comment that he was, for once, solvent, there was room for improvement and the arrival of Ian Major from the Virgin Islands with a commission for the survey of Scrub Island was a welcome boost, as well as another wonderful distraction. Tragically, this was not to take place for on 30 November, 1973, Blondie heard of Ian's murder (that day) at his home in the Virgin Islands.[7] Not only would he miss a very great friend but he had lost the companionship of a mind nearly as fertile, inventive and questioning as his own. Blondie missed

---

[7.] Having discovered "crookedness in high places", Ian was stabbed outside his front door where Cynthia found him dying. The murderer was never brought to trial.

too, though he would never have commented such, a man who appreciated his value and who had stood by him in the low days with practical
help and support.

Loss of friends was always a hard blow to Blondie. Later, he was to
lose another valued colleague and enthusiastic sounding board when, in
October, 1980, the yacht designer Angus Primrose was lost at sea. This
was another severe loss, but Blondie willingly took up his duties as
executor of the estate and increased his contacts with his godson, Dan
Primrose.

Scotland beckoned more strongly now and, with only the sketch of an
idea for the future, a valuation of The Old Forge was undertaken in
January, 1974, from which it was estimated that between £16,000 and
£17,000 might be realized on the market. But while it was still in his
hands, and still called The Old Forge, it had better earn its keep and thus
had Blondie been encouraged to attend the blacksmith's course in
February that he mentioned in his list of Doomsday projects.

In March Bridget's parents, who lived in Argyll, were persuaded to
look for a house (in Scotland) from which their daughter and son-in-law
could practise a life of true self-sufficiency, leaving any consultancy
income for modern-world essentials. Blondie and Bridget's dreams
reached further than just 'the good life' and while they knew it was what
they wanted they knew, very well indeed, that it would not, in practical
terms, be easy. Nine months later Ralph and Ursula Fisher were able to
suggest a farm off 'the road to the isles' and barely a hundred yards from
the upper reaches of a long sea loch. The estate was owned by Sir Stewart
MacTier[8] and, providing agreements on boundaries could be reached, it
sounded ideal.

Nautical transactions also flourished that summer with an agreement
to sell *Sumner* to an almost wholly paralysed Frenchman, Bernard Brecy,
for £1900, followed swiftly by the purchase of the prototype 'Hasler-
Kingfisher 20 Plus' that Blondie and Bridget named *Pilmer*.[9]

Despite an horrific driving accident that had left him, aged nineteen,
severely handicapped, Brecy continued to sail but only with the greatest

---

[8.] Sir Stewart MacTier, Kt, CBE, onetime Director of the The Ocean
Steamship Company and the Glen Line, who had served as the Director of the
Port and Transport Control in the Ministry of War Transport between 1940
and 1945. he gave his recreation as 'sailing' in *Who's Who* but never did so with
Blondie.

[9.] "The fine rain so frequent on our western coasts". Admiral Smythe in his
1867 *The Sailor's Word Book*.

of difficulty and immense help from his wife Rolande. In 1972 (eight years after his accident) he had written to Blondie seeking advice and help in incorporating some of *Jester's* features into his own boat so that he could sail alone. Blondie was so thrilled that such an enterprising and exceptional man should want *Sumner* that he, at his own expense, adapted her to Brecy's needs before the sale was completed. The two families became great and lasting friends.

GRAVE DANGER AHEAD

SHE MAY RUN OFF WITH A YACHTSMAN WHO HAS FITTED A HASLER VANE GEAR

# CHAPTER TWENTY-ONE

## The Road to the Isles

An inspection of the farm and the instant decision to make an offer began 1975 with an air of anticipation and excitement. An ex-Royal Marines officer, Jeff Douglas, agreed to buy The Old Forge and the amount of his offer appeared a good sum to suggest to the Argyll farm's owner but Sir Stewart hoped for rather more than was likely to be realized by The Old Forge's sale. At this precise moment an extraordinary stroke of financial luck came Bridget's way – she won a £5000 Premium Bond and on 31 January their new offer was accepted and the terms agreed. Years later they heard that in the short time between their first and second suggestions Sir Stewart had been offered a considerably larger sum which, without hesitation, he had refused in favour of the Haslers.

Take the Dumbarton Road out of Glasgow and eventually the housing estates and blocks of flats give way to the beauty of Loch Lomond. From here the stunning scenery is lochs and steep-sided glens with, in winter, few other motorists to disturb the journey. Once round the head of Loch Fyne and past the smokery (it is impossible to pass the smokery without stopping) the road to Inveraray winds down the western shore. On, then, to a glimpse of the islands and Scotland at her finest. Blondie and Bridget chose magnificently.

If anyone thought that at the age of 61 Blondie was searching for peaceful obscurity then they were wrong. Escape though it might have seemed, the move to Scotland was not a bolt for retirement, nor was it an attempt to hide from the world of experiments, designs and consultations. A set sum of money tends to buy more and more the further north one travels and, at the farm, Blondie and Bridget had reached the optimum distance for what they could afford – less money and they would have travelled even further from the crowded south.

The move was completed on 2 April and heralded six days of 'camping' with the builders still in semi-permanent residence. But the south of England cast a long shadow and, satisfied with progress, if not the rate of it, the Hasler family returned on 16 April to join *Pilmer* for a week's cruising along the north French coast. A general tidying up of affairs followed, included the packing of "endless bits of wood, metal and old boats plus two canoes" prior to permanent emigration north of the border in a removal van and a small lorry which Blondie drove for two round journeys; not forgetting the piano which had its own transport as it totally filled the Austin Mini-van.

There was time for Blondie to vote 'no' in the 5 June Referendum on whether or not the United Kingdom should join the Common Market before he was able to enter his diary with the words:

> June 21: Complete sale of Old Forge to Jeff Douglas. 22: Arrive farm. Builders still working. Chaos. 25th: 29th: buy Border Collie pup – Jess, born March '75.

A number of mentors passed through Blondie Hasler's life and from each of these he would absorb knowledge and experience in a continual search for improvement with the genuine belief that little ever reaches its ultimate stage of evolution. Before the war Pat Phibbs had encouraged sailing as an extension of some aspects of 'military' prowess; Lord Mountbatten, Professor Solly Zuckerman (as he had then been) and Uffa Fox were three such influences during the war; for sailing post 1945 it was Bobby Somerset[1] and John Illingworth's turn to influence; for his drawings and painting skills he was coached and encouraged by his friend Siegfried Charoux[2] the noted, internationally recognized artist and sculptor for whom Blondie held a deep admiration and respect; in the 'inventing' world there were Sir Kenneth Hutchison[3] and Sir William Hawthorne[4] of Dracone Limited and the Loch Ness Patrol and in this final, and certainly most contented, but probably most difficult stage (for he was, literally, about to break new ground) there was Hardie Telfer.

Hardie was a Perthshire man, ex-game keeper, deer-stalker, ghillie and now a tenant hill farmer of Argyll. He had served through the war in the Scottish Horse and had at some time been seconded to Popski's Private

---

[1] One of the most successful British ocean racing skippers who had a house in Majorca to which Blondie would be invited for discussions. He was drowned at sea.

[2] 1896–1967. Born in Austria he lived in, and admired, England. He was known for the manner in which he used his sculptures to highlight humanity and express his view that human feelings count above everything else.

[3] See Appendix One.

[4] See Chapter Seventeen.

Army as the Colonel's bodyguard: to his total regret, though, he had never been a full part of that daring organization. Now, he was to admit freely, Blondie would better him in a number of his skills. Hardie, who had never been to sea other than in a rowing boat on the rivers and a troopship to the Middle East, was, in return, to understudy Blondie in the ways of a yacht until, if not perfect, then at least able to take his watch unsupervised, even when racing and especially when running before the wind.

Hardie was a tenant of Sir Stewart's and rented the grazing around the Haslers' farm. As soon as the new owners moved in he called on them, by invitation, to discuss cutting the hay, thus beginning an enduring friendship. With the cut completed on 2 July a landmark in self-reliance was reached for which, perhaps subconsciously, Blondie had been striving all his life. Now there were two young children to be brought up in the ways of the sea and the land – both hard taskmasters – and there was a community to be joined, a community that lived by the sea and one that was, thankfully, far from the frenetic south. From the very first days Blondie and Bridget felt at home, this feeling being reciprocated many-fold.

Some years later when summing up the community's initial reaction to the arrival of the Hasler family, David Montgomery, the village minister, was to write:

> When he came to live with Bridget and their two young children, Dinah and Tom, we took them to our hearts because of their openness and friendliness. There were whispers at first that Blondie was some kind of celebrity, but he and his family were soon cherished, loved and honoured for what they were in themselves among us.

Here was a place where Blondie could devote time to bring up his family in exactly the social and practical conditions for work and play that he and Bridget considered perfect. Dinah and Tom were already accomplished seamen for they had taken part in, and often won, various rowing and sailing regattas on the Hamble and had, naturally, accompanied their parents in the four cross-channel cruises that *Sumner* had undertaken before she was permanently 'seconded' to that part of France.

But bringing up the children was not all sailing and regattas; instead of reading his offspring to sleep as a conventional form of paternal contact (or 'bonding' in the dreadful modern idiom) Blondie chose a more practical way to bring each day to a close. When ready for bed Dinah, and eventually Tom, would creep into the office where he would draw a cartoon showing the main event of the day, sometimes as a 'lesson learnt', or a similar sketch forecasting the morrow's programme. These would then be coloured by the young at a later date in the large books kept for the purpose and which now exist as a vivid, pictorial diary of their growing up.

The village, down the loch and towards the sea, sprawls around the northern and western edge of a land-locked bay and it was to this community that Blondie and Bridget now devoted many of their interests. They could hardly wait to tell David Astor of their new find:

> We can see Jura if we walk up the hill. For years we've been looking for a house with a few acres and a sheltered anchorage, and we were very lucky to hear of this just before Christmas.
>
> Our present cruising boat – a fibreglass potty only 22 feet long – is still down at Poole, but I hope to sail her up here in August. After that we would be able to sail her over and see you all if you were in Jura, which would be nice for us. Meanwhile we are digging in here, having got rid of the builders while still solvent and now will slowly get the inside of the house painted and organized. Dinah and Tom are going to the very good village school.

Fittingly (and touchingly) their first visitors were Bernard and Rolande Brecy (plus five year old daughter) who sailed up the Loch from France at the end of July 1975.

At the beginning of September Blondie sailed *Pilmer* to her new home, single-handed from Poole without a steering gear (this had been stolen just before departure) and with her arrival all was finally in place and the last physical contact with the south cut.

Designing and consulting could begin again, with a welcome boost of substantial orders for the Hasler-rigged Kingfisher, the successful prototype of which was now lying to her moorings less than a mile away. Scotland's west coast climate is not the same as that of Hampshire, and so a mini wood-burning stove suitable for tiny twenty-two foot yachts was one of the first developments to be sketched in blue ink in the small notebooks kept for the purpose.

Past adventures would occasionally catch up with Blondie in his Scottish retreat and few were received with more pleasure than those that related to his Loch Ness Patrol of 1962. In October news had reached

*The Observer's* editor of a "monster corpse" being dragged up by Japanese fishermen, prompting an immediate comment from Blondie:

> The fins in the photograph look *exactly* like the underwater photograph of the Loch Ness fins and I have no doubt that it was one of the various unidentified families of 'sea serpent'. I have just this morning written a letter to a French Admiral who had a sea serpent sighting off the west coast of Scotland and never reported it for fear of ridicule.
>
> It is crazy that there is no 'report centre' to which one can send such reports with any hope that they will be treated seriously and filed for use by interested people. At least the UFOs (one was seen in these parts recently) have some sort of Society that collects reports, but the Sea Serpent has none.

By far the most important project, though, was a definitive book on modern junk rigged vessels on which he and Jock now embarked. This *tour de force* was to take many years of dedicated research starting with a comprehensive introduction ready by that November, 1975. *Practical Junk Rig* stemmed from a desire to tabulate, in progressive form, the results of over two decades of empirical experiments and intellectual study. It demonstrates, as it was intended to do, the fascination, and admiration for, the Chinese lug-sail and the thinking behind its modern development.

It was also a natural progression from the folio system that Blondie and Jock used as they became inundated with requests for individual instructions and drawings in order that clients could undertake design work themselves. Once the book was published, just after Blondie's death, this system was discontinued. The Foreword sets the scene:

> Sail enthusiasts all over the world are showing an increasing interest in the Chinese, or Junk, rig. This is because the rig is incomparably safe, seamanlike and easy to handle and is particularly suitable for small boats and for short-handed or family sailing in open water and in unpredictable conditions . . . our qualifications are simply that we have worked together on the development of the Chinese rig for twenty-five years, using it on our own boats and designing rigs for other yachtsmen in various parts of the world. Between us we have sailed . . . ten crossings of the Atlantic . . . The more we sail it the more we like it and this is true both on ocean passages and when cruising in coastal

waters . . . Our most distinguished client is undoubtably Bill King whose forty-two foot *Galway Blazer II* carried him across 40,000 miles of ocean . . . we believe she may have been the first junk-rigged vessel in history to have sailed round the world and round the Horn . . . The adaptation of this ancient rig to modern needs is still in an early stage but we have tried to provide a starting point from which other enthusiasts will make further headway . . .

The farm was the overriding passion and to that Blondie and Bridget now devoted their considerable, corporate inventiveness and energies. Very few days passed without the help and advice of the previous tenants, Duncan and Chrissie McLullich, and Hardie Telfer, whether called for or not, and when 'not' it was usually high time that it was, especially as the farm, when they bought it, was economically viable, although Bridget was to say later that it was the last time that it was so! Fields were planted with all manner of crops, often throwing up problems to tax even the Hasler ingenuity and humour. For example, when finishing the sowing of 110 pounds of wheat the sewage system that ran beneath the field decided to burst: "Ah, good; now we will have to dig out the ancient cesspit" – and he did.

Preparation of the fields continued into late spring, when the un-finished *Mizpah* was sold for £700, the first potatoes were lifted, the cesspit was in full use, water had been successfully dowsed and was irrigating the land and the first wheat was ready for threshing at the end of October. Not everything was manual and, despite assuring Hardie that a chain saw and a small rotavator were the last things he needed, they were also the first mechanical aids that Blondie bought. There were dead trees to be felled for there was winter fuel for the house and boat to be stored – it was all, in the modern idiom, a very steep learning curve for Blondie and Bridget but one that was climbed with laughter and great energy, with, all the time, much advice, help and practical support from new friends in the village.

Hardie was attracted to Blondie as he had been to no other:

He was a wonderful man, out of this world, and would make us all feel that we were not Tom, Dick or Harry; when you were with Blondie you were part of his life. He taught me that class didn't really exist, that it was imaginary and that was part of the lesson that he had for all of us.

Hardie taught Blondie the practical aspects such as hand-scything, stook-tying and, later, the eccentric ways of the old binder.

> But he had the theory of everything stored in his mind before he started: the theory of agriculture, the rotating of crops, drainage and the right seasons for planting and harvesting. The practical things I would teach him only once, such as how to use the five-pronged fork for throwing dung. People who have never handled these things are hopeless and you cannot learn that from a book but at this as with everything, Blondie became proficient.

From Duncan McLullich he learnt the intricate pattern and flow of the land drains as together they probed and cleared them while Blondie charted their underground courses – a vital record using nautical methods of position-finding. As a result, years later, Bridget was able to pinpoint immediately the exact position of a sewage pipe and clear a blockage.

There were concessions to some modern ideas; the chain saw had been one and the grey Ferguson TEF 20 tractor and Begg plough, bought with Hardie's assistance at Campbeltown in November, were others. The first ploughing attempts took place a week later with intense concentration and the grudging approval of the mentor. But all this help was not a one-way flow:

> I'm telling you about me helping him but that was only half of the thing. Blondie came down to my place picking potatoes and he would help me with a milk round. I liked his company and he must have liked my company too because if I was two or three days absent he would ask me where on earth I had been. He grew every kind of crop but he needed to water them so we went up the hill seeking for water. So many people would say that there was a shortage of underground water here but not Blondie. He dowsed for his own, dug a well and devised a siphon system so that his crops would remain properly looked after.[5]

Following a demonstration on 27 September the next day was worthy of a special diary entry:

[5.] He designed a modern version of the middle-east Shadouf system for drawing water from a well using a counterbalance to the goat skin at the opposite end of a long, asymetrically-pivoted arm.

Demonstration of flail threshing by Ronnie McLaughlin.
Winnow enough for first loaf.

It was a move forward but there were others. Butchery was learned
through considerable trials and many errors until the day that a red stag
was successfully cut up in the kitchen; afterwards the family never looked
back in that regard. Hand-milking and butter-making were natural
extensions of keeping cattle with Hardie's old churn brought out of
retirement for the purpose.

*Pilmer* was now part of the village scenery and, as well as being used
as a test-bed for a new-style steering gear and an efficient source of
mackerel, she took her part in the local regatta that first year at which all
distinguished themselves. And so life settled into one of near total
contentment for Blondie and his family. It was not always easy and it was
often not financially productive but it was satisfying, definitely fulfilling
and always fun.

Inevitably local responsibilities were offered and accepted, the most
'productive' being the Village Hall Committee where his project for the
Silver Jubilee Green was carried out with all the dedication and attention
that he had given to the various military operations for which he had been
responsible. Even closer to his heart was the secretaryship of the Harbour
Committee where he is particularly remembered for "bringing order out
of chaos to the moorings". He also stood his share of 'door duty' at the
village hall dances, helped at barbecues, regattas and, inevitably, Sunday
afternoon sailing races.

Occasionally a slight shadow would be cast over the idyll; while dis-
appointing, none received more than a cursory mention and certainly
were not considered a real threat to the happiness they all shared. The
sales of vane-gears began to collapse, due largely to a sudden proliferation of other models backed with commercial money. The refusal of the
yacht builders, Westerly, to countenance the fitting of a junk rig option
on their various models brought brief, initial frustration, but with the
shutting of one door another would often open: for instance he was asked
to design a Chinese rig for the Halmatic 30, a most seaworthy yacht with
an underwater hull form much to Blondie's liking. Meanwhile progress
on 'the book' was steady with the first draft complete by 21 June, 1978
– but there was a long way to go.

April, 1979, marked the surprising end to the floating breakwater
when Rhu Marina, on the Gareloch, decided not to bring the Seabreaker
model 001 to Scotland. Following this decision, the whole project was
scrapped, although not before he had attended a meeting with the

NRDC in London later in the year to see what might be salvaged. Hugh Bruce and Peter Hamilton's company, Sea Services Agency, acted as the sole United Kingdom agents for the Hasler Seabreaker, and had, among others, been close to signing contracts with the city of Chicago but this had not materialized either. As Peter was to write:[6]

> I was struck by the vast quantity of technical information he had acquired on wave motion and structural engineering. In trying to market the device, all possible clients came up with the remark: "Yes. I grant you it does seem to work. Seems to work very well in fact." (Which it did). "But how on earth can a Royal Marine colonel *know* all this. He's not a qualified engineer." It was a very real drawback. People love to have strings of letters after inventor's names if they are going to buy the invention.

This was a blow, for Blondie had felt that here had been an excellent idea with good commercial possibilities, but, "Ah well, now we know," and so be it. He looked forward again.

Blondie became eligible for an old age pension on 27 February, 1979, but was surprised to learn that he was not to receive one as his "earnings are just too high". It was not until after his sixty-sixth birthday that he managed to persuade an unimpressed Department of Social Security that he was worth the pension to which he had contributed in kind and effort for so long.

Despite appearing to shut himself away in a remote part of Scotland, Blondie's views were still sought, as proved by an invitation from the Royal Institute of Naval Architects to present a paper at a symposium on Commercial Sail that they were holding on 14 June, 1979, to be attended by HRH The Duke of Edinburgh.

The Duke opened the proceedings by stating:

> The successful development of wind-driven ships . . . will depend on the support and encouragement made available to research projects in the future and the judgement exercised in their control and evaluation. I cannot wait to hear what people are going to say this morning.

The Chairman, Sir Frederic Bolton, ended his opening words with the news that the Department of Industry's Ship and Marine Technology

---

[6.] Letter to the author dated 28 September, 1996.

Requirements Board had already sponsored two studies, one into conventional sailing ships and one into

> more exotic ways in which wind can be used to drive ships. At the end of the day we shall have proper publicity for the various arguments and this should . . . help us in deciding what we should encourage with government funds.

Blondie's ideas, as presented, contained the following opinions:

> The papers read at this symposium have been concerned with the use of sail to reduce the consumption of diesel and fuel in ocean going ships, but fuel will also be scarce and expensive for coastal and inshore vessels and for road and rail transport ashore. There must exist a parallel requirement for the revival of sail in coastal waters with the twin aim of reducing the consumption of fuel by existing coastal vessels and for taking back from the road and rail systems bulk cargo trades traditionally, until very recently, carried by sea, estuary river and canal.
>
> To be as brief as possible I suggest that the scope of the ship and the marine technology requirements aboard could, with advantage, include research into the following headings
>
> 1. The use of sail to reduce fuel consumption in existing coastal shipping trades, passenger, cargo and fishing and services such as pilot cutters.
> 2. The possible introduction of sailing coasters to reduce the fuel consumption of road and rail services by opening or re-opening alternative sea-routes.
> 3. The possible use of small sailing vessels to extend the depleted services now offered to many of our isolated but inhabited islands.
> 4. Design studies of modernized sailing coasters and their methods of handling different cargoes including containers . . .
> 5. Designing studies of modernized sailing fishermen and their methods of fishing including the processing of fish on board before landing.
>
> Coastal sailing vessels will obviously require different kinds of rig and different hull forms from those of ocean-going ships with a strong bias towards rigs that are suitable for working into

narrow waters and hulls of shallow draft that are able to take the ground fully loaded . . .

From the practical point of view it would be much easier and cheaper to make a start on sailing coasters than deep water ships. In spite of the fundamental differences there would be many lessons from one that would be applicable to the other.

Finally in order to avoid any possibility of being considered a crank and because I sense it is outside the scope of this symposium I have avoided suggesting that we could make use of deserted railways with a development of the Pacific Railways Sailing Power that could once cover forty miles in one hour, or of deserted motorways as a successor to Bishop Wilkin's sailing chariot of 1648.

In February 1980, Sir Stewart and Lady MacTier decided to emigrate to Australia later that year, a decision which allowed Blondie to negotiate, successfully, for increased grazing rights and the next month a French television team interviewed him on the single-handed trans-Atlantic races for he was still remembered as the man who had given France a new national sport and a new generation of heroes.

But none of this brought in serious money. There were writing commissions at irregular intervals which certainly helped, the new Pentab steering gear system was proving to be a success, (if still in limited numbers) and Bridget helped Hardie by gathering his sheep on a regular basis.

His library, which once contained books mainly on sailing, monsters and jazz, was now filled with well-thumbed titles such as *Down to Earth Gardening*, *Self Sufficiency*, *Old Farms*, *Keeping Pigs*, *Practical Beekeeping*, *Crofting – A Culture*, *The Farm and the Village*, *Old Farm Tools and Machinery*, *Victorian Farming* and the *Illustrated Blacksmith's Manual*. There was still much that he wanted to learn.

Hardie Telfer takes up the story again:

> He invented another thing; apart from an arrangement for making it easier to cut wood in the most dangerous positions, he invented a better tractor box. A three-cornered affair that fitted into the bolts already on the tractor so that you were carrying your load in the centre of the tractor. If you were carrying too heavy a load on a tractor and you were going up a steep hill you couldn't with a transport box but this was right in the centre, yet he never marketed it. It was a brilliant thing.

Although physically strong, Blondie's body, for so long affected by spondylitis, now began to complain at the punishing routine of harvesting, shifting and placing sixteen telegraph poles to make a sheaf drying rack to an ancient design, laying moorings, tussling successfully, with the Highlands and Islands Development Board for money to repair the village's post office pier, digging potatoes, collecting and distributing seaweed, surveying and marking the approaches to the anchorage, cattle rearing and general crofting duties. It was hardly surprising that in the early 1980s a hip needed replacing and that he began to suffer badly, but uncomplainingly, from arthritis for which he embarked on the Dong[7] diet. This, and a swim in the loch before breakfast five mornings a week, produced some (but not total) beneficial effects.

Dinah left the village school in 1977 to attend Gordonstoun's preparatory school, Aberlour, from where she passed into the public school in 1981; Tom followed the same route a year later with generous help from Cynthia Major, widow of his godfather. After working abroad, Dinah gained a first in Philosophy from Aberdeen University and now works with the *Aberdeen Press and Journal* while Tom's '2:1' in Mechanical Engineering from Edinburgh took him and some friends into a small company, Seafloor Dynamex whose expertise is aimed at sea bed operations with the North Sea oil industry.

Another family move, in January, 1981, was that of Bridget's parents, Ralph and Ursula Fisher, to a cottage at the bottom of the farm's drive. This was not the in-laws moving in against his wishes for Blondie was caring and loving towards Ralph and Ursula; the Lieutenant-Colonel and the Rear-Admiral shared similar outlooks and would extract great amusement from dissecting the smallest item until, together, they had understood why it existed, how it worked and whether or not it could be improved.

These days were filled with visitors and visiting, so much so that at one point a plaintive but sympathetic note appears that "the time set aside for sailing has been filled up by friends".

> When our two children come home from school for the holidays all hell is let loose with hordes of visitors coming up from England to stay with us and poor Bridget nearly out of her mind trying to feed them all.[8]

---

[7] Among other restriction – no red meat. Plenty of vegetables and nothing acid.

[8] Letter to Murray Davis dated 5 September, 1981.

But everyone was welcome, no matter how full the bedrooms, for all were genuine friends, interested in the Hasler family activities. The house was permanently brimming with laughter and plans, wet sailing clothes and music from the banjo-ukele or piano. Although never able to read music, Blondie could produce any tune requested much to the amusement of the young who never tired of trying to catch him out.

Letters continued to arrive from all quarters seeking advice or moral support for some project or other with every request given precise attention, sometimes being answered with additional information far from the original subject, as Bill Wallace[9] from Houston, Texas, discovered in June, 1985:

> Any comments I may make are of little value, being largely conjecture from someone who has operated only spasmodically, and on the lunatic fringe of sailing for the past thirty years . . .
>
> As regards the 57 foot design, the canoe shape is pretty and reminds me of a 10 sq m. canoe but the bow rudder worries me . . . I feel that the ideal downwind bow is spoon-shaped like a surf board, able to hunt from side to side when running down the face of a wave while the boat is held firmly on the rails by the (deeper) stern end. I have longed for an actual spoon that hinges over the sharp bow and hinged back over the bow when going to windward . . .
>
> About the whisky: I am not an expert as I never drink the stuff unless social etiquette demands it (which is frequent in Scotland) but in my opinion the smartest usage is to ask for a dram (only in Scotland, the term is not in general use in England) when you will be given a glass of whisky and (usually) a small jug of water (at room temperature) with which to dilute it if you wish. At least half the Scots will add water. Ice is out, soda unheard of, but to our astonishment when we migrated to Scotland we found that many women, and even some men, add *lemonade* (ugh) to it! If you are feeling rich you try a single malt whisky, preferably undiluted, which makes a very soft and mellow liqueur liquor liqueur (I need three shots at spelling it). We hope to offer you a dram when you visit.

---

[9.] Bill had taken part in the 1980 and 1984 single-handed trans-Atlantic races.

Putting friends, the farm, spondylitis, arthritis and suspected gout aside, Blondie could still find plenty of time for sailing with Bridget and the children, despite *Pilmer* becoming a little small for all of them together. Although never commenting, he may have yearned for the wider expanses of the Atlantic but he now believed that it would be wrong to leave Bridget, Dinah and Tom at home. It would matter more than it ever had if "he didn't get back" and that responsibility weighed heavily against him making any further lone offshore voyages – nor, mindful of his age, did he want to miss one moment more than was necessary with the children. And, as the editor's sub-title to an article he wrote for *Yachting Monthly*[10] he called *"Round Jura?"* suggests, suitable enough drama lay close at hand to satisfy him:

> Blondie Hasler, the veteran of many single-handed trans-Atlantic crossings, finds the weather near home can equal anything in mid-ocean . . .

a point Blondie himself had always made. This was a wonderful four-day cruise with just the two of them and indicated that, despite two hernia operations, and the first of two hip replacements due in two months, Blondie had, at sixty-nine, lost none of his skills nor enthusiasm.

> My two teenage children had just gone back to school. We had got our acre of oats safely in and the potatoes could wait in the ground a little longer. My wife Bridget said, "Why don't we go off for a little cruise, just us two. Perhaps we could sail round Jura?" . . . It was September and my experience is that summer finishes at the end of August on the west coast of Scotland. Luckily Bridget is not much more than half my age and has been sailing so long that she does the right thing automatically, like breathing. Was I man or mouse, I pondered, not for the first time, and so it was agreed that we would start if there was a prospect of three days of reasonably settled weather.

The weather did not stay settled. Indeed the log speaks of almost continual fresh or gale force winds from the south-east to south-west,

[10] September, 1985.

and Jura was not circumnavigated, but by many criteria it was a hard four days conducted with impeccable style:

> We had . . . given *Pilmer* a good testing and had no fault to find in her response. All she needs now is an enclosed cockpit such as we had in *Jester* and *Sumner* in which you keep watch with only your head out of a small hatch, protected by a rotatable pram-hood. We had not used . . . the engine after the first evening, but had made a total of twenty-one changes of sail area whilst under way, without once ever leaving the cockpit, all but one of them in less than 30 seconds.

It belongs to Hardie Telfer to sum up sailing in those twilight years of Blondie's life. Hardie, who had never set foot in a yacht until the Haslers bought the farm and who, until then, would no more have considered sailing with a 'toff' than joining the league against blood sports, relished this new life and the company of the man who introduced him to it. His devotion to his sailing instructor was as complete as was Blondie's to his crofting mentor:

> I only ever sailed with Blondie Hasler and there is not many who can make that boast. Every Sunday, and many days between, and it was wonderful. While we were out Bridget would be sailing in the Mirror dinghy.
> Blondie was terrible keen on self-sufficiency and, when not racing, going for the mackerel was part of that business – broad beans, mackerel and rotation farming. The crop that requires nitrogen next year is where you grow your beans this year for they add nitrogen to the soil . . . He understood all this yet he had not done any of these things before he came up here.

They would swop yarns over the statutory drams, Blondie recounting tales of others' nautical deeds and Hardie recalling his time in Popski's Private Army.

> The great thing about Blondie's life was that he was a character and he attracted and was attracted to people who were characters. No one with whom he was involved ever came away the same – if they were an ordinary sort of fellow before they met

him they certainly were not afterwards! In many respects the story of Blondie is the story of all those he came in contact with – and that includes the young. He loved the young people and they loved him.

The rough and tumble continued to extract its toll: new hips in 1984 and 1985 were followed by what he described as a "minor heart attack" in April, 1986. Tragically, a more severe attack followed, despite, typically, "enjoying trying to get everything stronger simultaneously" after the hip and heart setback. The most severe attack occurred on 7 April, 1987, requiring a fortnight in hospital. Friends from very far and near made excuses to visit him to find an unchanged Blondie planning for the future; but his health was deteriorating rapidly and nobody was taken in by his cheerful and remarkable optimism. On Monday 4 May at an address in Glasgow from where Bridget was "keeping watch" she wrote to Mike Richey:

He's allowed home on Wednesday but will have to take things pretty easily. He so hates drugs – it's hellish that he has to rely on them now. He's cheerful as usual though – in fact he has been all the time.

Blondie Hasler died on the morrow, seventy years and a day after his father.

Tributes from all corners of the military and sailing worlds and, of greater significance, from men and women from every possible walk of life, arrived at the farm. Obituaries appeared in the 'usual' newspapers and yachting press and while all were unanimous in their praise and coverage of the Bordeaux raid few, if any, acknowledged what he had considered to be his finest wartime hours; those spent in north Norway. Nor did any pay tribute to the months he had spent establishing and then directing the remarkable series of morale-sapping raids into Japanese-occupied Burma. *Jester* and the steering gears came in for generous compliments as did the contentment and success of farming with his family in Scotland. If he had been asked he would probably have liked his sense of humour and the Loch Ness Patrol to have been given honourable mentions as well.

The funeral was held in the village kirk: the noises of nature that had been the permanent backdrop to his life's work – the gulls, the wind and the sea – filled the nave from just a few yards away. The Royal Marines in general and the Special Boat Service in particular were represented by two officers, both of whom had, coincidentally, taken part in his races.[11] There were, too, representatives from the RMBPD[12] and 385 Detachment but the kirk was largely packed with members of the local community. The yachting and military worlds would have their opportunity to say goodbye and honour his life later in the year when they would fill Portsmouth's cathedral, but for the moment it was the village that paid respects to 'their' man. The minister's address on that 11 May, 1987, summed-up not just local feelings but those of everyone with whom he had fought, sailed, farmed and laughed:

> Blondie was not a medal-wearer, living in the glow of past exploits – rather that we knew that his life was all of one piece, in that whatever he did, he did with a high sense of responsibility and with an exceptional thoroughness – whether it was in his distinguished service career during the war (and he would have been embarrassed and abashed to know that we had even mentioned it) or in his single-handed ocean sailing which he pioneered and others followed, or in his numerous inventions; he gave to everything he did careful and thorough thought and the incisiveness of a keen and inquiring mind . . . Blondie was a complete man, courageous far beyond the average, yet quiet in his ways; a strong man physically and mentally yet with infinite gentleness; single-minded yet tolerant and sympathetic towards others. Blondie was a good man, a man of the most complete Christian character.

Later, after a cremation in Glasgow, his ashes were scattered over his favourite anchorage – remote and unfrequented.

It is right that Bridget, with whom he shared so much love and happiness, and whose ideals absolutely matched his, should have the last words: words written to Mike Richey when confirming that she would like him to give the address at the Thanksgiving Service to be held at noon on 19 June, 1987, in Old Portsmouth's cathedral, close to the waters over which he had sailed his first punt sixty years before:

> It's very kind of you to say that you'll give the Address, or Tribute, at Blondie's Service. I know it's a burden in a way;

[11.] Respectively Ewen Southby-Tailyour and Richard Clifford.
[12.] Bill Ladbroke.

specially on top of all you're trying to do – but thank you. Blondie would be horrified at the idea of you having to perhaps mess up your sailing in *Jester* and I was loath to ask you in lots of ways. The trouble is just about all his marine friends are no longer around – either that or they are people who know and appreciate all his exploits but maybe don't appreciate what a wonderful person he was: he never did a mean thing to anyone. I am deeply grateful to him for everything he ever did.

David Astor wrote; "I know he didn't like to be praised but it's hard not to think of him as someone who really was far superior to others – including the genuiness of his modesty. In strength of character and boldness and originality of mind he was in the highest class – an eternal inspiration."

The service is being taken by Basil Watson[13] . . . I hope it"ll be very much a Thanksgiving Service and not gloomy.

He was incredibly brave and courageous and calm about things these last few months.

As I think you know, he loved this farm and taught himself to do everything the proper, traditional craftsman's way. He ploughed beautifully – it's a real art.

*He ploughed beautifully – it's a real art* and, as with everything else in his life, it had also been immense fun, conducted with much laughter.

At the Service of Thanksgiving Mike Richey did give the address and Colonel Johnnie Coke read from Chaucer:

> A knight there was and that a worthy man
> Who from the day on which he first began
> To ride abroad had followed chivalry,
> Truth, honour, generousness and courtesy.
> He was of sovereign value in all eyes.
> And though so much distinguished, he was wise
> And in his bearing modest as a maid.
> He never yet a boorish thing had said
> In all his life to any, come what might;
> He was a very perfect, gentle knight.

---

[13.] Lately a Royal Navy Chaplain. Although a long friend of the Royal Marines, he had never met Blondie.

The Royal Marines buglers then played Sunset before the Prayers of Thanksgiving concluded with a Celtic Blessing:

> Deep peace of the Running Wave to you
> Deep peace of the Flowing Air to you
> Deep peace of the Quiet Earth to you
> Deep peace of the Shining Stars to you
> Deep peace of the Son of Peace to you.

## THE END

# APPENDIX ONE

It was generally accepted that Blondie Hasler was too modest to write his own story, and while that is true he did have one teasing attempt enigmatically titled *Hasler – The Man Behind the Façade* A second, more serious, undertaking remained unknown until, seven years after his death, a draft manuscript was unearthed. This was to have been an anthology of various nautical endeavours with the more apt title of *Experimenting with Boats*. He planned "70,000 words, plenty of sketches and not more than sixteen pages of photographs" covering the craft with which he had been involved from 1925 to the summer of 1966. While considerable thought went into its preparation it remains doubtful that it was intended for publication. What remains are the Synopsis (highlighting what he though was significant), a Foreword (of sorts), the last half of Chapter Seven and the first half of Chapter Eight. It could be argued that he might have preferred that a biographer (towards whom, perhaps, this effort was aimed) keep to his original layout and content but that would be to ignore much that he was too modest to expose.

Yet it must be right to allow his own expressions and phrases to describe the few events he did record in manuscript. Repetition has been edited out but, where possible his common-sense, whimsy, advice and humour have been retained, highlighting the regret that he did not complete the job – perhaps the only significant task in his life that he left unfinished.

On 6 April, 1967, he wrote to David Astor:

> Idiotically, I have got myself under contract to write a book on the general theme of Experiments in Boats. It will be a pseudo-technical book strung on a thin autobiographical thread.[1]

---

[1]   With the lack of any clues to support this statement it is unlikely that he had a contract: it is more probable that his modesty required this "excuse".

The following (except those brief comments in italics) was written by Blondie:

# Chapter I 1914–1932

CANOE LAKE AND ENGLISH CHANNEL

*Canoe Lake, Southsea*: Models, paddle boats, steam boats, canoes, rowing boats.

*First Boat*: Canvas canoe. Sailing downwind. Envy of sailing boats.

*Failed Dartmouth*: Frustrated seaman at inland school.[2] (Conjecture if passed.)

*Inland School*: No teachers, no critics – conjecture if had had them.

*The Schoolboy Pundit*: OTC Dreams.

*Second Boat*: Home-built, flat-iron "sharpie". Its development – tarred bottom. Mud Harbours. Solent cruising. Barges and fishermen.

*Entered Marines*: Perfect situation for sailing. (Conjecture if Navy.) A sail in *Westward*.

*Third Boat* (uniform allowance) *The Voilit* (sic) – reaction to her loss.

*Fourth Boat*: Dinghy. Portsmouth Sailing Club.

*Fifth Boat*: *Trivia* – first thoroughbred dinghy. Coastal cruising, Plymouth to Portsmouth and return. *Bluenose*.

# Chapter II. 1932–1939

AMPHIBIOUS DOINGS

*Fleet Flagship*: Malta and Greek Islands. Main derrick. Sail in a Star. Abyssinian crisis.

*Back in England.*

*Sixth Boat*: Rectangular canoe/punt of hardboard.

*Seventh Boat*: RNSA/Island dinghy.

*RNSA Journal.* Assistant Editor.

*Eighth Boat*: *Mandy*. RNSA 14 ft.

*MNBDO Landing Officer*: Piers and beach roadways. MLC 10. Diving course. ISTDC. Coronation Review. Munich Crisis. Scapa Flow. *Wanda* (Gerald Potter) and RORC.

*Ninth Boat*: Felucca.[3]

---

[2]  Interestingly, there is no other evidence that he wanted to join the Royal Navy nor that he "failed Dartmouth" nor, indeed, that he was unhappy at Wellington because of its distance from the sea.

[3]  The only mention he makes of this Nile craft.

*Return of Peace* – Another canoe/punt. (Tenth boat.) Mansfield's gun. Buying a *Vallam*. (Eleventh boat). Home again.

## Chapter VI

*TRE-SANG* AND OTHERS
*Twelth Boat*: *Tre-Sang* – Modifications. Characteristics. Lessons.
*Thirteenth Boat*: Fairey Canoe – Planning and twin spinnakers.
*Surfing*: Surfboats. Coble.
*Coble Model*: Reversible hull and rig.
*Myth of Malham*: 1st Season. Fastnet, La Rochelle and Channel Races.
*Firefly*.
*Leaving the Marines*
*Finding a Boat* – *Petula*. (Fourteenth Boat.)

## Chapter VII

ON THE LOOSE
*Myth of Malham*: Bermuda race. sail home.
*Petula*: Rig. Griping. Handling. Protection. Crew. Single-handed. Rockall. Norway. Spain. Ornithologists. Winter living. *Harbours and Anchorages*. Long cruise frustrated. Boat or Cottage? Requirements for new boat. End of romantic period.
*End of Conventional Period*: Cruising less attractive. Onset of inventor's syndrome. *Petula's* end.

## Chapter VIII

Trying to Achieve Something 1953–1966
*Spearfisth*.
*Jester (Lapwing)*: (Fifteenth Boat). Vospers. Model trials. (Ian Major). Twin hulls. Aerofoil sails. Perfect running rig.
*Autogyro Sail*.
*Umbrella foils*.
*Rigid foils*.
*Child's Squaresail*.
*Cabin heaters*. Condenser heater – balanced flue.
*Fin Locomotion*.
*Single-handed Transatlantic Race – Origins*.
*Ropewheel Winch*.
*Dracones*.
*Warwick Films*.

---

[4]   No known mention was made in any correspondence or article written by Blondie – this is the only single-word reference to this affliction.
[5]   Jock McLeod.

## Chapter XIII

## Chapter XIV

## Index

## Bibliography

## Foreword

This is not a "scientific" book, unless you are using the word in its 19th century sense. I am not a scientist and soon get out of my depth when confronted with scientific theory, much of which stirs in me a sort of peasant's mistrust, an attitude of sulky disbelief.

This is an account of various experiments undertaken as a form of recreation but occasionally for sterner purposes such as earning a living or co-operating in a war. Many were set up without spending any appreciable money and this kind has often seemed to get the best results . . .

In the field of small boats the reading public flinches under a barrage of pseudo science and risks being engulfed by a great, wet avalanche of unsupported conjecture presented as fact. We need fewer pundits and more experiments . . .

The amateur experimenter or inventor must often carry enthusiasm to the brink of madness if he is to struggle with a hostile world as well as with nature, but at least he can take heart from the history of modern invention which shows an astonishingly high proportion of success achieved initially by laymen working outside their own sphere of specialist knowledge.

A great scientist once said to me "All radical development takes place in the teeth of opposition from the expert". Perhaps the most difficult thing to guard against, as you get older, is the danger of becoming an Expert.

HGH. January 1967

## Introduction

In May 1960 I shut up my flat at Curdridge and sailed off in *Jester* to take part in the first Single-handed Transatlantic Race, returning on October 2nd after a very enjoyable expedition . . . That winter *Jester* was taken to London by the *Daily Express* while . . . nearby, in the Boating Information Bureau, I sat periodically at a table and got asked the most extraordinary questions. I can't believe I was really very much help to the man who wanted a financial analysis of the prospects of setting up a business which would charter small motor boats by the hour from a beach in Wales, and nobody voiced a particular need, which I was at that time planning to satisfy: the smallest possible "heads" for use in midget cruising boats and cruising dinghies.

The idea had started with a thunderbox that had reached me as part of *Tre Sang's* inventory and in my improved design I sought to provide a complete unit comprising a standard *vase de nuit* (who would speak English when the French is so elegant?) provided with a fitted lid for use while carrying it around to be emptied. The *vase de nuit* fitted into a plastic box which made it more stable to sit on at sea and contained the *papier hygiénique* attached to a second lid which could be removed and placed somewhere handy to the user. When not in use a nylon strap held everything together and provided the carrying handle. It seems barely credible that the boating, motoring and camping public is still muddling along without the benefit of this unit.

*Here the introduction suddenly ends.*

## Chapter VII (continued)[6]

## On The Loose

. . . I remember reading, when I was quite young, that there were only three ways in which a man could remain happy on a long voyage in a

---

[6]  Although he wrote "continued" it is certain he had not written either Chapters 1 to 6 nor the earlier part of this Chapter 7.

small boat: by himself, with a woman or with a non-communicating aboriginal native. This still seems to be greatly true, although I have misgivings about this aborigine.

Anyway I was getting tired of *Petula* herself . . . She now seemed to me to be an unsuccessful compromise: as a home for a single man she was smaller and less convenient than a flat or cottage yet she was too big for easy maintenance or for easy single-handed cruising . . . Luckily some nice young men from London University turned up looking for a cheap and seaworthy cruising boat which would be capable of doing a sort of Kon-Tiki Expedition from Dakar to the West Indies towing a Carley Float and doing oceanographic work (plankton sampling and the like) all the way across . . .

I realise all too well that the very word "inventor" has a comic ring to it and conjures up a picture of a man suffering from a peculiar syndrome of which the symptoms are a neglect or rejection of current scientific teaching; total obsession with some far-fetched and unconvincing hypothesis; inability to see or understand any argument which runs counter to his own; a conviction that the rest of the world is trying to steal his brainchild from him leaving him without reward or credit for it and a marked tendency to sacrifice everything he possesses in the furious pursuit of his particular mirage. It is no wonder that the private inventor is a figure of fun to the public, and a dreaded apparition in the corridors of science and commerce.

Yet the awkward fact of history is that a large proportion of useful technical innovation has originated in the brains of these embarrassing lunatics, mainly because they do not know how to admit defeat in the face of failure.

Wise friends have often told me not to call myself an inventor if I hope to get help or sympathy from a hard world, but unfortunately there is no other word that means the same thing. As I see it, an inventor is one whose chosen role is to operate, on a mixture of guesswork, imagination and experiment, in a chosen technical field but outside the limits of existing scientific knowledge and often in a field to which he is himself a stranger. By contrast, a research worker is a technician operating inside the framework of conventional technology and engaged either on pure research to enlarge the fund of available knowledge that somebody has handed to him. As I can seldom claim to be a research worker I have had to accept the stigma of being a would-be inventor and to learn to live with the inventors syndrome.

*Here ended "Chapter VII (continued)": Chapter VIII began straight-away:*

## Trying to Achieve Something 1953–1966

. . . I spent the winter of 1952/53 designing *Jester* . . . Ian Major and I were (also) experimenting with long, thin, single-hullers with various other experimental sails on them (and) producing a stream of different wind-vane steering gears in model size.

I often remember those rigid aerofoil sails and would like to find time one day to do some work on them. To be efficient in light or moderate winds a rigid aerofoil must have a strongly arched asymmetrical section and the best arrangement we finished up with was the "umbrella foil", so called because in its original form it resembled an umbrella although this likeness became rather remote towards the end . . . When sailing, the foil is normally arranged vertically in such a way that its hollow side is to windward and "sheeted" by turning the wheel assembly by means of the boom. "Reefing", if the wind is on or forward of the beam, is achieved by causing the foil to feather progressively into the wind. The sail will tend to feather itself and can be made to reef automatically by means of an adjustable tension spring . . . A feature of rigid aerofoil sails is their extreme sensitivity to the exact angle of incidence. Whereas a soft sail seems to me to be never fully "un-stalled" and indeed to collapse at or before the time it reaches its "high lift" attitude the rigid aerofoil seemed to develop a strong peak of lift from time to time, presumably when the incidence of the apparent wind was just right while being pretty "dead" at angles slightly above or below this. When actually sailing, the boats seemed to be hit by a succession of hammer blows and to proceed in jerks.

In 1955 Vospers (very wisely) withdrew from sponsoring the Lapwing Rig and I had to make plans for fitting *Jester* with the final version of it from my own resources . . . By the spring of 1956 I had her in commission with the new Lapwing rig, but found little time to sail because I had become absorbed in trying to write plays: a fascinating art which I never came anywhere near mastering but which has unfortunately made all other forms of writing (including this book) boring for ever afterwards . . .

Ian Major and I spent some time doing a design study for a project that we called "*Spearfish*". The object was to produce the smallest possible *motor* boat capable of making long ocean passages and we saw this partly as a piece of amusing research that might attract support from the makers of small marine diesel engines and partly as an attempt to produce a boat that would enlarge the scope of small-scale amphibious operations in wartime.[7]

We set ourselves the specific target of designing the smallest motor boat that would carry one man non-stop from London to New York (3,300 miles) taking the northern route and encountering head winds most of the way. No provision was made for the boat's possible wartime role other than keeping the silhouette down to the minimum.

She got as far as outline design stage since Ian and I got enmeshed in other occupations before we could take the planning further. In retrospect I can see no difficulty about this scheme except for the morale of the solo crew who might be hard put to it to remain fit and sane in such a *very small* cabin and with so little to occupy his time. Occupational therapy would need to be carefully planned and conscientiously carried out. It would have been fun to try it.

Another joint activity with Ian Major was to have a go at the Committee of the Royal Ocean Racing Club in an attempt to make them admit experimental boats to ordinary offshore races. The root of our complaint was that the RORC rules assumed that a yacht could only be rigged as a sloop, cutter, yawl, ketch or schooner and that any sails which weren't jibs, staysails or spinnakers could only be ordinary gaff or Bermudian sails. Every possible departure from this pre-conceived idea seemed either to run into a positive Prohibition or to be un-measurable under their Rules of Measurement.

I think it will be a pity if the RORC continues to elect to insulate itself from radical experiment and thereby encourages the formation of a splinter group who will have to organize their ocean races for experimental boats. But the pattern is a familiar one; such clubs are often founded by small groups of progressive enthusiasts and just as often become, in a few years, citadels of conservatism. If the Royal Cruising Club had been on its toes there would have been no need to start the Royal Ocean Racing Club. Soon we shall be able to say that if the RORC had been on its toes there would have been no need to start the Royal Outcasts Offshore Experimental Club.[8] Unfortunately it all becomes rather expensive if you want to belong to all of them.

Towards the end of 1957 I started part-time work with Dracone Developments Ltd. Next year I signed on as whole-time Operations Manager for the firm, and set up a small base at Marchwood, opposite

---

[7]   Thus pre-dating by over forty years various such craft based on the same principles and which are now operated by the SBS

[8]   Which, in effect, he was to do!

Southampton docks. The project was fascinating but my role in the company inevitably contained too little development and too much administration for my tastes.

Another private development project that got crowded into 1959 is best described by quoting directly from my enthusiastic prospectus:

> For the past 25 years the "Folbot" type of folding canoe has sold more successfully than any type of rigid canoe both for civil and military use even in circumstances where its folding ability is unimportant. The reasons for its success are that it has a good shape, is strong and resilient, is easy to repair, needs little maintenance and is easy to stow away when laid up. The Hasler Folding Boat is intended to score the same points against existing rigid boats, and to be obviously superior in amphibious warfare . . . for yachtsmen, for small children . . .

Since 1953 I had also been working intermittently on the development of a new kind of winch, with the help of John Chamier . . . My ideal winch was required to pull rope in at one side and push it out the other in a continuous smooth movement which could be reversed for veering and which needed no backing-up or adjustment whatever for the variations in loading on the rope . . . When the prototype winch began to show encouraging results we filed a provisional patent which (under British Patent Law) gave us 12 months to try to find a backer before it became necessary to complete the more expensive and more difficult stage of filing detailed specifications as a preliminary to being granted actual legal patents. Having been told that a good "presentation" would carry weight we prepared a demonstration model in polished brass accompanied by some elegant paper work. We then got in touch with the Deputy Chairman of a firm that manufactured winches and winding gear. John Chamier provided a rather good, non-temperance lunch in London at which we explained the idea of the winch and gave him a copy of our provisional specification.

In our innocence, we made rather a point of offering him first refusal and assured him that we would not offer the idea elsewhere until he had rejected it. We thought vaguely that he seemed rather formal and that he managed not to laugh very heartily at our jokes (which were, as usual, extremely witty) but he went away promising to get in touch with us quite soon. By this time 7 of our 12 month's grace had somehow slipped away. Two months later I wrote asking if he could yet say "yes" or "no", and got a reply from his clerk saying that the Deputy Chairman was expected back in the office in a week's time. Another month later I wrote again; no answer. Three weeks later I wrote again, shyly enquiring if he had received my previous letter; his clerk replied that the Deputy Chairman would probably return in about a week's time and that my letter would be placed before him. Since then I have had no word of any sort and the Provisional Patent expired peacefully, leaving John and me somewhat wiser in our understanding of the business of selling inventions, and without the urge to proceed any further into this particular thicket.[9]

In theory, the British Patent Laws give inexpensive protection to the individual inventor, and provide him with the power to license a commercial firm to make and sell his invention in return for royalty payments. Eminently fair, but unfortunately it doesn't work.

Commercial firms are run by businessmen (often by sharp businessmen) and no businessman worth his salt would dream of paying royalties to a private inventor. If he thinks the inventor has something useful left inside his head he will want to buy him, to get him on the payroll. If not he will either get his own men to "design round" the invention or, more simply, he will just make use of the invention without a licence and wait to be sued. No private inventor of modest means can risk suing a large firm on a charge of patent infringement. Perhaps the only feasible way of upholding the inventor's rights would be for the Public Prosecutor to be charged with prosecuting an offending firm wherever a private inventor could show a clear case of infringement, but no doubt the net result of any such legislation would be twisted with the help of the amoral legal profession, to the ultimate advantage of any firm willing and able to pay the lawyers.

The private inventor soon learns that he might as well save himself the expense of filing endless patents. The two best courses open to him are either to try to get himself sponsored by a government-financed corporation (such as the NRDC) which labours under an effective political compulsion to be fair to the small man or to set up his own little manufacturing and selling outfit as we did with vane steering gears and hope that in a few year's time his know-how will acquire a commercial value of their own.

In October 1959 I was asked to plan and install a system of navigational marks in Loch Tarbert Jura and this appealed to me so much that I gladly agreed in spite of an increasing awareness that *Jester* would never be properly ready for the 1960 trans-Atlantic.

The island of Jura, 29 miles long and mountainous lies off the west coast

---

[9]  A few years later the revolutionary self-tailing winch came on the market.

of Scotland almost due west of Glasgow and is one of the most southerly of the Hebrides. In spite of its relative closeness to civilization it remains wild and undeveloped. A single road runs halfway round its coast and a few hundred people live scattered along it. Access is by steamer from Islay its prosperous and highly developed neighbouring island . . .

A few enquiries around London established the interesting fact that there was no government authority with any interest in the design of a navigational system for the loch. If I had chosen to put a row of starboard hand buoys on the port side of the channel there was apparently nobody to say me nay, although the Hydrographer would have been glad to know afterwards what I had done so that he could put them on his charts. It was a temptation that I was able to resist having always believed that navigational marks, like men's formal clothing, should be rigidly conventional.

The loch is splendidly rocky and positively spooky in the narrows where the tide rushes silently in and out between steep rock walls and you suddenly realise with a start that there is a deer up there watching you. I was taken up and down it in the old motor launch by Ruari Darroch, a marvellous highland boatman who for many years had been the only person who knew how to avoid the submerged dangers. Alas he was getting very old and had recently allowed the launch to run up on one of the rocks in the outer loch; hence the need for the navigational marks.

The possible means of marking the channels seemed to be by buoys, by iron or stone beacons on the submerged rocks or by pairs of leading marks. The first two would give the navigator a close-range mark that he could use in low visibility but would be expensive to install and difficult to maintain. I decided to rely on leading marks, all sited above high water mark and to add a few small marker buoys on single anchors.

Luckily, we had a good Admiralty chart and a Photostat of the original survey supplied by the Hydrographer for everything below the upper narrows, so I was able in the course of a couple of days to lay out the general framework of a system which involved 13 pairs of leading marks and 6 marker buoys.

The first half of 1960 was hectic and I don't think I'd ever had to work so feverishly since 1942. *Jester* was launched in March, with a trim tab fitted to her rudder but as yet no means of turning it . . . Early in May I dropped everything and returned to Jura for a week. For the leading marks we would first plant a pair of flags on posts in the approximate positions then go out in the launch or dinghy at low water and test the clearance of the line from its nearest dangers, signalling for the front flag to be moved left or right as necessary; then we built the temporary marks over these exact points. It was fascinating to be able to test for ourselves the extreme accuracy of the transits, even when observed from positions a couple of miles distant.

In 1934 Uffa Fox commented that, "The best ocean racer is the best ocean cruiser" and I have often wondered if this is true. Ocean racing seems to me to be purely a sport comparable with dinghy racing or playing tennis. The best ocean racer is the one which provides the maximum amount of hard work and exposure for the maximum number of men. That's what they came for. That's what will give them the strength to go back to another five days of sitting in a warm office and wondering about their secretaries. They want ocean racing to be difficult, to call for every ounce of skill or endurance they can muster.

Would anyone play golf if it consisted of picking up the ball with a pair of long-handled tongs carrying it to the next hole and dropping it in? Consider that huge bag of golf clubs, towed around on its little wheels. Nobody, I imagine, would claim that it provides a logical means of persuading a golf ball to visit eighteen holes in a chosen sequence. In the same way, ocean racers are not a logical means of transport and are not trying to get anywhere.

Cruising seems to me to be different. You are trying to get somewhere and you want to arrive there in a civilised state, ready either to go ashore or to have visitors on board. Your crew may be few in number and may include children, wives, landlubbers or dotards. So it seems fair to say that a cruising boat should be designed to be sailed by a very small crew of weaklings and as far as possible to be sailed without great skill and endurance.

However rough the passage, she should not arrive in harbour full of wet sails, wet clothes or wet people. It may even be worth remembering – for such things still happen, even in the welfare state that there may be on board a gentleman and a lady who regard each other with something warmer than mere tolerance, and would like to have an opportunity of proving it.

Alas! Very few yacht designers have ever done any serious work on improvement of cruising boats. If a professional designer is asked to produce an out-and-out cruising boat, his mind seems to wander backwards towards pilot cutters and baggywrinkle. For the past 35 years at any rate, nearly all development work in the design of small seagoing sailing yachts has been devoted to producing boats that do well on corrected time under the ocean racing rules of measurement. The results are only too well known. Designers have danced a fandango with rule-makers. Loopholes have been discovered, and exploited for a year or so before being plugged by a belated amendment . . . Under the influence of ocean racing, great changes have taken place in the design of yachts, and most of them have been good. It seems a long time since Claud Worth felt it necessary to apologise for putting a single wire guardrail round *Tern II* and to explain that it was scarcely visible a hundred yards away. But some of the changes (parachute spinnakers . . . !) seem to be like that bag of golf clubs – a preposterous means of achieving a given end, but a means that gives the experts a chance to shine and dooms the weakling and the fumbler to ridicule and disgrace . . .

Even if the modern ocean racer seems to be a triumph of rational design, where do we go from here? . . . What are all those wires and spreaders for? Aeroplanes stopped looking like that ages ago . . . Man overboard! No panic, now. Let us just think rather carefully. Do we gybe on to it, or luff it aback, or go creaming on towards France while we get the thing down? Wave good-bye to him, somebody. Tell him through the loudhailer that we'll be back in a jiffy, just as soon as we've solved one or two problems in elementary seamanship. How wise of the Club to make us carry a life-buoy with a light on it, all ready to let go! It really ought to have a tin of 24-hour rations on it and a waterproof copy of *Lolita* . . .

We are always being assured that the act of shifting headsails on a sloping foredeck under a refreshing cascade of salt water is "by far the easiest means of shortening sail". I am hoping to design a yachtsman's motor car which has no gear box but which carries, in place of the back seat passengers, several pairs of different-sized rear wheels. Then all that will be needed, instead of bothersome gear-changing, will be to stop, get out in the rain, jack up the rear of the car and change the wheels. I shall, of course, take a good deal of trouble over the design of the jacks and the wheel fastenings, so as to make the whole operation simple and trouble-free.

The ocean racing rules contain curious prohibitions, such as fully battened mainsails – something that must, surely, become common in the future of sailing boats of all kinds? And even if an unorthodox rig is not prohibited, the chances are that it cannot be measured. Even a dipping lug, the traditional fisherman's sail of England and one of the best seagoing rigs ever invented, cannot be measured under the RORC rule. This seems to preclude an interesting experiment, because it is at least possible that the dipping lug could be developed into a very good ocean crossing rig. And be easier to handle than a masthead sloop with genoa and spinnaker.

So it is that we must regretfully abandon any hope of developing futuristic sailing boats under ocean racing rules. But racing of some sort is the best possible incentive and we must have some sort of handicapping. Shall we now revert, then to the traditional system of handicapping each boat arbitrarily according to the judgement of a handicapper? I, personally, would welcome it but, alas, the modern age has already rejected him, and I doubt if anything could bring him back. Yet the only thing wrong with this system is the mean minds of the owners who object to it. A handicapper once told me that he had been accosted by a frothing owner after a race: "Under RORC rating, I'd have beaten that boat by half an hour!" he shouted. "Exactly" replied my friend, "and under my handicap you lost by two minutes. You can judge for yourself which is the better handicapping" I need hardly say that this argument was well beyond the scope of the owner's intellect . . . So handicappers are out. Good luck to them as they leave us; for they were public-spirited men who did much good and earned much hatred.

Is there any other way of handicapping if we rule out both formulae and handicappers? I believe there is, but I do not think it has yet been tried out. I call it Mutual Handicapping, and the main idea is that the best judges of the potential performance of any boat are its owners and the owners of other boats in the same class. Therefore the best handicapping system will be one that harnesses this expert knowledge.

In my proposed system each owner is required to volunteer his own time allowance (Volunteered Time Allowance or VTA) for a given race. This encourages a sporting spirit at the outset, since it is obviously unsporting to volunteer an allowance that is too favourable to yourself. But for those owners – do such people really exist? – who would rather win races than be a good sportsman, there is a more positive incentive to be fair: every other owner in the race will be laying odds against you, by wagering "points" on his chances of beating you at your VTA. If he does not think he has much chance of doing this, he will not wager many points against you – and the results of the race depend on the total points won by each boat from those boats she has defeated on VTA.

Thus, in a specified race, Mr A's VTA may favour himself, D's may do the opposite, and B's and C's may be fair. Everybody, therefore, lays the minimum number of points on his chance of defeating A, average points on his chance of defeating B and C and maximum points on his chance of defeating D.

After the race, on "corrected time" (ie after applying VTA) A defeats B, C and D; but B defeats C and D; C defeats D; and D defeats nobody. But when we add up the points won by each boat from the boats it has defeated on corrected time, we fine that:

A wins 3 points
B wins 6 points
C wins 4 points
D wins 0 points

The finishing order is therefore BCAD. Next time they race, in his own interest A will penalise himself less.

In this way a balance is struck and the whole system provides a sensitive and constantly fluctuating index of the true performance potential of each boat. In this it will also make a lot of extra fun in the process. It will also make rule cheating impossible – or at any rate unprofitable – for the man who is known to be ready to win by low cunning will never get any odds against him even when he is blameless. It will do away with the ridiculous and expensive business of measuring each yacht as though she were some fascinating unknown species. No racing boat will ever become outclassed. And it will take the shackles off yacht design by allowing everybody to have the kind of boat he wants, instead of the kind of boat the rule-makers want.

I want to sum up the new features that I believe our future offshore boats will show. The rig must have no "alternative" sails. If the most sail the boat will ever carry at one time is 500 sq. ft., then 500 sq. ft. is the total area that you carry on board and it is up on deck all the time, not using up your lockers or bunks. The same sail(s) must serve efficiently in all wind strengths and on all points of sailing. It follows that reefing must be quick and easy in successive stages all the way down to nothing, and that the sail(s) must be efficient when reefed. If the area is big enough for running in light airs, as it should be, she will obviously have to reef very early when on the wind. In other words, we may regard it as normal to reef for windward work instead of setting spinnakers for running. Preferably, all reefing and un-reefing should be done by the helmsman – without leaving the helm . . .

We hardly know anything about the aerodynamics of sails and I have often felt that more harm than good has been done by the bland application of aircraft theory to boat sails. A great cloud of theorists is constantly telling us what sails ought to behave like and supporting their views with quite a large part of the Greek alphabet. But alas! The sails themselves are quite uneducated and do not seem to understand very clearly what they are supposed to do. It is a subject that needs an empirical approach. First we have got to find out, by comparative experiment, how sails do behave. Then we can turn the theorists on to explaining why . . .

I have read that one sign of a mature civilisation is that the men actually enjoy the companionship of their women and I like to think that all properly organised yachts have women on board. It is a pity that these seagoing women have not raised their voices more loudly. Most of them would like the business of handling the boat to be easier and to need less brute strength so that they could play a bigger part in it. I think they would all like to keep dry and to keep the inside of the boat dry. And however much they may be prepared to pig it if they have to, I think they would all like some cabin privacy at sea and even more so in harbour. Our forefathers understood this and had "ladies cabins". The wide-open layout of the modern ocean racer denies it altogether. But even the smallest cabin boat can offer privacy once the designer makes it possible to sail the boat with a very small crew, to handle the rig from the helm and to keep wet sails up on deck.

I said at the beginning that the fanatical offshore racing man, snatching a week-end off from his business, may have an inherent need for a different and more difficult boat than the ideal offshore cruising boat. I still like to think, however, that these superb cruising boats of the future will be able to sail effectively in offshore races and do it without having to embark any extra muscle. It will be a great day when the Fastnet is won by a middle-age man and his wife, as an interlude in the middle of their summer cruise . . .

*. . . and here Blondie's autobiography came to an end.* Even in the late 1990s there is much radical and perceptive thought in the above – perhaps someone as far sighted will now take up those of Blondie's various "challenges" that have still to be developed.

Clipped to this manuscript was a list of the various inventions that had passed through his inky note books, or were about to be developed into working designs and drawings in them. He tabulated these under various headings and while this list is certainly not complete (and, here, has been edited to avoid repetition) it is in the order in which he wrote it over the years since 25 May, 1956. Red lines were drawn through those that had reached fruition and a tick placed against those that were simply "started". Not all are "inventions" in the accepted sense of the word for many are writing or drawing projects, some of which illustrate this biography. Many are just outline ideas waiting to be developed and some are unintelligible without further explanation – which does not exist.

Pen and ink drawings and cartoons. Rope winch cum rope drive. Folding boats. *Ferret* drain cleaner. *Spearfish*. Dracone. Wife management (as picture book). Ski vangs. Chinese lug. Americas cup. Windicator. Hosegrip. Vintage machinery. Walking lizard. Beach raft. Trundle hut. Centrifugal gun. Breakfast oven. Universal camouflage system. *Petula's* table. Ratchet lever for chain. Toasting fork. Coathanger. Plasticising of sails. Tree saw. Bathtub boat. Cork extractor. Captive kite. Light vent. Bow spoon. Propeller designs. Table models for sailing instruction. Inflatable catamarans. Horracle (a form of coracle with whale-fluke propulsion). Hasler heater for boats (fuelled by wood). Double-hulled dinghies. Foam plastic hulls with or without strengthening skins. Broad, shallow hulls that can be fitted on edge to form deep, narrow hulls. Asymmetrical surf boat to surf ride storms without steering. Buoyancy supplied by fully submerged hulls. Sailing raft based on the true catamarans of the Palk Straits. Fin propulsion by the rolling and pitching of the hull. Fin propulsion by mechanical linkage. Swim fins which take up the line of the lower leg rather than the foot and whose incidence (angle of attack) is controllable. Swim fins that reproduce the action of a duck's feet and can be used on the swimmer's feet at or above water level. Combined oar, rudder or yuloh. Chin float for swimmer's chin and arms. Variable groove rope winch. Portable, canvas clothes locker like a partitioned kit-bag. Power take-off from current of air for oscillating fins. Diving bell. Balanced flue cabin heater. Automatic filters. Long, narrow hull stablilized by hydrofoils. Long-range approach craft as opposed to assault craft. Ratchet lever for hauling-chain. Ski vangs. Stall indicator for sails. Ornithopter using vibrating wing action. Toasting fork. Wind mill/log charging set for boats. Yacht's diving gear. Yacht stove. Watch cover. Mud skis. Sectional nesting boats, Swim fins – folding. Toy diver. Fully gimballed galley. Yachts sounding poles. Deep sea diving. Long, inflatable hull stabilizing fins. Horizontal pendulum generator. Commercial coasting sail. Midget, wood-burning stove for 20' yachts. Rotary floating fish cages.

To which should be added the windsurfer (which appeared in his working drawing books years in advance of those that we know today) surf boats and canoes (that can be used on edge as well as flat), a drill guide, slab reefing gear (again, well before its time) and numerous unnamed, miscellaneous ideas and drawings in his notebooks.

Additionally, he wrote twenty-one notes analysing the style of cartoon drawings that he felt would best suit what he wanted to project: in fact they reveal rather more about himself:

1. Morning may be a good time? Perhaps brain wants to be rather sleepy?
2. Learn to draw first – go for realism to start with.
3. Sensitive pen work calls for comfortable position.
4. All thin lines may be best.
5. I think I like shaded faces and skins. (This is then crossed out).
6. Arrange them like toy soldiers, with the suggestion of a base?
7. Nothing quite black – mouths etc.
8. Be careful not to overcharge pen.
9. Late at night seems best.
10. (Missing)
11. Lean towards understatement in treatment, even if over-stated in form.
12. They seem to be getting too big.
13. Hatching should be done with the pen.
14. Small chins.
15. THINK – WEAVE – SCRIBBLE – STOP.
16. Do tiny stick group first for composition.
17. Try doing final drawings.
18. Stop between each figure and think.
19. Max economy of line. Leave out everything.
20. Single-line mouths.
21. Be calm, not excitable.

Mention has been made in a number of places throughout the narrative of the damage suffered by *Jester* off Inverness on his way to Loch Ness in 1961 and of the lessons learned. Perhaps the greatest lesson was that it is not necessary to travel into the deep oceans in order to meet dangerous seas. Under the heading Storm Seas Survival he wrote of his experience in the North Sea in 1961:

> I must dispute . . . the assertion that "quite certainly there is no danger of falling into the trough" when a small yacht is at sea under storm conditions.

In my opinion, this danger arises when an individual wave develops into a "plunging breaker" in contrast to the "spilling breakers" that make up the great majority of storm waves. A plunging breaker is similar to the waves that break on a steep beach in onshore winds, in that the leading face of the wave becomes more and more vertical until the whole crest overhangs and crashes into the trough in front of it. Any small light-displacement boat that is unfortunate enough to be in the crest at that moment will fall with it.

I believe that individual plunging breakers can develop in deep-water conditions through the random synchronisation of different wave trains, and in particular just before or just after a change in wind direction. Here the sea created by the ambient wind is distorted by a swell running in a different direction, whether in advance of the new wind or as an after-effect of the old wind – usually the former. From time to time this creates the "rogue waves" that can suddenly throw a light-displacement boat upside-down even when the gale has taken off and the crew are about to set sail.

Another potential cause of plunging breakers is the wind-against-tide condition and this was, I think, the cause of the knockdown that nearly sank . . . *Jester* on 16th September 1961, not in the Atlantic but in the North Sea, 15 miles off Aberdeen. In a severe gale of short duration that blew a lot of trees down in Scotland, I was lying a-hull in *Jester* single-handed, with the junk sail furled and secured in its lifts and the original pendulum-servo vane steering gear still mounted on the stern, but unlatched. Conditions worsened as night fell, so I secured all hatches as strongly as I could and lay down on my bunk, hating the impact of the waves on her hull.

Suddenly the feeling was of accelerating upwards as in an express lift, a pause, and then she dropped a long way on to what felt like concrete. There was a loud structural bang and I seemed to be swimming in a great quantity of North Sea that had suddenly invaded the cabin. She righted herself instantly and I found that a hole, big enough for me to crawl through, had been smashed high up *on the lee side* of her curved roof. At that time her upper works were admittedly too light, and I had the ply skin doubled up later . . .

I don't *think* she did a full role but all the glass jars on her heavily-fiddled galley shelf shot straight up and smashed against the deckhead, strewing broken glass everywhere to add to the problems of stuffing up the hole (with a large kitbag full of blankets) and pumping her out.

It was this knock-down that led Blondie to insist that yachts should be as strongly built above the waterline as below, but this is not a view that, even to this day, is held by many designers of offshore yachts.

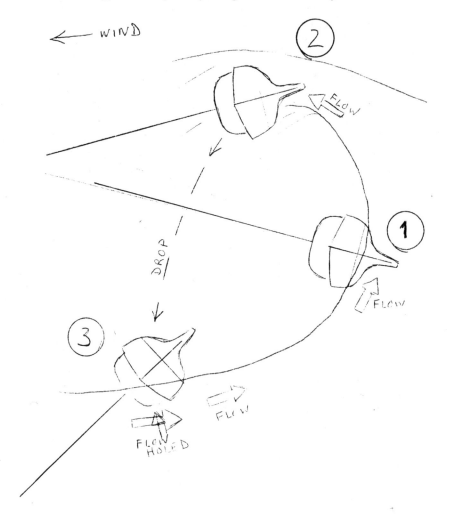

# APPENDIX TWO

## Consequences or "Competitors should die with dignity"

Blondie's single-handed trans-Atlantic and two-handed round-Britain races started it all and the next logical challenge was a circumnavigation of the world, which Francis Chichester, predictably, took up. Confirmation of the success of the Hasler servo pendulum, wind-vane steering gear during the second trans-Atlantic race came with the commissioning of a similar system for Chichester's proposed single-handed, one-stop[1] round-the-world attempt in the yet-unbuilt *Gipsy Moth IV*. This was a coup for Blondie as Chichester was by now a "household" name whose exploits were being followed closely by the British public.

*Gipsy Moth* was designed by John Illingworth and built by Camper and Nicholson and while only the best was acceptable to Chichester, this did not stop him having qualms over some aspects of the project and especially the steering gear. But he was unnecessarily harsh for, in truth, he had not divulged his intentions and when they became obvious it was too late to alter the gear's design. Blondie wrote to him, "If you had told me, you would have got a different gear."[2]

Chichester's attempt started from the RWYC line on 27 August, 1966, and ended across the same line on 28 May, 1967: it was by any standard of the day a remarkable voyage. Blondie, though, regarded him as a man to be kept at arm's length: this removed none of the admiration for his achievements but the two men were of very different psychological make-up with Blondie placid and phlegmatic while Chichester tended towards the mercurial – occasionally intolerant and blinkered to others' ideas and techniques. Jock McLeod wrote:

> We developed a specially large gear for *Gipsy Moth IV*; and supervised the fitting of this trying all the while to get Francis to

---

[1]  Sydney
[2]  Letter from Jock McLeod to the author.

understand how to get the best out of it . . . He never liked it nor understood the subtleties or the importance of the lead counter-balance on the vane. At some stage he lists the stowage of various bits of kit in the forepeak and amongst them is 'a large lump of lead on a stainless steel arm'. This should have been on the vane gear and not stowed away! Blondie regarded Francis as an interesting man, but with limitations.

Blondie's steering gear had now sailed round the world with success, despite Chichester's strictures: it was to do so again in what many regarded as an even more interesting voyage, that of Alec Rose between July 1967 and July 1968. Rose had entered the second trans-Atlantic race in his *Lively Lady* using a Hasler gear as Blondie records in an appendix to Rose's own book *My Lively Lady*:[3]

When Jock McLeod and I first went over to Attril's yard at Bembridge in December 1963 to advise on the fitting of the gear, all we knew was that an unknown Mr Rose had bought the boat with the intention of entering for the 1964 single-handed trans-Atlantic race for the *Observer Trophy* and had commissioned Illingworth and Primrose to re-rig her for single-handed sailing.

Three months later we sailed in the Solent with Alec and found him so quiet and retiring that we could not really decide whether he fully understood what he was tackling or not. These doubts began to be dispelled a few days after the start of the race when . . . my own boat, *Jester*, and *Lively Lady* found themselves converging close to each other out of an empty sea on three separate occasions and I could see Alec always seemed to have her beautifully under control tramping along with the right number of reefs down and an obvious absence of drama. When I finally got to Newport, Rhode Island, it was no surprise to find that he had finished 4th out of 15 starters and over a day ahead of me.

It was with this same veteran steering gear that he started off round the world in 1967, leaving us anxiously wondering what components were going to wear out first, and whether he had taken enough spare parts.

Our biggest relief came when he was photographed off the Horn with the gear still working and when it finally brought him up the English Channel we were able to see for ourselves what

[3]    Nautical Publishing Company, 1968.

signs of age it was showing after steering for a total of at least 36,000 nautical miles of open water and how well Alec looked after it . . .

Alec was very much a man after Blondie's own heart – uncomplaining, self sufficient and modest.

Now there had to be a non-stop circumnavigation and the first to consider this seriously was Blondie's fellow crewman from *Myth of Malham*, the man who had bought *Tre Sang*, Bill King. In 1967, before Alec Rose had completed his one-stop marathon, there was no question of a race but a number of yachtsmen, mostly British, had decided quite separately that a full circumnavigation should be attempted and Bill was determined to lead the pack.

> Blondie was intrigued and persuaded him to ask Angus Primrose to design a hull specially for the purpose and to take full advantage of the Chinese rig. There were two false starts – at the first attempt he was capsized and broke the masts but erected "the cunning jury rig" we had designed and sailed to Cape Town. The second attempt ended at Gibraltar . . . Bill did finally complete a circumnavigation in 1973 but he had to stop in Australia after a collision with a whale.[4]

Bill's boat, *Galway Blazer*, was of ultra-light build, 4½ tons on a 30 foot waterline; 42 feet overall with four laminations of plywood, cold-moulded and glued, with a total thickness of ¾ inch and high freeboard. Her cockpit was below the deck and had two circular access hatches into which hurricane covers could be fitted, one of which had a plastic observation dome. The two masts were un-stayed and supported Chinese lug sails.

With a number of other skippers declaring their intention to be the first single-handed, non-stop circumnavigator, the *Sunday Times* now offered *The Golden Globe* award for the first and £5,000 for the fastest, thereby acknowledging that not all would start from the same place nor at the same time. In the end there was to be only one finisher, Robin Knox-Johnston, on 2 April, 1969.[5]

The trans-Atlantic had spawned the *Sunday Times* race and this led, subsequently, to the proliferation of similar single-handed events run

4    Jock McLeod to the author 5 April, 1996.
5    See his book *A World of my Own.*

(for the most part) by various British and French sponsors. Conception
for the first fully-crewed Round the World Race was achieved at Barra
in June, 1970, while a number of competitors in the second two-handed
round-Britain rode out a gale during their compulsory forty-eight hour
stop-over. Roger Dillon, Michael Shuttleworth, Ewen Tailyour, Martin
Read, Mike McMullen, (by coincidence all officers in the Royal Marines
and all but one members – or about to be – of the Royal Cruising Club,
who knew Blondie and whose three yachts carried Hasler steering gears)
believed that if yachts could race round Britain via pre-planned stops
they should do so round the world. This suggestion was put to the
journalists and public relations specialists following the race and while
the yachts continued on their way Anthony Churchill and Guy Peirce
established what they named the *Clipper Race* due to start in 1973. The
yachts would be fully crewed and there would be stops and mass re-
starts, unlike the round-Britain race where yachts start each leg
individually forty-eight hours after arrival. The *Clipper Race*, for which
numerous brochures were despatched touting for entries, did not take
place but the baton was taken up by the RNSA and sponsored by
brewers, Whitbreads. It was natural that this race would, itself, develop,
and in 1975 the *Financial Times* ran a race with just one stop, Sydney.
This was not run again but "The Whitbread" flourished to spawn yet
more imitators such as British Telecom's "round the wrong way with
stops" challenge for amateur crews in celebration of Chay Blyth's non-
stop first. Yet more such races grew from those beginnings including the
Three Peaks Race whose founding father is often given as the legendary
Bill Tilman whereas it was the Royal Marine yachtsman and mountaineer Mike McMullen who first mooted the idea to him in the autumn
of 1970.

There is yet the one unattempted round-the-world route that is the
truest circumnavigation of all for it follows, very nearly, the only great
circle that can be drawn on the surface of the globe without crossing land.
Apart from a couple of "wiggles" it is possible by traversing the north-
west passage, cutting diagonally down the Atlantic to the south of Africa,
before "turning" north between Tasmania and Australia and on up
towards the Bering Sea. This passage was named the "McMullen Route"
by the author after Mike first suggested it to him as the only "true"
cicumnavigation: he intended to try it one day and discussed the
possibility with Blondie but he was to be lost at sea during the 1976
single-handed trans-Atlantic.

The French have always acknowledged the supremacy of the Royal
Western Yacht Club's single-handed trans-Atlantic race despite con-

tinuing to develop their own: the Route de Rhum from St Malo to Guadeloupe being one such example and the Mini-Transat for boats not exceeding 21.3 feet overall, being another[6] and the short-lived, single-handed round Majorca race from Leucate in the south of France designed as a 'qualifier' for the RWYC's single-handed trans-Atlantic being yet another. The AZAB – Azores and Back Race – from Falmouth and the Round North Island, New Zealand, Race plus the Bermuda One-Two, first sailed in 1977 as a single-handed race to the island with a two-handed return to America, are among other clones that have their antecedents in "Hasler's amazing idea", as Lloyd Foster dubbed the original concept in his book *Ostar*.

Among the present single-handed, global marathons the British BOC Race,[7] with stops, and the French non-stop, *Vendée Globe*[8] complete the current evolution.

In 1996 the Royal Western Yacht Club decided to stop the two-handed trans-Atlantic Race (first raced in 1981) and replace it with a two-handed race to Iceland in 1997 aimed to fit in with a proposed round-Iceland race organized by the Reykjavik Yacht Club.

The third single-handed trans-Atlantic race, held in 1968, produced the largest number of retirements but no casualties, although for the first time five competitors had to be rescued from liferafts. Always unhappy with the thought of a single-handed crew unable to keep a continual lookout while at sea the 'antis' were now able to state that single-handed sailing was proving to be dangerous (in fact only one competitor put down 'collision' as the reason for retiring and that was not with another vessel but whale) and someone had to pay for the rescues.

Commander Lloyd Foster, then the secretary of the RWYC and thus of the race committee,[9] had a stock answer to those who said it was

6    The Mini-Transat from Penzance to Tenerife and thence to Antigua was the brainchild of the English single-handed yachtsman, Bob Salmon, who competed in it and ran four races (one every two years) from 1977 without the support or sponsorship of an organizing club. When he could no longer do so the race was taken up by the French over a different course. For yachts under 21.3 feet the race was designed for those with a limited budget; now modern technology tends to dictate an increase in costs. See *OSTAR* by Lloyd Foster.
7    About to suffer a name change.
8    In which, in 1997, the ex-Royal Marine Pete Goss became another British sailing hero for the French.
9    Lloyd's calm but firm guidance was to influence the development of the race along the original lines established by Blondie and Jack Odling-Smee. His talents were rewarded by his later "promotion" to Commodore of the RWYC from which position he was able to continue this invaluable direction.

dangerous, "Of course its dangerous, that's why they do it!" and in reply to the cost of such rescues a senior Royal Air Force officer said, "You can't equate a human life with pounds, shillings and pence. Besides, its jolly good practice for us".[10] Some years before, during a night search for a trawler in trouble off Iceland a sailor in the Operations Room of the British frigate *Undine* turned to his Captain (by coincidence, Lloyd Foster) with the succinct comment that, "This is far better than all those NATO exercises – these are real people."[11] Lloyd would quote this often as an example of the opinions of those whose actual duty it is to effect the searches. Blondie's own views were equally as robust:

> This year's (1968) *Observer* single-handed trans-Atlantic race has suffered more mishaps and aroused more hostile criticism than either of its two predecessors . . .
>
> Five weeks ago 35 starters left Plymouth . . . and 13 of these were multi-hulled. At the time of writing 3 monos, 2 multis have finished; 5 monos and 6 multis have returned to harbour and given up; 1 mono and 2 multis have been abandoned at sea and their crew rescued; 13 monos and 3 multis are believed to be still at sea, of whom 2 monos have had to put into harbour for repairs. Criticisms of the event seem to revolve around a few general themes:
>
> Multi-hulls should be excluded.
>
> The committee should be more strict in barring boats whose design they consider to be unseaworthy.
>
> The committee should be more strict barring skippers who are inexperienced or female.
>
> There shouldn't be such a race anyway.
>
> Various taxpayers have also protested about the cost of air/sea rescue operations, but it seems possible that what they really object to is rescuing *foreigners* . . . Would it be outrageous to suggest that rescuing foreigners from the sea does more to further international goodwill than our traditional pre-occupation of trying to drown them in it?
>
> Since 1960 the race has grown rapidly in size and importance,

[10] Much the same was said by the Australian authorities after rescuing Tony Bullimore – a regular entrant in Blondie's races – from his upturned yacht in 1997.

[11] Paraphrased from Lloyd Foster's *OSTAR* (Haynes 1989) – and papers in the Hasler archives.

with entries from 10 different countries this year. This international interest sets up strong pressures on the organizers who have a pretty rough ride in the three months before the start. What, for example, will be the French reactions if a fast French trimaran is barred from the race because the British committee don't think she looks quite right for the job? Perfidious Albion reacting to the French victory of 1964. Any 'expert yacht designer' of 1888 would have condemned the 1968 boat on sight as being quite unsuitable for open water and would have been particularly horrified by (its) features. Conversely, few 'expert yacht designers' of today could tolerate the features of the boat of 1988. There is no doubt that the modern yacht is very much more seaworthy, as well as being faster and more easily handled. Progress has been made but its form could not have been foreseen.

So what are we to think of the boat of 2048? I doubt whether any orthodox yacht designer would risk the attempt . . . but we can say with certainty that the boat of 2048 will be quite different from that of 1968, that it will be the survivor of a vast number of experiments and that the road to success will be littered with failure. *You cannot have the success without the failures.*

My personal view is that the race is being guided along the right lines and that it should be allowed to continue and develop. No doubt it will always stir up its share of criticism but so do many other progressive activities. What heartens me is the large number of people, both seaman and landsmen, who think it is an exciting and worthwhile thing.[12]

If Blondie thought the third single-handed race had produced problems that were easily answered, then the fourth in 1972 was altogether a different affair which culminated in the first serious re-think of the rules.

The catalyst for these changes was the decision by the Frenchman Jean Yves Terlain to enter a 123 foot long mono-hull, *Vendredi Treize*, with a view to winning by sheer size alone. Although within the rules this was not considered to be in accord with the spirit of the race: in the event she did not win and was beaten by Tabarly's 70 foot trimaran, *Pen Duick IV* sailed by Alain Colas. The even greater *Club Méditerranée* at 236 feet was entered for the next race . . . and, inevitably, the British Department of

---

[12] Hasler papers, draft for publication in a number of journals.

Trade now began to take an interest . . . meanwhile the history of the single-handed trans-Atlantic race is best studied in Lloyd Foster's book *OSTAR*. Blondie, although no longer a member of the committee, remained the prime consultant receiving all committee agenda and minutes.

He always insisted on keeping rules to the minimum believing that the free-spirit nature of the competition was of paramount importance, yet even he could not have foreseen the size of vessels now being entered nor the proliferation of navigation aids available only to those with almost unlimited sponsorship money. Even before *Club Méditerranée* and the renamed *Vendredi Treize* (now *ITT Oceanic*) were declared for the next race in which for the first time there would be fatalities, a worried Blondie wrote on 6 April, 1976, a "Strictly Confidential Paper for Private Discussion", which he is not believed to have shown anyone and which has only recently been unearthed. On 13 August, 1976, Blondie aired his outline views in a letter marked 'Confidential' to Jack Odling-Smee in which he congratulated the RWYC's Commodore for again running a successful event with his "usual firmness and calmness in the teeth of hysterical reactions all round". He went on to lament the "two presumed deaths" but expressed relief that it was not as many as he might have feared bearing in mind "the reported conditions and the number of starters" – 125.

What was worrying him was a rumour that *The Observer* would be pulling out and that, possibly, the Royal Western would follow.[13] This perceived possibility, coupled with the increasing number of 'nannies' who wanted to dominate and emasculate the race, caused him to consider the future carefully. Without actually showing him the 6 April paper, he elaborated his views to Jack:

> As I see it, the race (like the Olympics) is in danger of being killed by success. Excessive publicity leads to an excessive number of entries, excessive competitiveness and attempts to gain an unfair advantage by finding loopholes in the rules. Various self-appointed Nannies then get busy attacking the race organization and the rules, for their own ends rather than for the good of the competitors . . . If the worst should happen I would

[13] Lloyd Foster. "Those of us involved in running the races never considered abandoning the event nor thought we had lost control of it. We were much heartened by the support we had from the RYA and David Edwards in particular." David was then Deputy Chairman of the RYA, a late Commodore of the RORC and a solicitor.

. . . initiate a new series which would try to avoid our present pitfalls . . . with the help of a handful of the hard-core British entrants and without any sponsor or organizing club . . . there would be nobody the Nannies could snipe at except the competitors themselves who would be ordinary yachtsmen going about their business . . . My ideas would only work if there was no club or sponsor . . . they would also cut down the entry list by about 90%! . . . Keep me in touch with the way things go between you, *The Observer* and the Nannies.

The findings of his 'private' paper, announcing the end of the single-handed trans-Atlantic race, were not, in the end, evoked, despite the unwelcome imposition of the very rules and restrictions which, Blondie believed, would be the cause of the race's demise[14] – but they are worth recording:

The Single-Handed Trans-Atlantic Race – Series 2.
The Series 1 Single-handed trans-Atlantic Races, organized by the Royal Western Yacht Club of England and sponsored by the London *Observer* were held in 1960, 1964, 1968, 1972 and 1976 and achieved unprecedented success. The race became a famous international event attracting entries from all over the world, but this very success contained the seeds of its own death, for the following reasons:
  a.  Too many would-be entrants came forward, many of them so unsuitable that it was felt necessary to devise elaborate rules for rejecting them, but the field of accepted entries still became embarrassingly large.
  b.  The rules of the race, deliberately permissive about boat design, contained a fatal loophole in not having an upper size limit. It had originally been thought, wrongly, the size would automatically be limited by the size of crew. These giant boats, although less than 50% of the entrants, taken together with the vast size of the competing fleet, attracted increasingly hostile comment from the outside world, although not from many competitors.

[14] This paper was not discovered until research revealed its existence seven years after his death.

   c.  The hard-pressed Race Committee felt unable to reject giant entries without giving at least four years notice, since boats had already been laid down or built, did not contravene the rule and were mainly French, creating a problem of international feeling. The sponsoring newspapers naturally favoured the giants as having great news value.

   d.  Feeling responsible for the safe and seamanlike conduct of the race, the committee felt forced to introduce more and more safety regulations which reached a new peak when the Royal Yachting Association persuaded them to lay down a rule about 'not under command' signals which, had it been intelligible, could not possibly have been obeyed by the smaller competitors. Such rules are for the benefit of the organisers but against the interests of the competitors.

   e.  The increase in the size and speed of the larger entries tended to bring the smaller boats (ie those that would normally be used for single-handed sailing) into faint disrepute. There was a feeling that they took too long to finish, were too liable to have to give up and were not really what the race was all about. This feeling was not shared by the owners of small boats, who came forward in large numbers and hammered continually at the lower size limit. It is a unique feature of the race that the honour of finishing far outweighs the honour of being on the prize list.

In retrospect, it is evident that the Series 1 was killed by over-organization, because the Club and the Sponsors, under fire from the outside world, felt morally and perhaps legally, responsible for taking every possible step to silence criticism and promote the safety of the competitors. In so doing they acted throughout with sensitvity and tact but the competitors themselves never wanted to be nannied, and found the proliferation of rules and restrictions somewhat irksome and increasingly comic. In spite of this they sustained to the end a fine sporting attitude towards the race and strong feeling of solidarity with all competitors.

The Series 2 Races have been planned in the hope of offering competitors the kind of sporting event they want whilst treating them as adults who can plan their own methods and take their own risks.

This was the 'down-side' to Blondie's feelings but it was now followed by positive, forward-looking suggestions for the future which, it has to be conjectured, might have been what Blondie really would have preferred all along. As it is, the race (close to its original form) continues to be the most prestigious and successful of all the short-handed and long-distance marathons. The single-handed trans-Atlantic race has never needed to look back nor has it ever again been necessary to alter the rules by any radical degree. It came of age just in time to save the following taking place – and yet . . .:

Single-handed trans-Atlantic Races – Series 2

1. The purpose of the race is to provide the participants with an enjoyable sporting contest.
2. The first race of the new series will start at 1300 BST on the first Thursday in June 1980. The starting line will be an extension of the line of Plymouth breakwater to the shore in both directions. Participants will start themselves using the BBC 1300 time signal as the starting gun. Having crossed the line from north to south, the course will be by any route to the finishing line, which is a line from which the Brenton Reef light tower[15] bears (. . .) magnetic. Participants will take their own finishing times.
3. The race will have no sponsor, no organising clubs, no rules, no official acceptances, no pre-arranged facilities or festivities at either end, no entrance fee, no handicaps, no disqualifications, no race numbers, no official finishing order, no prizes and no official dinner.
3a. Each skipper should regard himself as sailing a match against each of the other boats and may make his own estimate of a reasonable handicap for each match. Some may wish to make private wagers on the results of such matches.
4. The race will be open to any sailing vessel crewed by one person only. The object is to reach the finish as quickly as

---

[15] Off Newport, Rhode Island – the finish line for all but the first race.

possible. Powered hauling devices should not be used, except for anchor work. Auxiliary propulsion by muscle power is permissible but power propulsion should not be used in such a way as to advance the boat any nearer the finish.

5. Each skipper takes part in the race on his own responsibility as an ordinary yachtsman making an independent passage. The design, condition, equipment and handling of the boat are entirely his own affair. No search or rescue operation will be mounted. *Any skipper who is unable to remain alive by his own efforts is expected to die with dignity.*[16]

5a. There will be no qualifying procedure but it is obvious nobody should enter unless he has extensive sea-going experience and has sailed extended sea trials in that actual boat in winds of up to gale force.

6. Entry procedure. About a month before the start of the race the British yachting magazines will be asked to publish information about the Starting Recorder – an individual who has nothing to do with running the race but who will, at a stated place in Plymouth and at stated times during the week before the start, be available to record particulars of those intending to start. These particulars will be duplicated and made available at cost price plus 50% to anyone who has applied for them. Each skipper should go to the Recorder in person but the boat need not be brought into Plymouth. He should bring measurement details of the boat and a good profile photograph of her under sail which should be left with the Recorder who in exchange will issue him with blank sheets for use in making out his Log Summary, together with instructions for filling them in. There will be no further formalities at the starting end. Starters may be recorded up to 7 days after the starting time.

7. Finishing Procedure. On arrival in Newport, participants should find the Finishing Recorder, who has nothing to do with running the race but who will receive their Log Summaries. The Log Summaries will be duplicated, and made available at cost price plus 50% to anybody who applies for them. There will be no time limit for finishing. There will be no further formalities at the finishing end.

---

[16] Author's italics.

8. An archivist (who will have nothing to do with the conduct of the race) will be appointed in Britain to hold the original copies of the entry details and the original Log Summaries after the Starting Recorder and the Finishing Recorder have completed their work. Copies of any material held by the archivist will be available at cost price plus 50% to anyone who applies for them.

9. The race organization, other than this notice which is being distributed to selected yachting magazines, is published by the undersigned, each of whom has completed at least two single-handed trans-Atlantic races. We regret that we cannot enter into correspondence or discussion about the race, either as individuals or as a group. A further notice will be published not later than 31 Dec 1980 on the subject of any future race.

There were, of course, no signatories.

This was simplicity itself and showed a great faith in human honesty or, at least, a belief in the honesty of those who go to sea in small yachts. Nobody, least of all Blondie, believed that the competitors themselves would have brought about the death of the race and he continued in public, and with conviction, to defend the "Series 1" race against those whose criticisms were not well-founded. One such example came in a letter he wrote to *The Times*:

Sir,

Writing in your issue of June 6th (1980)[17] about the Royal Western/*Observer* single-handed trans-Atlantic race, Mr John Young says, "There are those, including, reputedly, Hasler, who was not at Plymouth and was said to be in Scotland, who regret the degree to which the race has been commercialised by sponsorship".

I do not regret anything of the sort. Until shortly before we moved to Scotland I served as a member of the race committee and I have always felt that the organizers and the sponsors have guided the development of the race in a responsible and imaginative way in spite of being subjected to strong conflicting pressures and a certain amount of downright opposition. I am delighted with their success and grateful to the race's many friends and helpers on both sides of the Atlantic.

[17] The day before the start on 7 June, 1980.

Before the start of the sixth race in 1980 Blondie wrote, originally for his own private, mind-clearing purposes, a résumé of the story so far and his predictions for the future. Although the race had by then been 'stabilised' under considerable public and official scrutiny, the question he now asked himself was, *Is the OSTAR*[18] *on Course?*

The main thrust of the answer to his own question was contained in a philosophical look at the whole business of going to sea, short-handed, in small boats. The following is an amalgamation of various articles that he wrote for the international yachting press based on this one, self-imposed question:

> The brochure and race instructions are now printed in a neat, blue brochure, like those issued for important orthodox races – Dear God, we are becoming respectable. The race has become far more successful than I could possibly have imagined with the numbers of starters climbing from five to 125 and the nations represented from two to fifteen. People sometimes ask me if I approve of the way in which the race has developed, hoping (I think) to get a negative answer. If so they are disappointed. It is true that the race is now a very different affair, with a number of boats being built to win it, many of them fully sponsored by commercial firms and sailed by men who could reasonably be called professionals. These boats appeal to the media but do not necessarily excite any great interest among the other competitors. The great majority of entrants still are unsponsored amateurs sailing the race just for the thrill of doing it rather than with any appreciable chance of winning an award. As long as this continues to be true, I shall feel that the spirit of the race is unimpaired . . .
>
> On the whole I think the first object of the race ("a sporting event, to encourage the development of suitable gear, supplies, and techniques for single-handed ocean crossing under sail") is being achieved, but on the development side progress has been patchy. Some things, such as wind-vane steering gears and methods of generating electricity from wind and water flow, have evolved rapidly under the stimulus of the race.

[18] OSTAR – *Observer* Single-Handed Trans-Atlantic Race – the popular title. To avoid confusion the acronym has not be used throughout this account of Blondie's life – especially as the race is now no longer sponsored by that newspaper – except when quoting directly.

More important, the evolution of seaworthy multi-hulls is now in full spate. This race and the related two man Round Britain Race were the first to permit multi-hulls and mono-hulls to race together in the open sea without handicap and we have all learned a great deal from the multi's success and failures.

By contrast, and disappointingly, no radical new rigs have emerged and in 1976 the only boats that did not carry more or less conventional Bermudian mainsails and staysails were five that sailed under Chinese rig, a case of development reaching backwards a thousand years . . .

You can hardly open a yachting magazine without finding details of yet another 'space age' rig intended to revolutionize the small sailing yacht. I wish some of them could just get over the hump of sailing the 500 mile non-stop single-handed passage to qualify for entering the race . . .

Permissiveness has always been the essence of the race and there has never been any restriction on the TYPE of boat that could enter, provided that the inspection team considered her to be seaworthy. For the first three races there were no limitations on size and boats ranged between 19 feet and 67 feet in length. In the rules for the 1972 race the only limitation was the sentence, "It is unlikely that the committee will admit a yacht of less than 20 feet overall on deck" but after prolonged negoti-ation David Blagdon was allowed to enter *Willing Griffin* . . . 19 feet overall and 17 feet 3 inches on the waterline . . . but the real headache appeared simultaneously at the other end of the scale in the person of Jean-Yves Terlain with the three-masted staysail schooner *Vendredi Treize* at 128 feet overall.

It seemed that the French, who were by now trying harder than any other nation to win the race, had settled on two parallel lines of development: fast multi-hulls of up to 65 feet in length and long narrow mono-hulls of nearly twice that length, arguing that only by going to enormous lengths could the mono-hulls hope to beat the multi-hulls . . .

In 1972 *Vendredi Treize* was opposed by Tabarly's four year old trimaran, *Pen Duick IV* then owned by Alain Colas . . . Those of us who disliked the giant schooner were relieved when Colas won in 20 days and 13 hours with Terlain in second place 16 hours behind.

The race committee debated whether to impose an upper limit

of size for the 1976 race but were reluctant to apply new restrictions particularly if they could be interpreted as being aimed at the French. So they left it open in the hope that even the French would feel that giant mono-hulls were a dubious proposition.

But the French felt nothing of the kind for in 1976 Alain Colas entered a four-masted schooner of 236 feet which is appreciably longer than the *Cutty Sark*. I think we were all horrified at the idea of this huge vessel charging along with only one man aboard but Colas was keeping strictly within the rules and the committee felt honour-bound to do the same. Colas finished second . . . and Tabarly won again . . . with a 73 foot ketch whose self steering had failed on the fourth day out . . .

After this race a great deal of criticism was aimed at the Club and the sponsors. It was alleged, with considerable truth, that giant single-handed vessels were a danger to other vessels, being perfectly capable of sinking a fishing boat or a coaster if they should run into one at speed. It was also acknowledged that the number of starters had become too great for shipping lanes around Land's End also from the point of view of overloading the potential of any rescue services that might be needed.

Heavy pressures were brought to bear and for a time it looked as if the race would be discontinued, but the committee showed itself willing to make substantial changes in the rules and the race was saved for 1980, at least. Now we have a minimum size limit of 25 feet overall, but multi-hulls of less than 30 feet are not accepted without special consideration by the committee. The upper size limit is 56 feet overall and 46 feet waterline length, plus a limitation on the profile shape to prevent very flat overhangs. As in 1976 the fleet is divided into small, medium and large classes, each equal to the others in importance and each having its own awards. The number is limited to 100 plus an additional 10 at the committee's discretion. The number of starters, as always, will be appreciably less than the number of entries.

When these rules were first published there were fresh cries of woe from the professional critics, claiming that the committee was now interfering with the freedom of design that had always been a feature of the race and the French contingent would be driven elsewhere. I don't agree. The elimination of monster boats will bring the race closer to its original spirit, and the biggest boats will now be of a reasonable size for single-handing.

As for our French friends, there are now 19 of them entered, including Tabarly with a 55 foot space-age trimaran, so the competition should still be hot. It is also heartening to find 28 entries from the USA now coming on strong after having been largely absent from the earlier races.

I am in favour of these rule changes and in particular of the maximum size limit, even though it would have ruled out the winners of the last three races.

We have always tried our hardest to allow total freedom of design but there is something inherently silly about trying to win a single-handed race by entering an enormously large boat. I had thought originally that no single-hander would want to sail a huge boat, just as I thought that he would be dissatisfied with conventional rigs, but in both these cases I was quickly proved wrong. Being middle-age and lazy I had forgotten that young men often like to seek out the most severe challenges. These "nautical athletes" will always be welcome in the race but their wilder excesses have now been curtailed because they threatened the existence of the race itself. Another bad guess was that nobody would enter the race unless he was an experienced seagoing sailor and had a seaworthy boat to sail. This proved to be too optimistic . . . Eliminating the half-baked exhibitionist was tackled by progressively tightening up the single-handed qualifying cruise . . . but even then we were outwitted by a beginner who was discovered to have made this cruise in company with a sailing instructor in another boat . . .

From the beginning I have been against any attempt to handicap entries according to a rule of measurement, having seen the result only too often, notably in the RORC and IOR systems. Rules of measurement are fine until designers start drawing boats to defeat them instead of drawing boats that are fast and seaworthy . . .

In 1957 I had proposed that radio transmitters be prohibited because I felt that calling for help in mid-ocean would bring discredit on the race and that it would be more seemly for the entrant to die like a gentleman . . . Since 1964 transmitting has been permitted . . . Now in 1980 . . . all entries are to be compulsorily fitted with the System Argos at Plymouth before the start . . . Its coded signal is picked up by a satellite that passes it to a station in France where it is decoded to reveal the yacht's position. If in distress the skipper can actuate an alarm signal . . .

I am not against Argos which makes no demands on the skipper and does not in any way assist him to sail the race.

Will the race continue in future years? The worst penalty of its success is that it increasingly attracts the attention of outside authorities who are invariably against it. These authorities exert pressure on the club and sponsors who in self defence then have to start nannying the competitors by introducing more and more safety measures and restrictions . . . Few, if any, of the competitors want to be nannied and to this extent the race begins to depart from the ideal concept of being organised by sporting yachtsmen for the benefits of the participants alone.

What if these outside pressures should finally cause the race to be discontinued? Perhaps then we would have to make a fresh start. Knowing what we know now, it might be possible to find a way of getting back to the old idea in which the race was really a series of matches between individual yachtsmen and perhaps we could avoid having any organizers or sponsors for the critics to get their sharp little teeth into. But I hope it doesn't come to that.[19] The race organisers, sponsors, and many helpers on both sides of the Atlantic have done us proud so far and deserve to be allowed to continue with this successful international event without having to endure constant sniping from non-participants.

The success and the growth of the race have not been achieved without problems but they are problems of success and not of failure.

Blondie was not entirely devoted to the Chinese rig – although he preferred it as it came closest to his ideal for energy saving at sea – for in 1970 he collaborated with Angus Primrose in designing a 73 foot, three-masted schooner to be built in ferro-cement which, at that length and in those days, would be lighter and stronger than most other materials. She was to be entered for the 1972 trans-Atlantic race with an eye on a later single-handed round the world attempt. For eighteen months she was sponsored by Blue Circle Cement; her hull was designed by Blondie and Angus while Blondie, alone, drew the radical sail plan that allowed the main and mizzen rigs to be altered from Bermudian mainsails to staysails in a few moments in order that the best use could be made, instantly, of changing wind directions and strengths. The sails not in use would fall

---

[19] The proposed Series 2 format.

into a deep, self-draining well that ran nearly the length of the ship. At the last minute the company withdrew their sponsorship and the project collapsed – the designs still exist.[20]

Other projects, too, caught Blondie's eye or would be brought to his attention for comment: Rob Denney, who had lost his catamaran *Jan II* during the 1982 round-Britain race wrote to Lloyd Foster:

> My plans for a windmill powered boat are slowly coming together . . . At the moment *Jan III* is going to be a 30 foot Iroquois catamaran with a horizontal axis, three-bladed windmill driving a large underwater propeller . . .

After much deliberation within the Royal Western Yacht Club, Lloyd wrote to Blondie on 9 December, 1982.

> We seem to have a new boat being devised for the next OSTAR (1984) and it looks as though we are going to have to decide whether it is a sailing boat or a power boat driven by wind-generated electricity. We have asked him to explain in more detail just how the boat will work but we would very much like to know how you would view a boat driven either by a wind-powered propeller or a propeller driven by wind-generated electricity . . .

Blondie had no doubt about how he should view this innovative thinking and so within the week replied with sympathy for the designer battling against conventional "wisdom".

> I support attempts to develop windmills for marine propulsion. As you know, they are being taken seriously by various bodies interested in the revival of commercial sail, in both their vertical and horizontal forms. (The windmills I mean, not the bodies).
>
> I'm not sure how your latest rules are worded, but my original rules would have permitted windmills, whether with mechanical drive or with dynamo/battery/electric motor drive. If nothing but wind power has been fed into the boat then it must be held to be propelled by wind power alone?
>
> With dynamo drive, I suppose it would be necessary to consider the state of the batteries before the start, but I would

[20] She was to have been sailed by the author.

like an electrical opinion as to whether it is reasonable to ask for them to be fully discharged, if not, a state of half charge would seem to be reasonable. He would not in any case get very far across the Atlantic on a pre-charge, although he might briefly take the lead if the start was in a flat calm.

The project is so experimental that I find it inconceivable that he would have any chance of winning, and would have thought less than a 25% chance of qualifying in time as he doesn't seem to have made much of a start yet.

It seems to be a typical case of our relying on stiff qualifying requirements to eliminate an entry that will, in my opinion, be hard put to it to be ready for the 1988 race, if then. The technical problems are enormous even with mechanical drive but I am all for letting such an entry eliminate himself rather than artibrarily excluding him and leaving him with a grudge to air.

I seem to remember that on some previous occasion we have at least considered adding to the qualification requirements a demand for evidence that the boat has been in the open sea in Force 8 or more without damage. This seems a reasonable demand for any very experimental boat?

Blondie had come across these ideas before and knew some of the problems, not least of all those of running downwind and wave clearance for the turbine propeller when rolling. In the event the Committee met on 10 January, 1983 at which the proposed entry of the "Wind Turbine Driven Water Propelled Yacht" was discussed and came to the, probably inevitable, conclusion that:

. . . since the craft is capable of going directly to windward it should not be regarded as a sailing vessel but should be treated as coming under the category of a wind-power driven vessel and observe the appropriate Rules of the Road (for a power drive vessel) . . .

More conventional concerns dogged the committee for by September 1984 the multi-hull fleet had reached a stage of development that Blondie had long forecast prompting Lieutenant-Colonel Johnny Dacre, now the Commodore of the RWYC, to asked Blondie:

Your views will be more than welcome to all of us and especially to the new committee which is about to form to organise the

1988!! Whilst on that, what do you think about 60 foot multis streaking across at say 25–28 knots single-handed . . . I know that one argument will be that if we don't let them the French will . . .

Blondie was delighted and replied on 15 September:

I would be against banning multis, since this race has been the biggest single factor in the developing of seagoing high-speed multis, which is still continuing at full spate. In any case, the big monos now seem to be equally lethal.

I would not oppose reducing the max length overall say to 50 feet but I imagine this would raise many problems for you. At the other end of the scale, I beg you not to increase the minimum size limit above 25 feet, particularly if you still call it the *Jester* class! This class is of major interest to a lot of ordinary yachtsmen and is also one which the British seem to dominate.

In general I am in favour of the race being organised by amateur yachtsmen for amateur yachtsmen and not by sponsors for other sponsors although I can see such a purist policy may not always be feasible.

This letter gave Blondie the opportunity to comment on another development in racing – that of transferring ballast. While agreeing to the general principle of the system he insisted that the rules state that the ballast be liquid in order to reduce the risk of heavy weights being moved around the inside of a small boat in a gale:

I am happy about the use of liquid transferable ballast but think it should be sea water, fresh water or fuel, ie not mercury and not solid or granular ballast. I accept the idea of ordinary stores being transferred to windward. I think the liquid ballast should be in rigid tanks fixed permanently inside the boat and connected by permanently fitted pipes. All this of course to prevent heavy weights from getting loose below decks or liquid from being released into the hull.

Blondie remained much in control of many aspects of his races. This was not through any expressed desire but no committee would have dared suggest any radical change without consultation: as long as Blondie's influence remained, even in the apparent background, the races were safe from the more extreme "antis" and would continue to be run for the benefit of the competitors . . . and if he failed then, unknown to the RWYC and the *Observer*, he still had "Series 2" ready up his sleeve.

Perhaps some of the last words should go to the Frenchman Olivier le Diouris when, in a letter to the Royal Western Yacht Club, he explained why he preferred the Royal Western Yacht Club/*Observer* races:

> The big difference between the English and the French Races is that the English ones are organised for the competitors and not the sponsors.

But the final words belong, respectively, to an American, an Englishman and an Australian. The 1976 race had been the first in which fatalities had occurred and they were not among those huge craft that had otherwise set that year's race apart; they were from comparatively conventional craft, indeed the very types that Blondie felt personified the race. Mike Flanagan was lost from the 38 foot mono-hull *Galloping Gael* and Mike McMullen was lost along with his fast, expected-to-win, 46 foot trimaran, *Three Cheers*. To add to this double tragedy, Mike's wife, Lizzie, had been killed a few days before the start of the race when she was electrocuted as she polished *Three Cheers'* hull.

Stuart Woods, an American entry in the race and friend of both of those skippers who were lost, summed up the feeling at the time in his book *Blue Water, Green Skipper*.[21]

> Two lives were lost, the first ever in this event. It was inevitable that it would happen in one of these Races and now it has. Both men knew that it might, though neither probably expected it would happen to him. Both, in a sense, died defending the right of men to risk dying in adventurous living.
>
> No one has proposed, with any effect, that motor racing be prohibited or that men stop trying to climb Everest. It is simply accepted that those who participate in these enterprises do so at their own risk, and good luck to them. Those of us who race single-handed ask no more than that. Leave us alone; ignore us if you like, but let us get on with it. Let us, as Jack Odling-Smee, commodore of the Royal Western Yacht Club, has said, ". . . enjoy and profit by what surely must be one of the last great freedoms granted to us in this ever contracting world."

[21] Stanford Maritime. London. 1977.

The Australian Poet, Adam Lindsay Gordon, stated what most still think:

> No game was ever yet worth a rap
> For a rational man to play
> Into which no accident, no mishap,
> Could possibly find its way.

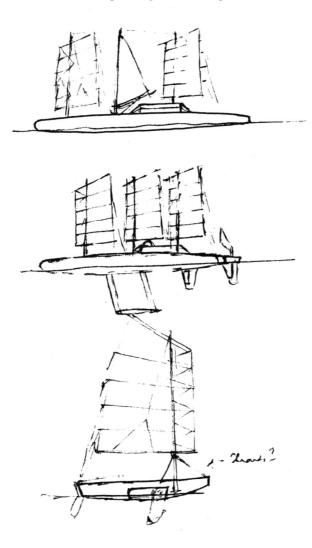

# APPENDIX THREE

## *Jester, Sumner* and the Cockle Mark II

At the end of 1964 *Jester* was sold to Mike Richey who described her as

> a work of genius, so effortless was sailing her in almost every
> condition.

Angus Primrose had already dubbed her to be the

> only radical advance in yacht design this century.

When Mike bought her she had completed four trans-Atlantic crossings
and was to complete (or nearly so) another ten. Her fastest east to west
crossing of just under thirty-eight days had been under Blondie's
command in 1962 and her fastest west to east journey of thirty days
between Bermuda and the Lizard had been with Mike in 1981. In 1986
she was overwhelmed, not without considerable resistance from skipper
and yacht, by a gale about three hundred miles west of Ushant which
resulted in her dismasting and being hoisted aboard an England-bound
ship, the SS *Geestbay*, under the command of Captain David Boon exercising superb seamanship under trying conditions. Repaired, she was
entered for the 1988 race but, under similar conditions, was lost at sea
four hundred and seventy miles from Halifax and just six hundred miles
from the finish.

In fact Mike abandoned her in a sinking condition at 39° 08'N,
58° 43'N on 15 July and while the decision was undoubtedly correct he
has never quite forgiven himself:

> Men personalize their boats as no other artefact. I felt that I had
> failed her and that I should have stayed with her. Better to pass

into that other world in the full glory of some passion than fade and wither dismally with age.[1]

By now Blondie had died but Bridget was able to console Mike with the following words:

> I'm sure, Mike, the odds are you didn't make the wrong decision, in spite of having no time to think. The only thing Blondie would have been sad about would be if all the achievement and happiness she's given to him and to you was destroyed by her end being the cause of your end. I'm so very sorry – for you – but if she's lost I feel it's a kind of suitable place for her to be.

It was not the end of the *Jester* name for the *Jester Trust* was formed to raise money to build a replica, and this it has done thus perpetuating the *Jester* name and spirit in subsequent trans-Atlantic races without a break. Her final resting place may be assured by the *Conservatoire International Plaisance de Bordeaux's* decision to offer her a berth in the permanent memorial to Blondie Hasler, not only for his achievement in that city in December 1942, but to those subsequently and more peacefully in which she and *Sumner* played key rôles.

As for *Sumner*, she was given to the *Conservatoire* by Bernard Brecy in 1995 and when last seen by the author was stripped to her component parts ready for a definitive refit before taking her place alongside other immortals of the experimental sailing world: this she has now done and is sailed regularly on the Garonne River with her junk-rig.

A replica of Blondie's wartime Cockle Mark II is also displayed in the old submarine base, from where, once a year it is taken to Blaquefort and the precise spot where Sergeant Wallace and Marine Ewart were shot. It forms the centrepiece to a short ceremony reminding the young of that community "of the remarkable deeds of brave men when facing the worst of odds". The French remember their sacrifice with humility and honour.

An original *Sleeping Beauty* is on display in the Royal Marines Museum at Eastney (housed in and around the old Officers' Mess) where a

---

[1] For fuller descriptions see, *inter alia*, the RCC's *Roving Commissions* for 1986 and 1988, and the yachting press at the time.

selection of wartime cockles, including the Mark II, can be seen. Among other artefacts are a limpet mine, a hold-fast, the mittens worn by Blondie during *Operation Frankton* and the pair of boots given to him by a French farmer during his escape.

# APPENDIX FOUR

## Vane Gears

*So we made fast the braces and we rested, letting the wind
and the steersman work the ship.*

(The Odyssey of Homer.)

The self-steering of yachts through the use of wind vanes was a life-long
fascination that led Blondie to design the first commercially acceptable
and successful systems to harness the power of the sea to steer the vessel.
The following is an edited version of Blondie's potted history and operating instructions.[1]

> A wind-vane self-steering gear is a device that will steer a yacht
> on a desired course relative to the direction of the wind. It does
> this without any power input simply by harnessing the force of
> the wind and the force of the water flowing past the yacht's hull.
> It differs in principle from the "automatic pilot" which steers a
> yacht on a desired compass course and needs a large generator
> or batteries to provide the power for the electric motor to turn
> the yacht's rudder.
>
> Vane gears first appeared in the model racing yacht classes
> developed in the Thirties but it was not until 1955 that effective
> vane gears appeared in full sized sailing boats: Ian Major's
> *Buttercup* and Michael Henderson's *Mick the Miller*.
>
> I started developing gears on sailing models in 1953 and
> gained practical experience from four single-handed crossings of
> the North Atlantic in the 25ft *Jester*. Out of a total of 12,000
> miles *Jester* was steered by hand for less than fifty. The value of
> these steering gears on long voyages is obvious but many owners
> have no intention of crossing oceans and use their gears when

---

[1]   Culled from a number of drafts in the Hasler archives.

cruising to save having to call on unwanted crew members. A good vane gear will steer the yacht on all points of sailing whenever there is a wind and can be regarded as the equivalent of at least one, if not two, extra men.

It is occasionally suggested that vane gears are in some way "dangerous". This is nonsense. I do not recommend that yachts should sail around blindly with nobody on watch: vane gears enable a solitary watch-keeper to keep a better look-out (for example he can move position to where he can see under the genoa or can stand up and use binoculars) and he can frequently visit the chart table when piloting through coastal waters. All my gears may be thrown out of action by pulling the latch line leading to the cockpit enabling the watch-keeper to revert instantly to manual steering in an emergency.

There are two types of Hasler wind-vane steering gears: Trim-Tab and Pendulum-Servo. Both work on the servo principle in which a small wind-vane is used to turn an underwater servo blade, whereupon the force of the water acting on the servo blade develops the power to turn the yacht's main rudder which is left free. The type of gear is determined by the type of rudder and not by the owner's preference.

Trim-Tab gears must be ordered for all boats with externally-mounted rudders, ie with transom or lifeboat sterns. In this system the wind vane V turns the trim-tab T and the flow of water past the tab causes the rudder to swing in the opposite direction. (See figure 1.)

I designed the Pendulum-Servo gear (figure 2) specifically to meet the demand for a fully portable vane gear that can be fitted to yachts with internal rudder stocks without underwater modifications. This type of gear only fits boats whose rudder stocks are internal.

In this system a servo-blade S is hung vertically over the stern and is carried by a servo box F which allows it to be turned like a rudder by means of the servo tiller A. The servo frame itself is carried in fore and aft bearings E on portable bumpkin B and can swing from side to side like an athwartships pendulum, taking the servo blade with it.

A quadrant P is integral with the servo box and steering ropes W lead from it through the sheaves C to the quadrant Q which is integral with the rudder stock. The wind vane V turns the servo tiller A which turns the servo blade S. The flow of water past the bottom of this blade causes this and the servo box to swing sideways (D) so that the quadrant P pulls the ropes W and so turns the quadrant Q and the rudder R.

There were those who took time to accept that having a self-steering gear actually made short handed sailing safer, as the following reply by Blondie on 3 January, 1966, reveals:

> In the middle of his interesting account of a cruise round Britain in *Sénéchal*, Mr Miller describes a close encounter with a ship which appeared on a collision course and adds, . . . *I was glad* Sénéchal *was not being wind vane steered as is now fashionable.*
>
> This is another example of a curious and fairly common belief that a vane gear somehow interferes with keeping a seamanlike look-out.
>
> May I suggest that in fact a vane gear makes it possible for a solitary watch-keeper to keep a *better* lookout than he otherwise could, and that any properly-designed vane gear permits instant reversion to manual steering in an emergency?

There are many variations on Blondie's theme in use now although electrically operated systems are wide-spread: their advantage is that they steer a compass course rather than a course at a set angle to the wind. With the advance of technology (including a greater use of solar panels) the pure wind vane will be seen less and less although for long, short-handed cruises it would be a foolish skipper who sailed without one. For more information see the Bibliography.

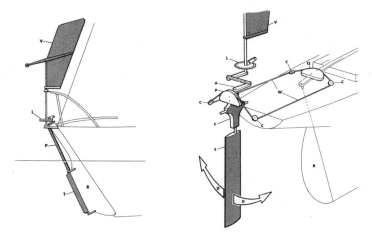

# APPENDIX FIVE

## Hasler Floating Breakwater

The following is taken from the National Research and Development Corporation's publicity brochure for Blondie's mobile, floating breakwater, the idea he believed to be his most important:[1]

> The advantages of using a floating breakwater over a fixed breakwater are:
>
> a.   The ability to operate in water that would be much too deep for an economical solid breakwater design.
> b    The ability to be towed from site to site or to be repositioned to give the best results at a particular location.
> c.   The ability to act as a moving breakwater to protect a moving vessel such as a pipe-laying barge or any floating structure under tow.
>
> The Hasler Floating Breakwater design was proposed by Col H.G. (Blondie) Hasler the well-known yacht consultant. Previous designs have generally presented considerable vertical surface area to the wind and waves, resulting in structures difficult to moor securely in storm conditions or in strong tidal streams.[2] The Hasler design operates on what is believed to be a new principle in which the primary means of disrupting the movement of water particles within waves is by means of a floating horizontal surface which is maintained in a stable

---

[1]   Advised and encouraged by Professor Sir William Hawthorne. See also Chapter Seventeen.
[2]   Blondie worked against the established principle and developed a system that moved with the sea rather than fought against it.

position by suitable design. The breakwater takes the form of a shallow pontoon whose length is approximately 20 times its width, moored so as to lie more or less broadside on to the advancing waves. A simple tubular superstructure limits flexing and torsional movements; rolling is minimised by the provision of an outrigger float on the sheltered side. The structure has less than 20% reserve buoyancy. These design features ensure that the structure cannot heave or pitch appreciably unless a large part of its length is lifted simultaneously by a wave. In practice, wind driven waves are found to have short crest lengths and these do not affect the breakwater but break locally over the raft without moving it bodily. A small baffle projecting above the surface of the raft along its inner edge assists in reflecting these breaking waves.

The breakwater is less effective against low swell waves and is not recommended for locations where such waves provide the major hazard.

Early flume tests showed promise and proving of the design was carried out in further flume tests at Wimpey's Hydraulics Laboratory and in trials on a 36 foot model moored in Portsmouth Harbour. The results of the trials have been assessed by the Hydraulics research station, Wallingford, who have produced a report . . .

It is now possible to recommend a design of breakwater for any given location. First, the scale and direction of the troublesome waves are predicted from a knowledge of wind conditions. Having then chosen the desired degree of attenuation of wave height, the scale of breakwater may be calculated. Attenuations of more than 60% of the incident wave height can be achieved with breakwaters of relatively modest size. To protect larger areas, several similar sections of breakwater may be coupled together. The design of the mooring system will depend upon the severity of the storm conditions at the particular location. Obviously the breakwater must be capable of remaining on station, and be undamaged, even in waves exceeding those for which it is designed.

The principle advantages of the Hasler Floating Breakwater may be summarized as follows:

    a.   Economical structure.
    b   Very low windage and hydrodynamic drag which

simplifies the mooring problem and makes towing
comparatively easy.

c.  Shallow draught facilitating its use in shallow water
or on drying beaches and enabling it to be laid up
conveniently when not in use.

Although it would not be prudent to encourage the immediate
construction of a very large breakwater, a progressive increase of
successive designs is envisaged commencing with structures
approximately 200 feet long . . .

# APPENDIX SIX

## Collision Regulations and Single-handed Watchkeeping

Watchkeeping when single-handed is an emotional subject and although, in theory, covered by Rule 5 of the 1972 International Regulations for the Prevention of Collision at Sea, this can be open to subjective interpretation. The Rule firmly states:

> *Every vessel shall at all times maintain a proper lookout by sight and hearing as well as by all available means appropriate in the prevailing circumstances and conditions so as to make a full appraisal of the situation and the risk of collision.*

There is no doubt that a single-handed yachtsman can not, to the letter of the law, keep a proper lookout at all times and thus the business of such ocean races could be brought into question. There continues to be much correspondence on the subject in the nautical press and within such bodies as the Royal Institute of Navigation and it is not the intention to enter that debate here. However it is appropriate to mention the subject and to offer an interpretation of Blondie's views.

His opinion suggested that Rule 5 was not, purposefully, specific enough for it does not make it clear whether one man is required to be on watch the whole time as a lookout and nothing else or whether this one man might also be steering, navigating, shaking his relief and carrying out the other duties required on the bridge or in the cockpit. "A proper lookout by sight and sound", he stated by way of example, "cannot be kept through the windows of a wheelhouse on a dark night in pouring rain with internal machinery running". He then continued by emphasizing that an experienced single-hander can maintain full mental and physical efficiency for an unlimited number of days without ever sleeping for more than twenty minutes at a time. "Catnaps often for as little as half a minute taken at frequent intervals throughout the twenty-four hour period should enable him to deal efficiently with the collision risks in congested waters."

It is also possible for the lone yachtsman to keep a lookout through the use of radar detecting devices which alert him to a ships' radar at, at least, horizon distance and the alarm device on his own radar (should he have one) which every two minutes (if he so sets it) switches on, takes a look and if nothing has changed or no new echo is detected switches off for another two minutes.

It has often been argued, convincingly, that an experienced single-hander can keep a better lookout from his open cockpit than can many a steamer's bridge-team – often also one man – from the all-too-snug confines of a wheelhouse with other distractions and the heavy reliance on a radar set, on which few yachts, anyway, show up in a heavy sea or normal ocean swell. But it is too easy to become embroiled in an 'us and them' argument when there are plenty of examples on both 'sides' of foolhardiness, crass stupidity and unprofessionalism.

The degree of vigilance which is necessary for a single-hander must, with common-sense, be related to the probability of encountering another vessel and in the open ocean some relaxation is justified especially in unrestricted waters where it is the duty of power vessels to give way to sail – although even the 'right of way vessel' has a legal duty to prevent collision – though it would, indeed, be a foolish yachtsman who relied on that 'let out' for his safety.

Despite not being covered by the law it is, too, recognised, perhaps unofficially, that (except in the case of the large French entries in two of the trans-Atlantic races) a yacht will cause negligible damage to an ocean-going power vessel and consequently the risk to the single-hander is entirely his own affair – and that lay at the heart of Blondie's opinion.

Nevertheless the 'nannies' (as he called them) continue to use the 'proper lookout at all times' argument to support their view that single-handed ocean sailing should be outlawed.

# APPENDIX SEVEN

Original score of the march *Cockleshell Heroes* by courtesy of the executors of the late Sir Vivian Dunn.

# BIBLIOGRAPHY AND RESEARCH

## Farming

Barrett, Thomas. *Harnessing the Earthworm*. Int. Home Fish Breeders
Assoc. 1942
Blandford, Percy. *Old Farm Tools and Machinery*. David and Charles.
1976
Garner, John. *How to Make and Set Nets*. Fishing (News) Books. 1962.
Iverson, ES. *Farming the Edge of the Sea*. Fishing (News) Books. 1968.
Jewkes, Sawers and Stillerman. *The Sources of Invention*. Macmillan.
1958.
Milne, PH. *Fish and Shellfish Farming in Coastal Waters*. Fishing (News)
Books. 1972.
Seymour, John. *The Complete Book of Self Sufficiency*. Faber. 1976.
Shewell-Cooper, WE. *Grow Your Own Food Supply*. English University
Press. 1939.

## Jazz

Condon, Eddie. *We Called it Music*. Transworld Publishers, Corgi. 1962.
Fox, Charles, *Jazz in Perspective*. BBC. 1969.
Harris, Rex and Rust, Brian. *Recorded Jazz. A Critical Guide*. Pelican.
1958.
Hentoff, Nat. *The Jazz Life*. Panther. 1964.
Newton, Francis. *The Jazz Scene*. Penguin. 1959.

## Loch Ness

Carruth, JA. *Loch Ness and its Monster*. Abbey Press. 1960.
Dinsdale, Tim. *The Leviathans*. Futura. 1966.
Dinsdale, Tim. *Loch Ness Monster*. Chilton.1962.
Gould, RT. *The Case for the Sea Serpent*. Philip Allan. 1930.
Gould, RT. *The Loch Ness Monster*. Geoffrey Bles. 1931.

Hevvelmans, Bernard. *In the Wake of the Sea Serpents*. Hart Davis. 1968.
White, Constance. *More Than a Legend*. Hamish Hamilton. 1957.

## Military

Amphibious Warfare Headquarters. *History of Combined Operations Organisation 1940–1945*. London. 1956.
Admiralty. *The Royal Marines. Admiralty Account of their Achievements. 1939–1943*. London. 1944.
Bruce Lockhart, RH. *The Marines Were There*, London, 1950.
Churchill, Winston. *The Second World War. Volume I. The Gathering Storm*. Cassell. 1948.
Courtney, GB. *SBS In World War Two*. Robert Hale. London. 1983.
Cunningham, Viscount, of Hyndhope. *A Sailor's Odyssey*. Hutchinson. London. 1951.
Evans, MHH. *Amphibious Operations. The Projection of Sea Power Ashore*. Brassey's. 1990.
Foot, MRD and Langley, JM. *MI9. Escape and Evasion 1939–1945*. BCA by arrangement with the Bodley Head. 1979.
The *Globe and Laurel*. The journal of the Royal Marines.
Hornby, Lawrence. *My Starboard Watch*. The Book Guild. 1984.
Ladd, James. *The Royal Marines 1919–1980*. Jane's. London. 1980.
Ladd, James. *Commandos and Rangers of World War II*. Maritime.
Ladd, James. *Amphibious Warfare*. Brassey's. London. 1987.
Ladd, James. *SBS. The Invisible Raiders*. David and Charles. 1983.
Lindell, Mary. *No Drums, No Trumpets*. Arthur Barker. London. 1961.
Lucas Phillips, CE. *The Cockleshell Heroes*. Heinemann. London. 1956.
Macintyre, Donald. *Narvik*. Evans Brothers. London. 1959.
Messenger, Charles. *The Commandos. 1940–1946*. William Kimber. London. 1985.
Moulton, JL. *The Royal Marines*. Leo Cooper. London. 1972.
Moulton, JL. *The Norwegian Campaign of 1940*. London. 1966.
Oakley, Derek. *Behind Japanese Lines*. Royal Marines Historical Society. 1996.
Pringle, Patrick. *Fighting Marines*. Evans Brothers. London. 1966.
Roskill, S. *History of the Second World War. The War at Sea*. London. 1954.
Seymour, William. *British Special Forces*. Sidgwick and Jackson. London. 1985.
Southby-Tailyour, Ewen. *Reasons in Writing*. Leo Cooper. London. 1993.

Warren, CET and Benson, James. *Above Us The Waves.* George Harrap. London. 1953

Warner, Philip. *The Secret Forces of World War II.* Granada. London. 1985.

Woods, Rex. *Special Commando. The Wartime Adventures of Lt Col Robert Wilson DSO and Bar.* William Kimber. London. 1985.

Ziegler, Philip. *Mountbatten.* HarperCollins. London. 1985.

## Sailing/Nautical

Amateur Yacht Research Society. *Self Steering.* 1967. 3rd Edition. 1974.

*Boys Own Paper* publication. *How To make Canoes, Dinghies and sailing Punts.* BOP. London. 1920.

Chichester, Francis. *Alone Across the Atlantic.* George Allen and Unwin. London.1961.

Chichester, Francis. *Gipsy Moth Circles the World.* Hodder and Stoughton. London. 1967.

Chichester, Francis. *The Lonely Sea and the Sky.* Hodder and Stoughton. London. 1964.

Childers, Erskine. *The Riddle of the Sands.* (1904) Collins. London. 1955.

Clarke, DH. *An Evolution of Singlehanders.* Adlard Coles. London. 1976.

Coles, Adlard. *Heavy Weather Sailing.* Adlard Coles. London. 1967.

Coles, Adlard. *Creeks and Harbours of the Solent.* Edward Arnold. London. 1933.

Dijkstra, Gerard. *Self Steering For Yachts.* Nautical Publishing. 1979.

Garrett, Alasdair and Wilkinson, Trevor. *The Royal Cruising Club 1880–1980.*

Gliksman, Alain. *La Voile en Solitaire.* Maritimes et d'Outre-Mer. Denoel. 1976.

Hamilton, Peter. *The Restless Wind.* William Blackwood. London. 1961.

Heiney, Paul and Purves, Libby. *The Sailing Week-End Book.* Nautical. London. 1985.

Hiscock, Eric. *Voyaging Under Sail.* OUP. London. 1970.

Heaton, Peter. *The Singlehanders.* Michael Joesph. London. 1976.

Illingworth, John. *Offshore.* Adlard Coles. London. 1949.

Kemp, Peter. Editor. *The Oxford Companion to Ships and the Sea.* OUP. London. 1976.

King, Bill. *The Wheeling Stars.* Faber and Faber. London. 1989.

Knox-Johnston, Robin. *A World of My Own.* Cassell. London. 1969.

Letcher, John. *Selfsteering For Sailing Craft.* Int. Marine Pub. Co. USA. 1974.

Malice, Jean Philippe. *Barrer Sans Barreur. Régulateurs d''Allure et Pilote Automatiques*. Neptune. Paris. 1981.

Moitessier, Bernard. *Cape Horn*. Grafton. London. 1977.

Moitessier, Bernard. *The Long Way*. Adlard Coles. London. 1974.

Neison, Adrian. *Practical Boat Building and Sailing*. Upcott Gill. London. 1900.

O'Brien, Conor. *From Three Yachts* Reprint. (1927) Hart-Davis. 1950.

O'Brien, Conor. *Across Three Oceans*. Reprint. (1927) Hart-Davis. 1950.

O'Brien, Conor. *Sea-Boats, Oars and Sails*. OUP. London. 1941.

O'Brien, Conor. *The Small Ocean-Going Yacht*. OUP. London. 1931.

O'Brien, Conor. *The Practical Man's Cruiser*. OUP. London. 1940.

Phillips-Birt, Douglas. *British Ocean Racing*. RORC and Adlard Coles. London. 1960.

Purves, Libby and Grove, Trevor. *Single Handed*. Ebury Press. London. 1984.

Rose, Alec. *My Lively Lady*. Nautical. London. 1968.

Roth, Hall. *The Longest Race*. WW Norton. USA. 1983.

*Royal Cruising Club* Journals.

*Royal Institute of Navigation* Journals.

*Royal Naval Sailing Association* Journals.

Slocum, Joshua. *Sailing Alone Around the World*. Reprint. Hart Davis. London. 1948.

Slocum, Joshua. *Voyage of the Liberdade*. Reprint. Hart Davis. London. 1948.

Smeeton, Miles. *Once is Enough*. Hart Davis. 1959.

Smyth's *The Sailor's Word Book*. Blackie and Son. London. 1867.

Society For Nautical Research. *The Mariners' Mirror*.

Spencer, JE. *Junks of Central China*. Texas A and M University Press. 1976.

Theroux, Paul. *Sailing Through China*. Michael Russell. 1983.

Tomalin and Hall. *The Strange Last Voyage of Donald Crowhurst*. Hodder and Stoughton. 1988.

Woods, Stuart. *Blue Water, Green Skipper*. Stanford Maritime, London. 1977.

Worcester, GRG. *Junks and Sampans of the Yangtze*. Customs Department, Shanghai. 1948.

Worcester, GRG, *Sail and Sweep in China*. HMSO. 1966.

Worth, Claud. *Yacht Navigation and Voyaging*. JD Potter. 1927.

# Archives

Mountbatten
MB1/1202        HG Hasler
MB1/B53C        *Operation Frankton*
MB1/B55–9       Combined Operations

# Public Record Office

ADM 1/12            Loss of HM Ships
ADM 2              RM HQ, MNBDO, RM Units
ADM 53             Ships logs
ADM173             Submarine Logs
ADM 202/310        RMBPD War Diaries
ADM 223            Enemy vessels sunk or damaged in home waters
                   during February 1943
DEFE 2/1           Combined Operations HQs. June 40 – Sept 41
DEFE 2/216–218     *Operation Frankton*
DEFE 675–676       Norway
DEFE 694           Small Scale Raids
DEFE 780           History of the SOG in SEAC
DEFE 798           Canoes and Cockles
DEFE 842           Folbots/Cockles
DEFE 2/951–953     Boom Patrol Boats/Intermediate Carriers/Lancaster
                   Project
DEFE 957           Small raids
DEFE 958           Submersible craft
DEFE 967           Canoes
DEFE 972           Canoes
DEFE 975           Boom Patrol Boats
DEFE 988           RMBPD 42–48
DEFE 1009          Midget submarines
DEFE 1034          Special Boat Units
DEFE 1035          RM Forces, RN Beach Commandos
DEFE 1038          RM Forces, RN Beach Commandos
DEFE 2/1078        *Suitcase*
DEFE 1093          Small Scale Raiding Forces

| | |
|---|---|
| DEFE 1094 | Small Scale Raiding Forces |
| DEFE 1144a/b | *Sleeping Beauty* |
| DEFE 1145 | Swimming in Combined Operations |
| DEFE 1181 | Bridging the watergap |
| DEFE 1196 | Provision of Landing Craft for SEAC |
| DEFE 1203 | SOG Formation |
| DEFE 1247 | SOG Organisation |
| PG 32060/ND | Naval Intelligence Reports. |
| PG 36917 | Naval Intelligence Reports. |
| PG 37729 | Naval Intelligence Reports. |
| PG7730 | Naval Intelligence Reports. |
| WO 165/39 | Main HQ Diary of MI9 |
| WO 170/3962B | Popski's Private Army |
| WO 208/3242 | Historical Record of MI9 |

## Royal Marines

| | |
|---|---|
| 2/15/4 | RMBPD |
| 2/15/7 | Det 385 |
| 2/14/1 | General Sir Alan Bourne. Interview dated 4 August, 1942. |
| 7/19/13 (1) | *Frankton* |
| 7/19/19 (8) | Puffers |

## Hasler papers/archives.

All letters received by the author during eight years of research (many of which are mentioned in the text or the footnotes) are now lodged with Blondie's papers to form the Hasler Archives. By kind permission of Bridget Hasler, his military documents will now be housed with the Royal Marines Archives.

## Hasler's Own Writing

The following list of books, plays, letters and short articles (plus the more complete drafts found with his papers but which have no obvious destination) is almost certainly incomplete but it should give researchers a useful starting point. His own military documents are not tabulated here.

## Books

*Harbours and Anchorages of The North Coast of Brittany*. Robert Ross. 1952.
*Practical Junk Rig*. With Jock McLeod. Adlard Coles. 1987.
*Experimenting with Boats*. Draft. Circa 1966. Synopsis and brief manuscript only. See Appendix One.
*HG Hasler, The Man Behind the Façade*. Draft idea for biography – no further details have been unearthed.
*Small Boat Voyaging – Everything Changes*. Brief, draft manuscript – possibly for longer article or short book.
*My Lively Lady*. Chapter in Sir Alec Rose's book. 1968.
Foreword for book by "Ghillie" Howe DCM MM RM on Devizes to Westminster Canoe Race. 1971.

## Plays

*The Tulip Major* With Rosamund Pilcher. Dundee Rep.
*The Veteran Yachtsman*. For the *Observer* play competition. No m/s remains.

## Film Scripts

*The Long Voyage*. For José Ferrer. No m/s remains.
Suggested ending to the *Cockleshell Heroes*. See Chapter Twelve.

## Letters

| | |
|---|---|
| 30 May 1931. | *Illustrated and Sporting Life*. Madame Heriot's yacht. |
| 11 December 1931. | *Yachting World*. Bermudian Rig for Cruisers. |
| 7 January 1938. | *Yachting World*. "Why Not Canoes?" |
| November 1946. | *Yachting Monthly and Motor Cruising*. "Sailing in Tre Sang." |
| November 1946. | *Motor Boat and Yachting*. Changes in RORC rating rules. |
| December 1946. | *Yachting Monthly and Motor Cruising*. "Some Notions tried out in a "Thirty"." |
| February 1950. | *Yachting Monthly*. Bottled gas in yachts. |

April 1953          *Yachting World.* Letter from "Veteran" asking for yachtsmen's girl friends to entertain ships at anchor for the Coronation Review.

February 1960.      *Yachting World.* The National Trust and Lantic Bay.

21 October 1960.   *Yachts and Yachting. Jester's* Passage from New York.

January 1961.       *Yachting. Jester* sails home.

May 1962.           *Yachting World.* Rolling down wind.

3 January 1966.     *Yachting Monthly.* Self steering gear and keeping a good look out.

4 August 1966.     *Yachting Monthly.* Round Britain Race.

2 February 1968.   *Yachts and Yachting.* Single-handed trans-Atlantic.

3 July 1968.        *Observer.* Single-handed trans-Atlantic Race.

11 October 1977.   *Yachting Monthly.* Lifting heavy weights – parbuckle versus runner.

6 June 1980.        *The Times.* The single-handed trans-Atlantic race and sponsorship.

17 March 1985.     *Observer.* Rescue of HM Submarine *Stubborn.*

## Articles

January 1944.       *Yachting World.* "Why Not?" Coastal cruising in a dinghy.

February 1944.     *Yachting World.* Plymouth to Portsmouth in a 12' dinghy.

October 1946.      *Yachting World.* Portsmouth to Plymouth in a 12' dinghy.

November 1946.    *Motor Boat and Yachting.* Changes in RORC ratings.

November 1946.    *The Globe and Laurel.* "The Value of Sailing and Small Boat Work in the Royal Marines."

November 1946.    *Yachting Monthly.* Sailing in *Tre Sang.*

December 1946.    *Yachting Monthly.* Sailing in *Tre Sang.*

28 March 1947.    *Yachts and Yachting. Tre Sang.*

Summer 1948.     *Sail.* With *Myth of Malham* to Bermuda

Winter 1948        *Sail.* Passage in *Tre Sang*

February 1950.     *Mariners Mirror.* Balance Boards of the Palk Straits.

Spring 1950.       *Sailing. Petula* on the north and West Seabord.

Winter 1950.       *The Yachtsman.* Morlaiz – taken from *Harbours and Anchorages of the North Coast of Brittany.*

| | |
|---|---|
| 1949/1950. | *Yachtsman's Annual.* "Westabout to Rockall". Cruising in *Petula*. |
| 4 February 1950. | *Leader Magazine.* Small Boats versus the Atlantic. |
| April 1951. | *Yachting World. Petula* to Norway, Part I. |
| May 1951. | *Yachting World. Petula* to Norway, Part II. |
| 23 December 1955. | *Yachts and Yachting.* Below Deck Seamanship |
| 11 November 1956. | *Observer.* "New style Ocean Voyaging". *Buttercup* to the West Indies. |
| January 1957. | *Observer.* "Building a Boat". |
| 7 April 1957. | *Observer. "The Mayflower* Part I". |
| 14 April 1957. | *Observer. "The Mayflower* Part II". |
| 28 April 1957. | *Observer. "Mayflower*'s main worry is Victuals". |
| 19 May 1957. | *Observer. "Mayflower* becalmed halfway". |
| 9 June 1957. | *Observer. "Mayflower* is almost there". |
| 22 September 1957. | *Observer.* "Alone Across the Atlantic". Proposals put to the Slocum Society. |
| 11 October 1957. | *Yachts and Yachting.* "The Long and lonely Road", the single-handed trans-Atlantic Race. |
| 12 December 1957. | *Observer.* "Mine Always Light".[1] (By "Charles Tindall".) |
| January 1958. | *Yachting World.* "New Kind of cruising Yacht". *Jester* and the Lapwing Rig. |
| January 1958. | *Observer.* The Show Boats of 1958. |
| January 1960. | *Observer.* An Exhibition at Anchor in Earls Court. |
| 11 March 1960. | *Yachts and Yachting.* Advice and help for the ship-wrecked. |
| 21 October 1960. | *Yachts and Yachting. Jester*'s Passage from New York. |
| November 1960. | *Yachting Monthly.* Return of *Jester* from America. |
| November 1960. | *Yachting "Jester* – Seagoing Single-hander". |
| December 1960. | *Yachting. Jester*'s return from Sheepshead Bay. |
| 8 January 1961. | *Observer.* "Waiting for a Plastic Yacht". London Boat Show. |

---

[1] From the Editor of *The Observer*'s Foreign News Service to H.G. Hasler, 27 April, 1962: "In a new school textbook entitled *Contemporary Extracts in English and French for Advanced Translation* George Harrap and Co wish to include a passage from your article. . ." Blondie replied: "I am of course highly flattered that Harraps should want to include a passage . . . for advanced translation, even though I feel sure the translation will probably be more advanced than the article . . ."

January 1961.         *Yachting World* "Technically Speaking". Aspects of
                      *Jester.*
April 1961.           *Royal Institute of Navigation Journal.* Sailing the
                      North Atlantic.
19 August 1962.       *Observer.* "*Jester* in Search of the Joker".
22 August 1965.       *Observer.* "Time the Midgets Called it a Day".
17 October 1965.      *Observer.* "Design for Speed".
16 March 1966.        *Yachting and Boating Weekly.* Interview.
26 June 1966          *Observer.* Colour Supplement on building and
                      launch of *Sumner.* Interview and report.
10 July 1966.         *Observer.* "Painless Sail from Plymouth to Cork".
17 July 1966.         *Observer.* Report of retirement from the Round
                      Britain Race.
7 August 1966.        *Observer.* "Multi-hullers sweep the seas".
16 August 1966.       *Observer.* "This Must Come Close to Summit of
                      Sailing Skills".
11 September 1966.    *Observer.* "Rules of the Waves". Trans-Atlantic
                      rowing.
June 1968.            *Yachting Monthly.* The Wreck of *Ra.* Contributor
                      to article.
July 1968.            *Observer.* A Crucial Transatlantic Race.
18 June 1972.         *Observer.* "Battle of the Atlantic 1972". Single-
                      handed trans-Atlantic race.
March 1975.           *Cruising World.* Food – the "Beggar's Bowl".
September 1975.       *Yachting Monthly.* Sailing in *Pilmer.*
1976.                 Central Office of Information. Article about self
                      steering gears.
1976?                 Draft for *Cruising World.* Cooking tips for being at
                      sea.
20 July 1978.         *Cruising World.* "Banishing the Phantoms".
                      Hallucinations at sea.
June 1980.            *Yachting Monthly.* "Is OSTAR on Course".
June 1980.            *Cruising World.* "Is OSTAR on Course".
September 1985.       *Yachting Monthly.* "What I don't understand
                      is . . ." A cruise around Jura.
December 1985.        *Cruising World.* "Pilgrimage in *Pilmer*".
19 October 1986.      *Yachting Monthly. Jester's* survival of a knockdown,
                      with Mike Richey.

# Reviews

| | |
|---|---|
| 17 November 1957. | *Observer*. Reviews of *The Voyage of the Mayflower* by Warwick Charlton and *The Western Ocean* by Alan Villiers. |
| 11 June 1961. | *Observer*. Review of *The Restless Wind* by Peter Hamilton. |
| June 1961. | Draft for unknown destination – possibly a review of *The Ship Would Not Travel Due West* by David Lewis, Templer Press. |
| June 1961. | *Observer*. Review of *When the Crew Matter Most* by Errol Bruce. |
| January 1980. | Royal Institute of Navigation Journal. Review of *Self Steering for Yachts* by Gerard Dijkstra. |
| 1984. | Draft review of *Single Handed* by Libby Purves and Trevor Grove. |
| 1982. | Draft Review of *The West – A sailing companion to the West Coast of Scotland* by Ronald Faux. |
| Autumn 1985. | Royal Institute of Navigation Journal. Review of *Falkland Islands Shores* by Ewen Southby-Tailyour. |

## Miscellaneous drafts

| | |
|---|---|
| 1947. | Draft. "Some Impressions of *Myth of Malham*." |
| 1948? | Draft: Bermuda to Brixham in *Myth of Malham*. |
| 9 June 1952. | Letter sent to unknown publication. Light Displacement Yachts. |
| 1956. | Letter sent on Dead Reckoning and the Ocean Voyagers of the Past. |
| January 1958? | Draft: unknown destination "The Show Boats of 1958". |
| Autumn 1959? | Draft: Unusual Rig – *Jester* and the Lapwing Rig. |
| 1960 | Draft by "Plunger" on the use of privileged ensigns. |
| Spring 1966? | Draft for unknown publication. Two-handed, round-Britain sailing race. |
| 5 December 1966. | Vane Steering. For publication in an undesignated February issue. |
| ?? | Draft. "Seaworthiness – the Forgotten Factor". |
| ?? | "Is it Insane?" Single-handed trans-Atlantic Race. |
| ?? | Modern close-hauled sailing. |

??              "There are tunny down there." *Petula* and the tunny fishermen.

NB. These lists do not include the articles written about Blondie Hasler nor the books in which he is mentioned.

# Index